3 FREE Minutes
of weather information and save up to 60% on long distance calls!

Let The Weather Channel® help you pack! Get all the information you need before you leave.

- Current conditions & forecasts for over 900 cities worldwide
- Severe weather information including winter and tropical storm updates
- Wake-up call complete with your local forecast
- Special interest forecasts featuring ski resort, boating and other outdoor conditions

Remove card and see instructions on back.

Plus:

After selecting any additional payment option, you will receive 5 FREE MINUTES of long distance service!

Easy. Convenient. Fast.

It's The Only Phone Card You Will Ever Need!

During your free call, an automated operator will offer you an option to add $10, $20 or $30 to your phone card using any major credit card.

Use your card to:

- Save 20% on comprehensive weather information!
- Save up to 60% on long distance calls to **anywhere** in the U.S., **anytime**!
- Save 20% on other helpful information including lottery, sports, and more!

Domestic long distance service costs $0.25 per minute and all other options cost $0.75 per minute when using your TWC phone card.

Take the worry out of wondering! Carry the power to access all of these essential services with you in your wallet, wherever **Frommer's** may take you!

No place on Earth has better weather.™

Travel Discount Coupon

This coupon entitles you to special discounts
when you book your trip through the

TRAVEL NETWORK®
RESERVATION SERVICE

**Hotels ◆ Airlines ◆ Car Rentals ◆ Cruises
All Your Travel Needs**

Here's what you get: *

◆ A discount of $50 USD on a booking of $1,000** or more for two or more people!

◆ A discount of $25 USD on a booking of $500** or more for one person!

◆ Free membership for three years, and 1,000 free miles on enrollment in the unique Miles-to-Go™ frequent-traveler program. Earn one mile for every dollar spent through the program. Earn free hotel stays starting at 5,000 miles. Earn free roundtrip airline tickets starting at 25,000 miles.

◆ Personal help in planning your own, customized trip.

◆ Fast, confirmed reservations at any property recommended in this guide, subject to availability.***

◆ Special discounts on bookings in the U.S. and around the world.

◆ Low-cost visa and passport service.

◆ Reduced-rate cruise packages.

Visit our website at http://www.travnet.com/Frommer or call us globally at 201-567-8500, ext. 55. In the U.S., call toll-free at 1-888-940-5000, or fax 201-567-1838. In Canada, call toll-free at 1-800-883-9959, or fax 416-922-6053. In Asia, call 60-3-7191044, or fax 60-3-7185415.

---

* To qualify for these travel discounts, at least a portion of your trip must include destinations covered in this guide. No more than one coupon discount may be used in any 12-month period, for destinations covered in this guide. Cannot be combined with any other discount or program.
**These are U.S. dollars spent on commissionable bookings.
***A $10 USD fee, plus fax and/or phone charges, will be added to the cost of bookings at each hotel not linked to the reservation service. Customers must approve these fees in advance.

Valid until December 31, 1997. Terms and conditions of the Miles-to-Go™ program are available on request by calling 201-567-8500, ext 55.

SAN123

Frommer's® 97

Santa Fe, Taos & Albuquerque

by Lisa Legarde

Macmillan • USA

ABOUT THE AUTHOR

Lisa Legarde was born in New Orleans and is a graduate of Wellesley College. She worked as an assistant editor at Macmillan Travel before embarking on her career as a travel writer. Lisa has traveled extensively in Europe and North America and is author or coauthor of numerous Frommer's travel guides, including *Frommer's New Mexico* and *Frommer's New Orleans*.

MACMILLAN TRAVEL

A Simon & Schuster Macmillan Company
1633 Broadway
New York, NY 10019

Find us online at **http://www.mgr.com/travel** or
on America Online at Keyword: **Frommer's.**

ISBN 0-02-860908-5
ISSN 0899-2789

Editor: Charlotte Allstrom
Production Editor: Lynn Northrup
Design by Michele Laseau
Digital Cartography: John Decamillis
Maps copyright © by Simon & Schuster, Inc.

SPECIAL SALES

Bulk purchases (10+ copies) of Frommer's and selected Macmillan travel guides are available to corporations, organizations, mail-order catalogs, institutions, and charities at special discounts, and can be customized to suit individual needs. For more information write to: Special Sales, Macmillan General Reference, 1633 Broadway, New York, NY 10019.

Manufactured in the United States of America

Contents

List of Maps

AN INVITATION TO THE READER

In researching this book, I have discovered many wonderful places—hotels, restaurants, shops, and more. I'm sure you'll find others. Please tell me about them, so I can share the information with your fellow travelers in upcoming editions. If you were disappointed with a recommendation, I want to know that, too. Please write to:

Lisa Legarde
Frommer's Santa Fe, Taos & Albuquerque '97
Macmillan Travel
1633 Broadway
New York, NY 10019

AN ADDITIONAL NOTE

Please be advised that travel information is subject to change at any time—and this is especially true of prices. We therefore suggest that you write or call ahead for confirmation when making your travel plans. The authors, editors, and publisher cannot be held responsible for the experiences of readers while traveling. Your safety is important to us, however, so we encourage you to stay alert and be aware of your surroundings. Keep a close eye on cameras, purses, and wallets, all favorite targets of thieves and pickpockets.

WHAT THE SYMBOLS MEAN

✪ Frommer's Favorites

Hotels, restaurants, attractions, and entertainment you should not miss.

Ⓢ Super-Special Values

Hotels and restaurants that offer great value for your money.

The following abbreviations are used for credit cards:

AE	American Express	EU	Eurocard
CB	Carte Blanche	JCB	Japan Credit Bank
DC	Diners Club	MC	MasterCard
DISC	Discover	V	Visa
ER	enRoute		

Introducing Northern New Mexico

Santa Fe is the center of the fast-growing northern New Mexico tourist region, an area that also includes Taos, a one-time frontier town now famed worldwide as an art colony and downhill-skiing center; Albuquerque, a booming high-tech metropolis of half a million people; the 19 surviving settlements and numerous ruins of the centuries-old Native American Pueblo culture; and a spectacular outdoors appealing to wilderness lovers of all ages and fitness levels with its outstanding skiing, backpacking, fishing, hunting, rafting, and other pursuits. In short, there is more to do than you'll ever have time for on one trip.

1 Frommer's Favorite Northern New Mexico Experiences

- **Experiencing Acoma Pueblo:** This spectacular Native American pueblo, known as "Sky City," sits atop a 365-foot-high sheer rock mesa (6,600 feet above the valley floor). There you can see a church that dates from 1639 and also the beautiful thin-walled polychrome pottery made by pueblo members. The views are spectacular.
- **Riding the Sandia Peak Tramway:** The world's longest tramway will take you from Albuquerque's city limits to the summit of the 10,378-foot Sandia Peak. On your way up you'll see a variety of wildlife; at the top your view will span more than 11,000 square miles.
- **Viewing the Van Vechten Lineberry Taos Art Museum:** The newest art museum in Taos is a veritable treasure trove. It includes the varied and incredibly well-executed paintings of Duane Van Vechten, the late wife of the museum's creator.
- **Enjoying the Santa Fe Opera:** This is one of the finest opera companies in the United States, and its performances are held in a lovely hilltop open-air amphitheater.
- **Reliving History at the Albuquerque Museum:** This museum has the largest collection of Spanish colonial artifacts in the United States; there are also medieval religious artifacts, a marvelous collection of arms and armor, and old maps and coins.
- **Gaining Insight at the Indian Pueblo Cultural Center:** This Albuquerque museum is owned by 19 New Mexico pueblos. Its exhibits trace the evolution of the pueblos from prehistoric times to the present; there is also an enormous gift shop featuring original pueblo artwork.

- **Appreciating Turn-of-the-Century Taos at the Kit Carson Historic Museums:** This comprises three historic homes in Taos: the Martinez Hacienda, the Kit Carson Home and Museum of the West, and the Blumenschein Home and Museum. Together, the homes re-create the feeling of what life was like in Taos during the 19th and early 20th centuries.
- **Broadening One's Horizons at the Museum of International Folk Art:** This Santa Fe institution is the largest folk art museum in the world; its collection includes objects from more than 100 countries.
- **Marveling at the Kodak International Balloon Fiesta:** Visually, this is New Mexico's most spectacular event. More than 600 balloonists participate in the two-day event that features mass ascensions and a number of contests.
- **Exploring the Millicent Rogers Museum:** Located in Taos, this museum has one of the finest collections of Native American arts and crafts.
- **Spending Time in Old Town:** This was Albuquerque's commercial center until about 1880. Interesting shops surround the peaceful tree-shaded Plaza, and Native Americans sell jewelry, pottery, and weavings on the sidewalks in front of the Plaza shops.
- **Savoring the Vineyards:** Northern New Mexico has several excellent vineyards; it's fun to stop in for a tour and tasting. Two excellent wineries in Albuquerque are Anderson Valley Vineyards and the Gruet Winery; near Santa Fe, there is Santa Fe Vineyards.
- **Strolling Leisurely Along Canyon Road:** Art galleries line both sides of Santa Fe's Canyon Road, and it's great fun to spend time browsing there to see the works of new artists and learn about new trends in contemporary art.
- **Appreciating a Special Santa Fe Tradition—Indian Market:** This is the largest all-Native American market anywhere in the country. In Santa Fe during August, more than 800 artists display and sell their work; there is also costumed tribal dancing.
- **Traveling Back in Time—A Visit to El Rancho de las Golondrinas:** This 18th- and 19th-century living Spanish village/museum is located not far outside Santa Fe. It includes (among other things) a village store, blacksmith shops, a winery and vineyard, and a working molasses mill.
- **Sitting at a Cafe in Taos:** In Taos, it's great fun to sit at a cafe with a large cup of coffee and a good book or magazine and watch some of Taos's more colorful residents. People-watching and sitting around talking with friends are favorite pastimes among Taos residents, and it's a good way for visitors to become acquainted with this charming little town.
- **Visiting the Puye Cliff Dwellings:** Located at Santa Clara Pueblo, just north of Santa Fe in Española, these dwellings were once home to the Anasazi. All together there are 740 rooms as well as some interesting petroglyphs.

2 Northern New Mexico Today

With a long history of uninterrupted habitation, Santa Fe was founded by Spanish colonists a full decade before the pilgrims set foot on Plymouth Rock. It is caught in a time warp between the 17th and 21st centuries, between traditional Native American and Hispanic cultures and a current-day onslaught of tourism.

A carefully considered plan to preserve and perpetuate pre-20th-century architecture has made downtown Santa Fe look like an adobe enclave. Much of the rest of this city has followed suit. For miles in all directions, flat-topped earth-colored homes, many of them valued in the millions of dollars, speckle the hills amid sparse piñon and mesquite forests. Most of the construction is actually stuccoed concrete. A standing joke in Santa Fe art circles is that the city sanctions the use of 42 shades of brown.

It's no laughing matter, however, that Santa Fe is fast becoming a victim of its own uniqueness. Known to residents and visitors as "The City Different," Santa Fe is rapidly attracting large numbers of new residents from around the country who want to escape the crime, pace of life, and closed-in spaces created by concrete skyscrapers. Unfortunately, these new residents are bringing all of those things (except skyscrapers) with them. The real estate market was the first to fall victim to the onslaught of newcomers. At first, when the wealthy newcomers moved in, real estate prices went up. But then, as the area's less fortunate moved out because they could not afford these higher prices, home sales dropped. In the past few years, especially, real estate has taken a nosedive. The level of crime has increased: Muggings, almost unheard of in the past, are becoming commonplace; graffiti is showing up all over the city; homelessness is growing; and noise pollution is on the rise. (It should be noted, however, that comparatively speaking, Santa Fe is still one of this country's safest cities.) Due to these changes, tourism has declined and the city has begun to suffer economically. Some believe this is good news in its own way because hotel room rates have come down somewhat (though not significantly), and it's not as difficult as it once was to get a table at the more popular restaurants. Though Santa Fe remains a popular tourist destination, it is showing some wear and tear and has lost some of its original charm.

Taos, on the other hand, remains much the same as it was five years ago. Still a quaint small town, Taos seems to be attracting more visitors than it had in the past (perhaps due to Santa Fe's decline in popularity). The most significant event of late may have been the opening of a new museum—the Van Vechten Lineberry Taos Art Museum. It highlights the work of the 11 original Taos artists as well as Duane Van Vechten, the very talented wife of the museum's founder, Edwin C. Lineberry. This isn't to say that Taos has escaped the push for growth to which Santa Fe has fallen victim. There are plans to develop the land to the west of NM 68 (the road that leads into Taos town) just beyond Ranchos de Taos. Such plans would change not only the landscape, but the whole ambience of this charming little town. Fortunately, Taoseños have seen the negative consequences of changes in Santa Fe and are thus more aware of the problems that come with extensive development. It is my sincere hope that efforts will be made to keep Taos and its inhabitants from following in its neighbor's footsteps.

Albuquerque is completely different from Santa Fe and Taos in that it is truly a big city, skyscrapers and all. Most visitors to northern New Mexico fly into Albuquerque International Airport, rent a car, and head (literally) for the hills without stopping to take in the pleasures of the city. There are some wonderful museums, such as the New Mexico Museum of Natural History and Science, the Albuquerque Museum, and the Indian Pueblo Cultural Center, that should not be missed on a trip to New Mexico. They are constantly growing and changing. In addition, the nightlife offerings are expanding along Central Avenue in downtown Albuquerque. Furthermore, Albuquerque hosts the annual Kodak International Balloon Fiesta every October (it's the largest of its kind in the world) and is within a short driving distance of the spectacular Acoma Pueblo. For those who want to make an extended visit to Albuquerque but don't want to stay in a big downtown hotel, the good news is that many bed-and-breakfast inns are opening on the outskirts of the city in areas that are relatively free of the noise and traffic you'd experience downtown.

In the areas that surround and connect these three major tourist destinations, you will notice the development of many casinos and gaming palaces associated with the pueblos. These developments began in 1994 when a law was passed to permit gambling on Indian reservations. Not surprisingly, just about every pueblo, including Taos Pueblo, has taken advantage of this legislation. The casinos are a source of great debate among both area residents and politicians; undoubtedly, the debate will continue in the years to come.

Over the past two years New Mexico has witnessed more changes than it had in the previous four—some good, some bad. No matter what happens, I'd like to believe that this wonderful state will be able to retain enough of the qualities that make it different from every other state and that it will remain a unique and exciting place to visit.

3 History 101

The Pueblo tribes of the upper Rio Grande valley are believed to be descendants of the Anasazi, who lived from the 9th to the 13th century in the Four Corners region, where the states of New Mexico, Arizona, Colorado, and Utah now meet. The Anasazi built spectacular structures; you can get an idea of their scale and intricacy if you see the ruins at Chaco Canyon and Mesa Verde. It isn't known exactly why the Anasazi abandoned their homes (some archaeologists suggest it was due to drought; others say it was social unrest), but by the time the first Spanish arrived in the 1500s they were long gone, and the Pueblo culture was well established throughout northern and western New Mexico.

A distinguishing and unifying mark of the otherwise diverse Anasazi and Pueblo cultures was architectural style. Both built condominium-style communities of stone and mud adobe bricks, three and four stories high. Grouped around central plazas, their villages incorporated circular spiritual chambers called *kivas*. As farmers, these people used the waters of the Rio Grande and its tributaries to irrigate their fields of corn, beans, and squash, and they created elaborate works of pottery.

THE SPANISH OCCUPATION The Spanish ventured into the upper Rio Grande after conquering Mexico's Aztecs in 1519–21. In 1540 Francisco Vásquez de Coronado led an expedition in search of the fabled Seven Cities of Cíbola, coincidentally introducing horses and sheep to the region. Neither Coronado nor a succession of wealth-hungry conquistadors could locate the legendary cities of gold, so the Spanish focused on exploiting the Native Americans.

Franciscan priests attempted to turn the Pueblo people into model Hispanic peasants. Their churches became the focal points of every pueblo, with Catholic schools an essential adjunct. By 1625 there were approximately 50 churches in the valley. (Two of the pueblo missions, at Isleta and Acoma, are still in use today.) But the Pueblos weren't enthused about doing "God's work"—building new adobe missions, tilling fields for the Spanish, and weaving garments for export to Mexico—so soldiers came north to back the padres in extracting labor. For all practical purposes, the Pueblos were forced into slavery.

Santa Fe was founded in 1610 as the seat of Spanish government in the upper Rio Grande. Governor Don Pedro de Peralta named the settlement "La Villa Real de la Santa Fe de San Francisco de Asis" ("The Royal City of the Holy Faith of St. Francis of Assisi"). His capital, the Palace of the Governors, has been in continuous use as a public building ever since by the Spanish, Mexicans, Americans,

Confederate troops (briefly), and the Pueblos (1680–92). Today it's the flagship of the state museum system.

The Pueblo occupation signaled the culmination of decades of resentment against the Spanish colonials. Rebellions in the 1630s at Taos and Jemez left village priests dead and led to savage repression. In 1680 a unified Pueblo rebellion, orchestrated from Taos, succeeded in driving all Spanish from the upper Rio Grande. Forced to retreat to Mexico, the colonists could not reconquer Santa Fe until 12 years later. Bloody battles continued for the next several years, but by the beginning of the 18th century Nuevo Mexico was firmly in Spanish hands.

It remained so until Mexico gained its independence from Spain in 1821. The most notable event in the intervening years was the departure in the mid-1700s of the Franciscans, exasperated by their failure to wipe out all vestiges of traditional Pueblo religion—eight generations of Pueblos had clung tenaciously to their way of life through the Spanish occupation. But by that time the number of Pueblo villages had shrunk by half.

ARRIVAL OF THE ANGLOS The first Anglos to spend time in the upper Rio Grande valley were mountain men: itinerant hunters, trappers, and traders. Trailblazers of the United States' westward expansion, they began entering New Mexico in the first decade of the 19th century. Many married into Pueblo or Hispanic families. Perhaps the best known was Kit Carson, a sometime federal agent, sometime Native American scout, whose legend is inextricably interwoven with that of early Taos. The home where he lived for 40 years, until his death in 1868, is now a museum.

Wagon trains and eastern merchants followed Carson and the other early settlers. Santa Fe, Taos, and Albuquerque, already major trading and commercial centers at the end of the Chihuahua Trail (the Camino Real from Veracruz, Mexico, 1,000 miles south), likewise became the western termini of the new Santa Fe Trail (from Independence, Missouri, 800 miles east).

Even though independent Mexico granted the Pueblo people full citizenship and abandoned the restrictive trade laws of their former Spanish rulers, 25 years of direct rule from Mexico City were not peaceful in the upper Rio Grande. Instead, they were marked by ongoing rebellions against severe taxation, especially in Taos. Neither did things quiet down when the United States assumed control during the Mexican War. Shortly after Gen. Stephen Kearney occupied Santa Fe (in a bloodless takeover) on orders of Pres. James Polk in 1846, a revolt in Taos in 1847 led to the slaying of the new governor of New Mexico, Charles Bent. In 1848 the Treaty of Guadalupe Hidalgo officially transferred to the United States title to New Mexico, along with Texas, Arizona, and California.

Aside from Kit Carson, perhaps the two most notable personalities of 19th-century New Mexico were priests. Father José Martinez (1793–1867) was one of the first native-born priests to serve his people. Ordained in Durango, Mexico, he jolted the Catholic church by some of his actions after assuming control of the Taos parish: Martinez abolished the obligatory church tithe because it was a hardship on poor parishioners, published the first newspaper in the territory (in 1835) and fought large land acquisitions by Anglos after the United States annexed the territory.

On all these issues Martinez was at loggerheads with Bishop Jean-Baptiste (1814–88), a Frenchman appointed in 1851 to supervise the affairs of the independent New Mexican diocese. Lamy, on whose life Willa Cather based her novel *Death Comes for the Archbishop,* served the diocese for 37 years. He

kindly to Martinez's independent streak and, after repeated conflicts, excommunicated the maverick priest in 1857. But Martinez kept preaching. He established an independent church and continued as northern New Mexico's spiritual leader until his death.

Nevertheless, Lamy made many positive contributions to New Mexico, especially in the fields of education and architecture. Santa Fe's Romanesque Cathedral of St. Francis and the nearby Gothic-style Loretto Chapel, for instance, were constructed under his aegis. But he was adamant about adhering to strict Catholic religious views. Martinez, on the other hand, embraced the folk tradition, including the craft of *santero* (religious icon) carving and a tolerance of the Penitentes, a flagellant sect that flourished after the departure of the Franciscans in the mid-18th century.

With the advent of the Atchison, Topeka & Santa Fe Railway in 1879, New Mexico began to boom. Albuquerque in particular blossomed in the wake of a series of major gold strikes in the Madrid valley, close to ancient Native American turquoise mines. By the time the gold lodes began to shrink in the 1890s, cattle and sheep ranching had become well entrenched. The territory's growth culminated in statehood in 1912.

Territorial governor Lew Wallace, who served from 1878 to 1881, helped promote an interest in the arts that today flourish in northern New Mexico. Wallace penned the great biblical novel *Ben Hur* while occupying the Palace of the Governors. In the 1890s the Taos art colony was launched by Ernest Blumenschein, Bert Phillips, and Joseph Sharp; it boomed in the decade following World War I when Mabel Dodge Luhan, D. H. Lawrence, Georgia O'Keeffe, Willa Cather, and many others visited or established residence in the area.

During World War II the federal government purchased an isolated boys camp west of Santa Fe and turned it into the Los Alamos National Laboratory, where the Manhattan Project and other top-secret atomic experiments were developed and perfected. Today Albuquerque is among the nation's leaders in defense contracts and high technology.

4   Desert Landscape Inspires Artistic Creativity

PAINTING & CRAFTS   Since prehistoric times New Mexico has been a cradle of artistic genius for its native peoples. Prehistoric Anasazi pottery is unique in its design and color. Today's Pueblo people are noted not only for their pottery—each pueblo has its distinctive touch—but also for their weaving.

Hispanic art was by nature either religious or rustic—or both. Cut off for centuries from much of the world, Hispanic artisans handcrafted their own ornate furnishings while their paintings *(retablos)* and carved icons *(santos)* underscored their devotion to the Roman Catholic faith. Their traditional decorative tinwork and furniture are popular today, along with weaving and silversmithing.

Taos took its place in the world of art with the founding of the Taos Society of Artists in 1915. The society members—Kenneth Adams, Oscar Beringhaus, Ernest Blumenschein, Irving Couse, Herbert Dunton, E. Martin Hennings, Victor Higgins, Bert Phillips, Joseph Sharp, Walter Ufer, and the lesser-known Catherine Crichter—chose Taos because of the remarkable play of light on its landscape. Though disbanded in 1927, the society was so successful in widely marketing the work of Taos's geographically isolated masters that it established a solid foundation for the prolific art community of today. Works by society members are proudly displayed in museums and private collections throughout northern New Mexico and beyond, including the Metropolitan Museum of Art in New York.

Santa Fe grew as an art community on the heels of Taos. By 1921, Los Cinco Pintores, a group of five avant-garde painters—Jozef Bakos, Fremont Ellis, Walter Mruk, Willard Nash, and Will Shuster—were establishing names of their own.

Perhaps the best-known artist who worked extensively and lived most of her later years in the area was Georgia O'Keeffe (1887–1986). Her first stay in New Mexico in 1929 inspired her extraordinary paintings of the area's desert landscape and bleached animal skulls. The house where she lived in Abiquiu (42 miles northwest of Santa Fe on US 84) is now open for limited public tours (see Chapter 10 for details).

The number of full-time professional artists in Santa Fe and Taos today easily exceeds 1,000, and thousands more dabble in the arts. Studios and galleries are scattered throughout the region. Santa Fe, despite its relatively small size, is the third-largest art market in the United States.

Santa Fe is home to the Institute of American Indian Arts and the School of Indian Art, where many of today's leading Native American artists studied, including Apache sculptor Allan Houser. The best-known Native American painter today is R. C. Gorman, an Arizona Navajo who has made his home in Taos for more than two decades. Now in his late fifties, Gorman is internationally acclaimed for his bright, somewhat surrealistic depictions of Navajo women.

ARCHITECTURE   Traditional New Mexican homes are built of adobe—sun-dried clay bricks mixed with grasses for strength, mortared with simple mud, and then covered with additional protective layers of mud. Their roofs are supported by a network of *vigas*, long beams whose ends protrude through the outer façades, and *latillas*, smaller stripped branches layered between the vigas. Other architectural elements may include a *portal*, or ground-floor porch, usually shading a brick floor set into the ground; *corbels*, carved wooden supports for the vertical posts and the vigas; and a plastered adobe-brick *banco* fireplace set into an outside wall. Adobe homes are distinguished by their flat roofs and soft, rounded contours.

Santa Fe, Taos, and Albuquerque were once modest towns characterized by one- and two-story adobes. When the United States acquired most of the territory of New Mexico from Mexico in 1848 and goods began arriving by stagecoach and (later) by train from the eastern states, new tools and materials (such as red bricks and large logs) began to change the face of the city. The old adobes were modified with brick façades and roof decorations in what became known as Territorial style.

In Santa Fe and Taos the flat roofs were retained, so that these cities never lost their unique low profiles. Santa Fe has a serenity not found in other American cities and found in only a few of the smaller towns of the Southwest, such as Taos.

Santa Fe has very few true adobe homes today. The majority, of imitation adobe, are made of stuccoed concrete. But the imitations are effective. Strict building codes have been enforced by the city's Historic Design Review Board since 1957, requiring that all new structures within the circumference of the Paseo de Peralta conform to one of two revival styles: Pueblo (reflecting the mud-daubed adobe look of the Pueblos) or Territorial (reflecting that of the early Spanish colonists). Much of the rest of the city has followed the example set by downtown. In 1988 citywide standards were established to assure good architectural taste in new developments and to restrict the use of neon, large signs, and the like.

5 Basic Beliefs

Religion has always been central in the life of the Pueblo people, who view the cosmos as a single whole within which all living creatures are mutually dependent.

Thus every relationship, whether with another person, an animal, or even a plant, has spiritual significance. A hunter will pray before killing a deer, for instance, to ask the creature to give itself to the tribe. The slain deer is then treated as a guest of honor before the hunter ritually sends its soul back to its comrades to be reborn. Even the harvesting of a plant requires prayer, thanks, and ritual.

The Pueblos believe that their ancestors originally lived underground, the source of life (and the place from which plants spring). Encouraged by burrowing animals, they entered the world of humans—the "fifth" world—through a hole, a *sipapu*, by clinging to a web woven for them by Spider Woman.

They honor Mother Earth and Father Sun. In this dry land, the sun can mean life and death. The tribes watch the skies closely, tracking solstices and planetary movements, to determine the optimum time for crop planting.

Dances are ritual occasions. Usually held in conjunction with the feast days of Catholic saints (including Christmas Eve for Jesus), the ceremonies demonstrate how the Pueblos absorbed certain aspects of Christianity from the Spanish without surrendering their traditional beliefs. In a personal universe such as ours, they feel, spiritual beings actively participate in the material world—and the more, the merrier.

There are medicine dances, fertility rites, and prayers for rain and for good harvests. The spring and summer corn, or *tablita*, dances are among the most impressive. Ceremonies begin with an early-morning mass and a procession to the plaza with an image of the saint being honored. The rest of the day is devoted to song, dance, and feasting, with performers masked and clad as deer, buffalo, eagles, or other creatures.

Visitors are normally welcome to attend Pueblo dances but should respect the tribe's requests not to be photographed or tape-recorded. It was a lack of such respect that led the Zunis to ban outsiders from attending their famous Shalako ceremony.

Aside from the pueblos, the most visible places of worship are those of the Roman Catholics. Santa Fe's Cathedral of St. Francis is the state's best-known church, but a close second is El Santuario de Chimayo, an hour's drive north of the state capital. Constructed in 1816, it has long been a pilgrimage site for Catholics who attribute miraculous healing powers to the earth in the chapel's anteroom. Hispanic Catholics believe strongly in miracles.

6 Chiles, Sopaipillas & Other New Mexican Specialties

Santa Feans take their eating seriously. In fact, they've coined a name for their unique blend of Hispanic and Pueblo recipes: "Northern New Mexico Cuisine."

This isn't the same as Mexican cooking or even those American distortions sometimes called "Tex-Mex" or "Cal-Mex." It's a product of southwestern history: As Native Americans taught the Spanish conquerors about their corn—how to roast it and how to make corn pudding, stewed corn, cornbread, cornmeal, and *posole* (hominy)—the Spanish introduced their beloved chiles, adding spice to the cuisine and ultimately developing such famous strains of chile as Chimayo, Pojoaque, and Española Improved.

The basic ingredients of northern New Mexico cooking are three locally grown vegetables: chile, beans, and corn. Of these, perhaps the most crucial is the **chile,** brilliant red or green, with various levels of spicy bite. Green chile is hotter if the

You Say Chili, They Say Chile

It's never "chili" in New Mexico. New Mexicans are adamant that *chile*, the Spanish spelling of the word, is the only way to spell it—no matter what your dictionary might say.

Go ahead, look up *chile*. It's not in your dictionary; I guarantee it. Well, maybe it is, but only as a secondary spelling for the word *chili*; personally, I think it has been included there just to appease New Mexicans. They have such a personal attachment to their famous agricultural product that in 1983 they directed their senior U.S. Senator, Pete Domenici, to enter New Mexico's official position on the spelling of *chile* into the *Congressional Record*.

Chiles are grown throughout the state, which provides the perfect climate for cultivating and drying the small but powerful red and green New Mexican varieties; the town of Hatch, New Mexico, bills itself as "the chile capital of the world." Regardless of where you travel in the state, chiles appear on every menu. Virtually everything you'll order in a restaurant during your stay in New Mexico will be covered with a chile sauce. As a general rule, green chile sauce is hotter than red, but be sure to ask. If you're not accustomed to spicy food, red or green chile will make your eyes water, your sinuses drain, and your palate feel as if it's on fire after just one heaping forkful. *Warning:* No amount of water or beer will take the sting away. (Drink milk. A sopaipilla drizzled with honey is also helpful.)

Don't let my words of caution scare you away from genuine New Mexico chiles. The pleasure of eating them far outweighs the pain. Start slow, with salsas and chile sauces first, perhaps *rellenos* (stuffed peppers) next, followed by *rajas* (roasted peeled chiles cut into strips). Before long, you'll be buying *chile ristras* (dried chiles strung together for cooking as well as decorative use). You might even purchase bags of chile powder or a chile plant to take home. By then you will understand the difference between *chile* and *chili*.

---

seeds are left in; red chile is green chile at its ripest stage. Strung together like a garland (a *ristra*) to dry in the sun, chile forms the base for the red sauce known everywhere in the Southwest as *salsa*. Both red and green salsas are served in most restaurants; the red is usually the hotter of the two, but it's wise to ask before tasting.

Beans—spotted or painted pinto beans with a nutty taste—are simmered with garlic, onion, cumin, and red chile powder to be served as a side dish. When mashed and refried in oil, they become *frijoles refritos*.

Corn supplies the vital dough called *masa* for tortillas. New Mexican corn comes in six colors, of which yellow, white, and blue are the most common.

Even if you are familiar with Mexican cooking, the dishes you know and love are likely to be prepared differently here. The following is a rundown of some of the regional dishes that are not widely known outside the Southwest:

biscochito   A cookie made with anise.

carne adovada   Tender pork marinated in red chile sauce, herbs, and spices, and then baked.

chile rellenos   Peppers stuffed with cheese, deep-fried, then covered with green chile sauce.

chorizo burrito   (also called a "breakfast burrito") Mexican sausage, scrambled eggs, potatoes, and scallions wrapped in a flour tortilla with red or green chile sauce and melted Jack cheese.

empanada   A fried pie with nuts and currants.

enchiladas   Tortillas filled with peppers or other foods.

fajitas   Strips of beef or chicken sautéed with onions, green peppers, and other vegetables and served on a sizzling platter.

green chile stew   Locally grown chiles cooked in a stew with chunks of meat, beans, and potatoes.

huevos rancheros   Fried eggs on corn tortillas, topped with cheese and red or green chile, served with pinto beans.

pan dulce   A Native American sweet bread.

posole   A corn soup or stew (called hominy in other parts of the South), sometimes prepared with pork and chile.

sopaipillas   A lightly fried puff pastry served with honey as a dessert or stuffed with meat and vegetables as a side dish. Sopaipillas with honey are also often served with your meal—the honey has a cooling effect on your palate after you've eaten a spicy dish.

tacos   More often served as soft rolled tortillas than as crispy shells.

tamales   Made from cornmeal mush, wrapped in husks and steamed.

vegetables and nuts   Unusual local ingredients, such as piñon nuts, jicama, and prickly pear cactus, will often be a part of your meals.

7   Recommended Books

Many well-known writers have made their home in northern New Mexico in the 20th century. In the 1920s, the most noted were D. H. Lawrence and Willa Cather, both short-term Taos residents. Lawrence, the romantic and controversial English novelist, was here intermittently during 1922–25 and reflected on that period in *Mornings in Mexico* and *Etruscan Places.* Lawrence's Taos period is described in *Lorenzo in Taos,* written by his patron, Mabel Dodge Luhan. Cather, a Pulitzer Prize winner famous for her depictions of the pioneer spirit, penned *Death Comes for the Archbishop,* a fictionalized story of the 19th-century Santa Fe Bishop Jean-Baptiste Lamy, as a result of her stay.

Many contemporary authors live in and write about New Mexico. John Nichols of Taos, whose *Milagro Beanfield War* was turned into a popular movie in 1987, writes with insight about the problems of poor Hispanic farming communities. Tony Hillerman of Albuquerque is renowned for two decades of weaving mysteries around Navajo tribal police in such books as *Listening Woman* and *A Thief of Time.* Hispanic novelist Rudolfo Anaya's *Bless Me, Ultima,* and Pueblo writer Leslie Marmon Silko's *Ceremony* capture the lifestyles of their respective peoples. Of the desert environment and politics, no one wrote better than the late Edward Abbey; *Fire on the Mountain,* set in New Mexico, was one of his most powerful works.

OTHER SUGGESTED READING

Excellent works about New Mexican Native Americans include *The Pueblo Indians of North America* (Holt, Rinehart & Winston, 1970) by Edward P. Dozier and *Living the Sky: The Cosmos of the American Indian* (University of Oklahoma Press, 1987) by Ray A. Williamson.

For general histories of the state, try Myra Ellen Jenkins and Albert H. Schroeder's *A Brief History of New Mexico* (University of New Mexico Press, 1974) and Marc Simmons's *New Mexico: An Interpretive History* (University of New Mexico Press, 1988). In addition, Claire Morrill's *A Taos Mosaic: Portrait of a New Mexico Village* (University of New Mexico Press, 1973) does an excellent job of portraying the history of that small New Mexican town. I have also enjoyed Tony

Hillerman's (ed.) *The Spell of New Mexico* (University of New Mexico Press, 1976) and John Nichols and William Davis's *If Mountains Die: A New Mexico Memoir* (Alfred A. Knopf, 1979).

THE ARTS

Enduring Visions: 1,000 Years of Southwestern Indian Art by the Aspen Center for the Visual Arts (Publishing Center for Cultural Resources, 1969) and Roland F. Dickey's *New Mexico Village Arts* (University of New Mexico Press, 1990) are both great resources for those who are interested in Indian art.

If you've become intrigued with Spanish art during your visit to New Mexico, you'll find E. Boyd's *Popular Arts of Spanish New Mexico* (Museum of New Mexico Press, 1974) to be quite informative.

2

Planning a Trip to Santa Fe, Taos & Albuquerque

As with any trip, a little preparation is essential before you start. This chapter will provide you with a variety of planning tools, including information on when to go and how to get there.

1 Visitor Information

Numerous agencies can assist you with planning your trip. The Tourism and Travel Division of the **New Mexico Department of Tourism** is located in Room 751, 491 Old Santa Fe Trail, Santa Fe, NM 87503 (☎ 800/545-2040). Santa Fe, Taos, and Albuquerque each has its own information service for visitors (see the "Orientation" sections in Chapters 4, 11, and 15, respectively).

Information about northern New Mexico is also available on the Internet at the following World Wide Web addresses:

For general New Mexico information try:

http://www.swcp.com/nm/

For Internet addresses of individual cities see Chapters 4, 11, and 15.

2 When to Go

THE CLIMATE   Forget any preconceptions you may have about the New Mexico "desert." The high desert climate of this part of the world is generally dry but not always warm. Santa Fe and Taos, at 7,000 feet above sea level, have midsummer highs in the 80s and lows in the 50s. Spring and fall highs run in the 60s, with lows in the 30s. Typical midwinter daytime temperatures are in the low 40s, and overnight lows are in the teens. Temperatures in Albuquerque, at 5,300 feet, often run about 10°F warmer.

The average annual precipitation ranges from 8 inches at Albuquerque to 12 inches at Taos and 14 at Santa Fe, most of it coming in July and August as afternoon thunderstorms. Snowfall is common from November through March and sometimes as late as May, though the snow seldom lasts long. Santa Fe averages 32 inches total annual snowfall. At the high-mountain ski resorts, as much as 300 inches (25 feet) of snow may fall in a season—and stay.

Average Temperatures (°F) and Annual Rainfall

	Jan High–Low	Apr High–Low	July High–Low	Oct High–Low	Rainfall (Inches)
Albuquerque	47–28	70–41	91–66	72–45	8.9
Santa Fe	40–18	59–35	80–57	62–38	14.0
Taos	40–10	62–30	87–50	64–32	12.1

NORTHERN NEW MEXICO CALENDAR OF EVENTS

January

- **New Year's Day.** Parades, traditional dances, and masses at several pueblos, including Picuris, San Ildefonso, and Taos. January 1. Call **800/732-8267** for more information.
- **Winter Wine Festival.** A variety of food and wine offerings and tastings prepared by local chefs takes place mid-January in the Taos Ski Valley. Call **505/776-2291** for details.

February

- **Candelaria Day Celebration,** San Felipe Pueblo. Traditional dances. February 2. Call **505/843-7270** for more information.
- ✪ **Winter Fiesta.** Santa Fe's annual retreat from the midwinter doldrums appeals to skiers and nonskiers alike. Highlights include the Great Santa Fe Chili Cookoff; ski races, both serious and frivolous snow-sculpture contests; snowshoe races; and hot-air balloon rides.

  Where: Santa Fe Ski Area. **When:** The last weekend in February. **How:** Most events are free. Call **505/982-4429** for information.

March

- **Fiery Food Show**. This annual trade show, which takes place in Albuquerque in early March, features chiles and products that can be made from them. Call **505/873-9103** for details.
- **Rio Grande Arts and Crafts Festival**, a juried show featuring 200 artists and crafts-people from around the country takes place at the State Fairgrounds in Albuquerque during the second week of March. Call **505/292-7457** for more information.

April

- **Easter Weekend Celebration,** Nambe, Picuris, and San Ildefonso Pueblos. Celebrations include masses, parades, and corn and other dances. Call **505/843-7270** for information.
- **Easter Sunday Celebration,** Indian Pueblo Cultural Center, Albuquerque. Traditional dances are performed by Native Americans. Call **505/843-7270.**
- **American Indian Week,** Indian Pueblo Cultural Center, Albuquerque. A celebration of Native American traditions and culture. Begins late in the second week of April. Call **505/843-7270.**
- **Gathering of Nations Powwow,** University Arena, Albuquerque. Dance competitions, arts-and-crafts exhibitions, and Miss Indian World contest. Mid- to late April. Call **505/836-2810.**
- **Albuquerque Founder's Day Celebration,** Old Town Plaza, Albuquerque. On April 22 Albuquerque residents celebrate the city's founding by Gov. Francisco Cuervo Valdes. Call **505/768-3561.**

May

- ✪ **Taos Spring Arts Celebration.** Contemporary visual, performing, and literary arts are highlighted over two weeks of gallery openings, studio tours, performances by

visiting theatrical and dance troupes, live musical events, traditional ethnic entertainment, an Indian Market, a film festival, fashion shows, literary readings, and more.
Where: Venues throughout Taos and Taos County. **When:** The first two weeks in May. **How:** Tickets are available from the Taos County Chamber of Commerce, P.O. Box 1691, Taos, NM 87571 (☎ **800/732-TAOS** or 505/ 758-3873).

- **¡Magnifico! Albuquerque Festival of the Arts,** a 17-day celebration featuring more than 200 special events, attractions, and exhibits. The visual, performing, literary, and culinary arts are honored throughout the city. Early to mid-May. Call **800/284-2282** or 505/842-9918 for a schedule.

June

- **Rodeo de Taos,** County Fairgrounds, Taos. The fourth weekend in June.
- ✪ **New Mexico Arts and Crafts Fair.** This is the second-largest event of its type in the United States. More than 200 New Mexico artisans demonstrate and sell their crafts, and there is nonstop entertainment for the whole family. Hispanic arts and crafts are also on display.
  Where: State Fairgrounds, Albuquerque. **When:** The last weekend in June (on Friday and Saturday from 10am to 10pm and on Sunday from 10am to 6pm). **How:** Admission varies. For information, call **505/884-9043.**

July

- **Fourth of July celebrations** (including fireworks displays) are held all over New Mexico. Call the chambers of commerce in specific towns and cities for information.
- **Picuris Arts and Crafts Fair,** Picuris, Pueblo. Traditional dances and other events. Proceeds go to the restoration of the San Lorenzo Mission. The first weekend in July. Call **505/843-7270** for details.
- **Seventh Annual Jazz Festival,** Albuquerque. The one-day Albuquerque Jazz Festival takes place in early July and features both in- and out-of-state musicians. Admission is charged. Call **505/881-6383** for schedule and ticket information.
- ✪ **Rodeo de Santa Fe.** This four-day event features a western parade, rodeo dance, and four rodeo performances. It attracts hundreds of cowboys from all over the Southwest who compete for a sizable purse in such events as Brahma bull and bronco riding, calf roping, steer wrestling, barrel racing, trick riding, clown and animal acts, and a local version of bullfighting in which neither the bull nor the matador is hurt.
  Where: Rodeo grounds, 4801 Rodeo Rd., off Cerrillos Road, 5½ miles south of the Plaza. **When:** The first weekend following the Fourth of July (starting at 8pm Thursday through Saturday and at 2:30pm on Sunday). **How:** For tickets and information, call **505/471-4300.**
- **Taos Pueblo Powwow.** Intertribal competition in traditional and contemporary dances. The second weekend in July. Call **505/758-9593** for more information.
- **Eight Northern Pueblos Artist and Craftsman Show.** More than 600 Native American artists exhibit their work at one of the eight northern pueblos. Traditional dances and food booths. The third weekend in July. Call **505/852-4265** for location and exact dates.
- ✪ **Fiestas de Santiago y Santa Ana.** The celebration begins with a Friday-night mass at Our Lady of Guadelupe Church, where the fiesta queen is crowned. During the weekend there are candlelight processions, special Masses, music, dancing, parades, crafts, and food booths.
  Where: Taos Plaza. **When:** A three-day weekend in late July. **How:** Most events are free. For information, contact the Taos Fiesta Council, P.O. Box 3300, Taos, NM 87571 (☎ **800/732-8267**).

✪ **The Spanish Markets.** More than 300 Hispanic artists from New Mexico and southern Colorado exhibit and sell their work in this lively community event. Artists are featured in special demonstrations, while an entertaining mix of traditional Hispanic music, dance, foods, and pageantry create the ambience of a village celebration. Artwork for sale includes painted and carved saints, textiles, tinwork, furniture, straw appliqué, and metalwork.

   Where: Santa Fe Plaza, Santa Fe. **When:** The last full weekend in July. **How:** Markets are free. For information, contact the Spanish Colonial Arts Society, P.O. Box 1611, Santa Fe, NM 87504 (☎ **505/983-4038**).

August

✪ **The Indian Market.** This is the largest all-Native American market in the country. About 800 artisans display their baskets and blankets, jewelry, pottery, wood carvings, rugs, sand paintings, and sculptures at rows of booths. Sales are brisk. Costumed tribal dancing and crafts demonstrations are scheduled in the afternoon.

   Where: Santa Fe Plaza, surrounding streets, and DeVargas Mall. **When:** The third weekend in August. **How:** The market is free and hotels are booked months in advance. For information, contact the Southwestern Association on Indian Affairs, P.O. Box 1964, Santa Fe, NM 87501 (☎ **505/983-5220**).

• **Gourmet Jubilee,** Angel Fire. Farmer's market highlighting New Mexico–made products as well as wines. Cooking classes and dinners are available. Late August. Call **800/494-9117** for information.

• **Music from Angel Fire,** Angel Fire. World-class musicians perform classical and chamber music. Last week in August to first week in September. Call **505/377-3233** for information and schedules.

September

• **New Mexico Wine Festival at Bernalillo,** near Albuquerque. New Mexico wines are showcased at this annual event. Wine tastings, art show, and live entertainment. Early September. For schedule of events call **800/374-3061** or 505/867-3311.

✪ **La Fiesta de Santa Fe.** An exuberant combination of spirit, history, and general merrymaking, La Fiesta is the oldest community celebration in the United States. The first fiesta was celebrated in 1712, 20 years after the peaceful resettlement of New Mexico by Spanish conquistadors in 1692, following the Pueblo revolt of 1670. *La Conquistadora,* a carved Madonna credited with the victory, is the focus of the celebration, which includes masses, a parade for children and their pets, a historical/hysterical parade, mariachi concerts, dances, food, and arts, as well as local entertainment on the Plaza. Zozobra, "Old Man Gloom," a 40-foot-tall effigy of wood, canvas, and paper, is burned at dusk on Friday to revitalize the community.

   Where: Santa Fe. **When:** The first Friday after Labor Day. **How:** For information, contact the Santa Fe Fiesta Council, P.O. Box 4516, Santa Fe, NM 87502-4516 (☎ **505/988-7575**).

✪ **New Mexico State Fair and Rodeo.** One of America's top 10 state fairs, it features parimutuel horse racing, a nationally acclaimed rodeo, entertainment by top country artists, Native American and Spanish villages, the requisite midway livestock shows, and arts and crafts.

   Where: State Fairgrounds, Albuquerque. **When:** 17 days in September. **How:** Advance tickets can be ordered. Call **505/265-1791** for information.

✪ **Taos Fall Arts Festival.** Highlights include arts-and-crafts exhibitions and competitions, studio tours, gallery openings, lectures, films, concerts, dances, and stage plays. Simultaneous events include the Old Taos Trade Fair, the Wool Festival, and San Geronimo Day at Taos Pueblo.

Where: Throughout Taos and Taos County. **When:** 17 days, from mid-September (or the third weekend) through the first week in October. **How:** Events, schedules, and tickets (where required) can be obtained from the Taos County Chamber of Commerce, P.O. Drawer I, Taos, NM 87571 (☎ **800/732-8267**).

❂ **Old Taos Trade Fair,** Martinez Hacienda, Lower Ranchitos Road, Taos. This two-day affair reenacts Spanish colonial life of the mid-1820s with Hispanic and Native American music, weaving and crafts demonstrations, traditional foods, dancing, and "visits" by mountain men. The last full weekend in September. Call **505/758-0505**.

❂ **San Geronimo Vespers Sundown Dance and Trade Fair,** Taos Pueblo. A mass and procession; traditional corn, buffalo, and Comanche dances; an arts-and-crafts fair; footraces; and pole climbs by clowns. The last weekend in September. Call **505/758-1028** for details.

October

❂ **Kodak Albuquerque International Balloon Fiesta.** The world's largest balloon rally brings together more than 800 colorful balloons, and includes races and contests. There is a sunrise mass ascension. Various special events are staged all week long.

Where: Balloon Fiesta Park (at I-25 and Alameda NE) on Albuquerque's northern city limits. **When:** Second week in October. **How:** For information, call **800/733-9918**.

• **Taos Mountain Balloon Rally** and **Taste of Taos.** The Albuquerque fiesta's "little brother" offers mass dawn ascensions, tethered balloon rides for the public, and a Saturday parade of balloon baskets (in pickup trucks) from Kit Carson Parkaround the Plaza. Taste of Taos includes food and product fairs, chile cookoffs, and creation of the "world's biggest burrito." The last full weekend in October. Call **800/732-8267** for more information.

November

• **Weems Artfest,** State Fairgrounds, Albuquerque. Approximately 260 artisans, who work in mixed media, from throughout the world attend this fair. It's one of the top 100 arts-and-crafts fairs in the country. A three-day weekend in early November. For details call **505/293-6133**.

December

❂ **Yuletide in Taos.** This pre-Christmas event emphasizes New Mexican traditions, cultures, and arts with carols, festive classical music, Hispanic and Native American songs and dances, historic walking tours, art exhibitions, dance performances, candlelight dinners, and more.

Where: Throughout Taos. **When:** December 1–15. **How:** Events are staged by the Taos County Chamber of Commerce, P.O. Drawer I, Taos, NM 87571 (☎ **800/732-TAOS**).

• **Torchlight Procession** Taos Ski Valley, December 31. Call **505/776-2291** for information.

• **Winter Spanish Market,** La Fonda Hotel, Santa Fe. See the Spanish Markets in July (above) for more information. The last full weekend in December. Call **505/983-4038**.

3   Health & Insurance

HEALTH   One thing that sets New Mexico apart from most other states is its altitude. Santa Fe and Taos are about 7,000 feet above sea level, Albuquerque more than 5,000. The reduced oxygen and humidity can precipitate some unique problems, not the least of which is acute **mountain sickness.** In its early stages you may experience headaches, shortness of breath, appetite loss and/or nausea, tingling in the fingers or toes, lethargy, and insomnia. It can usually be treated by taking aspirin as well as getting plenty of rest, avoiding large meals, and drinking lots of nonalcoholic fluids (especially water). If it persists or worsens, you must return to a lower altitude. Other dangers of higher elevations include sunburn and hypothermia, and these should be taken seriously. To avoid dehydration, drink water as often as possible.

It is important to monitor your children's health while in New Mexico. They are just as susceptible to mountain sickness, hypothermia, sunburn, and dehydration as you are.

Other things to be wary of are **arroyos,** or flash floods, which can occur without warning in the desert. If water is flowing across a road, DO NOT try to drive through it because chances are the water is deeper and is flowing faster than you think. Just wait it out. Arroyos don't last long.

Finally, if you're an outdoorsperson, be on the lookout for **snakes**—particularly rattlers. Avoid them. Don't even get close enough to take a picture (unless you have a very good zoom lens).

INSURANCE   Before setting out on your trip, check your medical insurance policy to be sure it covers you away from home. If it doesn't, it's wise to purchase a relatively inexpensive traveler's policy, widely available at banks, travel agencies, and automobile clubs. In addition to medical assistance, including hospitalization and surgery, the policy should include the cost of an accident, death, or repatriation; loss or theft of baggage; the cost of trip cancellation; and guaranteed bail in the event of an arrest or other legal difficulties.

4 Tips for Travelers with Special Needs

FOR TRAVELERS WITH DISABILITIES   Throughout the state of New Mexico measures have been taken to provide access for the disabled. Several bed-and-breakfast inns have made one or more of their rooms completely wheelchair accessible, and in Taos there is a completely wheelchair-accessible trail in the state park. If you call the Developmental Disabilities Planning Council (☎ 800/ 552-8195), they will provide you with free information about traveling with disabilities in New Mexico. The brochure *Art of Accessibility* lists hotels, restaurants, and attractions in Albuquerque that are accessible to disabled travelers. *The Directory of Recreational Activities for Children with Disabilities* is a list of accessible camps, national forest campgrounds, amusement parks, and individual city services throughout New Mexico. And *Access Santa Fe* lists accessible hotels, attractions, and restaurants in the state capital. The Taos Chamber of Commerce will answer questions regarding accessibility in Taos. No matter what, it is advisable to call hotels, restaurants, and attractions in advance to be sure that they are fully accessible.

FOR SENIORS   Travelers over the age of 65—in many cases 60, sometimes even 55—may qualify for discounts not available to the younger adult traveler. Some hotels offer rates 10% to 20% lower than the published rate; inquire at the time you make reservations. Many attractions give seniors discounts of up to half the regular adult admission price. Get in the habit of asking about discounts. Seniors who plan to visit national parks and monuments in New Mexico should consider getting a

Golden Age Passport, which gives anyone over 62 lifetime access to any national park, monument, historic site, recreational area, or wildlife refuge that charges an entrance fee. Golden Age Passports can be obtained at any National Park Office in the country. There is a one-time $10 processing fee. In New Mexico, contact the National Park Service Office of Communications at **505/988-6021** for more information.

If you're retired and are not already a member of the American Association of Retired Persons (AARP), consider joining. The AARP card is valuable throughout North America in your search for travel bargains.

In addition, there are 24 active Elderhostel locations throughout the state. For information, call New Mexico Elderhostel at **505/473-6267.**

A note about health: Senior travelers are often more susceptible to changes in altitude and may experience heart or respiratory problems. Consult your physician before your trip.

FOR FAMILIES   Children are often given discounts that adults, even seniors, never dream of. For instance, many hotels allow children to stay free with their parents in the same room. The upper age limit may vary from 12 to 18.

Youngsters are almost always entitled to discounts on public transportation and admission to attractions. Though every entrance requirement is different, you'll often find that admission for kids 5 and under is free and for elementary-school-age children it's half price; older students (through high school) may also be offered significant discounts.

FOR STUDENTS   Always carry your student identification with you. Tourist attractions, transportation systems, and other services may offer discounts if you have appropriate proof of your student status. Don't be afraid to ask. A high-school or college ID card or International Student Card will suffice.

Student-oriented activities abound on and around college campuses, especially at the University of New Mexico in Albuquerque. In Santa Fe, there are two small four-year colleges: the College of Santa Fe and St. John's College.

5   Getting There

BY PLANE   The gateway to Santa Fe, Taos, and other northern New Mexico communities is the **Albuquerque International Sunport** (☎ **505/842-4366** for the administrative offices; call the individual airlines for flight information).

Airlines serving Albuquerque include American (☎ **800/433-7300**), America West (☎ **800/235-9292**), Continental (☎ **800/525-0280**), Delta (☎ **800/221-1212**), Southwest (☎ **800/435-9792**), TWA (☎ **800/221-2000**), and United (☎ **800/241-6522**).

BY TRAIN   Amtrak (☎ **800/USA-RAIL** or 505/842-9650) passes through northern New Mexico twice daily. The *Southwest Chief,* which runs between Chicago and Los Angeles, stops once eastbound and once westbound in Gallup, Grants, Albuquerque, Lamy (for Santa Fe), Las Vegas, and Raton.

You can get a copy of Amtrak's National Timetable from any Amtrak station, from travel agents, or by writing Amtrak, 400 N. Capitol St. NW, Washington, DC 20001.

BY BUS   Because Santa Fe is only about 58 miles northeast of Albuquerque via I-40, most visitors to Santa Fe take the bus directly from the Albuquerque airport. **Shuttlejack** buses (☎ **505/243-3244** in Albuquerque, **505/982-4311** in Santa Fe), make the 70-minute run between the airport and Santa Fe hotels 7 to 10 times daily each way, from 5am to 10:15pm (cost is $20, one way, payable to the driver). Reservations are required. Three other bus services shuttle between Albuquerque and Taos (via Santa Fe) for $35 one-way, $65 round-trip: **Pride of Taos Tours/ Shuttles** (☎ **505/758-8340**), **Faust's Transportation** (☎ **505/758-3410**), and **Twin Heart Express & Transportation** (☎ **505/751-1201**).

The public bus depot in Albuquerque is located on 2nd Street at Silver Avenue (300 2nd Street SW). Contact **Texas, New Mexico and Oklahoma** (T.N.M.& O.) ☎ **505/242-4998** for information and schedules. Fares run about $11 to Santa Fe and $20 to Taos. However, the bus stations in Santa Fe (858 St. Michael's Dr.; ☎ **505/471-0008**) and Taos (at the Chevron bypass station at the corner of US 64 and NM 68; ☎ **505/758-1144**) are several miles south of each city center. Because additional taxi or shuttle service is needed to reach most accommodations, travelers usually find it more convenient to pay a few extra dollars for an airport-to-hotel shuttle.

BY CAR   The most convenient way to get around the Santa Fe region is by private car. **Auto and RV rentals** are widely available for those who arrive without their own transportation, either at the Albuquerque airport or at locations around each city.

I have received good rates and service from **Avis** at the Albuquerque airport (☎ **800/331-1212**, 505/842-4080, or 505/982-4361 in Santa Fe); **Thrifty**, 2039 Yale Blvd. SE, Albuquerque (☎ **800/367-2277** or 505/842-8733); **Hertz**, Albuquerque International Airport (☎ **800/654-3131** or 505/842-4235); **Dollar**, Albuquerque International Airport (☎ **800/369-4226** or 505/842-4304); **Budget**, Albuquerque International Airport (☎ **505/768-5900**); **Alamo**, 2601 Yale SE (☎ **800/327-9633**); and **Rent-A-Wreck of Albuquerque**, 501 Yale SE (☎ **800/247-9556** or 505/242-9556).

Drivers who need wheelchair-accessible transportation should call **Wheelchair Getaways of New Mexico**, 1015 Tramway Lane NE (☎ **800/408-2626** or 505/247-2626); it rents vans by the day, week, or month.

If you're **arriving by car** from elsewhere in North America, Albuquerque is at the crossroads of two major interstate highways. **I-40** runs from Wilmington, North Carolina (1,870 miles east), to Barstow, California (580 miles west). I-25 extends from Buffalo, Wyoming (850 miles north), to El Paso, Texas (265 miles south). **I-25** skims past Santa Fe's southern city limits. To reach Taos, you'll have to leave I-25 at Santa Fe and travel north 74 miles via **US 84/285** and **NM 68**, or exit I-25 9 miles south of Raton, near the Colorado border, and proceed 100 miles west on **US 64**.

The table on page 20 shows the approximate mileage to Santa Fe from various cities around the United States.

PACKAGE TOURS   Of course, you don't really need to take a package tour when traveling in New Mexico, but they are available and may be less expensive than if you booked the trip yourself because group tour operators often secure better rates than individual travelers. Tours within the state of New Mexico are offered by the following inbound operators:

Destination Southwest, Inc., 121 Tijeras NE, Suite 1100, Albuquerque, NM 87102 (☎ **800/999-3109** or 505/766-9068; fax 505/766-9065).

Gray Line Tours, 800 Rio Grande NW, Suite 22, Albuquerque, NM 87104 (☎ **800/256-8991** or 505/242-3880; fax 505/243-0692).

Distances to Santa Fe (in miles)

From	Distance	From	Distance
Atlanta	1,417	Minneapolis	1,199
Boston	2,190	New Orleans	1,181
Chicago	1,293	New York	1,971
Cleveland	1,558	Oklahoma City	533
Dallas	663	Phoenix	595
Denver	391	St. Louis	993
Detroit	1,514	Salt Lake City	634
Houston	900	San Francisco	1,149
Los Angeles	860	Seattle	1,477
Miami	2,011	Washington, D.C.	1,825

Rojotours & Services, P.O. Box 15744, Santa Fe, NM 87506-5744 (☎ **505/474-8333;** fax 505/474-2992).

Sun Tours, Ltd., 4300 San Mateo Blvd. NE, Suite B-155, Albuquerque, NM 87110 (☎ **505/889-8888**).

Travel New Mexico, Inc., 6101 Candelaria NE, Albuquerque, NM 87110 (☎ **800/333-7159** or 505/883-9178; e-mail travelnm@swcp.com; Internet World Wide Web home page http://www.viva.com/nm/travelnm.html).

CWT-A to Z Travelink, 6020 Indian School Rd., Albuquerque, NM 87110 (☎ **800/366-0282** or 505/883-5865; fax 505/883-0038).

For Foreign Visitors 3

Although American fads and fashions have spread across Europe and other parts of the world so much that the United States may seem like familiar territory before your arrival, there are still many peculiarities and uniquely American situations that any foreign visitor may encounter.

1 Preparing for Your Trip

ENTRY REQUIREMENTS

DOCUMENT REQUIREMENTS   Canadian citizens may enter the United States without passports or visas; they need only proof of residence.

Citizens of the United Kingdom, New Zealand, Japan, and most Western European countries traveling on valid passports may not need a visa for fewer than 90 days of holiday or business travel to the United States, provided that they hold a round-trip or return ticket and enter the United States on an airline or cruise line participating in the visa waiver program. (Note that citizens of these visa-exempt countries who first enter the United States may then visit Mexico, Canada, Bermuda, and/or the Caribbean Islands and then reenter the United States by any mode of transportation, without needing a visa. Further information is available from any U.S. embassy or consulate.)

Citizens of countries other than those stipulated above, including citizens of Australia, must have two documents: (1) a valid **passport** with an expiration date at least six months later than the scheduled end of their visit to the United States; and (2) a **tourist visa,** available without charge from the nearest U.S. consulate.

To obtain a visa, the traveler must submit a completed application form (either in person or by mail) with a $1\frac{1}{2}$-inch-square photo and must demonstrate binding ties to a residence abroad. Usually you can obtain a visa immediately or within 24 hours, but it may take longer during the summer rush from June to August. If you cannot go in person, contact the nearest U.S. embassy or consulate for directions on applying by mail. Your travel agent or airline office may also be able to provide you with visa applications and instructions. The U.S. embassy or consulate that issues your visa will determine whether you will be given a multiple- or single-entry visa and any restrictions regarding the length of your stay.

MEDICAL REQUIREMENTS   No inoculations are needed to enter the United States unless you're coming from, or have stopped over in, areas known to be suffering from epidemics, particularly cholera or yellow fever.

If you have a disease that needs treatment with medications containing narcotics or drugs requiring a syringe, carry a valid signed prescription from your physician to allay any suspicions that you are smuggling drugs.

CUSTOMS REQUIREMENTS   Every adult visitor may bring in free of duty: 1 liter of wine or hard liquor; 200 cigarettes or 100 cigars (but no cigars from Cuba) or 3 pounds of smoking tobacco; and $100 worth of gifts. These exemptions are offered to travelers who spend at least 72 hours in the United States and who have not claimed them within the preceding six months. It's altogether forbidden to bring into the country foodstuffs (particularly cheese, fruit, cooked meats, and canned goods) and plants (vegetables, seeds, tropical plants, and so on). Foreign tourists may bring in or take out up to $10,000 in U.S. or foreign currency with no formalities; larger sums must be declared to Customs on entering or leaving the country.

INSURANCE

Unlike Canada and Europe, there is no national health-care system in the United States. Because the cost of medical care is extremely high, I strongly advise every traveler to secure health insurance coverage before setting out.

You may want to take out a comprehensive travel policy that covers (for a relatively low premium) sickness or injury costs (medical, surgical, and hospital); loss or theft of your baggage; trip-cancellation costs; guarantee of bail in case you are arrested; costs of accidents, repatriation, or death. Such packages (for example, "Europe Assistance Worldwide Services" in Europe) are sold by automobile clubs at attractive rates, as well as by insurance companies and travel agencies.

MONEY

CURRENCY & EXCHANGE   The U.S. monetary system has a decimal base: one American **dollar** ($1) = 100 **cents** (100¢).

Dollar bills commonly come in $1 ("a buck"), $5, $10, $20, $50, and $100 denominations (the last two are not welcome when paying for small purchases and are not accepted in taxis or at subway ticket booths). There are also $2 bills (seldom encountered).

There are six denominations of coins: 1¢ (one cent or "penny"), 5¢ (five cents or "nickel"), 10¢ (ten cents or "dime"), 25¢ (twenty-five cents or "quarter"), 50¢ (fifty cents or "half dollar"), and the rare $1 piece.

Note: The "foreign-exchange bureaus" so common in Europe are rare even at airports in the United States and nonexistent outside major cities. Try to avoid having to change foreign money (or traveler's checks denominated in a currency other than U.S. dollars) at a small-town bank or even a branch bank in a big city. In fact, leave any currency other than U.S. dollars at home—it may prove a greater nuisance to you than it's worth.

TRAVELER'S CHECKS   Traveler's checks denominated in U.S. dollars are readily accepted at most hotels, motels, restaurants, and large stores. But the best place to change traveler's checks is at a bank. Do not bring traveler's checks denominated in other currencies.

CREDIT & CHARGE CARDS   The method of payment most widely used is credit and charge cards: Visa (BarclayCard in Britain), MasterCard (EuroCard in

Europe, Access in Britain, Chargex in Canada), American Express, Diners Club, Discover, and Carte Blanche. You can save yourself trouble by using "plastic money" rather than cash or traveler's checks in most hotels, motels, restaurants, and retail stores (a growing number of food and liquor stores now accept credit/charge cards). You must have a credit or charge card to rent a car. It can also be used as proof of identity (often carrying more weight than a passport) or as a "cash card," enabling you to draw money from banks and automated-teller machines (ATMs) that accept it.

SAFETY

GENERAL   While tourist areas are generally safe, crime is on the increase everywhere, especially in large U.S. cities. It would be wise to check with the tourist offices in Santa Fe, Taos, and Albuquerque if you are in doubt about which neighborhoods are safe. (See the "Orientation" sections in chapters 4, 11, and 15 for the names and addresses of the specific tourist bureaus.)

Remember that hotels are open to the public, and in a large hotel, security may not be able to screen everyone who enters. Always lock your room door; don't assume that once inside your hotel you are automatically safe and no longer need to be aware of your surroundings.

DRIVING   Question your rental agency about personal safety, or ask for a brochure of traveler safety tips when you pick up your car. Obtain written directions, or a map with the route clearly marked, from the agency to show you how to get to your destination. And, if possible, arrive and depart during daylight hours.

In recent years, a crime that targets both cars and drivers, known as "car-jacking," has been on the rise in all U.S. cities. If you exit off a highway into a questionable neighborhood, leave the area as quickly as possible. If you have an accident, even on the highway, stay in your car with the doors locked until you assess the situation or until the police arrive. If you are bumped from behind by another car on the street or are involved in a minor accident with no injuries and the situation appears to be suspicious, motion to the other driver to follow you to the nearest police precinct, a well-lit service station, or an all-night store. *Never* get out of your car in such situations.

If you see someone on the road who indicates a need for help, do *not* stop. Take note of the location, drive on to a well-lighted area, and telephone the police by dialing **911.**

Also, make sure that you have enough gasoline in your tank to reach your intended destination, so that you're not forced to look for a service station in an unfamiliar and possibly unsafe neighborhood—especially at night.

SPECIAL SERVICES

The Santa Fe Council on International Relations, P.O. Box 1223, Santa Fe, NM 87501 (☎ 505/982-4931; fax 505/982-4931), assists foreign visitors by providing community information. An office in Room 281 of La Fonda Hotel on the Plaza is open Monday through Friday from 9:30am to 12:30pm.

2 Getting to the U.S.

Travelers from overseas can take advantage of the **APEX (Advance-Purchase Excursion) fares** offered by all the major international carriers. Aside from these, attractive values are offered by **Icelandair** on flights from Luxembourg to New York and by **Virgin Atlantic Airways** from London to New York/Newark and to Los Angeles. To reach northern New Mexico from Europe, you'll probably have to stop at one of these airports anyway to catch a connecting flight.

British travelers should check out **British Airways** (☎ 0345/222-111 in the U.K., or 800/247-9297 in the U.S.), which offers direct flights from London to New York and to Los Angeles, as does **Virgin Atlantic Airways** (☎ 0293/747-747 in the U.K., or 800/862-8621 in the U.S.). Canadian readers might book flights on **Air Canada** (☎ 800/268-7240 in Canada, or 800/776-3000 in the U.S.), which offers service from Toronto, Montréal, and Calgary to New York and to Los Angeles. In addition, many other international carriers also serve the New York and Los Angeles airports, including: **Air France** (☎ 800/237-2747), **Alitalia** (☎ 800/223-5730), **Japan Airlines** (☎ 800/525-3663), **Lufthansa** (☎ 800/645-3880), **Quantas** (☎ 008/177-767 in Australia), **Swissair** (☎ 800/221-4750), and **SAS** (☎ 800/221-2350).

Visitors arriving by air, no matter what the port of entry, should cultivate patience and resignation before setting foot on U.S. soil. Getting through Immigration control may take as long as two hours on some days, especially summer weekends. Add the time it takes to clear Customs and you'll see that you should allow extra time for delays when planning connections between international and domestic flights—an average of two to three hours at least.

In contrast, travelers arriving by car or by rail from Canada will find that the border-crossing formalities have been streamlined practically to the vanishing point. And air travelers from Canada, Bermuda, and some places in the Caribbean can sometimes go through Customs and Immigration at the point of departure, which is much quicker and less painful.

For further information about transportation to Santa Fe, Taos, and Albuquerque, see "Orientation" Chapters 4, 11, and 15, respectively.

3 Getting Around the U.S.

BY PLANE On transatlantic or transpacific flights, some prominent American airlines (for example, American Airlines, Delta, Northwest, TWA, and United) offer travelers special discount tickets under the name **Visit USA,** allowing travel between any U.S. destinations at minimum rates. These tickets not on sale in the United States, and must, therefore, be purchased before you leave your foreign point of departure. This system is the best, easiest, and fastest way to see the United States at low cost. You should obtain information well in advance from your travel agent or the office of the airline concerned, since the conditions attached to these discount tickets can be changed without advance notice.

BY TRAIN Long-distance trains in the United States are operated by Amtrak, the national rail passenger corporation. International visitors can buy a **USA Railpass,** good for 15 or 30 days of unlimited travel on Amtrak. The pass is available through many foreign travel agents. In 1996 prices for a 15-day pass were $245 off-peak, $355 peak; a 30-day pass costs $350 off-peak, $440 peak. (With a foreign passport, you can also buy passes at some Amtrak offices in the United States, including locations in Boston, Chicago, Los Angeles, Miami, New York, San Francisco, and Washington, D.C.) Reservations are generally required and should be made for each part of your trip as early as possible. Even cheaper than the above are **regional USA Railpasses,** allowing unlimited travel through a specific section of the United

States. Reservations are generally required and should be made for each part of your trip as early as possible.

Visitors should be aware of the limitations of long-distance rail travel in the United States. With a few notable exceptions, service is rarely up to European standards: Delays are common, routes are limited and often infrequently served, and fares are rarely much lower than discount airfares. Thus, cross-country train travel should be approached with caution.

BY BUS   The cheapest way to travel around the United States is by bus. Greyhound/Trailways, the sole nationwide bus line, offers an **Ameripass** for unlimited travel for 7 days (for $179), 15 days (for $289), 30 days (for $399), and 60 days (for $559). Bus travel in the United States can be both slow and uncomfortable, so this option is not for everyone. Furthermore, bus stations are often situated in undesirable neighborhoods.

BY CAR   Travel by car gives visitors the freedom to make—and alter—their itineraries to suit their own needs and interests. And it offers the opportunity to visit some of the off-the-beaten-path locations, places that cannot be reached easily by public transportation. For information on renting cars in the United States, see "Automobile Organizations" and "Automobile Rentals" in "Fast Facts: For the Foreign Traveler," below; "By Car" in "Getting There," in Chapter 2; and "By Car" in "Getting Around," in Chapters 4, 11, and 15.

FAST FACTS: For the Foreign Traveler

Automobile Organizations   Auto clubs will supply maps, suggested routes, guidebooks, accident and bail-bond insurance, and emergency road service. The major auto club in the United States, with 955 offices nationwide, is the **American Automobile Association (AAA).** Members of some foreign auto clubs have reciprocal arrangements with the AAA and enjoy its services at no charge. If you belong to an auto club in your home country, inquire about AAA reciprocity before you leave. You may be able to join the AAA even if you're not a member of a reciprocal club; to inquire, call the AAA (☎ **800/222-4357**). The AAA can provide you with an **International Driving Permit,** validating your foreign license.

In addition, some automobile-rental agencies now provide many of these same services. Inquire about their availability when you rent your car.

Automobile Rentals   To rent a car you will need a major credit or charge card and a valid driver's license. In addition, you usually need to be at least 25 years old (some companies do rent to younger people but add a daily surcharge). Be sure to return your car with the same amount of gas you started out with; rental companies charge excessive prices for gasoline. See "By Car" in "Getting Around," in chapters 4, 11, and 15, for the phone numbers of car-rental companies in Santa Fe, Taos, and Albuquerque, respectively.

Business Hours   See "Fast Facts" in chapters 4, 11, and 15.

Climate   See "When to Go," in Chapter 2.

Currency Exchange   You'll find currency-exchange services at major airports with international service. Elsewhere, they may be quite difficult to come by. In the United States, a very reliable choice is **Thomas Cook Currency Services, Inc.** They sell commission-free foreign and U.S. traveler's checks, drafts, and wire transfers; they also do check collections (including Eurochecks). Their rates are competitive and the service excellent. Thomas Cook maintains several offices in New York City, including one at 511 Madison Ave. (☎ **212/757-6915**), and at the JFK Airport International Arrivals Terminal (☎ **718/656-8444**).

For Santa Fe, Taos, and Albuquerque banks that handle foreign-currency exchange, see the "Fast Facts" sections in Chapters 4, 11, and 15, respectively.

Drinking Laws   You must be 21 to purchase alcoholic beverages in New Mexico.

Electric Current   The United States uses 110–120 volts A, 60 cycles, compared with 220–240 volts A, 50 cycles, as in most of Europe. In addition to a 100-volt transformer, small appliances of non-American manufacture, such as hair dryers or shavers, will require a plug adapter, with two flat, parallel pins.

Embassies/Consulates   All embassies are located in the national capital, Washington, D.C.; some consulates are located in major U.S. cities, and most countries maintain a mission to the United Nations in New York City. The embassies and consulates of the major English-speaking countries—Australia, Canada, the Republic of Ireland, New Zealand, and the United Kingdom—are listed below. If you are from another country, you can get the telephone number of your embassy by calling "Information" in Washington, D.C. (☎ **202/555-1212**).

The embassy of **Australia** is at 1601 Massachusetts Ave. NW, Washington, D.C. 20036 (☎ **202/797-3000**). There is an Australian consulate at Century Plaza Towers, 19th Floor, 2049 Century Park East, Los Angeles, CA 90007 (☎ **310/229-4800**). The consulate in New York is located at the International Building, 630 Fifth Ave., Suite 420, New York, NY 10111 (☎ **212/408-8400**).

The embassy of **Canada** is at 501 Pennsylvania Ave. NW, Washington, D.C. 20001 (☎ **202/682-1740**). There's a Canadian consulate in Los Angeles at 550 S. Hope St., 9th floor, Los Angeles, CA 90071 (☎ **213/346-2700**). The one in New York is located at 1251 Avenue of the Americas, New York, NY 10020 (☎ **212/596-1600**).

The embassy of the **Republic of Ireland** is at 2234 Massachusetts Ave. NW, Washington, D.C. 20008 (☎ **202/462-3939**). The consulate in New York is located at 345 Park Ave., 17th floor, New York, NY 10022 (☎ **212/319-2555**). The consulate in San Francisco is at 655 Montgomery St., Suite 930, San Francisco, CA 94111 (☎ **415/392-4214**).

The embassy of **New Zealand** is at 37 Observatory Circle NW, Washington, D.C. 20008 (☎ **202/328-4800**). The consulate in New York is located at 780 3rd Ave., Suite 1904, New York, NY 10017-2024 (☎ **212/832-4038**). The consulate in Los Angeles is located at 12400 Wilshire Blvd., Suite 1150, Los Angeles, CA 90025 (☎ **310/207-1605**).

The embassy of the **United Kingdom** is at 3100 Massachusetts Ave. NW, Washington, D.C. 20008 (☎ **202/462-1340**). The consulate in New York is located at 845 Third Ave., New York, NY 10022 (☎ **212/745-0200**). The consulate in Los Angeles is located at 11766 Wilshire Blvd., Suite 400, Los Angeles, CA 90025 (☎ **310/477-3322**).

Emergencies   Call **911** to report a fire, call the police, or get an ambulance. This is a toll-free call (no coins are required at a public telephone).

If you encounter traveler's problems, check the local telephone directory to find an office of the Traveler's Aid Society, a nationwide, nonprofit, social-service organization geared to helping travelers in difficult straits. Their services might include reuniting families separated while traveling, providing food and/or shelter to people stranded without cash, or even offering emotional counseling. If you're in trouble, seek them out.

Gasoline (Petrol)   One U.S. gallon equal 3.8 liters or .83 Imperial gallon. There are usually several grades (and price levels) of gasoline available at most gas stations, and their names change from company to company. Unleaded gas with the highest octane ratings are the most expensive; however, most rental cars take the least expensive—"regular" unleaded gas. Furthermore, the price is often lower if you pay in cash rather than by credit or charge card.

Finally, many gas stations now offer lower-priced self-service gas pumps—in fact, some gas stations, particularly at night, are all self-service.

Holidays   On the following legal national holidays, banks, government offices, post offices, and many stores, restaurants, and museums are closed: January 1 (New Year's Day), the third Monday in January (Martin Luther King, Jr.'s Birthday [observed]), the third Monday in February (Presidents' Day, Washington's Birthday), the last Monday in May (Memorial Day), July 4 (Independence Day), the first Monday in September (Labor Day), the second Monday in October (Columbus Day), November 11 (Veterans' Day/Armistice Day), fourth Thursday in November (Thanksgiving Day), and December 25 (Christmas). Also, the Tuesday following the first Monday in November is Election Day and is a legal holiday in presidential-election years (next in 2000).

Legal Aid   The well-meaning foreign visitor will probably never become involved with the American legal system. However, there are a few things you should know just in case. If you are stopped for a minor infraction of the highway code (for example, speeding), never attempt to pay the fine directly to a police officer; you may wind up arrested on the much more serious charge of attempted bribery. Pay fines by mail or directly to the clerk of the court. If you're accused of a more serious offense, it's wise to say and do nothing before consulting a lawyer. Under U.S. law, an arrested person is allowed one telephone call to a party of his or her choice. Call your embassy or consulate.

Mail   If you want your mail to follow you on your vacation and you aren't sure of your address, your mail can be sent to you, in your name, **c/o General Delivery** (Poste Restante) at the main post office of the city or region where you expect to be. (For the addresses and telephone numbers in Santa Fe, Taos, and Albuquerque, see the "Fast Facts" sections in chapters 4, 11, and 15, respectively.) The addressee must pick up the mail in person and must produce proof of identity (driver's license, credit or charge card, passport, etc.).

Domestic **postage rates** are 20¢ for a postcard and 32¢ for a letter. Check with any local post office for current international postage rates to your home country.

Generally found at intersections, **mailboxes** are blue with a red-and-white stripe and carry the designation **U.S. Mail.** If your mail is addressed to a U.S. destination, don't forget to add the five-digit **postal code,** or ZIP (Zone Improvement Plan) code, after the two-letter abbreviation of the state to which the mail is addressed (CA for California, NM for New Mexico, NY for New York, and so on).

Newspapers and Magazines   National newspapers include *The New York Times, USA Today,* and the *Wall Street Journal.* National news weeklies include *Newsweek, Time,* and *U.S. News and World Report.* In large cities most newsstands offer a small selection of the most popular foreign periodicals and newspapers, such as the *Economist, Le Monde,* and *Der Spiegel.* For information on local publications, see the "Fast Facts" sections in chapters 4, 11, and 15.

Radio/Television   Audiovisual media, with four coast-to-coast networks—ABC, CBS, NBC, and Fox—joined in recent years by the Public Broadcasting System (PBS) and the cable network CNN, play a major part in American life. In big cities, televiewers have a choice of several dozen channels (including basic cable), most of them transmitting 24 hours a day, not counting the pay-TV channels that show recent movies or sports events. All options are usually indicated on your hotel TV set. You'll also find a wide choice of local radio stations, both AM and FM, each broadcasting particular kinds of talk shows and/or music—classical, country, jazz, pop, gospel—punctuated by news broadcasts and frequent commercials.

Restrooms   Visitors can usually find a restroom in a bar, restaurant, hotel, museum, department store, service station, or train station.

Safety   See "Safety" in "Preparing for Your Trip," earlier in this chapter.

Taxes   In the United States there is no VAT (value-added tax) or other indirect tax at a national level. Every state, and each county and city in it, has the right to levy its own local tax on purchases, including hotel and restaurant checks, airline tickets, and so on. Taxes are already included in the price of certain services, such as public transportation, cab fares, telephone calls, and gasoline. The amount of sales tax varies from about 4% to 12%, depending on the state and city, so when you're making major purchases, such as photographic equipment, clothing, or stereo components, it can be a significant part of the cost.

Telephone/Telegraph/Telex   The telephone system in the United States is run by private corporations, so rates, especially for long-distance service and operator-assisted calls, can vary widely—even on calls made from public telephones. Local calls in the United States usually cost 25¢ (they're 25¢ throughout New Mexico).

Generally, hotel surcharges on long-distance and local calls are astronomical. It's generally cheaper to call collect, use a telephone charge card, or use a **public pay telephone,** which you'll find clearly marked in most public buildings and private establishments as well as on the street. Outside metropolitan areas, public telephones are more difficult to find. Stores and gas stations are your best bet.

Most **long-distance and international calls** can be dialed directly from any phone (stock up on quarters if you're calling from a pay phone or use a telephone charge card). For calls to Canada and other parts of the United States, dial **1** followed by the area code and the seven-digit number. For international calls, dial **011** followed by the country code (Australia, 61; Republic of Ireland, 353; New Zealand, 64; United Kingdom, 44), then the city code (for example, 171 or 181 for London, 121 for Birmingham) and the telephone number of the person you wish to call.

For reversed-charge or collect calls, and for person-to-person calls, dial **0** (zero, not the letter "O") followed by the area code and number you want; an operator will then come on the line, and you should specify that you are calling collect, or person-to-person, or both. If your operator-assisted call is international, ask for the overseas operator.

For local **directory assistance** ("information"), dial **411;** for long-distance information, dial **1,** then the appropriate area code and **555-1212.**

Like the telephone system, **telegraph** and **telex** services are provided by private corporations like ITT, MCI, and above all, Western Union, the most important. You can bring your telegram in to the nearest Western Union office (there are hundreds across the country) or dictate it over the phone (☎ **800/325-6000**). You can also telegraph money (using a major credit or charge card), or have it telegraphed to you, very quickly over the Western Union system. (Note, however, that this service can be very expensive—the charge can run as high as 15% to 25% of the amount sent.)

Most hotels have **fax** machines available for guest use (be sure to ask about the charge to use it), and many hotel rooms are even wired for guests' fax machines. You'll probably also see signs for public faxes in the windows of local shops.

Telephone Directory   There are two kinds of telephone directories available to you. The general directory is the so-called **White Pages,** in which private and business subscribers are listed in alphabetical order. The inside front cover lists the emergency number for police, fire, and ambulance, and other vital numbers (like the poison-control center, crime-victims hotline, and so on). The first few pages are devoted to community-service numbers, including a guide to long-distance and international calling, complete with country codes and area codes.

The second directory, printed on yellow paper (hence its name, **Yellow Pages**), lists all local services, businesses, and industries by type of activity, with an index at the back. The listings cover not only such obvious items as automobile repairs by make of car or drugstores (pharmacies), often by geographical location, but also restaurants by type of cuisine and geographical location, bookstores by special subject and/or language, places of worship by religious denomination, and other information that the tourist might otherwise not readily find. The **Yellow Pages** also often include city plans or detailed area maps, often showing ZIP codes and public transportation routes.

Time The United States is divided into six **time zones:** From east to west, Eastern standard time (EST), Central standard time (CST), Mountain standard time (MST), Pacific standard time (PST), Alaska standard time (AST), and Hawaii standard time (HST). Always keep the changing time zones in mind if you are traveling (or even telephoning) long distances in the United States. For example, noon in New York City (EST) is 11am in Chicago (CST), 10am in Santa Fe (MST), 9am in Los Angeles (PST), 8am in Anchorage (AST), and 7am in Honolulu (HST).

New Mexico is on Mountain standard time (MST), seven hours behind Greenwich Mean Time. **Daylight saving time** is in effect from the first Sunday in April through the last Saturday in October (actually, the change is made at 2am on Sunday), except in Arizona, Hawaii, part of Indiana, and Puerto Rico. Daylight saving time moves the clock one hour ahead of standard time. (Americans use the adage "Spring ahead, fall back" to remember which way to change their clocks and watches.)

Tipping This is part of the American way of life, based on the principle that one should pay for any special service received. (Often service personnel receive little direct salary and must depend on tips for their income.) Here are some rules of thumb:

In **hotels,** tip bellhops $1 per piece of luggage carried, and tip the chamber staff $1 per day. Tip the doorman or concierge only if he or she has provided some specific service (for example, calling a cab for you or obtaining difficult-to-get theater tickets).

In **restaurants, bars, and nightclubs,** tip the service staff 15% of the check, tip bartenders 10% to 15%, tip checkroom attendants $1 per garment, and tip valet-parking attendants $1 per vehicle. Tip the doorman only if he has provided some specific service (such as calling a cab for you). Tipping is not expected in cafeterias and fast-food restaurants.

Tip **cab drivers** 15% of the fare.

As for **other service personnel,** tip redcaps at airports or railroad stations $1 per piece of luggage, and tip hairdressers and barbers 15% to 20%.

Tipping ushers in cinemas, movies, and theaters and gas-station attendants is not expected.

THE AMERICAN SYSTEM OF MEASUREMENTS

Length

1 inch (in.)			=	2.54cm		
1 foot (ft.)	=	12 in.	=	30.48cm	=	.305m
1 yard (yd.)	=	3 ft.			=	.915m
1 mile (m)	=	5,280 ft.			=	1.609km

To convert miles to kilometers, multiply the number of miles by 1.61 (for example, 50 mi. X 1.61 = 80.5km). Note that this conversion can also be used to convert speeds from miles per hour (m.p.h.) to kilometers per hour (kmph).

To convert kilometers to miles, multiply the number of kilometers by .62 (for example, 25km X .62 = 15.5 mi.). Note that this same conversion can be used to convert speeds from kmph to m.p.h.

Capacity

1 fluid ounce (fl. oz.)			=	.03 liter		
1 pint (pt.)	=	16 fl. oz.	=	.47 liter		
1 quart (qt.)	=	2 pints	=	.94 liter		
1 gallon (gal.)	=	4 quarts	=	3.79 liters	=	.83 Imperial gal.

To convert U.S. gallons to liters, multiply the number of gallons by 3.79 (for example, 12 gal. ✕ 3.79 = 45.48 liters).

To convert liters to U.S. gallons, multiply the number of liters by .26 (for example, 50 liters ✕ .26 = 13 U.S. gal.).

To convert U.S. gallons to Imperial gallons, multiply the number of U.S. gallons by .83 (for example, 12 U.S. gal. ✕ .83 = 9.96 Imperial gal.).

To convert Imperial gallons to U.S. gallons, multiply the number of Imperial gallons by 1.2 (for example, 8 Imperial gal. ✕ 1.2 = 9.6 U.S. gal.).

Weight

1 ounce (oz.)			=	28.35g				
1 pound (lb.)	=	16 oz.	=	453.6g	=	.45 kg		
1 ton	=	2,000 lb.			=	907kg	=	.91 metric ton

To convert pounds to kilograms, multiply the number of pounds by .45 (for example, 90 lb. ✕ .45 = 40.5kg).

To convert kilograms to pounds, multiply the number of kilograms by 2.2 (for example, 75kg ✕ 2.2 = 165 lb.).

Area

1 acre			=	.41ha		
1 square mile	=	640 acres	=	2.59ha	=	2.6km^2

To convert acres to hectares, multiply the number of acres by .41 (for example, 40 acres ✕ .41 = 16.4ha).

To convert hectares to acres, multiply the number of hectares by 2.47 (for example, 20ha ✕ 2.47 = 49.4 acres).

To convert square miles to square kilometers, multiply the number of square miles by 2.6 (for example, 80 sq. mi. ✕ 2.6 = 208 sq. km).

To convert square kilometers to square miles, multiply the number of square kilometers by .39 (for example, 150 sq. km ✕ .39 = 58.5 sq. mi.).

Temperature

°C –18°	–10		0		10		20		30		40
°F 0°	10	20	32	40	50	60	70	80	90	100	

To convert degrees Fahrenheit to degrees Celsius, subtract 32 from °F, multiply by 5, then divide by 9 (for example, 85°F – 32 ✕ 5 ÷ 9 = 29.4°C).

To convert degrees Celsius to degrees Fahrenheit, multiply °C by 9, divide by 5, and add 32 (for example, 20°C ✕ 9 ÷ 5 + 32 = 68°F).

Getting to Know Santa Fe

4

As far as cities go, Santa Fe is fairly easy to get around. Like most cities of Hispanic origin, it was built around a parklike central plaza, with its centuries-old adobe buildings and churches lining the narrow streets. Many of these buildings now house shops, restaurants, art galleries, and museums.

Santa Fe is situated high and dry at the foot of the rugged Sangre de Cristo range. Santa Fe Baldy (with an elevation of more than 12,600 feet) is located just 12 miles northeast of the Plaza. The city's downtown straddles the Santa Fe River, a tiny tributary of the Rio Grande which is little more than a trickle for much of the year.

North is the Española valley (offering a beautiful view from the Santa Fe Opera grounds) and beyond that, the village of Taos, about 66 miles away. South of the city are ancient Native American turquoise mines in the Cerrillos Hills, and to the southwest is metropolitan Albuquerque, some 58 miles away. To the west, across the Caja del Rio Plateau, is the Rio Grande, and beyond that, the 11,000-foot Jemez Mountains and Valle Grande—an ancient and massive volcanic caldera. Pueblos dot the entire Rio Grande valley an hour's drive in any direction.

1 Orientation

ARRIVING

By PLANE The **Santa Fe Municipal Airport** (☎ 505/473-7243), just outside the southwestern city limits on Airport Road off Cerrillos Road, has three paved runways, used primarily by private planes. In conjunction with United Airlines, commuter flights are offered by **United Express,** which is operated by Mountain West Airlines (☎ 800/241-6522). There are four daily departures from Denver during the week and three on weekends. When departing from Santa Fe, passengers can connect to other United Airlines flights in Denver. Call for schedules and fares. For charter services call **Santa Fe Aviation** (☎ 505/471-6533).

Getting to and from the airport: Virtually all air travelers to Santa Fe arrive in Albuquerque, where they either rent a car or take one of the bus services. See "Getting There," in Chapter 2, for details.

BY TRAIN & BUS For detailed information about train and bus service to Santa Fe, see "Getting There," in Chapter 2.

BY CAR   I-25 skims past Santa Fe's southern city limits, connecting it along one continuous highway from Billings, Montana, to El Paso, Texas. I-40, the state's major east-west thoroughfare, which   bisects Albuquerque, affords coast-to-coast access to "The City Different." (From the west, motorists leave I-40 in Albuquerque and take I-25 north; from the east, travelers exit I-40 at Clines Corners and continue 52 miles to Santa Fe on US 285.) For those coming from the northwest, the most direct route is via Durango, Colorado, on US 160, entering Santa Fe on US 84.

For information on **car rentals** in Albuquerque, see "Getting There," in Chapter 2; and for agencies in Santa Fe, see "Getting Around," later in this chapter.

VISITOR INFORMATION

The **Santa Fe Convention and Visitors Bureau** is located at 201 W. Marcy Street, in Sweeney Center at the corner of Grant Street downtown (P.O. Box 909), Santa Fe, NM 87504-0909 (☎ **800/777-CITY** or 505/984-6760). If you would like information before you leave home but don't want to wait for it to arrive by mail, try this web site address: http://www.santafe.org. It will take you directly to the Santa Fe Convention and Visitors Bureau's home page.

CITY LAYOUT

MAIN ARTERIES & STREETS   The limits of downtown Santa Fe are demarcated on three sides by the horseshoe-shaped **Paseo de Peralta** and on the west by **St. Francis Drive,** otherwise known as US 84/285. **Alameda Street** follows the north shore of the Santa Fe River through downtown, with the State Capitol and other federal buildings on the south side of the river and most buildings of historic and tourist interest on the north, east of Guadalupe Street.

The **Plaza** is Santa Fe's universally accepted point of orientation. Its four diagonal walkways meet at a central fountain, around which a strange and wonderful assortment of people of all ages, nationalities, and life-styles can be found at nearly any hour of the day or night.

If you stand in the center of the Plaza looking north, you'll be gazing directly at the Palace of the Governors. In front of you is Palace Avenue; behind you, San Francisco Street. To your left is Lincoln Avenue and to your right **Washington Avenue,** which divides the downtown avenues into "east" and "west." St. Francis Cathedral is the massive Romanesque structure a block east, down San Francisco Street. Alameda Street is two full blocks behind you.

Streaking diagonally to the southwest from the downtown area, beginning opposite the state office buildings on Galisteo Avenue, is **Cerrillos Road.** Once the main north-south highway connecting New Mexico's state capital with its largest city, it is now a 6-mile-long motel and fast-food "strip." St. Francis Drive, which crosses Cerrillos Road three blocks south of Guadalupe Street, is a far less tawdry byway, linking Santa Fe with I-25, located 4 miles southeast of downtown. The **Old Pecos Trail,** on the east side of the city, also joins downtown and the freeway. **St. Michael's Drive** interconnects the three arteries.

FINDING AN ADDRESS   Because of the way the city is laid out, it's often difficult to know exactly where to look for a particular street address. It's best to call ahead for directions.

MAPS   Free city and state maps can be obtained at tourist information offices. An excellent state highway map is published by the New Mexico Department of Tourism, 491 Old Santa Fe Trail, Santa Fe, NM 87504 (P.O. Box 20002, Santa Fe,

NM 87504, (☎ **800/733-6396** or 505/827-7336). There's also a Santa Fe Visitors Center in the same building. More specific county and city maps are available from the State Highway and Transportation Department, 1120 Cerrillos Rd., Santa Fe, NM 87501 (☎ **505/827-5100**). Members of the American Automobile Association, 1644 St. Michael's Dr. (☎ **505/471-6620**), can obtain free maps from the AAA office. Other good regional maps can be purchased at area bookstores. Gousha publishes a laminated "FastMap" of Santa Fe and Taos that has proved indispensable during my travels.

2   Getting Around

BY BUS   In 1993, Santa Fe opened **Santa Fe Trails** (☎ **505/984-6730**), its first public bus system. There are six routes, and visitors can pick up a map from the Convention and Visitors Bureau. Buses operate Monday through Friday from 6am to 9pm and on Saturday from 8am to 8pm. There is no service on Sunday or holidays. Call for current schedule and fare information.

BY CAR   Cars can be rented from any of the following firms in Santa Fe: **Avis,** Garrett's Desert Inn, 311 Old Santa Fe Trail (☎ **505/982-4361**); **Budget,** 1946 Cerrillos Rd. (☎ **505/984-8028**); **Enterprise,** 1911 Fifth St., Suite 102 (☎ **505/473-3600**); and **Hertz,** Santa Fe Hilton, 100 Sandoval St. (☎ **505/982-1844**).

If Santa Fe is merely your base for an extended self-driving exploration of New Mexico, be sure to give the vehicle a thorough road check before starting out. There are a lot of wide-open desert and wilderness spaces in New Mexico, and if your car were to break down you could be stranded for hours in extreme heat or cold before someone might pass by.

Make sure your driver's license and auto club membership (if you're a member) are valid before you leave home. Check with your auto insurance company to make sure you're covered when out of state and/or when driving a rental car.

Street **parking** is difficult to find during the summer months. There's a parking lot near the federal courthouse, two blocks north of the Plaza; another one behind Santa Fe Village, a block south of the Plaza; and a third at Water and Sandoval streets. If you stop by the Santa Fe Convention and Visitors Bureau, at the corner of Grant and Marcy Streets, you can pick up a wallet-size guide to Santa Fe parking areas. The map shows both street and lot parking.

Unless otherwise posted, the **speed limit** on freeways is 65 m.p.h.; on most other two-lane open roads it's 55 m.p.h. The minimum age for drivers is 16. Seat belts are required for drivers and all passengers age 5 and over; children under 5 must use approved child seats.

Since **Native American reservations** enjoy a measure of self-rule, they can enforce certain designated laws. For instance, on the Navajo reservation (New Mexico's largest), it is forbidden to transport alcoholic beverages, to leave established roadways, or to go without a seat belt. Motorcyclists must wear helmets. If you are caught breaking reservation laws, you are subject to reservation punishment.

The State Highway and Transportation Department has a toll-free hotline (☎ **800/432-4269**) providing up-to-the-hour information on **road closures and conditions.**

A word of warning: New Mexico has the highest per capita rate of traffic deaths of any American state. Drive carefully!

BY TAXI   It's best to telephone for a cab, for they are difficult to flag from the street. Taxis have no meters, but fares are set for given distances. Expect to pay an average of about $2.50 per mile. **Capital City Cab** (☎ 505/438-0000) is the main company in Santa Fe.

BY BICYCLE/ON FOOT   A bicycle is an excellent way to get around town. Check with **Palace Bike Rentals,** 409 E. Palace Ave. (☎ 505/984-2151), for rentals.

The best way to see downtown Santa Fe is on foot. Free walking-tour maps are available at the tourist information center in Sweeney Center, 201 W. Marcy St. (☎ 800/777-CITY or 505/984-6760), and several walking tours are included in Chapter 7.

FAST FACTS: Santa Fe

American Express   There is no office in Santa Fe; the nearest one is in Albuquerque (see "Fast Facts: Albuquerque," in Chapter 15).

Area Code   All of New Mexico is in area code **505.**

Airport   See "Orientation," above.

Baby-sitters   Most hotels can arrange for sitters on request. Alternatively, call the Santa Fe Kid Connection at **505/471-3100.**

Business Hours   **Offices and stores** are generally open Monday through Friday from 9am to 5pm, with many stores also open Friday nights, Saturday, and Sunday in the summer season. Most **banks** are open Monday through Thursday from 10am to 3pm and on Friday from 10am to 6pm; drive-up windows may be open later. Some may also be open Saturday mornings. Most branches have cash machines available 24 hours. See also "Liquor Laws," below.

Car Rentals   See "Getting Around," above.

Climate   Santa Fe is consistently 10°F cooler than the nearby desert but has the same sunny skies, averaging more than 300 days of sunshine out of 365. Midsummer (July and August) days are dry and sunny (around 80°F), often with brief afternoon thunderstorms; evenings are typically in the upper 50s. Winters are mild and fair, with occasional and short-lived snow (average annual snowfall is 32 inches, although the ski basin gets an average of 225 inches). The average annual rainfall is 14 inches, most of it in summer; the relative humidity is 45%. (See also "When to Go" in Chapter 2.)

Currency Exchange   You can exchange foreign currency at two banks in Santa Fe: Sun West Bank, 1234 St. Michael's Dr. (☎ 505/471-1234) and First Security Bank, 121 Sandoval St. (☎ 505/983-4312).

Dentists   Located in the geographic center of the city is Dr. Leslie E. La Kind, at 400 Botulph Lane (☎ 505/988-3500). Dr. La Kind offers emergency service. You might also call the Dental Referral Services (☎ 800/917-6453) for help in finding a dentist.

Doctors   The Lovelace Alameda Clinic, 901 W. Alameda St. (☎ 505/995-2900), is in the Solano Center near St. Francis Drive. It's open daily from 8am to 8pm for urgent care, with no appointments required. For Physicians and Surgeons Referral and Information Services, call the American Board of Medical Specialties at **800/776-2378.**

Embassies/Consulates   See Chapter 3, "For Foreign Visitors."

Emergencies   For police, fire, or ambulance emergency, dial **911**.

Eyeglass Repair   The Quintana Optical Dispensary, 109 E. Marcy St. (☎ **505/988-4234**), provides one-hour prescription service Monday through Friday from 9am to 5pm and on Saturday from 9am to noon. They will also repair your current glasses.

Hospitals   St. Vincent Hospital, 455 St. Michael's Dr. (☎ **505/983-3361**), is a 268-bed regional health center. Patient services include urgent and emergency-room care and ambulatory surgery. Other health services include the AIDS Wellness Program (☎ **505/983-1822**) and Women's Health Services Family Care and Counseling Center (☎ **505/988-8869**). Lovelace Health Systems has a walk-in office at 901 W. Alameda St. (☎ **505/995-2900**).

Hotlines   The following hotlines are available in Santa Fe: battered families (☎ **505/473-5200**), poison control (☎ **800/432-6866**), psychiatric emergencies (☎ **505/983-3361**), and sexual assault (☎ **505/473-7818**).

Information   See "Visitor Information," above.

Libraries   The Santa Fe Public Library is half a block from the Plaza at 145 Washington Ave. (☎ **505/984-6780**). There are branch libraries at Villa Linda Mall and at 1713 Llano St., just off St. Michael's Drive. The New Mexico State Library is at 325 Don Gaspar Ave. (☎ **505/827-3800**). Specialty libraries include the Archives of New Mexico, 404 Montezuma St., and the New Mexico History Library, 110 Washington Ave.

Liquor Laws   The legal drinking age is 21 throughout New Mexico. Bars may remain open until 2am Monday through Saturday and until midnight on Sunday. Wine, beer, and spirits are sold at licensed supermarkets and liquor stores. There are no package sales on Sunday and no sales of any alcohol on election days. It is illegal to transport liquor through most Native American reservations.

Lost Property   Contact the city police at **505/473-5000**.

Newspapers and Magazines   The *New Mexican*—Santa Fe's daily paper—is the oldest newspaper in the West. Its offices are at 202 E. Marcy St. (☎ **505/983-3303**). The weekly *Santa Fe Reporter*, published on Wednesday, is often more willing to be controversial; its entertainment listings are excellent. Regional magazines published locally are *New Mexico Magazine* (monthly, statewide interest), the *Santa Fean Magazine* (monthly, local interest), *Santa Fe Lifestyle* (quarterly, local interest), and *Southwest Profile* (eight times a year, regional art).

Pharmacies   The **R&R Professional Pharmacy,** at 1691 Galisteo St. (☎ **505/988-9797**), is open Monday through Friday from 9am to 6pm and on Saturday from 9am to noon. Emergency and delivery service is available.

Photographic Needs   Everything from film purchases to camera repairs to one-hour processing can be handled by the Camera Shop, 109 E. San Francisco St. (☎ **505/983-6591**). Twenty-four-hour processing is available at Camera & Darkroom, 216 Galisteo St. (☎ **505/983-2948**).

Police   In case of emergency, dial **911**.

Post Offices   The Main Post Office is at 120 S. Federal Place (☎ **505/988-6351**), two blocks north and a block west of the Plaza. The Coronado Station branch is at 541 W. Cordova Rd. (☎ **505/438-8452**). Both are open Monday through Friday from 8am to 4pm and on Saturday from 9am to 1pm.

Most of the major hotels have stamp machines and mailboxes with twice-daily pickup. The ZIP code for central Santa Fe is 87501.

Radio   Santa Fe's radio stations include KMIK-AM 810 (all-news CBS affiliate), KTRC-AM 1400 (nostalgia music and early radio dramas), KSFR-FM 90.7 (classical), KNYN-FM 95.5 (country), KBAC-FM 98.1 (adult contemporary), KLSK-FM 104.1 (adult alternative), KBOM-FM 106.7 (Spanish), and KVSF, 1260 AM (news and talk). Albuquerque stations are easily received in Santa Fe.

Safety   Generally speaking, Santa Fe is an extremely safe city; however, as changes take place (see "Northern New Mexico Today" in Chapter 1), Santa Fe is becoming more and more like any large American city. Indeed, there have been increased reports of crime in recent years. It's easy to get a false sense of security in a city as attractive and friendly as Santa Fe, but I would advise visitors today to be as aware of their surroundings as they would be in any other major city in this country.

Taxes   A city bed tax of 3.875% and the state gross-receipts tax of 6.875% are added to all lodging bills.

Taxis   See "Getting Around," above.

Television   Two local independent television stations are KKTO-TV (Channel 2) and KCHF-TV (Channel 11); the latter offers Christian programming. The three Albuquerque network affiliates—KOB-TV (Channel 4, NBC), KOAT-TV (Channel 7, ABC), and KQRE-TV (Channel 13, CBS) all have offices at the State Capitol.

Time Zone   New Mexico is on Mountain standard time, one hour ahead of the West Coast and two hours behind the East Coast. When it's 10am in Santa Fe, it's noon in New York, 11am in Chicago, and 9am in San Francisco. Daylight saving time is in effect from early April to late October.

Useful Telephone Numbers   Information on road conditions in the Santa Fe area can be obtained from the state police (☎ **505/827-9300**). For time and temperature, call **505/473-2211**.

Weather   For weather forecasts, call **505/988-5151.**

Santa Fe Accommodations

5

There may not be a "bad" place to stay in Santa Fe. From downtown hotels to Cerrillos Road motels, from ranch-style resorts to quaint bed-and-breakfasts, the standard of accommodation is universally high.

When perusing the following listings, be aware of the highly seasonal nature of the tourist industry in Santa Fe. Accommodations are often booked solid through the summer months, and most establishments raise their prices accordingly. Rates go up even higher during Indian Market, the third weekend of August. During these periods, it's essential to make reservations well in advance.

But there's little agreement on what constitutes the tourist season; one hotel may raise its rates July 1 and lower them again in mid-September, while another may raise its rates from May to November. Some hotels raise their rates again over the Christmas holidays or recognize a shoulder season. It pays to shop around during the "in-between" seasons of May to June and September to October.

No matter what the season, discounts are often available to seniors, affiliated groups, corporate employees, and others. If you have any questions about your eligibility for these lower rates, be sure to ask.

A combined city-state tax of 10.75% is added to every hotel bill in Santa Fe. And, unless otherwise indicated, all my recommended accommodations come with private bath.

ACCOMMODATIONS CATEGORIES   In this chapter, hotels/motels are listed first by geographical area (downtown, Northside, or Southside) and then by price range, based on midsummer rates for doubles: **Very Expensive** refers to rooms that average $150 or more per night; **Expensive** includes those that go for $110 to $150; **Moderate** encompasses those that charge $75 to $110; and **Inexpensive** comprises those that cost up to $75.

Following my hotel/motel and bed-and-breakfast recommendations, you'll find suggestions for campgrounds and RV parks.

RESERVATIONS SERVICES   Although Santa Fe has more than 50 hotels, motels, bed-and-breakfast establishments, and other accommodations, it can still be difficult to find available rooms at the peak of the tourist season. Year-round assistance is available from **Santa Fe Central Reservations,** 320 Artist Rd., Suite 10 (☎ **800/776-7669** or 505/983-8200; fax 505/984-8682). This service will also book tickets for the Santa Fe Opera, Chamber Music Festival, Maria Benitez Teatro Flamenco, and the Desert Chorale, as well as jeep trips into the High Country, white-water rafting, horseback riding, mountain bike tours, and golf packages. **Emergency Lodging Assistance**—especially helpful around Fiesta time in September—is available free after 4pm daily (☎ **505/986-0043**).

1 Best Bets

- **Best Historic Hotel: La Fonda,** 100 E. San Francisco St. (☎ 505/ 982-5511), is the oldest (and one of the nicest) hotels in Santa Fe. It has hosted a long list of notables, including Ulysses S. Grant and Kit Carson. Billy the Kid is rumored to have once been a dishwasher there.
- **Best for a Romantic Getaway:** Bed-and-breakfast inns are always my first choice for a romantic getaway, and in Santa Fe I would recommend the cottage at **Spencer House,** 222 McKenzie St. (☎ 505/988-3024).
- **Best for Families: Bishop's Lodge,** Bishop's Lodge Rd. (☎ 505/ 983-6377), offers a wide variety of activities for children (pony ring, trail rides, a pool, and a day program) and is a good bet for families who can afford to spend a little extra money. Otherwise, **Homewood Suites,** 400 Griffin St. (☎ **505/988-3000**), which offers units with full kitchens, a 24-hour convenience store and video rental shop, and features a swimming pool, is a true bargain for families.
- **Best Location:** There are a number of centrally located hotels. Among them, **La Fonda** (see address and telephone above), is the only hotel right on the Plaza; the **Hotel Plaza Real,** 125 Washington Ave. (☎ **505/988-4900**), and the **Inn of the Anasazi,** 113 Washington Ave. (☎ **505/988-3030**) are both just a half block from the Plaza.
- **Best Fitness Facilities:** The **Eldorado Hotel,** 309 W. San Francisco St. (☎ **505/ 988-4455**), has a wonderful heated rooftop pool and Jacuzzi, an exercise room, professional masseuse, and his-and-hers saunas.
- **Best Southwestern Bed-and-Breakfast:** If you want to stay in a southwestern–style bed-and-breakfast that reflects the unique style of its owner, try **Adobe Abode,** 202 Chapelle St. (☎ **505/983-3133**), which is within walking distance of the Plaza. Each of the rooms is individually and creatively decorated. In addition to traditional southwestern features, you'll find everything from Balinese puppets to Ralph Lauren and Oaxacan hand-loomed fabrics, as well as cowboy paraphernalia.

2 Downtown

Everything within the horseshoe-shaped Paseo de Peralta, and east a few blocks on either side of the Santa Fe River, is considered downtown Santa Fe. All of these accommodations are within walking distance of the Plaza.

VERY EXPENSIVE

Eldorado Hotel
309 W. San Francisco St., Santa Fe, NM 87501. ☎ **800/955-4455** or 505/988-4455. Fax 505/995-4544. 219 rms, 18 suites, 8 condo suites. A/C MINIBAR TV TEL. Jan 1–Feb 1, $129–$239 double; Feb 2–May 2 and Oct 27–Dec 19, $159–$269 double; May 3–June 26 and Aug 25–Oct 26, $199–$309 double; June 27–Aug 24, $229–$339 double; Dec 20–Dec 31, $179–$299 double. Year-round $249–$950 suite. Ski and other package rates are available. AE, DC, DISC, MC, V. 24-hour valet parking.

A five-story Pueblo-style structure built around a lovely courtyard one block west of the Plaza, the Eldorado boasts a southwestern interior with an art collection appraised at more than $1 million, including antique furniture, Native American pottery, carved animals, and other works mainly by local artists.

The guest rooms continue the regional theme. Many of them feature traditional kiva fireplaces, handmade furniture, and decks or terraces. The upper rooms in particular afford outstanding views of the surrounding mountains. Each room—tastefully appointed in southwestern colors—is furnished with one king-size bed or two double beds, easy chairs, double closet, remote-control TV in an armoire, and a minirefrigerator with an honor bar. Deluxe rooms and suites have the added luxury of butler service. Just down the street from the main hotel is Zona Rosa, which houses two-, three-, and four-bedroom condo suites with full kitchens.

Dining/Entertainment: The innovative and elegant **Old House** restaurant was built on the preserved foundation of an early 1800s Santa Fe house. Its viga-latilla ceiling, polished wood floor, and pottery and kachinas in nichos provide a distinct regional touch, found also in its creative southwestern cuisine. More casual meals are served in the spacious **Eldorado Court.** The lobby lounge offers low-key entertainment.

Services: Room service, concierge, butlers, laundry, twice-daily maid service, nightly turndown, safe-deposit boxes.

Facilities: Rooms for nonsmokers and travelers with disabilities; pets are welcome; heated rooftop swimming pool and Jacuzzi, exercise room, his-and-hers saunas, professional masseuse, beauty salon, shopping arcade, and business center.

Hilton of Santa Fe

100 Sandoval St. (P.O. Box 25104), Santa Fe, NM 87504-2387. ☎ **800/336-3676,** 800/HILTONS, or 505/988-2811. Fax 505/986-6439. 158 rms, 6 suites. A/C MINIBAR TV TEL. Jan 1–May 1 and Oct 29–Dec 21, $89–$219; May 2–June 29 and Sept 4–Oct 28, $119–$239; June 30–Sept 3, $139–$260; Dec 22–Dec 31, $160–$260. Year-round, $380–$520 suite. Extra person $20. AE, CB, DC, DISC, MC, V. Free parking.

With its city-landmark bell tower, the Hilton encompasses a full city block (between Sandoval, San Francisco, Guadalupe, and Alameda streets) and incorporates most of the historic landholdings of the 350-year-old Ortiz family estate. It's built around a central pool and patio area and is an excellent blend of ancient and modern styles.

Well-appointed and spacious guest rooms are furnished with king-size, queen-size, or double beds. Standard rooms are equipped with a deck or balcony, four-drawer credenza, in-room movies, and a coffee-maker. Executive rooms are larger and feature such added amenities as a couch or two easy chairs, iron and ironing board, bathrobes, and hair dryer.

In June 1994 the Hilton opened Casa Ortiz de Santa Fe, a small building adjacent to the main hotel, which houses three exclusive casitas. The building was once the coach house (c. 1625) of Nicholas Ortiz III. Today the thick adobe walls encompass two one-bedroom units and one two-bedroom suite. Each has a living room with kiva fireplace, fully stocked kitchenette, and bathroom with whirlpool tub. One of the one-bedroom units offers a fireplace in the bedroom.

Dining/Entertainment: Two restaurants occupy the premises of the early 18th-century Casa Ortiz. In the **Piñon Grill,** with its intimate candlelight dinner (as well as daily lunch) service, you can't miss the ancient beams and pillars that typify the structure of the main house. All main courses are prepared on the wood-fired grill, including fresh wild game and Rocky Mountain trout. The **Chamisa Courtyard,** which serves breakfast, features casual garden-style tables amid lush greenery under a large skylight; it's built on the home's enclosed patio. **El Cañon** wine and coffee bar specializes in fine wines by the glass and gourmet coffees. El Cañon also serves breakfast, lunch, and dinner. Specialties include freshly baked breads and pastries as well as tapas.

Services: Room service, concierge, courtesy car, valet laundry.

Facilities: Rooms for nonsmokers and travelers with disabilities; outdoor swimming pool, Jacuzzi, gift shop, car-rental agency, travel agency.

Homewood Suites

400 Griffin St., Santa Fe, NM 87501. ☎ **800/225-5466** or 505/988-3000. Fax 505/988-4700. 105 suites. A/C TV TEL. Jan 1–April 30 and Oct 16–Dec 15, $99–$119 one-bedroom suite; $225 two-bedroom suite. May 1–Oct 15 and Dec 16–31, $150–$170 one-bedroom suite; $310 two-bedroom suite. Rates include continental breakfast. AE, DC, DISC, MC, V. Free parking.

Homewood Suites is Santa Fe's only downtown all-suite hotel. The apartment-style units are perfect for families or single travelers who like to cook for themselves while on vacation. Each suite has a living room, bedroom, kitchen, and bathroom with separate dressing area. Master Suites are just larger versions of Homewood Suites with the addition of a gas fireplace. There are also a few suites with two bedrooms and two baths. The kitchens are fully equipped and have microwaves, two-burner stoves, and full-size refrigerators with ice makers. All suites offer ironing boards and irons, as well as recliner chairs and VCRs. Living rooms and bedrooms are both furnished with TVs, and the living room couches convert into full-size beds (perfect for kids). Many of the suites feature fireplaces. Business travelers can enjoy free use of a computer, copier, and typewriter at the hotel's business center. A complimentary continental breakfast is served in the lodge daily, and there are free social functions Monday through Thursday evenings.

Services: Complimentary shopping service and local shuttle service.

Facilities: Outdoor pool and hot tubs, exercise center (with bikes, weights, a step machine, and a rower), activity court, guest laundry, business center, "Suite Shop" (for sundries, food, and video rentals).

✪ Inn of the Anasazi

113 Washington Ave., Santa Fe, NM 87501. ☎ **800/688-8100** or 505/988-3030. Fax 505/988-3277. 59 rms. A/C MINIBAR TV TEL. Nov–Mar, $199–$345 double. Apr–Oct, $235–$395 double. Holiday and festival rates may be higher. AE, CB, DC, DISC, MC, V. Valet parking $10 per night.

Located near the Palace of the Governors, the Inn of the Anasazi is definitely a luxury hostelry. It's named for the "enduring and creative spirit" of the Native American people known as the Anasazi. Opened in 1991, it is a collaborative project of the Washington Avenue Limited Partnership, a group that wanted to blend cultural, community, and environmental concerns to create a unique Santa Fe hotel and restaurant. Every piece of paper used at the inn is recycled; the guest room fireplaces are gas- rather than wood-burning; the linens, soaps, and shampoos are all natural; and the food served in the restaurant is organic and free of chemicals.

This is not to say that the hotel skimps on amenities—there are TVs and VCRs in all rooms, as well as minibars, private safes, coffee-makers, bathroom telephones, and walk-in closets. Original artwork is featured throughout the hotel, and there's a living room with a fireplace, as well as a library where you can sit and relax before dinner.

Dining/Entertainment: The **Inn of the Anasazi Restaurant** serves breakfast, lunch, and dinner daily, and features Native American and northern New Mexican food. (See Chapter 6, "Santa Fe Dining," for a full description.)

Services: Room service, concierge, twice-daily maid service, complimentary newspaper, tours of galleries and museums, massage and aromatherapy treatments, stationary bicycles available for use in guest rooms; use of spas and fitness centers can easily be arranged.

✪ Inn on the Alameda

303 E. Alameda St., Santa Fe, NM 87501. ☎ **800/289-2122** or 505/984-2121. Fax 505/986-8325. 67 rms, 9 suites. A/C TV TEL. Nov–Feb, $150–$200 single or double; $210–$320 suite. Mar–June, $165–$220 single or double; $235–$345 suite. June–Oct, $180–$235 single or double; $250–$360 suite. Holiday and special-event rates may be higher. Rates include breakfast. AE, CB, DC, DISC, MC, V. Free parking.

This might be just the ticket for visitors who prefer more intimacy than large hotels can offer. Located opposite the Santa Fe River at the corner of Paseo de Peralta, the Inn on the Alameda preserves the spirit of old Santa Fe behind an exterior of adobe and adz-hewn wood pillars. You'll feel it as soon as you enter the lobby, with its traditional viga-latilla ceiling construction. Just past the unobtrusive reception desk is a sitting room/library with handcrafted furnishings, soft pillows, and a rocking chair grouped around an inviting kiva fireplace.

The theme continues in the guest rooms, which are decorated in warm pastel shades of contemporary southwestern decor. Each room features a king-size bed or two queen-size beds, desk with three-drawer credenza, and additional table and chairs. Fresh-cut flowers brighten each room, charming prints hang on the walls, and wood-slat blinds add warmth and privacy. Heating and air conditioning are individually controlled. Some rooms feature outdoor patios or private balconies, refrigerators, and kiva fireplaces.

A new wing provides 19 additional rooms, guest laundry, fitness facility, and massage room. Eight individually designed suites provide such luxuries as enclosed courtyards and portals, traditional kiva fireplaces, TVs in both living room and bedroom, and minirefrigerators. These suites, which have their own parking areas, are set away from the main building.

Dining/Entertainment: An elaborate continental "Breakfast of Enchantment" is served each morning in the Agoyo Room, outdoor courtyard, or your own room. A full-service bar is open nightly.

Services: Limited room service, concierge, valet laundry, complimentary morning newspaper; child care can be arranged; pets are welcome (the hotel offers a pet program that features pet amenities and pet-walking map).

Facilities: Two open-air Jacuzzi spas, fitness facility, massage room, guest laundry, rooms for nonsmokers and the disabled.

EXPENSIVE

Hotel St. Francis

210 Don Gaspar Ave., Santa Fe, NM 87501. ☎ **800/529-5700** or 505/983-5700. Fax 505/989-7690. 83 rms, 2 suites. A/C TV TEL. May 1–Oct 31 plus the weeks of Dec 25 and Jan 1, $118–$188 double; $228–$353 suite. Nov–Feb, $88–$138 double; $178–$278 suite. Mar–Apr, $98–$153 double; $178–$278 suite. Children under 12 stay free in parents' room. AE, CB, DC, DISC, MC, V. Free parking.

Listed in the National Register of Historic Places, this was once the DeVargas Hotel, a 1924-vintage politicians' gathering place where more business may have been conducted in the 1930s and 1940s than at the State Capitol. The DeVargas closed its doors in 1984, and following a $6 million makeover, reopened as the Hotel St. Francis in 1986. With its original tile floor, high-backed Edwardian chairs and sofas grouped around glass tables, and big fireplace (with Cupid designs), it's also an ideal setting for afternoon tea.

All rooms have high ceilings and casement windows. Thirty of them are "baby rooms" with barely enough room for a double bed, two chairs, and a table. But, as with all rooms, they feature a refrigerator, closet safe, and individual thermostat. Most units are furnished with maroon carpeting, big brass or iron beds with paisley bedspreads and drapes, brass lamps, cushioned rattan chairs, antique cherrywood desks or tables, remote-control cable TVs in hand-painted armoires, and full baths of Mexican marble.

Dining/Entertainment: On Water Street, the hotel's restaurant, is open daily for breakfast, lunch, and dinner. The DeVargas Bar, which incorporates the earlier hotel's copper-topped counter, offers sidewalk seating for people-watchers. Then there's the silver tea service offered daily in the lobby. Finger sandwiches, scones, and pastries are served with six varieties of tea from India, Sri Lanka, China, and France.

Services: Room service, valet laundry, concierge.

Facilities: Rooms for nonsmokers and one for travelers with disabilities, guest membership at nearby health club.

Hotel Santa Fe

1501 Paseo de Peralta, Santa Fe, NM 87505. ☎ **800/825-9876** or 505/982-1200. Fax 505/984-2211. 131 rms, 91 suites. A/C MINIBAR TV TEL. Jan 1–Apr 10, $89–$109 double, from $119 suite; Apr 11–June 19 and Sept 2–Oct 19, $139–$159 double, from $169 suite; June–Sept 1 and Dec 20–Dec 30, $159–$179 double, from $199 suite. Extra person $10; children 17 and under stay free in parents' room. AE, CB, DC, DISC, MC, V. Free parking.

This is the first-ever partnership in New Mexico between a Native American tribe—in this case, Picuris Pueblo—and a private business located off reservation trust land. The three-story Pueblo-style building, cruciform in shape and featuring Picuris tribal motifs throughout, is about five blocks south of the Plaza.

Most of the rooms feature California king-size beds, and all have Taos-style furnishings, remote-control TVs, and fully stocked minibars. Each suite has a separate living room and bedroom, with a TV and phone in each room, a safe-deposit box, and a microwave oven.

Dining/Entertainment: The hotel offers an extended continental breakfast menu and the Corn Dance Cantina offers Native American cuisine. The Lobby Lounge serves complimentary hors d'oeuvres daily from 5 to 7pm.

Services: Valet laundry, 24-hour security, safe-deposit boxes, courtesy shuttle to the Plaza and Canyon Road, in-room massage, limited room service, twice-daily maid service, baby-sitting, secretarial services, concierge.

Facilities: Rooms for nonsmokers and travelers with disabilities; massage room, guest laundry, Picuris Pueblo gift shop, pool, whirlpool; use of the Club International fitness center can be arranged.

Inn at Loretto

211 Old Santa Fe Trail (P.O. Box 1417), Santa Fe, NM 87501. ☎ **800/727-5531** or 505/988-5531. Fax 505/984-7988. 137 rms, 3 suites. A/C TV TEL. Jan 1–Mar 30, $105–$120 double; Mar 31–May 24, $145–$175 double; May 25–June 29, $165–$195 double; June 30–Sept 9, $185–$215 double; Sept 10–Oct 21, $170–$185; Oct 22–Dec 31 $120–$135 double. Year round, $300–$550 suites. Extra person $15; children 12 and under stay free in parents' room. AE, CB, DC, DISC, MC, V. Free parking.

This handsome, Pueblo Revival–style building stands on the site of the original Loretto Academy, a Catholic girls' school built in the late 19th century under the direction of Bishop Lamy. Although the building (which opened as a hotel in 1975) has been fully renovated and expanded, bits and pieces of the original academy

Downtown Santa Fe Accommodations

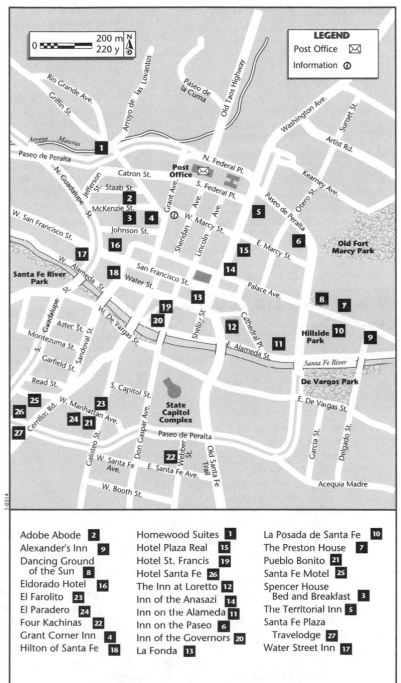

Adobe Abode **2**	Homewood Suites **1**	La Posada de Santa Fe **10**
Alexander's Inn **9**	Hotel Plaza Real **15**	The Preston House **7**
Dancing Ground of the Sun **8**	Hotel St. Francis **19**	Pueblo Bonito **21**
	Hotel Santa Fe **26**	Santa Fe Motel **25**
Eldorado Hotel **16**	The Inn at Loretto **12**	Spencer House Bed and Breakfast **3**
El Farolito **23**	Inn of the Anasazi **14**	
El Paradero **24**	Inn on the Alameda **11**	The Territorial Inn **5**
Four Kachinas **22**	Inn on the Paseo **6**	Santa Fe Plaza Travelodge **27**
Grant Corner Inn **4**	Inn of the Governors **20**	
Hilton of Santa Fe **18**	La Fonda **13**	Water Street Inn **17**

remain, including the famous Chapel of Our Lady of Light with its mysterious spiral staircase (see "More Attractions" in Chapter 7). Another unique element of the Inn at Loretto is the use of hand-painted Mimbres designs. There are about 1,000 of these colorful motifs, all different, throughout the building. Artist Ross Martinez re-created the patterns found on pottery of the 11th- and 12th-century Mimbres people of southwestern New Mexico.

The hotel, located about a block from the southeastern corner of the Plaza, is horseshoe-shaped, with room balconies or patios surrounding a landscaped outdoor courtyard and pool. Half the guest rooms are equipped with a king-size bed; the remainder, a pair of double beds. Southwestern decor dominates with etched-tin shades on intricate pottery-style lamps, Mexican tiles inset in writing and bedside tables, and colorful patterned comforters. All rooms have either a sofa or an easy chair or an activity table with two chairs, and in-room coffee-makers.

Dining/Entertainment: Bimi's, styled after the rambling haciendas of northern New Mexico, is open daily for all three meals. The warm, mezzanine-ringed hotel lounge features live entertainment nightly, and complimentary chips and salsa are available daily beginning at 4pm.

Services: Room service, concierge, valet laundry.

Facilities: Rooms for nonsmokers and the disabled; outdoor heated swimming pool (mid-May to mid-October), shopping arcade (with a fine-art gallery, four boutiques, gold designer, bookstore, three gift shops, sundries shop, and hair salon); tennis and golf privileges nearby can be arranged.

✪ Inn of the Governors

234 Don Gaspar Ave., Santa Fe, NM 87501. ☎ **800/234-4534** or 505/982-4333. Fax 505/989-9149. 100 rms. A/C TV TEL. Jan 1–Mar 6 $109–$189 double, $199–$219 suite; Mar 7–May 1 $129–$199 double, $209–$229 suite; May 2–June 26 $149–$219 double, $259 suite; June 27–Sept 2 $159–$229 double, $279 suite; Sept 3–Oct 26 $149–$229 double, $249–$269 suite; Oct 27–Dec 18 $129–$199 double, $209–$229 suite; Dec 19–Dec 31 $159–$239 double, $249–$269 suite. Extra person $10; children under 18 stay free in parents' room. AE, CB, DC, MC, V. Free parking.

Considered one of the best examples of Territorial architecture in downtown Santa Fe, the Inn of the Governors has been a city institution since 1965. Located two blocks from the Plaza, it consists of three sections—one wing with standard rooms, another with superior rooms, and a third with deluxe accommodations.

The guest rooms with white stuccoed walls and color schemes of coral and pale jade (accented by bedspreads done in a tribal-feather motif) all feature refrigerators, handcrafted Mexican furniture and headboards, folk art, wrought-iron lamps, hand-painted tin mirrors, Santa Fe–style armoires, and washed turquoise writing desks. The spacious deluxe rooms include wood balconies, wall-size 19th-century pueblo photographs, and L-shaped seating to divide the sleeping and living areas. Many of the superior and deluxe rooms have fireplaces (wood provided daily) and minibars. Stereos are available in some rooms.

Dining/Entertainment: The **Mañana Bar and Restaurant** serves three meals daily in a casual atmosphere. On warm days meals are served in an outdoor courtyard. The menu features light, healthy American cuisine. The adjacent bar is rustic, with cowhide chairs at a copper-topped bar beneath a viga ceiling; a pianist performs six nights a week.

Services: Room service, concierge, valet laundry, complimentary newspaper and refreshments in the lobby, in-room massage, baby-sitting.

Facilities: Rooms for nonsmokers and travelers with disabilities; year-round outdoor heated swimming pool with patio and outdoor kiva fireplace.

✪ La Fonda

100 E. San Francisco St. (P.O. Box 1209), Santa Fe, NM 87501. ☎ **800/523-5002** or 505/982-5511. Fax 505/988-2952. 153 rms, 21 suites. A/C TV TEL. $174 standard double, $189 deluxe double; $200–$500 suite. Extra person $15; children under 12 stay free in parents' room. AE, CB, DC, MC, V. Parking $4 per day in three-story garage.

"The Inn at the End of the Trail" occupies a full block between the southeast corner of the Plaza, where a marker denotes the terminus of the Santa Fe Trail, and Bishop Lamy's St. Francis Cathedral. When the first Americans who pioneered the trail arrived in Santa Fe in 1821, they found an inn—a *fonda*—on this site. As trappers, traders, and merchants began flocking to Santa Fe, a saloon and casino were added. Among the inn's 19th-century patrons were Pres. Rutherford B. Hayes, Gen. Ulysses S. Grant, and Gen. William Tecumseh Sherman. The original inn was dying of old age in 1920 when it was razed and replaced by the current La Fonda. Its architecture is Pueblo Revival, imitation adobe with wooden balconies and beam ends protruding over the tops of windows.

Every room is distinct. Each piece of handcarved Spanish-style furniture is individually painted with a Hispanic folk motif and is color-coordinated with other pieces in the room. Beds are king-size, queen-size, or double. Suites and deluxe rooms have minirefrigerators, tiled baths, and sophisticated artwork, including etched tin and stonework. Full suites feature fireplaces, private balconies, antique furniture, Oriental carpets, and lots of closet and shelf space. Two-bedroom suites offer kitchenettes.

Dining/Entertainment: La Plazuela Restaurant, a tiled skylit garden patio, is open for three meals daily. Cuisine is regional with a contemporary flair, ranging at dinner from blue-corn enchiladas to shrimp scampi cilantro. The adjacent **La Fiesta Lounge** offers nightly entertainment. The **Bell Tower Bar,** at the southwest corner of the hotel, is the highest point in downtown Santa Fe, a great place for a cocktail and a view of the city.

Services: Room service, concierge, tour desk, laundry.

Facilities: Rooms for nonsmokers and travelers with disabilities; outdoor swimming pool, two indoor Jacuzzis, cold plunge, massage room, ballroom, and shopping arcade.

✪ La Posada de Santa Fe

330 E. Palace Ave., Santa Fe, NM 87501. ☎ **800/727-5276** or 505/986-0000. Fax 505/982-6850. 119 rms, 40 suites. A/C TV TEL. May–Oct plus the Thanksgiving and Christmas seasons, $110–$297 single or double; $189–$397 suite. Nov–Apr (except holidays), $77–$215 single or double; $125–$285 suite. Various packages available. AE, CB, DC, DISC, MC, V. Free parking.

This lovely hotel has 119 adobe-style buildings spread across six acres of thoughtfully landscaped grounds. It's constructed around the Staab House, a historic mansion built two blocks east of the Plaza in 1882 by Abraham Staab, a German immigrant, for his bride, Julia. Santa Fe's first brick building, it was equally well known for its richly carved walnut interior woodwork and the decorative scrolls and fluting on its doors and windows. Today, several rooms have been fully restored in classical fashion as a Victorian lounge, with period furnishings and museum-quality 19th-century art. Julia Staab, who died in 1896, continues to haunt half a dozen upstairs bedrooms. Mischievous but good-natured, she is Santa Fe's best-known and most frequently witnessed ghost.

Each of the hotel's charming rooms is unique, with variations in size, shape, layout, and detail. Many objets d'art are one of a kind, which leads repeat visitors to request "their" room year after year. But the *casitas* ("little houses") share many common traits: outside entrances with carved wood portals, handcrafted furniture, wood floors with throw rugs, and painted tiles built into the walls. Eighty-six rooms are equipped with fireplaces or woodstoves; piñon firewood is provided daily. Some larger units have refrigerators, walk-in closets, and dressing tables. Since it may be confusing to find your way around the hotel grounds, it might be best to get a map from the front desk. The room numbers follow no particular sequence.

Dining/Entertainment: The **Staab House Restaurant,** open for three meals daily, has been fully restored with ceiling vigas, pueblo weavings, and tinwork on the walls. From spring to early fall, meals are also served outside on a big patio. New Mexican cuisine is a house specialty. The lounge has seasonal happy-hour entertainment (usually local musicians).

Services: Room service, concierge, valet laundry.

Facilities: Rooms for nonsmokers and travelers with disabilities; outdoor swimming pool, guest use of local health club, boutique, beauty salon.

MODERATE

Hotel Plaza Real

125 Washington Ave., Santa Fe, NM 87501. ☎ **800/279-7325** or 505/988-4900. Fax 505/983-9322. 56 rms, 44 suites. A/C TV TEL. Nov–Apr, $130–$209 double. May–June, $139–$219 double. July–Oct, $159–$249 double. Year round, $295–$475 suite. Extra person $15; children under 12 stay free in parents' room. Rates include breakfast. AE, CB, DC, DISC, MC, V. Parking $6 per day.

This three-story hotel, opened in 1990, is located half a block north of the Plaza. It's built in traditional Territorial style, with red-brick coping along the roof lines and white-trimmed windows. Native American designs and wood beams complement the Santa Fe-style furnishings in the rooms, most of which offer fireplaces and outdoor patios. Rooms overlook a peaceful inner courtyard, away from the bustle of the Plaza. Breakfast (plus the daily paper) is served in the Santa Clara Room and Patio or delivered to your room. **La Piazza** is the hotel's sidewalk cafe where guests can enjoy pastries, cappuccino, sandwiches, and cocktails. An intimate lounge also serves cocktails in the evening. Services include concierge, complimentary walking tour, 24-hour desk, valet laundry, and rooms for the disabled.

INEXPENSIVE

Santa Fe Motel

510 Cerrillos Rd., Santa Fe, NM 87501. ☎ **800/999-1039** or 505/982-1039. Fax 505/986-1275. 21 rms, 1 house. A/C TV TEL. May–Oct, $85–$95 double; $180 Thomas House. Nov–Apr, $70–$80 double; $150 Thomas House. Continental breakfast is included in the rates from May to Sept. AE, MC, V. Free parking.

One of the bonuses of staying at this adobe-style motel south of the Santa Fe River is that most rooms have kitchenettes, complete with two-burner stoves and mini-refrigerators, as well as pans, dishes, and utensils. Southwestern motifs predominate in the rooms, spread across four turn-of-the-century buildings. Fresh-brewed coffee is served each morning in the office, where a bulletin board lists Santa Fe activities. The nearby Thomas House, on West Manhattan Avenue, is a fully equipped rental home with living and dining rooms and off-street parking. A recent renovation at the Santa Fe Motel brought a new level of charm to eight of the hotel's rooms. One now has a fireplace, another features skylights, viga ceilings were added in some cases, and several have their own private patio entrances.

Santa Fe Plaza Travelodge

646 Cerrillos Rd., Santa Fe, NM 87501. ☎ **800/578-7878** or 505/982-3551. Fax 505/
983-8624. 48 rms. A/C TV TEL. Nov–Apr, $40–$60 single or double. May–Oct, $60–$75 single or double. AE, CB, DC, DISC, MC, V. Free parking.

Practically next door to the Santa Fe Motel (above) is this inn with a heated swimming pool. Each room has a king-size bed or two queen-size (or double) beds with floral-patterned bedspreads and drapes, two-drawer credenza, table and chairs, cable TV, and telephone (local calls are free). Some rooms also offer small desks.

3 Northside

Within easy reach of the Plaza, northside encompasses the area that lies north of the loop of the Paseo de Peralta.

VERY EXPENSIVE

✪ The Bishop's Lodge

Bishop's Lodge Rd. (P.O. Box 2367), Santa Fe, NM 87504. ☎ **505/983-6377**. Fax 505/
989-8739. 68 rms and 20 suites. A/C TV TEL. European Plan (meals not included), Mar 25–May 26 and Sept 6–Dec, $140 standard double, $215 deluxe double, $245 super-deluxe double; $170 standard suite, $285 deluxe suite. May 27–June 30, $160 standard double, $245 deluxe double, $275 super-deluxe double; $210 standard suite, $315 deluxe suite. July 1–Sept 5, $195 standard double, $295 deluxe double, $325 super-deluxe double; $245 standard suite, $355 deluxe suite. Modified American Plan (available May 27–Labor Day), $236–$271 standard double, $321–$371 deluxe double, $351–$401 super-deluxe double; $286–$321 standard suite, $391–$431 deluxe suite. Jan 1–Mar 24, $95 standard double, $175 deluxe double, $210 super-deluxe double; $125 standard suite, $249 deluxe suite. AE, DISC, MC, V. Free parking.

More than a century ago, when Bishop Jean-Baptiste Lamy was the spiritual leader of northern New Mexico's Roman Catholic population, he often escaped clerical politics by hiking 3 ½ miles north over a ridge into the Little Tesuque Valley. There he built a retreat he named Villa Pintoresca (Picturesque Villa) for its lovely vistas, and a humble chapel (now on the National Register of Historic Places) with high-vaulted ceilings and a hand-built altar. Today Lamy's 1,000-acre getaway has become the Bishop's Lodge. Purchased in 1918 from the Pulitzer family (of publishing fame) by Denver mining executive James R. Thorpe, it has remained in his family's hands to this day.

The guest rooms, spread through 10 buildings, all feature handcrafted cottonwood furniture and regional artwork. Guests receive a complimentary fruit basket upon arrival. Standard rooms provide balconies and either king-size beds or two twin beds. Deluxe rooms feature traditional kiva fireplaces, private decks or patios, and walk-in closets; some older units have flagstone floors and viga ceilings. Super-deluxe rooms offer a combination bedroom/sitting room. The deluxe suites are extremely spacious, with living rooms, separate bedrooms, private patios and decks, and artwork of near-museum quality. All "deluxe" units come with fireplaces, refrigerators, and in-room safes. The Lodge is an active resort three seasons of the year; in the winter, it takes on the character of a romantic country retreat. Furthermore, the room tax rate here is slightly lower than in downtown Santa Fe. The Bishop's Lodge is exceptionally well cared for—in fact, each year approximately 10 rooms are renovated.

Dining/Entertainment: Three large adjoining rooms with wrought-iron chandeliers and wall-size Native American–theme oil paintings comprise the Bishop's

Lodge dining room. Santa Feans flock here for breakfast, lunch, Sunday brunch, and dinner (featuring creative regional cuisine with continental flair). Attire is casual at breakfast and lunch but more formal at dinner (men generally wear a sport coat, though they aren't required). There's a full vintage wine list, and El Rincon Bar serves before- and after-dinner drinks.

Services: Room service, seasonal cookouts, valet laundry.

Facilities: Daily guided horseback rides, introductory riding lessons, children's pony ring; hiking and self-guided nature walk (the Lodge is a member of the Audubon Cooperative Sanctuary System); four surfaced tennis courts, pro shop and instruction; supervised skeet and trap shooting; outdoor pool with lifeguard, saunas, and whirlpool; aerobics classes; stocked trout pond for children; Ping-Pong; summer daytime program with counselors for children.

Rancho Encantado

Rte. 4, Box 57C, Santa Fe, NM 87501. ☎ **800/722-9339** or 505/982-3537. Fax 505/983-8269. 90 rms, 36 suites. A/C TV TEL. Nov 1–Apr 1 (excluding Thanksgiving and Dec 25), $115–$125 suite; $175 one-bedroom villa; $215 two-bedroom villa. Apr 2–Oct 31, $190–$210 suite; $315 one-bedroom villa; $375 two-bedroom villa. AE, DC, MC, V. Free parking.

Located 8 miles north of Santa Fe in the foothills of the Sangre de Cristo Mountains, Rancho Encantado, with its sweeping panoramic views, claims to be "where the magic of New Mexico comes to life." Indeed, it does have a rather magical history, which began when the ranch was the subject of the 1956 best-selling novel *Guestward Ho*. The book was later adapted for a television series of the same name which was filmed on location at the ranch. Shortly after the series' end, the property was sold, deteriorated, and eventually abandoned. Despite her lack of experience in the hospitality business, Betty Egan, a former World War II captain in the Women's Army Corps, purchased the property in the mid-1960s. Recently widowed, Mrs. Egan was determined to begin a new and prosperous life with her family, and so in 1968 the 168-acre ranch became Rancho Encantado. The property is still owned by the Egan family today.

The handsome main lodge is decorated in traditional southwestern style with hand-painted tiles, ceiling vigas, brick floors, antique furnishings, pueblo rugs, and Hispanic art objects hanging on stuccoed walls. The large fireplace in the living room/lounge is a focal point, especially on cold winter afternoons. In the main lodge and adjoining area there are seven standard rooms, five cottages with fireplaces, and 10 suites with living rooms, fireplaces, and refrigerators. All rooms provide coffee-makers plus coffee for those who couldn't make it out the front door otherwise. Across the street from the main building are two-bedroom/two-bath "villas." These split-level adobe units are equipped with fireplaces in the living room and master bedroom plus a full kitchen. Whatever you choose, you're sure to find the accommodations here more than adequate; satisfied guests have included Princess Anne, Robert Redford, Jimmy Stewart, Whoopi Goldberg, and John Wayne.

Dining/Entertainment: Rancho Encantado's **Cactus Rose Restaurant,** with its exceptional western decor, ranks among the most beautiful in the Santa Fe area. The west wall of the dining room has picture windows that overlook the Jemez Mountains, offering diners a first-rate view of the spectacular New Mexico sunset. Full dinners include prime grilled steaks, seafood, free-range chicken, and pork, in addition to a fine selection of appetizers and desserts. **The Cantina,** with its big-screen TV, is a popular gathering spot; there is also a snack bar on the premises.

Facilities: Tennis courts, horseback riding, hiking trails, pool, hot tub, library.

EXPENSIVE

Radisson Deluxe Hotel Santa Fe

750 N. St. Francis Dr., Santa Fe, NM 87501. ☎ **800/333-3333** or 505/982-5591. Fax 505/988-2821. 116 rms, 12 suites, 32 condo units. A/C TV TEL. Jan 1–May 15, $88–$138 double. May 16–Dec 31, $98–$178 double. Condos $119–$199 year round. AE, CB, DC, DISC, MC, V. Free parking.

If you're in town for the Santa Fe Opera, you'll have a hard time finding an accommodation any closer than the newly renovated Radisson Deluxe Hotel. The amphitheater is only about 3 miles north on US 84/285 and the Radisson Deluxe provides free drop-off and pickup. In fact, there's complimentary shuttle service anywhere within the city limits—including the Santa Fe Plaza, 1 mile southeast—from 7am to 10pm daily. Once you're in this landscaped garden-style hotel, though, you may find it hard to leave. Standard rooms, with soft southwestern decor, are equipped with either king-size beds or two double beds and subtle southwestern furnishings. Premium rooms are more spacious, with Santa Fe–style furnishings, TVs, and private balconies. Furthermore, each parlor suite has a Murphy bed and traditional kiva fireplace in the living room, a big dining area, a wet bar and refrigerator, and a jetted bathtub. Cielo Grande condo units come with fully equipped kitchens, fireplaces, and private decks.

Dining/Entertainment: The **Santa Fe Salsa Company Restaurant and Bar** serves three meals a day. Dinner main courses are international with a southwestern flair. A jazz combo plays Friday through Sunday in the bar, and the nightclub features the Spanish quick steps of New Mexico's best-known flamenco dancer and her Estampa Flamenco troupe.

Services: Room service, complimentary shuttle, valet laundry, complimentary *USA Today;* child care can be arranged.

Facilities: Rooms for nonsmokers and the disabled; outdoor swimming pool, hot tub, Santa Fe Spa (indoor pool, weights, massage, steam rooms, aerobics, dance, yoga, and karate classes), coin-op guest laundry.

⑤ Fort Marcy Condominium Resort Hotel/Las Palomas/527 Santa Fe

320 Artist Rd., Santa Fe, NM 87501. ☎ **800/745-9910** or 505/98-CONDO. Fax 505/984-8682. 140 units. A/C. Jan 6–Feb 28, Apr 1–May 14, and Nov 1–Dec 14, from $75 one-bedroom; $134 two-bedroom; $215 three-bedroom. Mar 1–Mar 31, May 15–June 30, and Sept 15–Oct 31, from $80 one-bedroom; $153 two-bedroom; $235 three-bedroom. July 1–Sept 15 and Dec 15–Jan 5, from $90 one-bedroom; $180 two-bedroom; $255 three-bedroom. Extra person $20. Children 18 and under stay free in parents' room. Rates include extended continental breakfast. AE, MC, V. Free on- and off-street parking.

These privately owned condos, nestled throughout Santa Fe's historic northeast side near the Plaza, on tastefully landscaped grounds, are an excellent choice. Each unit is a full apartment; most of them consist of a living and dining room, a full kitchen, one to three bedrooms, and two or two-and-a-half baths. A typical unit is equipped with handcrafted wood-and-leather furnishings and is decorated with regional arts and crafts. Most living rooms provide a sofa bed, easy chair with ottoman, coffee table, fireplace, cable TV with VCR (rentals are available), stereo tape deck, and private phone line with voice mail. In addition to a four-burner stove and refrigerator, each kitchen is furnished with a microwave, coffee-maker, and toaster, and the cupboards are stocked with some staples, as well as dishes, pots and pans, glasses, and cutlery. Bedding ranges from king-size to two twins, and most rooms offer private balconies (some are even equipped with private or semiprivate patios). Daily linen

⊕ Family-Friendly Hotels

The Bishop's Lodge *(see p. 47)*   A children's pony ring, riding lessons, tennis courts with instruction, a pool with lifeguard, stocked trout pond just for kids, a summer daytime program, horseback trail trips, and more make this a veritable day camp for all ages.

El Rey Inn *(see p. 51)*   Kids will enjoy the play area, table games, and pool; parents will appreciate the kitchenettes and laundry facilities.

Rancho Encantado *(see p. 48)*   Horseback riding (on trails or pony ring), pool, tennis courts, and many indoor and outdoor games will keep kids happily busy here.

exchange is available. The room rates listed above are for two in a one-bedroom unit, four in a two-bedroom unit, and six in a three-bedroom unit. Guests of Fort Marcy Compound have access to the swimming pool and hot tub on the premises; all other guests may use the facilities at Fort Marcy Sports Complex.

4   Southside

Santa Fe's major strip, Cerrillos Road, is US 85, the main route to and from Albuquerque and the I-25 freeway. It's about 5¼ miles from the Plaza to the Villa Linda Mall, which marks the southern boundary of the city. Most motels are on this strip, although several of them are east, closer to St. Francis Drive (US 84) or the Las Vegas Highway.

EXPENSIVE

⑤ Residence Inn

1698 Galisteo St., Santa Fe, NM 87505. ☎ **800/331-3131** or 505/988-7300. Fax 505/988-3243. 120 suites. A/C TV TEL. $99–$169 studio suite; $130–$170 penthouse suite. Rates vary according to season and include continental breakfast. AE, CB, DC, DISC, JCB, MC, V. Free parking.

This travelers' community, a division of Marriott, consists of 15 separate buildings on landscaped grounds. Three-quarters of the suites are one-bedroom studios; the remainder are deluxe penthouse suites. All are fully self-contained with their own water heaters.

Furnishings for each studio include a sofa sleeper or love seat and chair beside the fireplace, two spacious closets, and a remote-control TV. Each kitchen has a full refrigerator and range, a microwave oven, and a coffee-maker. A vanity with its own sink is located outside the bathroom. In addition, each penthouse suite has an open sleeping loft, a queen-size Murphy bed in the living room, a full dining room table, and two baths.

Dining/Entertainment: A social hour with complimentary hors d'oeuvres takes place on Monday through Thursday from 5 to 6:30pm.

Services: Valet laundry, complimentary local newspaper, grocery shopping service.

Facilities: Outdoor swimming pool, three hot tubs, jogging trail, sports court, guest membership at nearby health club, coin-op guest laundry, barbecue grills on patio.

Accommodations & Dining on Cerrillos Road

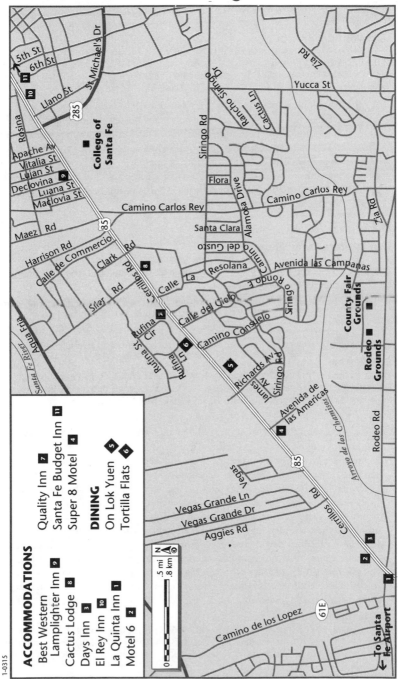

ACCOMMODATIONS

Best Western
Lamplighter Inn [9]
Cactus Lodge [8]
Days Inn [3]
El Rey Inn [10]
La Quinta Inn [1]
Motel 6 [2]

Quality Inn [7]
Santa Fe Budget Inn [11]
Super 8 Motel [4]

DINING
On Lok Yuen [5]
Tortilla Flats [6]

.5 mi
.8 km

1-0315

51

MODERATE

Days Inn

3650 Cerrillos Rd., Santa Fe, NM 87501. ☎ **800/325-2525** or 505/438-3822. Fax 505/ 438-3795. 96 rms, 20 suites. A/C TV TEL. Apr–Sept, $95–$105 double; $135–$155 suite. Oct–Mar, $45–$75 double; $85–$95 suite. Children 12 and under stay free in parents' room. Rates include continental breakfast. AE, CB, DC, DISC, MC, V. Free parking.

A three-story pink palace, the Days Inn opened in 1990 as an impressive new motel on Santa Fe's south side. It's a security-conscious hostelry; rooms can be entered only from interior corridors and there are private safes in each room. Typical rooms, decorated in soft southwestern style, feature a queen-size bed or two double beds plus a sofa or easy chair. Deluxe suites and 14 upgraded "king" rooms offer wet bars and refrigerators. Some suites also boast Jacuzzi tubs and private balconies. Amenities include a 24-hour desk, coin-op laundry, rooms for nonsmokers and the disabled, and a hot tub and swimming pool.

INEXPENSIVE

Best Western Lamplighter Inn

2405 Cerrillos Rd., Santa Fe, NM 87505. ☎ **800/767-5267** or 505/471-8000. Fax 505/ 471-8000. 80 rms. A/C TV TEL. $49–$95 depending on the season and type of room. AE, CB, DC, DISC, MC, V. Free parking.

Trees and shrubbery surround a grassy inner courtyard, located adjacent to a large heated indoor pool and hot tub. The motel consists of a well-kept older building plus two newer annexes. All rooms feature regional decor and in-room coffee-makers and refrigerators. Some rooms offer kitchenettes and five have VCRs.

✪ El Rey Inn

1862 Cerrillos Rd. (P.O. Box 130), Santa Fe, NM 87504. ☎ **800/521-1349** or 505/982-1931. Fax 505/989-9249. 86 rms, 8 suites. A/C TV TEL. $56–$115 single or double; $98–$207 suite. Rates include continental breakfast. AE, CB, DC, DISC, MC, V. Free parking.

"The King" is notable for its carefully tended, shaded grounds and thoughtfully maintained, recently renovated units. The white stucco buildings are adorned with bright trim around the doors and hand-painted Mexican tiles on the walls. No two rooms are alike. Most offer viga ceilings and Santa Fe–style wood furnishings, a walk-in closet, and a handsome blue-and-white-tiled bathroom. Some provide kitchenettes; others, refrigerators and/or fireplaces. Eight stylish poolside terrace units feature private patio areas. Facilities include a Territorial-style sitting room with library and games tables, swimming pool, hot tub, picnic area, children's play area, and guest laundry. The owners recently purchased the motel next door and have now added 10 new deluxe units around a Spanish Colonial–style courtyard. The new rooms offer more upscale amenities and gas log fireplaces, as well as distinctive furnishings and artwork. In addition, a spa area complete with sauna was under construction at press time. In my opinion, El Rey is Santa Fe's best inexpensively priced accommodation.

La Quinta Inn

4298 Cerrillos Rd., Santa Fe, NM 87505. ☎ **800/531-5900** or 505/471-1142. Fax 505/ 438-7219. 130 rms. A/C TV TEL. June–mid-Oct, $88 double. Late Oct–May, $66 double. Large discount for AAA members. Rates include continental breakfast. AE, CB, DC, DISC, MC, V. Free parking.

Right at Villa Linda Mall is La Quinta Motor Inn. The rooms are appointed with light-wood decor and a contemporary green color scheme. Each room has a king-size bed or two extra-long double beds and standard motel furnishings as well as a coffee-maker. Eight rooms are designed for travelers with disabilities, and nearly half are reserved for nonsmokers. Bathrooms have recently been completely rebuilt. **The Kettle,** a 24-hour coffee shop, is adjacent. La Quinta has an outdoor heated swimming pool, 24-hour desk, launderette (as well as valet laundry), and complimentary coffee at all times in the lobby. Continental breakfast includes fresh fruit, danish, cereal, bagels, coffee, tea, and juice. Pets are accepted.

Quality Inn

3011 Cerrillos Rd., Santa Fe, NM 87505. ☎ **800/228-5151** or 505/471-1211. 99 rms. A/C TV TEL. $55–$95 single or double. AE, CB, DC, DISC, ER, JCB, MC, V. Free parking.

An impressive outdoor pool is surrounded by balconies or patio decks extending from each guest room. Each unit features southwestern decor, queen-size bed (or two double beds), reading lamps, dresser with two deep drawers, table and chairs, and individual thermostat. Deluxe rooms offer king-size beds plus refrigerators and dressing tables. There are rooms for nonsmokers and a courtesy airport van. Pets are accepted and child care can be arranged. The Quality Inn coffee shop and dining room serves American and New Mexican fare.

Santa Fe Budget Inn

725 Cerrillos Rd., Santa Fe, NM 87501. ☎ **800/288-7600** or 505/982-5952. Fax 505/984-8879. 160 rms. A/C TV TEL. July 4–Oct 25 and Dec 25–Jan 2, $75–$86 double ($10–$20 higher during Indian Market). Rest of the year, $50–$58 double. A Sun–Thurs "supersaver" rate may apply in the off-season. AAA and AARP members receive $3 discounts. AE, CB, DC, MC, V. Free parking.

Santa Fe Opera and Fiesta posters add a splash of color to the predominantly brown rooms of this motel at the north end of Cerrillos Road. Each of its modest units is furnished with one queen-size or two double beds, striped bedspreads, reading lamps, and desk with built-in dresser. Each room has satellite TV. Rooms are available for nonsmokers and travelers with disabilities. Guests can enjoy an outdoor swimming pool, lots of parking space, and two restaurants adjacent to the motel. Santa Fe Budget Inn is within walking distance of the Plaza and historic downtown Santa Fe.

Super 8 Motel

3358 Cerrillos Rd., Santa Fe, NM 87501. ☎ **800/800-8000** or 505/471-8811. Fax 505/471-3239. 96 rms. A/C TV TEL. May–Sept, $49.88 double. Oct–Apr, $44.88 double. AE, CB, DC, DISC, MC, V. Free parking.

It's nothing flashy, but this boxlike motel attracts a regular following who know precisely what to expect—a clean, comfortable room with standard furnishings: double beds, working desk, TV, and phone that allows free local calls. Rooms for nonsmokers are available. The motel has a 24-hour desk.

5 Bed-and-Breakfasts

If you prefer a homey, intimate setting rather than the sometimes impersonal ambience of a large hotel, one of Santa Fe's bed-and-breakfast inns may be right for you. All those listed here are located in or close to the downtown area and offer comfortable accommodations at moderate to inexpensive prices.

✪ Adobe Abode

202 Chapelle St., Santa Fe, NM 87501. ☎ **505/983-3133.** 6 rms. TEL. $100–$155 double. Rates include breakfast. DISC, MC, V. Free parking.

Without a doubt, Adobe Abode is one of Santa Fe's most luxurious bed-and-breakfasts. The living room has a fireplace and is filled with everything from Mexican folk art and pottery to Buddhas and ethnic masks. The open kitchen features bar stools with cowhide seats, as well as Balinese puppets. The creativity of the owner/innkeeper Pat Harbour shines through in each of the guest rooms as well. The Bloomsbury Room, in the main house, is named for the English literary and artistic circle of the early part of this century. Laura Ashley created some Bloomsbury-inspired fabrics, which can be seen hanging from the queen-size four-poster bed in the Bloomsbury Room. Another unique feature in this room is the bathroom tiles that were handcrafted for the Adobe Abode by a local artist. The English Garden Room features Ralph Lauren floral fabrics, an antique marble-topped desk, and a French armoire. Casita de Corazon, known for its custom-designed aspen-pole twin beds, is the perfect room for friends who are traveling together. Amenities in the casita include a coffee-maker, minirefrigerator, skylights, and towel warmer in the bathroom. The artwork in Casita de Corazon is captivating. The Cactus Room displays a variety of fabrics that were hand-loomed in Oaxaca, Mexico, and colorful, hand-painted furnishings. The bathroom here also features locally handmade tiles as well as an oversize shower. The Bronco Room is just filled with cowboy paraphernalia: hats, Pendleton blankets, pioneer chests, and my favorite—an entire shelf lined with children's cowboy boots. Finally, Pat has added a new two-room suite—the Provence Suite—which she decorated in sunny yellow and bright blue. It has a queen bedroom and full living room. Two rooms have fireplaces and several have private patios. All rooms feature fine bed linens, writing desks, cable TV, and terry-cloth robes. Complimentary sherry, fruit, and Santa Fe cookies are served daily in the living room. Every morning a healthy breakfast of fresh-squeezed orange juice, fresh fruit, homemade muffins, scones or pastries, and a hot dish is served in the kitchen. You'll have no complaints if you stay at Adobe Abode.

Alexander's Inn

529 East Palace Ave., Santa Fe, NM 87501. ☎ **505/986-1431**. Fax 505/982-8572. 6 rms (4 with bath), 2 cottages. A/C TV TEL. $75–$150 double. Rates include continental breakfast. MC, V. Free parking.

Located not far from central downtown—in a quiet residential area—Alexander's Inn is quite different from other accommodations here because its decor is *not* southwestern style. Instead, the eight-year-old inn (whose building dates back to 1903) has a Victorian/New England style with stenciling on the walls, hook and Oriental rugs, muted colors such as apricot and lilac, and white iron or four-poster queen-size beds (there are some king-size beds as well). You might begin to think you're in a country inn in Vermont. One of the rooms has a private deck. There are also two cottages complete with kitchens and living rooms with kiva fireplaces. Fresh flowers adorn all the rooms throughout the year. Guests can enjoy privileges at El Gancho Tennis Club as well as the hot tub in the back garden. Mountain bikes are available for guest use. A continental breakfast of homemade baked goods is served on the veranda every morning, and afternoon tea and cookies are available. Alexander's Inn currently has plans to add two small houses to the property that will be great for families, so be sure to ask when you make your reservation. Pets are accepted.

✪ Dancing Ground of the Sun

711 Paseo de Peralta, Santa Fe, NM 87501. ☎ **800/645-5673** or 505/986-9797. 8 rooms. TV TEL. Nov–Apr, $75–$210 double. May–Oct, and all holidays $95–$245 double. Rates include breakfast. MC, V. Free parking.

Sometimes I am amazed at the new and creative theme ideas set forth by bed-and-breakfast owners, especially when I first saw Dancing Ground of the Sun. These owners put a great deal of thought and energy into decorating their units—and it shows. Each of the eight rooms, the majority of which are casitas, has been outfitted with handcrafted Santa Fe–style furnishings made by local artisans, and the decor of each room focuses on a mythological Native American figure, whose likeness has been hand-painted on the walls of that unit. Corn Dancer, who represents the anticipation of an abundant harvest, is the motif for the studio casita with a queen-size bed. The Kokopelli Casita is a one-bedroom unit with a dining room, living room, and king-size bed; Kokopelli, a flute player, is believed to bring good fortune and abundance to the Native American people. The Rainbow Dancer represents power, beauty, and strength through the colors of the rainbow. In the Buffalo Dancer Casita beautiful Native American drums are used as end tables and are meant to remind visitors of the rhythm of life. The one-bedroom Clown (or Koshari) Dancer Casita is a delightful representation of the "spirit of the classic Native American prankster." Four of the casitas feature fireplaces, and all have fully equipped kitchens; the Buffalo and Rainbow casitas are equipped with washers and dryers. Spirit Dancer and Deer Dancer, completed in 1996, are the inn's newest rooms. Spirit Dancer, the least expensive of all, is a studio with a queen bed, microwave, and refrigerator. Each morning a breakfast of healthful, fresh-baked food is delivered (along with the newspaper) to your front door in a basket for you to enjoy at your leisure. Smoking and pets are not permitted.

✪ Dos Casas Viejas

610 Agua Fria St., Santa Fe, NM 87501. ☎ **505/983-1636.** 6 rms. Fax 505/983-1749. TV TEL. $165–$275 double. Free off-street parking.

These two old houses (dos casas viejas), located not far from the Plaza on Agua Fria Street, have been beautifully restored by Jois and Irving Belfield who are now running them as a very well-kept bed-and-breakfast. The half-acre compound, surrounded by a wall, is not visible from the street, but after you pass through the security gates you'll find yourself in an adobe oasis. The grounds are nicely manicured and the rooms, each with a private entrance, are beautifully decorated. Furnished with southwestern antiques and original art (one room, for instance, displays figurines from an Indian tribe in South America—they were originally carved to help cure sick people), all rooms have Mexican-tile floors and kiva fireplaces. Some rooms are furnished with canopy beds and one has a beautiful sleigh bed; all are covered with fine linens and down comforters. Guests can use the library and dining area (where a European breakfast is served each morning) in the main building. Breakfast can also be enjoyed on the main patio or on your private patio (after you collect it in a basket). A lap pool is available for guest use.

El Farolito

514 Galisteo St., Santa Fe, NM 87501. ☎ **505/988-1631.** 7 casitas. TV TEL. $110–$125 casita for two. Rates include breakfast. MC, V. Free parking.

El Farolito is just a five-minute walk from downtown, but it's far enough away from the center of town so that guests can enjoy some peace and quiet after a long day of shopping and sightseeing. All seven of the casitas are equipped with kiva fireplaces and are decorated in true Santa Fe style. The floors in each unit are either brick or tile and are covered with Mexican rugs, the walls are adobe-colored, and the bedspreads are southwestern in style. Some rooms feature semiprivate patios and some have wet bars (not stocked). A continental breakfast of fruit, pastry, cereals, and coffee or tea is served each morning in the breakfast room (which also has a fireplace).

El Paradero

220 W. Manhattan Ave., Santa Fe, NM 87501. ☎ **505/988-1177.** 14 rms (8 with bath), 2 suites. A/C TEL. May 15–Oct 31, $70–$110 double; $130 suite. Nov 1–May 14, $60–$100 double; $120 suite. Rates include breakfast. MC, V. Free parking.

Located a few blocks south of the Santa Fe River, El Paradero (The Stopping Place) began about 1810 as a Spanish adobe farmhouse. It doubled in size in 1878, when Territorial-style details were added; and in 1912 Victorian touches were incorporated in the styling of its doors and windows. Nine ground-level rooms surround a central courtyard; they offer a clean white decor, hardwood floors, folk art, and hand-woven textiles on the walls. Three more luxurious upstairs rooms feature tile floors and baths as well as private balconies. Three rooms have fireplaces. Eight rooms offer private baths; four others share. There are no TVs in the main building. Two suites in a separate brick Victorian building provide living rooms with fireplaces, kitchen nooks, bedrooms with queen-size beds, full baths, TVs, and phones.

The ground floor of the main building, with its impressive viga-latilla ceiling, includes a parlor, a living room with a piano and fireplace, and the dining room, where a full gourmet breakfast and afternoon tea are served daily. Also, if you'd like to take a trip up the mountain and have a picnic, they'll prepare a lunch for you.

Four Kachinas Inn

512 Webber St., Santa Fe, NM 87501. ☎ **800/397-2564** or 505/982-2550. 4 rms. TV TEL. $88–$125 double. Rates include breakfast. DISC, MC, V. Free parking.

Located on a quiet, residential street, but still well within walking distance of downtown, the Four Kachinas Inn is a wonderful little bed-and-breakfast. The rooms are decorated with southwestern artwork, including beautiful antique Navajo rugs, kachinas, and handmade furniture (in fact, some of the furniture was made from the wood salvaged from the old barn that once stood on the property here). As you might have guessed, each of the rooms is named for a Hopi kachina: The Koyemsi Room is named for the "fun-loving, mudhead clown kachina"; the Poko Room, for the dog kachina which "represents the spirits of domestic animals"; the Hon Room, for the "powerful healing bear kachina"; and the Tawa Room, for the sun god kachina. Three of the rooms are on the ground floor. The upstairs room offers a beautiful view of the Sangre de Cristo Mountains. In a separate building, constructed of adobe bricks that were made on the property, there is a lounge where guests can gather at any time of day to enjoy complimentary beverages and snacks. The snacks, whatever they are, will be a treat—one of the owners won "Best Baker of Santa Fe" at the county fair a couple of years ago. In the guest lounge there is a library of art and travel books, and works of art are for sale. An extended continental breakfast of juice, coffee or tea, pastries, yogurt, and fresh fruit is brought to guests' rooms each morning. One of the rooms here is completely handicapped-accessible.

✪ Grant Corner Inn

122 Grant Ave., Santa Fe, NM 87501. ☎ **505/983-6678** for reservations, 505/984-9001 for guest rooms. Fax 505/983-1526. 12 rms (10 with bath), 1 hacienda. A/C TV TEL. $80–$120 single or double without bath; $100–$155 single or double with bath. Hacienda $105–$130 guest rooms rented separately; $215–$255 for entire house. Rates include full gourmet breakfast. MC, V.

This early 20th-century manor at the corner of Grant Avenue and Johnson Street is just two blocks west of the Plaza. Each room is furnished with antiques, from brass or four-poster beds to armoires and quilts, and monogrammed terry-cloth robes are available for those staying in rooms with shared baths. All rooms have ceiling fans and some are equipped with small refrigerators. Each room has its own character.

For example, no. 3 has a hand-painted German wardrobe closet dating from 1772 and a washbasin with brass fittings in the shape of a fish; no. 8 has an exclusive outdoor deck that catches the morning sun; and no. 11 has an antique collection of dolls and stuffed animals. Two rooms have kitchenettes and two also have laundry facilities. The inn's office doubles as a library and gift shop. Children 6 and under are accepted in specific rooms. In addition to the rooms mentioned above, Grant Corner Inn now offers accommodations in their Hacienda, located at 604 Griffin Street. It's a southwestern-style condominium with two bedrooms, living and dining rooms, and a kitchen. It can be rented in its entirety or the rooms can be rented separately, depending on your needs.

Breakfast, for both the inn and the Hacienda, is served each morning in front of the living-room fireplace or on the front veranda in summer. The meals are so good that an enthusiastic public arrives for brunch here every Saturday and Sunday (the inn is also open to the public for weekday breakfasts).

Inn on the Paseo

630 Paseo de Peralta, Santa Fe, NM 87501. ☎ **800/457-9045** or 505/984-8200. Fax 505/989-3979. 18 rms, 2 suites. A/C TV TEL. $85–$165 double. Rates include extended continental breakfast. AE, DC, MC, V. Free parking.

Located just a few blocks from the Plaza, the Inn on the Paseo is a good choice for travelers who want to be able to walk to the shops, galleries, and restaurants but would rather not stay at a larger hotel. As you enter the inn you'll be welcomed by the warmth of the large fireplace in the foyer. Southwestern furnishings dot the spacious public areas and the work of local artists adorns the walls. The guest rooms are large, meticulously clean, and very comfortable. One room boasts a fireplace and many feature four-poster beds and private entrances. The focal point of each room is an original handmade patchwork quilt. The owner is a third-generation quilter and she made all the quilts you'll see hanging throughout the inn (more than 25 of them). A breakfast buffet is served on the sundeck in warmer weather, and indoors by the fire on cooler days. It consists of muffins, breads, granola, fresh fruit, and coffee or tea. Complimentary refreshments are served every afternoon.

The Preston House

106 Faithway St., Santa Fe, NM 87501. ☎ **505/982-3465.** Fax 505/982-3465. 15 rms (13 with bath), 2 cottages, 1 adobe house. A/C TV TEL. High season, $75–$85 double without bath; $106–$160 double with bath; $150 cottage or adobe house. Low season, $48–$58 double without bath; $78–$98 double with bath; $115 cottage or adobe house. Additional person $20 extra. Rates include continental breakfast and afternoon tea. MC, V. Free parking.

This is a different type of building for "The City Different"—a century-old Queen Anne home. This style of architecture is rarely seen in New Mexico; it has been painted sky blue with white trim. The house's owner, noted silk-screen artist and muralist Signe Bergman, adores its original stained glass.

Located five blocks east of the Plaza, off Palace Avenue near La Posada hotel, the Preston House has several types of rooms. Six in the main house are furnished with period antiques and decorated with floral wallpaper and lace drapes. Many rooms feature brass beds covered with quilts; some have decks, several offer fireplaces, and only two require sharing a bath. All rooms are equipped with phones. Seven more rooms with bath are located in an adobe building catercorner from the house. Two private cottages behind Preston House and an adobe home across the street provide more deluxe facilities. All rooms are stocked with sherry and terry-cloth robes. A continental buffet breakfast is served daily, as is afternoon tea with homemade cookies, cakes, and pies. Children age 10 and under not accepted.

Pueblo Bonito

138 W. Manhattan Ave., Santa Fe, NM 87501. ☎ **800/461-4599** or 505/984-8001. Fax 505/984-3155. 20 rms, 6 suites. TV TEL. Jan–Feb, $70–$110 double. March–April and Nov–Dec, $80–$120 double. May–Sept, holidays, and special events, $95–$140 double. Rates include continental breakfast. MC, V. Free parking.

Private courtyards and narrow flagstone paths provide a look of elegance for this former circuit judge's 19th-century adobe hacienda and stables, located a few blocks south of the Santa Fe River. Adobe archways lead to hybrid rose gardens shaded by prolific apricot and pear trees; guests are invited to help themselves to the fruit.

Each guest room is named for a Pueblo tribe of the surrounding countryside. Every room—decorated with Native American rugs on wood or brick floors—is furnished with a queen-size bed, fireplace, cable TV, and radio/alarm clock. Bathrooms are small but attractively tiled. Six rooms are suites, each with an elaborate and fully stocked kitchen, living/dining room with fireside seating, and bedroom. A couple of other rooms offer refrigerators and wet bars. The remainder are standard units with locally made willow headboards and couches, dining alcoves, and old Spanish-style lace curtains. Continental breakfast is served daily from 8 to 10am in the dining room or on the sun deck; if you prefer, there's room service. Afternoon tea is served daily from 4 to 6pm. There's also a coin-op laundry and an indoor hot tub.

✪ Spencer House Bed & Breakfast Inn

222 McKenzie St., Santa Fe, NM 87501. ☎ **800/647-0530** (7am to 7pm) or 505/988-3024. 4 rms, 1 cottage. A/C. $85–$115 double. Rates include breakfast. MC, V. Free parking.

The Spencer House is unique among Santa Fe bed-and-breakfasts. Instead of southwestern–style furnishings, you'll find beautiful antiques from England, Ireland, and colonial America. One guest room features an antique brass bed, another a pencil-post bed, yet another an English panel bed, and all rooms utilize Ralph Lauren fabrics and linens (in fact, the Spencer House continues to be featured in Ralph Lauren ads). Each bed is also outfitted with a fluffy down comforter. All bathrooms are completely new, modern, and very spacious. Owners Keith and Michael take great pride in the Spencer House and keep it spotlessly clean. From the old Bissell carpet sweeper and drop-front desk in the reading nook to antique trunks in the bedrooms, no detail has been overlooked. In summer a full breakfast—coffee, tea, yogurt, cereal, fresh fruit, and main course—is served on the outdoor patio. In winter guests dine indoors by the wood-burning stove. A full afternoon tea is served in the breakfast room. Keith and Michael, who live next door, received an award from the Santa Fe Historical Board for the restoration of Spencer House. In 1995 they added two new rooms. One has a fireplace, private patio, TV, and private telephone. The second is an 800-square-foot cottage with a living room, dining area, full kitchen and bath, private patio, and screened-in porch.

The Territorial Inn

215 Washington Ave., Santa Fe, NM 87501. ☎ **505/989-7737.** Fax 505/986-9212, attn: Lela. 10 rms (8 with bath). TV TEL. $90–$100 single or double without bath; $130–$160 single or double with bath. Indian Market, Thanksgiving, and Dec 25, rates are higher. Additional person $15 extra. Rates include continental breakfast. MC, V. Free parking.

This two-story Territorial-style building, dating from the 1890s and situated one and a half blocks from the Plaza, is the last of the private homes on Washington Avenue. Constructed of stone and adobe with a pitched roof, it features a curving tiled stairway.

Eight of its rooms, typically furnished with Early American antiques, offer private baths; the remaining two share a bath. All rooms are equipped with ceiling fans and sitting areas, and two also have fireplaces. The back garden, shaded by large cottonwoods, boasts a patio where breakfast is served in warm weather, as well as a rose garden and a gazebo-enclosed hot tub.

Water Street Inn

427 Water St., Santa Fe, NM 87501. ☎ **505/984-1193**. 6 rms. A/C TV TEL. $115–$170 single or double. Rates include continental breakfast. AE, MC, V. Free parking.

An award-winning adobe restoration to the west of the Hilton hotel and four blocks from the Plaza, this friendly inn features beautiful Mexican-tile baths, several kiva fireplaces or woodstoves, and antique furnishings. Each room is packed with southwestern art and books. Wine, fruit, chips, and salsa are offered in the living room or on the upstairs portal in the afternoon.

All rooms have king-size or queen-size beds. Room 3 features a queen-size hideaway sofa to accommodate families. (Yes, children are welcomed, as are pets, with prior approval.) Room 4 provides special regional touches in its decor and boasts a chaise longue, fur rug, built-in seating, and corner fireplace. Five new rooms are currently under construction.

6   RV Parks & Campgrounds

RV PARKS

At least four private camping areas, mainly for recreational vehicles, are located within a few minutes' drive of downtown Santa Fe. Typical rates are $20 for full RV hookups, $15 for tents. Be sure to book ahead at busy times.

Babbitt's Los Campos RV Park

3574 Cerrillos Rd., Santa Fe, NM 87501. ☎ **505/473-1949**. Fax 505/471-9220.

The resort has 95 spaces with full hookups, picnic tables, showers, restrooms, laundry, and grocery store. It's just 5 miles south of the Plaza.

Rancheros de Santa Fe Campground

Exit 290 off I-25 (Rte. 3, Box 94, Santa Fe, NM 87505). ☎ **505/466-3482**.

Tents, motor homes, and trailers requiring full hookups are welcome here. The park's 130 sites are situated on 22 acres of piñon and juniper forest. Facilities include tables, grills and fireplaces, hot showers, restrooms, laundry, grocery store, swimming pool, playground, games room, free nightly movies, public telephones, and propane. Cabins are also available. It's located about 6 miles southeast of Santa Fe and is open from March 15 to October 31.

Santa Fe KOA

Exit 290 or 294 off I-25 (Rte. 3, Box 95A, Santa Fe, NM 87501). ☎ **505/466-1419** or 505/KOA-1514 for reservations.

This campground offers full hookups, pull-through sites, tent sites, picnic tables, showers, restrooms, laundry, store, "Santa Fe–style" gift shop, playground, recreation room, propane, and dumping station. It's located about 11 miles northeast of Santa Fe.

Tesuque Pueblo RV Campground

US 84/285 (Rte. 5, Box 360H, Santa Fe, NM 87501). ☎ **800/TRY-RV-PARK** or 505/ 455-2661.

This campground has full hookups, pull-through sites, tent sites, showers, restrooms, laundry, seasonal swimming pool and hot tub, and a store that sells Native American jewelry and fishing gear. It's approximately 10 miles north of Santa Fe.

CAMPGROUNDS

There are three forest sites along NM 475 going toward the Santa Fe Ski Basin. All are open from May to October. Overnight rates start at about $6, depending on the particular site.

Hyde Memorial State Park

NM 475 (P.O. Box 1147, Santa Fe, NM 87503). ☎ **505/983-7175.**

This park is about 8 miles from the city. Its campground includes shelters, water, tables, fireplaces, and pit toilets. Maps of Santa Fe showing where firewood can be found are supplied. Seven RV pads with electrical pedestals and an RV dump station are available. There are also a small ice-skating pond and nature trails.

Santa Fe National Forest

NM 475 (P.O. Box 1689, Santa Fe, NM 87504). ☎ **505/988-6940.**

Black Canyon campground, with 44 sites, is located just before you reach Hyde State Park. It has potable water and sites for trailers up to 32 feet long. Big Tesuque campground, with ten newly rehabilitated sites, is about 12 miles from town. Both Black Canyon and Big Tesuque campgrounds, located along the Santa Fe Scenic Byway, NM 475, are equipped with vault toilets.

Santa Fe Dining 6

There are literally hundreds of restaurants in Santa Fe, from luxury establishments with strict dress codes right down to corner hamburger stands. This is a sophisticated city where a large variety of cuisines flourish. Some chefs create dishes that incorporate traditional southwestern foods with nonindigenous ingredients; their restaurants are referred to in the listings as "creative southwestern." Others stick with steak and seafood. Many offer continental, European, or Asian menus.

Especially during peak tourist seasons, dinner reservations may be essential. Reservations are always recommended at the better restaurants.

In the listings below, **Very Expensive** refers to restaurants where most dinner main courses are priced above $25; **Expensive** includes those where the main courses generally cost between $18 and $25; **Moderate** means those in the $12 to $18 range; and **Inexpensive** refers to those charging $12 and under.

1   Best Bets

- **Best Value:** If you're looking for good food and large portions for little money, you'll find it at **Tortilla Flats,** 3139 Cerrillos Rd. (☎ 505/471-8685). Portions are gigantic and the atmosphere is quite friendly.
- **Best for Kids:** Without doubt, the **Cowgirl Hall of Fame,** 319 S. Guadalupe St. (☎ 505/982-2565), is great for children. The food on the kids menu is simple enough to suit their tastes, and they'll be endlessly amused in the children's play area.
- **Best Continental Cuisine:** These days continental cuisine is losing its popularity, but **Geronimo,** 724 Canyon Rd. (☎ 505/982-1500), isn't. Traditional continental specialties such as tournedos share the menu with a variety of more creative dishes. The atmosphere is lovely.
- **Best Creative American Cuisine:** Decor, service, and cuisine are top-notch at **Santacafé,** 231 Washington Ave. (☎ 505/984-1788). The chef has a magical way of combining Asian and southwestern spices.
- **Best French Cuisine: Encore Provence,** 548 Agua Fria St. (☎ 505/983-7470). Although this is the only real French restaurant in town, it happens to be excellent. The service, the wine list, and the crème brûlée are superb.
- **Best Italian Cuisine:** There are other good Italian restaurants in town, but my personal favorite is **Babbo Ganzo Trattoria,** 130 Lincoln Ave. (☎ 505/986-3835). Their thin-crust pizzas are the best, and their pastas and specialties are consistently good.

• **Best Spanish Cuisine: El Farol,** 808 Canyon Rd. (☎ **505/988-9912**) offers great ambience and local color, not to mention the longest and best tapas menu in Santa Fe.

2 Restaurants by Cuisine

AMERICAN
Real Burger (*I*, Downtown)
San Francisco Street Bar and Grill
(*I*, Downtown)

BARBECUE
Cowgirl Hall of Fame (*I*, Downtown)

CHINESE
Hunan Restaurant (*M*, Southside)
On Lok Yuen (*I*, Southside)
Szechwan Chinese Cuisine
(*M*, Southside)

CONTINENTAL
Bistro 315 (*M*, Downtown)
Cafe Escalera (*M*, Downtown)
The Compound (V*E*, Downtown)
The Evergreen (*E*, Out of Town)
Geronimo (*E*, Downtown)
The Pink Adobe (*E*, Downtown)
Poulet Patate (*E*, Downtown)

CREATIVE SOUTHWESTERN
Coyote Cafe (*E*, Downtown)
La Casa Sena (*E*, Downtown)

DELI/CAFE
Carlos' Gosp'l Cafe (*I*, Downtown)
Old Santa Fe Trail Bookstore &
Coffeehouse (*I*, Downtown)

ECLECTIC
Atalaya (*I*, Downtown)

FRENCH
Encore Provence (*M*, Downtown)

INTERNATIONAL
The Natural Cafe (*I*, Southside)
Paul's (*M*, Downtown)
Zia Diner (*I*, Downtown)

ITALIAN
Andiamo! (*M*, Downtown)
Babbo Ganzo Trattoria (*M*, Downtown)
Julian's (*M*, Downtown)
La Traviata (*M*, Downtown)
The Palace (*M*, Downtown)
Pranzo Italian Grill (*M*, Downtown)
Upper Crust Pizza (*I*, Downtown)

JAPANESE
Shohko-Cafe and Hiro Sushi
(*M*, Downtown)

MEXICAN
Old Mexico Grill (*M*, Southside)
Toushie's (*M*, Southside)

NEW AMERICAN
Cafe Cassis (*M*, Downtown)
Celebrations (*M*, Downtown)
Double A (*E*, Downtown)

NEW MEXICAN
Blue Corn Cafe (*I*, Downtown)
The Burrito Co. (*I*, Downtown)
Cafe Pasqual's (*M*, Downtown)
Green Onion (*I*, Southside)
Guadalupe Cafe (*I*, Downtown)
Inn of the Anasazi (*E*, Downtown)
La Choza (*I*, Downtown)
La Tertulia (*M*, Downtown)
Maria's New Mexican Kitchen
(*I*, Southside)
Santacafé (*E*, Downtown)
The Shed (*I*, Downtown)
Tecolote Cafe (*I*, Southside)
Tia Sophia's (*I*, Downtown)
Tomasita's Cafe (*I*, Downtown)
Tortilla Flats (*I*, Southside)

SPANISH
El Farol (*M*, Downtown)

STEAKS/SEAFOOD
Bobcat Bite (*I*, Southside)
The Bull Ring (*M*, Downtown)
El Nido (*E*, Northside)
The Legal Tender (*M*, Out of Town)
Ore House on the Plaza
(*M*, Downtown)
Steaksmith at El Gancho
(*M*, Southside)
Tiny's Restaurant & Lounge
(*I*, Southside)
Vanessie of Santa Fe (*M*, Downtown)

VIETNAMESE
Saigon Cafe (*I*, Southside)

Key to abbreviations: *I* = Inexpensive, *M* = Moderate, *E* = Expensive *VE* = Very Expensive

3 Downtown

This area includes the circle defined by the Paseo de Peralta and St. Francis Drive, as well as Canyon Road.

VERY EXPENSIVE

The Compound

653 Canyon Rd. ☎ **505/982-4353.** Reservations required. Main courses $17.50–$28. AE. Tues–Sat 6pm until the last diners leave. CONTINENTAL.

The Compound, designed by noted architect Alexander Girard, is set on beautifully landscaped grounds amid tall firs and pines on the south bank of the Santa Fe River. It's reached by a long driveway off Canyon Road, at the rear of an exclusive housing compound. The interior decor is simple but refined, yielding to the natural setting. Service is attentive and elegant: A coat and tie are de rigueur for gentlemen. Young children are not admitted.

Typically there's a wide choice of seafood, chicken, and meat dishes. Appetizers include pâté de foie gras and caviar. A favorite house special is roast rack of lamb with mint sauce. A different special is offered nightly. Main courses are served with rice, potatoes, a vegetable, and fresh-baked rolls. Seafood and vegetables are delivered to the restaurant daily; bread and pastries are baked on the premises. There is, of course, an extensive wine list.

EXPENSIVE

Coyote Cafe

132 Water St. ☎ **505/983-1615.** Reservations recommended. Main courses $6.50–$15.95 (Rooftop Cantina); fixed-price dinner $39.50 (Coyote Cafe). AE, DC, DISC, MC, V. Oct–Apr cafe daily lunch 11:30am–2pm, dinner 6–9pm; Apr–Oct cafe lunch Sat–Sun 11:30am–2pm, dinner daily 6–9pm, Rooftop Cantina daily 11am–9pm. CREATIVE SOUTHWESTERN.

This is still the number-one "trendy" place to dine in Santa Fe. Owner Mark Miller has talked extensively about his restaurant and cuisine on national television, which has invariably identified him with "Santa Fe cuisine." Tourists throng here: In fact, during the summer, reservations are recommended days in advance. The cafe overlooks Water Street from tall windows on the second floor of a downtown building. Beneath the skylight, set in a cathedral ceiling, is a veritable zoo of animal sculptures in modern folk-art forms. Smoking is not allowed here.

The cuisine, prepared on a pecan-wood grill in an open kitchen, is southwestern with a modern twist. The menu changes seasonally, but diners might start with roasted red pepper soup with grilled Yucatan chicken sausage and fennel confit or griddled buttermilk corn cakes with chipotle shrimp and salsa fresca. Main courses might include pecan-grilled fillet of beef served with red chile, huitlacoche taquitos, and a chanterelle-grilled yellow tomato salsa; or grilled ahi with a spicy tomato avocado sauce and tortilla salad. A vegetarian special is offered daily. Andrew Maclauchlan, the new pastry chef, has added a wonderfully creative variety of treats to the menu, including peach star anise upside-down cake with iced gingered peach sauce and vanilla bean ice cream and apricot and black mission fig linzer tart with brown sugar cream and blueberry ice cream. You can order drinks from the full bar or wine by the glass.

The Coyote Cafe has two adjunct establishments. The **Rooftop Cantina** serves light Mexican fare and cocktails. On the ground floor is the Coyote Cafe General Store, a retail gourmet southwestern food market, featuring the Coyote Cafe's own food line (called Coyote Cocina), as well as hot sauces and salsas from all over the world.

Double A

331 Sandoval ☎ **505/982-8999.** Reservations recommended. Main courses $7–$9 at lunch, $14–$26 at dinner. AE, MC, V. Mon–Fri lunch 11:30am–2pm, dinner 5:30–10pm; Sat–Sun dinner 5:30–10pm. The bar is open until 2am Mon–Sat and until 11pm on Sun. AMERICAN.

Every year a number of new restaurants open in Santa Fe, but only one or two keep the locals coming back for more—the Double A, which opened in June 1995, is destined to be one of those places. Chef Marion Gillchrist (previously chef at Santacafé) and sous chef Tom Atkins (previously a banquet chef at the Inn of the Anasazi) make a great team and, so far, turn out consistently good American fare night after night. I really enjoyed the penne with buffalo sausage in roasted tomato-garlic sauce, as well as the cowboy coffee, rubbed quail served with toasted grits and summer squash casserole. Other menu items include the Double A Burger with buttermilk onion rings or spaghettini with roasted corn, arugula, and shaved Parmesean. For an additional sum you can have a side order of toasted grits, oven-roasted potatoes, horseradish mashed potatoes, or match-stick potatoes. Desserts include sweet potato shortcake with brandied peaches and buttermilk-pecan cream and warm fudge cake served with peanut butter crunch ice cream, toasted bananas, and a warm chocolate sauce. The wine list is well chosen, but only a few bottles are priced at less than $25. Wines are available by the glass and there's an interesting selection of beers and mixed drinks.

Geronimo

724 Canyon Rd. ☎ **505/982-1500.** Reservations recommended. Main courses $16.50–$21. AE, MC, V. Daily 11:30am–2:15pm, Sun–Thurs 6–10pm, Fri–Sat 6–10:30pm. CREATIVE CONTINENTAL.

When Geronimo opened in 1991, no one was sure if it would succeed because so many previous restaurants at this site had failed miserably. But Geronimo has done more than just survive—it has flourished. Occupying an old adobe structure known as the Borrego House, built by Geronimo Lopez in 1756, the restaurant has been completely restored. Numerous small dining rooms help it retain the comfortable feel of an old Santa Fe home. On a recent visit, I enjoyed cornmeal-dusted, pan-seared, free-range chicken served with baby spinach and roasted new potatoes. Additional offerings included mesquite-grilled Black Angus ribeye burger with grilled Anaheim chile-pineapple salsa and Gruyère cheese served with chile-dusted shoestring potatoes, and chicken mole relleno served with jalapeño peach salsa and crème fraîche. For dessert try the mocha pot de creme—you won't be disappointed, especially if you're a chocoholic. The menu changes seasonally, and there is an excellent wine list. Outdoor dining is available in warm weather.

Inn of the Anasazi Restaurant

113 Washington Ave. ☎ **505/988-3236.** Reservations recommended. Main courses $8–$11.75 at lunch, $17.50–$29 at dinner; breakfast $5.25–$9.50. AE, DC, DISC, MC, V. Mon–Fri 7–10:30am, Sat–Sun 7–10:30am; daily 11:30am–2:30pm; daily 5:30–10pm. NORTHERN NEW MEXICAN/NATIVE AMERICAN.

In keeping with the principles of the Inn of the Anasazi (see Chapter 5), everything served at this restaurant is all natural. The meats are chemical-free and the fruits and vegetables are organic whenever possible. They serve water only upon request "in

Downtown Santa Fe Dining

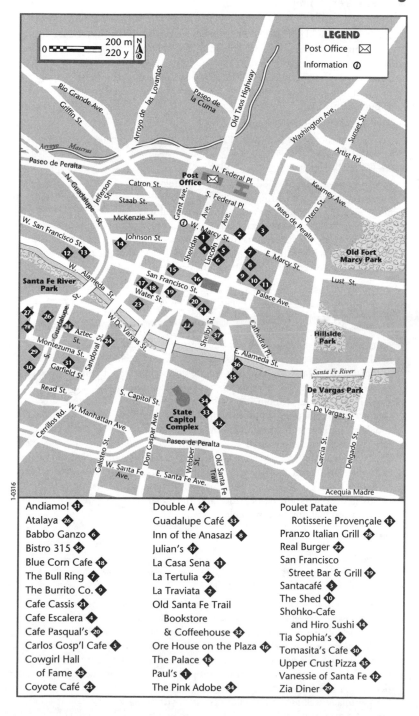

LEGEND
Post Office ✉
Information ⓘ

Andiamo! ㉛
Atalaya ㉖
Babbo Ganzo ⑥
Bistro 315 ㊱
Blue Corn Cafe ⑱
The Bull Ring ⑦
The Burrito Co. ⑨
Cafe Cassis ㉑
Cafe Escalera ④
Carlos Gosp'l Cafe ⑤
Cowgirl Hall
   of Fame ㉕
Coyote Café ㉓

Double A ㉔
Guadalupe Café ㉝
Inn of the Anasazi ⑧
Julian's ㊲
La Casa Sena ⑪
La Tertulia ㉗
La Traviata ②
Old Santa Fe Trail
   Bookstore
   & Coffeehouse ㉜
Ore House on the Plaza ⑯
The Palace ⑮
Paul's ①
The Pink Adobe ㉞

Poulet Patate
   Rotisserie Provençale ⑬
Pranzo Italian Grill ㉘
Real Burger ㉒
San Francisco
   Street Bar & Grill ⑲
Santacafé ③
The Shed ⑩
Shohko-Cafe
   and Hiro Sushi ⑭
Tia Sophia's ⑰
Tomasita's Cafe ㉚
Upper Crust Pizza ㉟
Vanessie of Santa Fe ⑫
Zia Diner ㉙

Smoking is allowed only in the **Dragon Room,** the lounge across the alleyway from the restaurant. Under the same ownership, the charming Dragon Room (which is much more popular with locals than the Pink Adobe's main dining room) has its own menu offering traditional Mexican food. The full bar is open daily from 11:30am to 2am, until midnight on Sunday, and there's live entertainment Sunday through Thursday.

Poulet Patate Rotisserie Provençale

446 W. San Francisco St. ☎ **505/820-2929.** Reservations recommended. Main courses $9–$18 at lunch, $14.25–$24 at dinner. AE, DISC, MC, V. Lunch daily 11am–2:30pm; dinner daily 6–10pm. CONTINENTAL.

Featuring a 6-by-6 foot wood-burning rotisserie oven, Poulet Patate is best known for its spit- or fire-roasted rotisserie chickens. The food is authentically French—the house specialty is herbes de Provence chicken and is excellently prepared. Another good choice is the rotisserie duck stuffed with oranges and rosemary and glazed with honey and lavender. The leg of lamb offered here is traditionally French in its preparation. Everybody's favorite dessert is Berries on a Cloud. In addition to dining room service, Poulet Patate also offers a takeout menu.

✪ Santacafé

231 Washington Ave. ☎ **505/984-1788.** Reservations recommended. Main courses $9–$12 at lunch, $18–$24 at dinner. AE, MC, V. Lunch Mon–Sat 11:30am–2pm; dinner daily 6–10pm. NEW AMERICAN.

A casually formal restaurant in the 18th-century Padre Gallegos House, 2 $1/_2$ blocks north of the Plaza, Santacafé's service and presentation are impeccable. Noted for its minimalist decor (and attractiveness to celebrities), art-free soft white adobe interior, and "Zen-inspired" courtyard, Santacafé has been a favorite of tourists and locals alike since 1983. Each room has a fireplace, and there's an outside courtyard for summer diners. Its unique modern American cooking has a hint of southwestern and Asian influences. Menus created by Chef Ming Tsai, change seasonally. Recent offerings included herb-roasted chicken with udon noodles and red-chile ravioli filled with goat and feta cheeses, fresh oregano, sun-dried tomato, and a basil/green-chile sauce or Atlantic salmon with roasted new potatoes. Another excellent choice is the Asian duck breast served with maple hoisin sauce and sesame bok choy. All breads and desserts are homemade, and the full bar offers wines by the glass. Outdoor seasonal dining is available.

MODERATE

Andiamo!

322 Garfield St. ☎ **505/995-9595.** Reservations recommended. Main courses $12–$18. AE, DISC, MC, V. Wed–Mon 5:30–10pm. ITALIAN.

Quite a few new restaurants have sprung up in Santa Fe over the past year, several of which were created by former staff members from some of the city's most popular eateries. Andiamo! is one of those that's making a successful go of it. Chris Galvin, once the sous chef at Cafe Escalera, has joined forces with business partner Joan Gillcrist at this fine restaurant to create an authentically Tuscan atmosphere in which a daily changing menu features antipasto, pasta, and excellent desserts. I particularly enjoyed the Caesar salad and the crispy polenta with rosemary and Gorgonzola as well as the cannelloni (stuffed with spinach). For dessert I'd recommend the polenta pound cake with lemon crème anglaise. Beer and wine are served at this nonsmoking restaurant.

the interest of conservation." The setting is comfortable, with an exposed-beam ceiling, exposed adobe walls, and traditional southwestern decor.

For breakfast you can have anything from fruit to scrambled egg quesadillas with apple smoked bacon, tomatoes, and guacamole. At lunch, you might try the Anasazi flatbread with fire-roasted sweet peppers and tomato-olive salsa to start, followed by coconut tempura prawns with jicama-poblano slaw and chile passion fruit coulis. For dinner, try tortilla soup with ginger pork potstickers, then perhaps follow with cinnamon- and chile-rubbed tenderloin of beef with chipotle and white Cheddar mashed potatoes and mango salsa. Or maybe you'd rather have plantain crusted halibut served with a peach-citrus coulis, green chile risotto, and tropical fruit salsa.

There are daily specials, as well as a nice list of wines by the glass and special wines of the day.

✪ La Casa Sena

125 E. Palace Ave. ☎ **505/988-9232.** Reservations recommended. Main courses $7.75–$10 at lunch; $29 fixed-price dinner. La Cantina, main courses $8.50–$17. AE, CB, DC, DISC, MC, V. Mon–Sat 11:30am–3pm; daily 5:30–10pm. Brunch Sun 11am–3pm. CREATIVE SOUTHWESTERN.

Opposite St. Francis Cathedral, two restaurants face a spacious garden patio. The elegant main dining room occupies a Territorial-style adobe house built in 1867 by Civil War hero Maj. José Sena for his wife and 23 children. Today it's a veritable art gallery with museum-quality landscapes on the walls and Taos-style handcrafted furniture. In the adjacent **La Cantina,** waiters and waitresses sing numbers from Broadway shows as they carry platters from the kitchen to the table.

The cuisine in the main dining room might be described as northern New Mexican with a continental flair. Lunches include chicken enchiladas on blue-corn tortillas and almond-encrusted salmon with gazpacho salsa. In the evening, diners might start with a salad of mixed organic greens, goat cheese, and a fresh herb vinaigrette, then move to American corn-fed lamb chops with habañero-papaya sauce, tropical fruit ensalada, and crispy root vegetables.

The more moderately priced **Cantina** menu offers the likes of country fried ribeye and carne adovada burrito (prime pork roasted with red-chile sauce, served with Hatch green chile and cheeses). Both restaurants have exquisite desserts. The award-winning wine list features more than 850 wines.

The Pink Adobe

406 Old Santa Fe Trail. ☎ **505/983-7712.** Reservations recommended. Main courses $4.75–$8.75 at lunch, $10.75–$23.25 at dinner. AE, CB, DC, DISC, MC, V. Mon–Fri 11:30am–2:30pm; daily 5:30–9:30pm. CONTINENTAL/SOUTHWESTERN.

San Pasqual, patron saint of the kitchen, keeps a close eye on this popular restaurant in the center of the 17th-century Barrio de Analco and across the street from the San Miguel mission. A Santa Fe institution since 1946, it occupies an adobe home believed to be at least 350 years old. Guests enter through a narrow side door into a series of quaint, informal dining rooms with tile or hardwood floors. Stuccoed walls display original modern art or Priscilla Hoback pottery on built-in shelves.

At the dinner hour the Pink Adobe offers the likes of escargots and shrimp rémoulade as appetizers. Main courses include shrimp rémoulade, poulet Marengo, steak Dunnigan (a house specialty), lamb curry, and porc Napoléone. Lunch has more New Mexican and Cajun dishes, including a house enchilada topped with an egg, turkey-seafood gumbo, and gypsy stew (chicken, green chile, tomatoes, and onions in sherry broth). The food here isn't the greatest, to be sure, but people don't flock here for the cuisine; they come for the atmosphere.

Babbo Ganzo Trattoria
130 Lincoln Ave. ☎ **505/986-3835.** Reservations recommended. Main courses at lunch $4–$9, at dinner $10–$22. MC, V. Mon–Sat 11:30am–2:30pm and 5:30–10pm. ITALIAN.

Located atop the only escalator in Santa Fe, the Babbo Ganzo is a great little Italian place that serves lunch and dinner. As you walk into the restaurant, you'll see on your right a wall of pasta for sale and on your left a large bar. There's a wonderful mural, as well as a fireplace and a wine rack.

For lunch you could start with bruschetta (grilled bread topped with garlic, tomato, and basil) and then follow with an allo zenzero pizza with red chile, tomato, and mozzarella cheese. Pizzas are baked in the wood-burning oven. At dinner, start with insalata e funghi fritti—shiitake and oyster mushrooms sautéed in balsamic vinegar and served over a bed of lettuce. Move on to pappardelle sui cinghiale (homemade pasta with wild boar in a light tomato sauce), or if you prefer fish, Babbo Ganzo offers a nice selection plus a fresh fish of the day. This is one of the more authentic Italian restaurants in the area.

Bistro 315
315 Old Santa Fe Trail. ☎ **505/986-9190.** Reservations recommended. Main courses $16–$24 at dinner. AE, DISC, MC, V. Lunch daily 11:30am–2pm; dinner daily 6–9pm. CONTINENTAL.

Bistro 315 has enjoyed instant success since it opened in 1995, and no wonder—with two powerhouses like Matt Yohalem, a graduate of Johnson and Wales and Chef Poissonier at Le Cirque under Chef Daniel Boulud, and Jack Shaab, who formerly worked with both Larry Forgione and Mark Miller (Coyote Cafe). The restaurant is tiny (only 27 tables), but always packed—and with good reason. The food is excellent. The menu changes seasonally; on my last visit there I started with croquettes of goat cheese and bell pepper coulis and moved on to piñon-crusted halibut served with spinach and scallion beignets (Yohalem's previous experience in the kitchen of Commander's Palace in New Orleans is evident in his preparation of dishes such as this). The grilled tomato soup was also excellent, and I was fortunate to be there on a night when grilled smoked chicken was on the menu. My favorite dessert here is the warm tarte tatin served with crème fraîche. Because the restaurant is so small and so popular, reservations are an absolute must.

The Bull Ring
150 Washington Ave. ☎ **505/983-3328.** Reservations recommended. Main courses $10.95–$25. AE, DISC, MC, V. Mon–Fri 11:30am–3pm; daily 5:30–10pm. Closed Sun in winter. STEAKS/SEAFOOD.

Legislators and lobbyists from the State Capitol still make a habit of dining and drinking at the Bull Ring even though it recently moved to a new location. Steaks are the dinner specialty. Much ballyhooed is the Bull Ring steak, a 12-ounce charcoal-broiled New York cut with sautéed mushrooms or onions, red or green chile, or au poivre sauce. Seafood dishes include grilled shrimp skewer served on a bed of rice with garlic-herb butter. Enchiladas Nuevo Mexico (blue-corn tortillas with red or green chile, cheese, beef, or chicken) highlight the small regional portion of the menu. Midday diners can also choose half-pound hamburgers or other sandwiches.

Cafe Cassis
103 E. Water St. ☎ **505/989-1717.** Reservations not required. Main courses $6.50–$15.75. AE, MC, V. Mon–Fri 11am–9pm; Sat–Sun brunch 9am–3pm and dinner 4–9pm. CONTEMPORARY AMERICAN.

A 20-foot-high ceiling makes the dining room at this small, contemporary restaurant seem much bigger, and entertainment is provided by cooks who throw pizza dough into the air as though they've been doing it all their life. The specialty here is oak-fired pizzas with perfectly crisp crusts and creative toppings (such as mushrooms and spinach pesto). One of Chef Ivan Walz's specialties is piñon-breaded pan-fried chicken which is served with a chipotle and lingonberry sauce. This is the place for good food at reasonable prices. There is a bar.

Cafe Escalera

130 Lincoln Ave., 2nd floor ☎ **505/989-8188.** Reservations recommended. Main courses $8.50–$14.50 at lunch, $14.50–$24.50 at dinner. AE, MC, V. Lunch Mon–Fri 11:30am–2:30pm; dinner Mon–Wed 5:30–9pm, Thurs–Sat 5:30–9:30pm. CREATIVE CONTINENTAL/MEDITERRANEAN.

Cafe Escalera has, over the past six years, become one of Santa Fe's best and most popular restaurants. The spacious, open, warehouselike space is bright, airy, and filled with energy. The decor is understated in a modern way—the focus here is on the food. At lunch I like to start with an order of Mediterranean olives and perhaps roasted almonds. If you're in the mood for a more substantial appetizer, try the roasted peppers and goat cheese or the vegetarian black-bean chile. On my last visit to Cafe Escalera for lunch, I enjoyed the mussels in a spicy broth. Lunch and dinner appetizers are usually the same, but the main courses differ greatly. The risotto timbale with summer squash, spinach, and basil pesto is a good choice, and so is the grilled king salmon with a tomato-basil vinaigrette. Those with a heartier appetite might like the Niman-Schell Ranch fillet steak with garlic mashed potatoes. The menu changes daily. For dessert you really can't go wrong by ordering the Blanco y Negro, the Crème Brolles, or pots de crèmes. The waitstaff here is among the best in Santa Fe.

ⓢ Cafe Pasqual's

121 Don Gaspar Ave. ☎ **505/983-9340.** Reservations recommended for dinner. Breakfast $4.75–$8.95; lunch $7.95–$9.95; dinner main courses $15.95–$24.75. AE, MC, V. Mon–Sat 7am–3pm and 11am–3pm; Mon–Thurs 6–10pm, Fri–Sat 6–10:30pm. Brunch Sun 8am–2pm. NEW MEXICAN.

This intimate establishment, located across from the Hotel St. Francis, has a common table where solo diners can get acquainted and an innovative menu that appeals to budget-watchers at breakfast and lunch. Omelets, pancakes, and huevos motuleños (two eggs over easy on blue-corn tortillas and black beans topped with sautéed bananas, feta cheese, salsa, and green chile) are among the breakfast options. Soups, salads, and Mexican dishes are popular at lunch, and there's a delectable grilled-salmon burrito with herbed goat cheese and cucumber salsa. The frequently changing dinner menu offers grilled meats and seafoods, plus vegetarian specials. Typical appetizers include warm French Brie with whole roasted garlic jalapeño salsa and tomatillo salsa, and chilled roasted corn and chipotle soup. Main courses might include Thai shrimp with lemongrass-coconut sauce, baby bok choy, and scallion cake, or pollo pibil (char-grilled Yucatan-spiced breast of free-range chicken with saffron rice and fire-roasted vegetables). Pasqual's also offers homemade desserts, imported beers, and wine by the bottle or glass.

Celebrations

613 Canyon Rd. ☎ **505/989-8904.** Reservations recommended. Dinner main courses $5.75–$14.95; breakfast/lunch $3.95–$8.25. AE, MC, V. Daily 7:30am–2pm; Wed–Sat 5:30–9pm. NEW AMERICAN.

Housed in a former art gallery with beautiful stained-glass windows and a kiva fireplace, Celebrations boasts "the ambience of a bistro and the simple charm of another era." In summer, guests can dine on a brick patio facing Canyon Road.

Three meals are served daily, starting with breakfast—an omelet with black beans or French toast with orange syrup, for example. Lunch choices include soup, salad, and pasta specials, Swiss raclette, sandwiches like the oyster poor boy, and ploughman's lunch. Casseroles, pot pies, and hearty soups are always available in winter. The dinner menu changes with the chef's whim, but recent specialties have included sautéed pecan trout, roasted rack of lamb, and crawfish étouffée. All desserts (including the red chile piñon ice cream) are homemade. There is a choice of beers and California wines by the bottle or glass.

⑤ El Farol

808 Canyon Rd. ☎ **505/988-9912.** Reservations recommended. Main courses $9.95–$23.95. DC, DISC, MC, V. Daily 11am–4pm and 6–10pm. SPANISH.

This is the place to head for local ambience and old-fashioned flavor. The Canyon Road artists' quarter's original neighborhood bar, El Farol means "The Lantern." Its low ceilings and dark-brown walls have now become the home of one of Santa Fe's largest and most unusual assortments of tapas (bar snacks and appetizers). Thirty-five varieties are offered, including such delicacies as pulpo a la Gallega (octopus with Spanish paprika sauce), grilled cactus with ramesco sauce, conejo y vino (rabbit with tomatoes, olives, and wine), and Moroccan eggplant. Diners who proceed to a main course often choose the Cornish game hen—butter fried, cooked with rosemary, and served with ginger sauce or the authentically Spanish paella. Jazz, folk, and ethnic musicians play almost every night beginning at 9:30pm. In summer, an outdoor patio, seating 50, is open to diners.

✪ Encore Provence

548 Agua Fria St. ☎ **505/983-7470.** Reservations recommended. Main courses $14–$18.50. AE, MC, V. Sun–Thurs 6–9pm; Fri–Sat 6–9:30pm. FRENCH.

Encore Provence, a delightful little restaurant decorated in French country style, is one of Santa Fe's lesser known jewels. The menu features dishes reminiscent of the heart of the French countryside. Begin with a lovely serving of mussels provençal (served off the shell in garlic and parsley butter) or the brandade (purée of salt cod, potatoes, garlic, and extra virgin olive oil served with sweet bell peppers and olive tapenade). My choice for a main course would be the seven-hour grilled leg of lamb served with mashed potatoes or the scallops wrapped in bacon and served with a cream of French lentils and spinach. For dessert, the crème brûlée, as might be expected, is quite good, as is the schuss (light raspberry and kirsch fromage blanc cheesecake with a raspberry coulis). The wine list here is superb.

✪ Julian's

221 Shelby St. ☎ **505/988-2355.** Reservations recommended. Main courses $14–$21. AE, CB, DC, DISC, MC, V. Daily 6pm until the last diners leave. ITALIAN.

Devotees of Julian's in Telluride, Colorado, may be pleased to discover that their favorite northern Italian restaurant resurfaced in Santa Fe in 1989. Elizabeth (Lou) McLeod and Wayne Gustafson have moved to an unpretentious setting just off Alameda Street. Meals are served in an atmosphere of simple elegance, around a central kiva fireplace, to the strains of light jazz music. The menu is primarily Tuscan, though other regional dishes have been known to pop up on occasion. Start with prosciutto di Parma con melone (fresh melon with Italian ham), ostriche alla Genovese (oysters baked with Parmesan cheese, pesto, and seasoned bread crumbs), or melanzana alla griglia con pepperoni (grilled eggplant with roasted peppers and balsamic vinegar). Then move on to the generous main courses—for instance, fresh fish (grilled fresh trout served with extra virgin olive oil and aromatic herbs), pollo agro dolci (chicken sautéed with shallots, raisins, and capers in a sweet brown sauce) or veal piccata alla limone. All main courses include bread and a side of pasta. You can order a salad à la carte. There is a full bar with an extensive list of Italian and Californian wines.

Ⓢ La Tertulia

416 Agua Fria St. ☎ **505/988-2769.** Reservations recommended. Lunch $5.50–$7.50, dinner $7.35–$18. AE, DC, DISC, MC, V. Tues–Sun 11:30am–2pm and 5–9pm. NEW MEXICAN.

Housed in a former 18th-century convent, La Tertulia's thick adobe walls separate six dining rooms, including the old chapel and a restored *sala* (living room) with a valuable Spanish Colonial art collection. There's also an outside garden patio for summer dining. Dim lighting and viga-beamed ceilings, shuttered windows and wrought-iron chandeliers, lace tablecloths, and handcarved santos in wall niches lend a feeling of historic authenticity. *La tertulia* means "the gathering place." Gourmet regional dishes include fillet y rellenos, carne adovada, pollo adovo, and camarones con pimientos y tomates (shrimp with peppers and tomatoes). If you feel like dessert, try the chocolate piñon-nut truffle torte or natillas (custard). The bar features homemade sangría.

La Traviata

95 W. Marcy St. ☎ **505/984-1091.** Reservations recommended. Main courses at lunch $6–$10, at dinner $14–$18. MC, V. Mon–Fri 8:30am–2:30pm; daily 6–10pm. SOUTHERN ITALIAN.

This simple Italian bistro, just a block off the Plaza, hits its stride during the annual July–August opera season. Photos of opera singers and classical composers share wall space with prints of Italian scenes amid the refined strains of classical music. The menu focuses on antipasti, pastas, and a handful of seasonal specials. Grilled eggplant, smoked salmon, and roast pepper dishes are popular starters. Favorite homemade pastas include linguine con gamberi (with shrimp in a tomato-saffron sauce) and tagliatelle arrabbiata (with mushrooms in a spicy tomato-basil sauce). Featured main dishes include fresh fish and shellfish and veal dishes—such as the costolette di vitello alla saltimbocca (a grilled veal chop with prosciutto, Fontina cheese, and sage). La Traviata also offers delectable desserts, espresso coffee, and a wine list full of Italian imports.

Ore House on the Plaza

50 Lincoln Ave. ☎ **505/983-8687.** Reservations recommended. Main courses $12–$23. AE, MC, V. Mon–Sat 10:30am–2:30pm, Sun noon–2:30pm; daily 5:30–10pm. STEAKS/SEAFOOD.

The Ore House's second-story balcony, at the southwest corner of the Plaza, is an ideal spot from which to watch the passing scene while you enjoy cocktails and hors d'oeuvres—in fact, it is the place to be between 4 and 6pm every night. The decor is southwestern, with plants and lanterns hanging amid white walls and booths. The menu, currently presided over by Chef Isaac Modivah, is heavy on fresh seafood and steaks. Daily fresh fish specials include salmon and swordfish (poached, blackened, teriyaki, or lemon), rainbow trout, lobster, and shellfish. Steak Ore House (wrapped in bacon and topped with crabmeat and béarnaise sauce) and chicken Ore House (a grilled breast stuffed with ham, Swiss cheese, green chile, and béarnaise) are local favorites. The Ore House also caters to non-meat-eaters with vegetable platters.

The bar, with solo music Wednesday through Saturday night, is proud of its 66 "custom margaritas." It offers a selection of domestic and imported beers and an excellent wine list. An appetizer menu is served from 2:30 to 5pm daily, and the bar stays open until midnight or later (on Sunday it closes at midnight).

The Palace

142 W. Palace Ave. ☎ **505/982-9891.** Reservations recommended. Dinner main courses $9.50–$18.95, lunch $5.25–$10.50. AE, MC, V. Lunch Mon–Sat 11:30am–4pm; dinner daily 5:45–10pm. NORTHERN ITALIAN/CONTINENTAL.

When the Burro Alley site of Doña Tules's 19th-century gambling hall was excavated in 1959, an unusual artifact was discovered: a brass door-knocker, half shaped like a horseshoe, and the other half like a saloon girl's stockinged leg. That knocker has become the logo of the Palace, which maintains the Victorian flavor but none of the negative associations of its predecessor.

The brothers Lino, Pietro, and Bruno Pertusini have brought a long family tradition into the restaurant business: Their father was chef at the Villa d'Este on Lake Como, Italy. The Pertusinis' menu is northern Italian with a few French and continental dishes. Lunch features Caesar salad and roasted "7 Aromas" chicken salad, bruschetta caprini, ruby trout, housemade pasta, and breads. Dinner includes crabstuffed shrimp, scaloppine di vitello Ortolana (veal, eggplant, and zucchini in a pinot grigio parsley sauce), New Mexican lamb, and a variety of vegetarian dishes. There are fresh pastas daily; the wine list is long and well considered.

There is outdoor dining, and the bar is open Monday through Saturday from 11:30am to 2am and Sunday from 5:45pm to midnight with nightly entertainment.

✪ Paul's

72 W. Marcy St. ☎ **505/982-8738.** Reservations recommended for dinner. Dinner main courses $12.95–$18.95, lunch $4.95–$7.50. AE, DISC, MC, V. Mon–Sat 11:30am–2:15pm; Sun–Thurs 5:30–9pm; Fri–Sat 6–10pm. INTERNATIONAL.

Once just a home-style deli, then a little gourmet restaurant called Santa Fe Gourmet, Paul's (which opened in 1990) is a wonderful place for lunch or dinner. The lunch menu presents a nice selection of main courses, such as salad Niçoise, dill salmon cakes, and an incredible pumpkin bread stuffed with pine nuts, corn, green chile, red chile sauce, queso blanco, and caramelized apples. Sandwiches are also available at lunch. At dinner, the lights are dimmed and the bright Santa Fe interior (with folk art on the walls and colorfully painted screens that divide the restaurant into smaller, more intimate areas) becomes a great place for a romantic dinner. The menu might include red chile duck wontons in a soy ginger cream to start, and pecan-herb crusted baked salmon with sorrel sauce as an entrée. The grilled ahi with roasted pepper, artichoke heart, and green olive salsa is excellent. Every dish is artistically exquisite in its presentation. Paul's won the "Taste of Santa Fe" award for the best main course in 1992 and the best dessert in 1994. His chocolate ganache is exquisite. A wine list is available. Smoking is not permitted anywhere in the restaurant.

✪ Pranzo Italian Grill

540 Montezuma St., Sanbusco Center. ☎ **505/984-2645.** Reservations recommended. Main courses $5.95–9.95 at lunch, $5.95–$18.50 at dinner. AE, DC, DISC, MC, V. Mon–Sat 11:30am–3pm; Sun–Thurs 5–10pm; Fri–Sat 5–11pm. REGIONAL ITALIAN.

Housed in a renovated warehouse, and freshly redecorated in warm Tuscan colors, this sister of Albuquerque's redoubtable Scalo restaurant caters to local Santa Feans with a contemporary atmosphere of modern abstract art and food prepared on an open grill. Homemade soups, salads, creative pizzas, and fresh pastas are among the less expensive menu items. Bianchi e nere al capesante (black-and-white linguine with bay scallops in a light seafood sauce) and pizza pollo affumicato (with smoked chicken, pesto, and roasted peppers) are consistent favorites. Steak, chicken, veal, and fresh seafood grills—heavy on the garlic—dominate the dinner menu. The bar offers the Southwest's largest collection of grappas, as well as a wide selection of wines and champagnes by the glass. The upstairs rooftop terrace is lovely for seasonal moon-watching over a glass of wine. **Portare Via Cafe,** adjacent to the restaurant, is a great place for a light breakfast or lunch. The cinnamon rolls and scones are particularly good, and cappuccino and pastries are served throughout the day. Sandwiches are available at lunch.

Shohko-Cafe and Hiro Sushi

321 Johnson St. ☎ **505/983-7288.** Reservations recommended. Lunch $4.25–$12, dinner $4.25–$18. AE, DISC, MC, V. Mon–Fri 11:30am–2pm; Mon–Thurs 5:30–9pm; Fri–Sat 5:30–9:30pm. JAPANESE.

Opened in 1976 as Santa Fe's first Japanese restaurant, Shohko, located in a 150-year-old adobe building that had been a bordello in the 19th century, celebrated its 20th anniversary in 1996. Its current owners have done a terrific job of blending New Mexican decor (such as ceiling vigas and Mexican tile floors) with traditional Japanese decorative touches (rice paper screens, for instance). Up to 30 fresh varieties of raw seafood, including sushi and sashimi, are served at the 36-foot sushi bar. Here is the place to indulge in teriyaki dishes, sukiyaki, yakitori (skewered chicken), and yakisoba (fried noodles), and two uniquely southwestern Japanese treats: green-chile tempura and, at the sushi bar, the Santa Fe Roll (with green chile, shrimp tempura, and masago). A brand-new menu item—chilled seafood noodle salad—is quite good. There are also some Chinese dishes, a bento box lunch special, and many vegetarian specialties. "Food for Health" is the motto of Shohko. Wine, imported beers, and hot saké are available.

Ⓢ Vanessie of Santa Fe

434 W. San Francisco St. ☎ **505/982-9966.** Reservations strongly recommended. Dinner $12.95–$17.95. AE, CB, DC, DISC, MC, V. Daily 5:30–10:30pm. STEAKS/SEAFOOD.

Vanessie is as much a piano bar as it is a restaurant. The talented Doug Montgomery and Charles Tichenor hold forth at the keyboard, caressing the ivories with a repertoire that ranges from Bach to Gershwin to Barry Manilow. A 10-item menu, served at large, round wooden tables beneath hanging plants in the main dining room or on a covered patio, never varies: roast chicken, fresh fish, New York sirloin, filet mignon, Australian rock lobster, grilled shrimp, and rack of lamb. Portions are large and come with baked potatoes or onion loaf. Fresh vegetables or sautéed mushrooms are available at an extra charge. For dessert, the slice of cheesecake served is large enough for three diners. There's a short wine list.

INEXPENSIVE

Atalaya Restaurant-Bakery

320 S. Guadalupe. ☎ **505/982-2709.** Reservations not required. Main courses $6–$12. AE, MC, V. Daily 7am–10pm. ECLECTIC.

Atalaya, a trendy bistro, is one of Santa Fe's newest restaurants. The hip decor (exposed brick walls and geometric wall partitions), low prices, and an interesting menu attract a cross-section of the city's population to this restaurant night after night. The shrimp and grits done "low country style" with mushrooms, bacon, green onions, and fried eggs is a great choice for breakfast. At lunch try a muffuletta sandwich (a New Orleans staple), filled with ham, salami, provolone, and olive salad. Other menu items include grilled lamb brisket with an orange serrano pepper sauce and mussels served with Thai green curry. Of course, if you'd rather just have a burger, go for the Green Chile Cheeseburger topped with roasted poblanos and Monterey Jack. The breads here are quite good. Desserts are as varied as the entrées and equally good, and there's an excellent selection of coffees and milkshakes.

Blue Corn Cafe

133 W. Water St. ☎ **505/984-1800.** Reservations accepted for parties of 8 or more. Main courses $4.95–$8.25. AE, DC, DISC, MC, V. Daily 11am–11pm. The bar stays open until 2am. NEW MEXICAN.

This lively, attractively decorated southwestern-style restaurant opened in 1992 and is just what downtown Santa Fe needed—great food at low prices. The interior is notable for its blue, green, red, and yellow painted patch floor. While you peruse the menu your waiter will bring freshly made tortilla chips to your table. The Blue Corn Cafe is known for its chile rellenos, and I have enjoyed the achiote grilled half chicken with epazote cream sauce as well as the carne adovada quesadilla (red chile marinated pork, wrapped in a flour tortilla with green chile and Jack and Cheddar cheeses served with guacamole and sour cream). For the more adventurous, the tortilla burger (beef patty covered with cheeses and red or green chile, wrapped in a flour tortilla and served with chile fries) is a good bet. And for those who can't decide, the combination plates offer a nice variety. For dessert, try the Mexican brownies, the homemade caramel flan, or the fried ice cream. The bar features 34 varieties of tequila and an interesting list of specialty margaritas. Live bands play on Friday and Saturday nights.

The Burrito Co.

111 Washington Ave. ☎ **505/982-4453.** Menu items $1.25–$4.75. MC, V. Mon–Sat 7:30am–11pm; Sun 10am–5pm. NEW MEXICAN.

This is probably downtown Santa Fe's best fast-food establishment. You can people-watch while you dine on the outdoor patio or enjoy the garden-style poster gallery indoors. Order and pick up your food at the counter. Breakfast burritos are popular in the morning; after 11am you can get traditional Mexican meals with lots of chile.

ⓢ Carlos' Gosp'l Cafe

125 Lincoln Ave. ☎ **505/983-1841.** Menu items $2.65–$6.90. No credit cards. Mon–Fri 11am–4pm; Sat 11am–3pm. DELI.

You may sing the praises of the "Say Amen" desserts at this cafe in the inner courtyard of the First Interstate Bank Building. First, though, try the tortilla or hangover (potato, corn, and green chile chowder with Monterey Jack cheese) soups, or the deli sandwiches. The Gertrude Stein sandwich, with Swiss cheese, tomato, red onion, sprouts, and mayonnaise is good (though Stein herself may have found it lacking). I prefer the unusual Miles Standish (fresh turkey breast with cranberries, cream cheese, and mayonnaise). Carlos's has outdoor tables, but many diners prefer to sit indoors, reading newspapers or chatting around the large common table. Gospel and soul music play continually; paintings of churches and performers cover the walls.

Cowgirl Hall of Fame

319 S. Guadalupe St. ☎ **505/982-2565.** Reservations recommended. Main courses at lunch $2.95–$7.50, at dinner $4.25–$12.95. AE, DISC, MC, V. Mon–Thurs 11am–10:30pm; Fri–Sat 11am–11:30pm; Sun 10am–10pm. The bar is open every night until 2am (Sun until midnight). REGIONAL AMERICAN/BARBECUE.

Mention the Cowgirl Hall of Fame to any Santa Fean and you'll hear one word: "fun." Everything at this restaurant has been done with a playful spirit—from the cowgirl paraphernalia decorating the walls to the menu featuring such items as "chicken wing dings" (eight chicken wings in a "dandy" citrus-Tabasco marinade served with a special dressing). The chuckwagon chile is another house favorite, and so is the honey-fried chicken. The bunkhouse smoked brisket with potato salad, barbecue beans, and cole slaw is excellent, as is the cracker-fried catfish with jalapeño-tartar sauce. Recent specialties of the house included butternut squash casserole and grilled salmon soft tacos. There's even a special "kid's corral" which has horseshoes, a ridin' rockin' horse, a horse-shaped rubber tire swing, hay bales, and a bean bag toss to keep children entertained during dinner. The dessert specialty of the house is the original ice cream baked potato (ice cream molded into a potato shape, rolled in spices, and topped with green pecans and whipped cream). Happy hour is from 4 to 6pm, and the bar stays open until 2am. There is live music or comedy performances almost every night.

⑤ Guadalupe Cafe

422 Old Santa Fe Trail ☎ **505/982-9762.** Main courses at dinner $6.95–$15.95, at breakfast $4.50–$8.75, at lunch $6–$12. DISC, MC, V. Tues–Fri 7am–2pm; Tues–Sat 5:30–10pm. Brunch Sat–Sun 8am–2pm. NEW MEXICAN.

Santa Feans line up at all hours to dine in this casually elegant cafe, which was recently featured in *Bon Appetit* magazine. Breakfasts include spinach-mushroom burritos and huevos rancheros, while the lunch menu features chalupas, stuffed sopaipillas, burritos, chimichangas, and burrito plates, as well as a wide variety of salads and burgers. Dinner specialties include breast of chicken relleno (boneless breast of chicken filled with Jack and Cheddar cheese, breaded in corn meal, deep fried, and finished in the oven with green chile and cheese), which is excellent, and fresh roasted ancho chiles (filled with a combination of Montrachet and Monterey Jack cheeses, piñon nuts, and topped with your choice of chile). For those who don't enjoy Mexican food, there are "hamberguesas" (hamburgers) and a selection of traditional favorites like chicken fried steak, turkey piñon meat loaf, and chicken salad. Daily specials are available; don't miss the famous chocolate-amaretto adobe pie for dessert. Beer, wine, and margaritas are served.

La Choza

905 Alarid St. ☎ **505/982-0909.** No reservations. Lunch $4.50–$5.50, dinner $5.50–$6.50. MC, V. Mon–Sat 11am–9pm. NEW MEXICAN.

The sister restaurant of the Shed (see below) is located near the intersection of Cerrillos Road and St. Francis Drive. A casual eatery with round tables beneath a viga ceiling, it's especially popular on cold days when diners gather around the wood-burning stove and fireplace. The menu offers traditional enchiladas, tacos, and burritos on blue-corn tortillas, as well as green-chile stew, chile con carne, and carne adovada. Vegetarians and children have their own menus. Beer and wine are available.

Real Burger

227 Don Gaspar Ave. ☎ **505/988-3717.** Menu items $2.25–$6. No credit cards. Mon–Sat 8am–5pm. AMERICAN/NEW MEXICAN.

Downtown Santa Fe's favorite hamburger stand is across the street from the St. Francis Hotel. Don't come for atmosphere—come for burgers with "the works," chile dogs, fajitas, or the enchilada plate. In the morning, you can order steak and eggs or a breakfast burrito.

⑤ San Francisco Street Bar and Grill

114 W. San Francisco St. ☎ **505/982-2044.** No reservations. Lunch $5.25–$6.75, dinner $5.25–$12.50. AE, DISC, MC, V. Daily 11am–11pm. AMERICAN.

This easygoing eatery offers casual dining amid simple decor in three seating areas: the main restaurant, an indoor courtyard beneath the three-story Plaza Mercado atrium, and an outdoor patio with its own summer grill. Although the restaurant is probably best known for its hamburgers, it also offers a variety of daily specials. The lunch menu consists mainly of soups, sandwiches, and salads; dinner dishes include a tasty chicken breast with roasted red pepper aioli, grilled pork tenderloin with apple and green chile salsa, and New York strip steak. There are also nightly pasta specials such as spinach linguini al Greque (homemade spinach linguini with sun-dried tomatoes, kalamata olives, feta cheese, olive oil, and garlic). The full bar service includes draft beers and daily wine specials.

⑤ The Shed

113¹/₂ E. Palace Ave. ☎ **505/982-9030.** Reservations accepted at dinner. Main courses $4.75–$7 at lunch, $6.75–$13.95 at dinner. DISC, MC, V. Mon–Sat 11am–2:30pm; Thurs–Sat 5:30–9pm. NEW MEXICAN.

Queues often form outside The Shed, half a block east of the Palace of the Governors. A luncheon institution since 1953, it occupies several rooms and the patio of a rambling hacienda that was built in 1692. Festive folk art adorns the doorways and walls. The food is basic but delicious, a compliment to traditional Hispanic Pueblo cooking. Enchiladas, tacos, and burritos, all served on blue-corn tortillas with pinto beans and posole, are menu staples. The green-chile soup is a local favorite. The Shed recently hired a new chef, Joshua Carswell, who has added vegetarian and low-fat Mexican foods to the menu as well as a wider variety of soups and salads. There are dessert specials, and beer and wine are available. The Shed is once again open for dinner (this meal had not been available for some 30 years).

Tia Sophia's

210 W. San Francisco St. ☎ **505/983-9880.** Breakfast $1.35–$7.50, lunch $3.50–$8.50. MC, V. Mon–Sat 7am–2pm. NEW MEXICAN.

Diners at this friendly downtown restaurant (now in its 23rd year) sit at big wooden booths. Daily breakfast specials include eggs with blue-corn enchiladas (Tuesday) and burritos with chorizo, potatoes, chile, and cheese (Saturday). A popular lunch is the Atrisco plate: two eggs, green-chile stew, a cheese enchilada, beans, posole, and a sopaipilla. Beware of what you order because, as the menu states, Tia Sophia's is "not responsible for too hot chile." Be prepared to wait for a table since this is a popular place.

⑤ Tomasita's Cafe

500 S. Guadalupe St. ☎ **505/983-5721.** No reservations. Main courses $4.25–$9.50 at lunch, $4.75–$9.95 at dinner. MC, V. Mon–Sat 11am–10pm. NEW MEXICAN.

This restaurant may be the one most often recommended by Santa Feans. Why? Some point to the atmosphere; others cite the food and prices. Hanging plants and wood decor accent this spacious brick building, adjacent to the old Santa Fe railroad station. The menu features such traditional New Mexican dishes as chile rellenos and enchiladas (house specialties), as well as stuffed sopaipillas, chalupas, and tacos. Vegetarian dishes, burgers, steaks, and daily specials are also offered. There's full bar service.

Upper Crust Pizza

329 Old Santa Fe Trail. ☎ **505/983-4140.** No reservations. $3.95–$12.95. No credit cards. Winter, Mon–Sat 11am–10pm; Sun noon–10pm. Summer, Mon–Sat 11am–11pm; Sun noon–11pm. PIZZA.

Santa Fe's best pizzas may be found here, in an adobe house where the front patio adjoins the old San Miguel mission. Meals-in-a-dish include the Grecian gourmet

pizza (feta and olives) and the whole-wheat vegetarian pizza (topped with ses.
seeds). You can either eat here or request free delivery (it takes about 30 minutes)
to your downtown hotel. Beer and wine are available, as are salads, calzones, and
stromboli.

Zia Diner

326 S. Guadalupe St. ☎ **505/988-7008.** Reservations accepted only for parties of six or
more. Main courses $3.50–$7.50 at lunch, $5.25–$14.95 at dinner. AE, MC, V. Daily
11:30am–10pm. INTERNATIONAL/AMERICAN.

In a renovated 1880 coal warehouse, this art deco diner with a turquoise-and-mauve
color scheme boasts a stainless-steel soda fountain and a shaded patio. The varied
menu features homemade soups, salads, fish and chips, meatloaf, and, of course,
enchiladas. Specials range from East Indian curry to spanakopita, Thai-style trout
to three-cheese calzone. There are fine wines, a full bar, great desserts (for example,
tapioca pudding, apple pie, and strawberry rhubarb pie), an espresso bar, and of
course, you can get malts, floats, and shakes anytime.

4 Northside

EXPENSIVE

El Nido

NM 22, Tesuque. ☎ **505/988-4340.** Reservations recommended. Main courses $9.95
$25.95. MC, V. Tues–Sat 11:30am–2pm; Tues–Sun 5:30–10pm. STEAK/SEAFOOD.

Life has never been dull at El Nido ("The Nest"). This 1920s adobe home had been
a dance hall and later Ma Nelson's brothel, before it became a restaurant in 1939.
Since then it's been attracting throngs of Santa Feans for the food, atmosphere,
lively bar, and occasional flamenco dance performances. Scandinavian wood tables
and chairs are surrounded by kiva fireplaces, and the stuccoed walls are covered with
local artwork.

Long-time favorite appetizers include steamed mussels or clams and deep-fried
oysters. As a main course I've enjoyed steak with a spicy anise, black-and-pink pep-
percorn crust and a deliciously moist reddened fresh grilled halibut steak served
with a nice light tequila lime butter. The best desserts here are the profiteroles and
the chocolate piñon torte.

5 Southside

Santa Fe's motel strip and other streets south of the Paseo de Peralta have their share
of good, reasonably priced restaurants.

MODERATE

Hunan Restaurant

2440 Cerrillos Rd., College Plaza South. ☎ **505/471-6688.** Reservations recommended.
Lunch buffet $5.55, dinner $6.95–$25.95. AE, MC, V. Mon–Thurs 11am–9:30pm; Fri
11am–10:30pm; Sat–Sun 11:30am–9:30pm. NORTHERN & CENTRAL CHINESE.

A pair of stone lions guard the ostentatious dragon-gate entrance to this Asian
delight. The red-and-white decor, together with a large aquarium and antique
Oriental furniture, reminds one of a Chinese palace. The hot, spicy Hunan- and
Peking-style recipes prepared by chef/owner Alex Lee are equally fascinating. Family
dinners of Hunan shredded pork, sha-cha beef, and spiced chicken and shrimp are

served with egg roll, wonton soup, fried rice, tea, and fortune cookies. Or you can order such à la carte dishes as whole fish with hot bean sauce or Peking duck. There's an 18-dish luncheon buffet (with children's prices), and food can be taken out.

✪ Old Mexico Grill

2434 Cerrillos Rd., College Plaza South. ☎ **505/473-0338.** Reservations recommended for large parties. Main courses at lunch $5.95–$9.95, at dinner, $8.75–$17.50. DISC, MC, V. Lunch Mon–Fri 11:30am–2:30pm; dinner Sun–Thurs 5:30–9pm, Fri–Sat 5:30–9:30pm. MEXICAN.

Here's something unique in Santa Fe: a restaurant that specializes not in northern New Mexico food, but in authentic Mexico City and regional Mexican cuisine. The servers are attentive. The restaurant's focal point is an exhibition cooking area with an open mesquite grill and French rôtisserie where a tempting array of fajitas, tacos al carbon, and other specialties are prepared. Popular dishes include turkey mole poblano, costillas de puerro en barbacou de Oaxaca (hickory-smoked baby back ribs baked in a chipotle and mulato chile, honey, mustard barbecue sauce), shrimp in orange-lime/tequila sauce, and paella mexicana. There is a nice selection of soups and salads at lunch and a variety of homemade desserts. A full bar serves Mexican beers (10 in all) and margaritas.

✪ Steaksmith at El Gancho

Old Las Vegas Hwy. ☎ **505/988-3333.** Reservations recommended. Main courses $8.95–$24.95. AE, CB, DC, MC, V. Mon–Sat 5:30–10pm; Sun 5–9pm. STEAKS/SEAFOOD.

Santa Fe's most highly regarded steakhouse is a 15-minute drive up the Old Pecos Trail toward Las Vegas. Guests enjoy attentive service in a pioneer atmosphere of brick walls and viga ceilings. New York sirloin, filet mignon, and other complete steak dinners are served, along with barbecued ribs and such nightly fresh seafood specials as oysters, trout, and salmon. In addition, the chef has added a few vegetarian entrées to the menu. A creative appetizer menu ranges from ceviche Acapulco to grilled pasilla peppers and beef chupadero. There is also a choice of salads, homemade desserts, and bread, plus a full bar and lounge (serving a tapas menu from 4pm) that even caters to cappuccino lovers.

Szechwan Chinese Cuisine

1965 Cerrillos Rd. ☎ **505/983-1558.** Reservations recommended. Lunch $5–$7, dinner $5.95–$11.95. DISC, MC, V. Daily 11am–9:30pm. NORTHERN CHINESE.

Spicy northern Chinese cuisine at this restaurant pleases the southwestern palate. The seafood platter of shrimp, scallops, crab, fish, and vegetables stir-fried in a wine sauce is excellent. Other specialties include Lake Tung Ting shrimp, sesame beef, and General Chung's chicken. Wine and Tsingtao beer from China are available.

Toushie's

4220 Airport Rd. ☎ **505/473-4159.** Reservations recommended on weekends. Main courses $3.95–$8.50 at lunch, $6.95–$14.95 at dinner. AE, CB, DC, MC, V. Mon–Fri 11am–midnight; Sat–Sun 4pm–midnight. MEXICAN/AMERICAN.

Located just one block from the Villa Linda Mall, this is an oft-overlooked surprise on the south side of town. Its spacious, semicircular seating area is an ideal place for listening to mellow dance music on Saturday nights and an intimate area for enjoying a relaxing meal at other times. Appetizers include escargots and sautéed mushrooms. The wide choice of main dishes includes a 16-ounce T-bone steak, prime rib and baked shrimp, and coquille of sea scallops and shrimp. Regional dishes highlight the lunch menu, from menudo (Spanish-style tripe stew) to a combination plate of taco, tamale, and rolled enchilada. A favorite dessert is Toushie's Delight—a flaming sopaipilla.

INEXPENSIVE

Ⓢ Bobcat Bite

Old Las Vegas Hwy. ☎ **505/983-5319.** No reservations. Menu items $3.50–$11.95. No credit cards. Tues–Sat 11am–7:50pm. STEAKS/BURGERS.

This local classic (in business for more than 40 years), located about 5 miles southeast of Santa Fe, is famed for its high-quality steaks—such as the 13-ounce ribeye—and huge hamburgers, including a remarkable green-chile cheeseburger. The ranch-style atmosphere appeals to families.

Green Onion

1851 St. Michael's Dr. ☎ **505/983-5198.** Lunch $1.75–$5.25, dinner $4.50–$9.50. AE, MC, V. Daily 11am–10pm. NEW MEXICAN.

The Onion offers up some of the hottest chiles and one of the liveliest local bars in Santa Fe. Roast-beef burritos and chicken enchiladas highlight an established menu, which also features a choice of sandwiches and a great many daily specials.

Ⓢ Maria's New Mexican Kitchen

555 W. Cordova Rd. near St. Francis Dr. ☎ **505/983 7929.** Main courses $5.25–$8.95 at lunch, $5.75–$15.95 at dinner. AE, CB, DC, DISC, MC, V. Mon–Fri 11am 10pm; Sat Sun noon–10pm. NEW MEXICAN.

Built in 1949 by Maria Lopez and her politician husband, Gilbert (the present owners are Al and Laurie Lucero), this restaurant is a prime example of how charm can be created by scavenging. The bricks used for its construction came from the old New Mexico State Penitentiary and most of the furniture once belonged to La Fonda Hotel. The five wall frescoes in the cantina were painted by master muralist Alfred Morang (1901–58) in exchange for food. Maria's boasts an open tortilla grill, where cooks can be seen making flour tortillas by hand. Generous portions of tortillas are served with every dish, from the award-winning beef, chicken, and vegetarian fajitas to blue-corn enchiladas, chile rellenos, green-chile and posole stews, and huge steaks. If you're a margarita fan, this is the place to sample a variety of them—Maria's features over 50 "real margaritas." In addition, Maria's now offers a tasting sampler of more than 50 tequilas. Strolling mariachi troubadours perform nightly. The restaurant provides patio dining in the summer, and two fireplaces warm the dining room in winter.

The Natural Cafe

1494 Cerrillos Rd. ☎ **505/983-1411.** Reservations recommended. Main courses $5–$7.25 at lunch, $8.50–$12 at dinner. DISC, MC, V. Tues–Fri 11:30am–2:30pm; Tues–Sun 5–9:30pm. CREATIVE INTERNATIONAL.

At the Natural Cafe an international menu of tasty and healthy dishes is served in an artsy garden atmosphere by a competent cosmopolitan staff. Seven national cuisines—Mexican (black-bean enchiladas), Chinese (Szechuan chicken), Indian (East Indian tempeh curry), Japanese (pan-broiled trout), Thai (vegetable gai tua), Italian (pasta of the day), and American—are represented on the menu. There are several seafood and chicken daily specials. A children's menu is available. Homemade desserts are sweetened with maple syrup, raw sugar, or honey. Wine and beer are served.

ⓘ Family-Friendly Restaurants

Bobcat Bite *(see p. 79)* The name and the ranch-style atmosphere will appeal to families that are looking for great steaks and huge hamburgers at low prices.

Cowgirl Hall of Fame *(see p. 74)* Kids love the Kid's Corral where, among other things, they can play a game of horseshoes.

Upper Crust Pizza *(see p. 76)* Many people feel they have the best pizza in town, and they'll deliver it to tired tots and their families at downtown hotels.

Old Santa Fe Trail Bookstore & Coffeehouse

613 Old Santa Fe Trail. ☎ **505/988-8878.** No reservations. Main courses $5–$10.50. AE, DISC, MC, V. Daily 8am–closing. Lunch/Dinner 11am–9:30pm.

If you're one of the literati (or just enjoy being around the literati), the Old Santa Fe Trail Bookstore & Coffeehouse is the place to see and be seen. Sandwiches, coffees, and pastries dominate the menu here, so you can grab a bite to eat while listening to the latest reading or attending the latest book-signing. Local talent is featured, and chocolate decadence dessert and cappuccino are the perfect way to enjoy the atmosphere.

On Lok Yuen

3242 Cerrillos Rd. ☎ **505/473-4133.** Reservations not accepted for Fri evenings. Lunch $2.95–$4.95, dinner $4.95–$7.95. MC, V. Mon–Thurs 11am–2:30pm and 4:30–9pm; Fri–Sat 11am–9pm. CHINESE/AMERICAN.

Behind the adobe walls you'll find typical Chinese-American fare—longtime favorites such as beef and chicken chow mein, chop suey, egg foo yung, sweet-and-sour pork, and shrimp fried rice. Luncheon specials include wonton soup, rice, and fortune cookie. There's a choice of several dinner combinations.

Saigon Cafe

501 W. Cordova Rd. ☎ **505/988-4951.** Lunch $3.25–$4.75, dinner $4.50–$8.95. AE, MC, V. Mon–Sat 11am–2:30pm and 5–8:30pm. VIETNAMESE/CHINESE.

Daily lunch buffets and low-priced dinner main courses, such as cashew chicken and egg rolls, are the fare here. The Saigon prepares orders to go, but for those who want to dine here, beer and wine are available.

Ⓢ Tecolote Cafe

1203 Cerrillos Rd. ☎ **505/988-1362.** Main dishes $2.95–$9.25. AE, CB, DC, DISC, MC, V. Tues–Sun 7am–2pm. NEW MEXICAN/AMERICAN.

This is a breakfast-lovers' favorite. The decor is simple, but the food is elaborate: eggs any style, omelets, huevos rancheros—all served with fresh-baked muffins or biscuits and maple syrup. Give the atole piñon hotcakes (made with blue cornmeal) a try. Luncheon specials include carne adovada burritos and green-chile stew, served with beer or wine.

Tiny's Restaurant & Lounge

In the Penn Road Shopping Center, 1015 Penn Rd. ☎ **505/983-9817.** Reservations recommended. Lunch $5.25–$8, dinner $6.95–$14.50. AE, CB, DC, MC, V. Mon–Fri 11:30am–2pm; Mon–Sat 6–10pm. Bar, Mon–Sat 10pm–2am. STEAKS/NEW MEXICAN.

A longtime favorite of Santa Feans, Tiny's first opened in 1948 and is appropriately decorated in 1950s style. There's also an indoor/outdoor patio and garden room

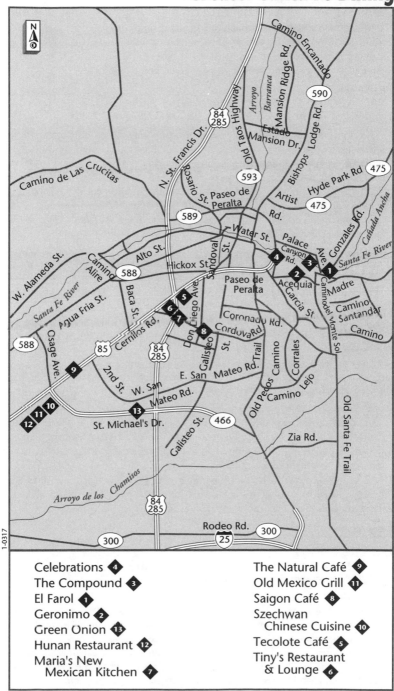

Greater Santa Fe Dining

Celebrations 4
The Compound 3
El Farol 1
Geronimo 2
Green Onion 13
Hunan Restaurant 12
Maria's New
    Mexican Kitchen 7

The Natural Café 9
Old Mexico Grill 11
Saigon Café 8
Szechwan
    Chinese Cuisine 10
Tecolote Café 5
Tiny's Restaurant
    & Lounge 6

with full food and cocktail service. Steaks and shrimp complement a menu that features fajitas and northern New Mexico main courses, such as chicken and guacamole tacos. Try the house specialty—baked chicken flautas. A very popular lounge has live entertainment weekends from 9pm.

Tortilla Flats

3139 Cerrillos Rd. ☎ **505/471-8685**. Breakfast $1.75–$6.25, lunch $5.25–$9, dinner $6.25–$11. DISC, MC, V. Sun–Thurs 7am–9pm; Fri–Sat 7am–10pm. NEW MEXICAN.

This casual restaurant takes pride in its all-natural ingredients and vegetarian menu offerings (its vegetarian burrito is famous around town). The restaurant serves such dishes as homemade blueberry pancakes; fajitas and eggs with a side of black beans; and blue-corn enchiladas, quesadillas, chile rellenos, tacos, and chimichangas. Santa Fe Trail steak (8 ounces of prime ribeye smothered with red or green chile and topped with grilled onions) and green-chile pork chops (smothered with green chile and topped with grilled tomatoes and onions) are house specialties. Beer and wine are served. A children's menu and take-out service are available.

6 Out of Town

A couple of very popular restaurants take a little extra effort to reach but they're worth it.

EXPENSIVE

The Evergreen

Hyde Park Rd. (NM 475), 8 miles east of Santa Fe. ☎ **505/984-8190.** Reservations recommended. Main courses $14.95–$23.50. AE, CB, DC, MC, V. Lunch seasonal (call for hours); Fri–Sun 6–9pm; brunch Sun 11am–2:30pm. CONTEMPORARY CONTINENTAL.

If the views en route to the Santa Fe Ski Basin don't take your breath away, the elevation might—you're 8,400 feet up in the Sangre de Cristo range. The restaurant is nestled in a grove of spruce and pine at the entrance to Hyde Memorial State Park. Diners can enjoy an intimate candlelit atmosphere beside the fireplace or, in summer, bask in twilight on a flagstone patio.

The menu, designed by award-winning chef Jonathan Coady, features applewood-smoked lamb, pheasant breast, free-range beef tenderloin, black- and white-bean sausages, fresh fish, and many daily specials.

MODERATE

✪ The Legal Tender

Lamy. ☎ **505/466-1223.** Reservations recommended. Main courses $12.50–$22.95. DISC, MC, V. Daily noon–3pm; Sun–Thurs 5–8:30pm; Fri–Sat 5–9pm. STEAKS/SEAFOOD.

Just across the road from the old Atchison, Topeka & Santa Fe Railway station in Lamy, the Legal Tender is spectacularly faithful to the Wild West theme of the late 19th century. Built as a general store in 1881, it has gone through a lot of changes—but the Victorian decor remains. The handcarved cherrywood bar is the same one its first owner imported from Germany. Two murals on the balcony, depicting the coming of the iron horse to the West, were commissioned for the 1916 Pan-Pacific Exposition in San Francisco. The tin ceiling in the Americana Room came from the original Hilton Hotel in San Francisco, and its drapes and chandeliers are from the presidential suite of Chicago's Sherman Hotel. Of course, the building is listed in the National Register of Historic Places.

The food is equally worthy of recognition. For lunch a Tender's beef sandwich is a good choice, as is the red snapper Veracruz. Dinner main courses include ribeye steak, a barbecue dish, quail, mountain rainbow trout, and top sirloin and shrimp. During lunch on Tuesday, Thursday, and Saturday a ragtime pianist entertains, and on Friday and Saturday nights, as well as at Sunday lunch, there's country music.

To reach Legal Tender, take I-25 north (actually southeast) toward Las Vegas, get off at Exit 290, and follow US 285 south until you see the signs for the Lamy turnoff.

7

What to See & Do in Santa Fe

Santa Fe is one of the oldest cities in the United States and has long been a center for both the creative and the performing arts, so it's not surprising that the city's major sights are related to history and the arts. The Museum of New Mexico system, the art galleries and studios, the historic churches, and the Native American and Hispanic communities all merit a visit. It would be easy to spend a full week sightseeing in the city without ever heading out to any nearby attractions. In addition to the following listings, you might want to inquire whether the brand new Georgia O'Keeffe museum (scheduled to be completed in the spring of 1997) is now open to visitors.

SUGGESTED ITINERARIES

If You Have 2 Days

For an overview, start your first day at the Palace of the Governors and, as you leave, visit the Native Americans selling their crafts and jewelry beneath the portal facing the Plaza. After lunch, take a self-guided walking tour of old Santa Fe, starting at the Plaza.

On Day 2, spend the morning at the Museum of Fine Arts and the afternoon browsing in the galleries, perhaps on Canyon Road.

If You Have 3 Days

On your first two days, follow the outline above.

On the third day, visit the cluster of museums on Camino Lejo— the Museum of International Folk Art, the Museum of Indian Arts and Crafts, and the Wheelwright Museum of the American Indian. Then wander through the historic Barrio de Analco and spend the rest of the afternoon shopping.

If You Have 4 Days or More

For the first three days, follow the outline above.

Devote your fourth day to exploring the pueblos, including San Juan Pueblo, headquarters of the Eight Northern Indian Pueblos Council, and Santa Clara Pueblo, with its Puye Cliff Dwellings.

On Day 5, go out along the High Road to Taos, with a stop at El Santuario de Chimayo, returning down the Rio Grande valley.

If you have more time, take a trip to Los Alamos, birthplace of the atomic bomb and home of the Bradbury Science Museum, and Bandelier National Monument.

1   The Top Attractions

✪ Palace of the Governors

North Plaza. ☎ **505/827-6483.** Admission $5 adults, free for children under 17. Four-day passes good at all four branches of the Museum of New Mexico cost $8 for adults. Jan–Feb, Tues–Sun 10am–5pm; Mar–Dec, daily 10am–5pm. Closed Jan 1, Mon in Feb, Thanksgiving, and Dec 25.

Built in 1610 as the original capital of New Mexico, the Palace has been in continuous public use longer than any other structure in the United States. Designated the Museum of New Mexico in 1909, it has become the state history museum, with an adjoining library and photo archives. Some cutaways of doors and windows reveal the early architecture.

A series of exhibits chronicles four centuries of New Mexico's Hispanic and American history, from the 16th-century Spanish explorations through the frontier era to modern times. Among Hispanic artifacts, there are maps dating from the early 1700s. There's even a whole mid–19th-century chapel, with a simple, bright-colored altarpiece made in 1830 for a Taos church by folk artist José Rafael Aragón.

Governors' offices from the Mexican and 19th-century U.S. eras have been restored and preserved. Displayed artifacts from early New Mexican life include a stagecoach, an early working printing press, and a collection of *mestizajes*, portraits of early Spanish colonists depicting typical costumes of the time. Also on display are pieces from the silver service used aboard the battleship U.S.S. *New Mexico* from 1918 to 1939 and a tiny New Mexico state flag (3 by 4 inches) that went to the moon on one of the *Apollo* missions.

Most Native American artifacts (previously housed here) have been moved to the Museum of Indian Arts and Culture. Those that remain include several pieces of ancient pottery from the Puye Plateau culture and photographs depicting a museum-sponsored study of Mayan sites in Mexico's Yucatán.

The bookstore has one of the finest selections of art, history, and anthropology books in the Southwest. There is also a fine print shop and bindery, where limited-edition works are produced on hand-operated presses.

Outside the museum, many Santa Fe visitors are impressed with the sight of Native American artisans sitting shoulder-to-shoulder beneath the long covered portal facing the Plaza. Here on the shaded sidewalk, several dozen colorfully dressed members of local Pueblo tribes, plus an occasional Navajo, Apache, or Hopi, spread out their handcrafts: mainly jewelry and pottery, but also woven carpets, beadwork, and paintings. The museum's Portal Program restricts selling space to Native Americans only.

The Palace is the flagship of the Museum of New Mexico system; the main office is at 113 Lincoln Ave. (☎ **505/982-6366** or 505/827-6463 for recorded information). The system comprises five state monuments and four Santa Fe museums—the Palace of the Governors, the Museum of Fine Arts, the Museum of International Folk Art, and the Museum of Indian Arts and Culture.

✪ Museum of Fine Arts

107 W. Palace (at Lincoln Ave.) ☎ **505/827-4455.** Admission $5 adults, seniors are admitted free on Wed, free for children under 17. Four-day passes are available ($8 for four museums). Jan–June, Tues–Sun 10am–5pm; July–Dec, daily 10am–5pm. Fri evenings the museum is open from 5–8pm. Closed Jan 1, Easter Sunday, Thanksgiving, and Dec 25.

Located catercorner from the Plaza and just opposite the Palace of the Governors, this was one of the first Pueblo Revival–style buildings constructed in Santa Fe (in

1917). As such, it was a major stimulus in Santa Fe's development as an art colony earlier in this century.

The museum's permanent collection of more than 8,000 works emphasizes regional art and includes landscapes and portraits by all the Taos masters and the contemporary artists R. C. Gorman, Amado Pena, Jr., and Georgia O'Keeffe, among others.

The museum also has a collection of photographic works by such masters as Ansel Adams, Edward Weston, and Elliot Porter. Modern artists, many of them far from the mainstream of traditional southwestern art, are featured in temporary exhibits throughout the year. Two sculpture gardens present a range of three-dimensional art from the traditional to the abstract.

Beautiful St. Francis Auditorium, patterned after the interiors of traditional Hispanic mission churches, adjoins the art museum (see Chapter 9). A museum shop sells books on southwestern art, prints, and postcards of the collection.

✪ St. Francis Cathedral

Cathedral Place at San Francisco St. ☎ **505/982-5619.** Donations appreciated. Open daily. Visitors may attend mass Mon–Sat at 5:15pm; Sun at 6, 8, and 10am, noon, and 7pm.

Santa Fe's grandest religious structure is just a block east of the Plaza. An architectural anomaly in Santa Fe, it was built between 1869 and 1886 by Archbishop Jean-Baptiste Lamy in the style of the great cathedrals of Europe. French architects designed the Romanesque building—named after Santa Fe's patron saint—and Italian masons assisted with its construction.

The small adobe Our Lady of the Rosary chapel on the northeast side of the cathedral has a Spanish look. Built in 1807, it's the only portion that remains from Our Lady of the Assumption Church, founded along with Santa Fe in 1610. The new cathedral was built over and around the old church.

A wooden icon set in a niche in the wall of the north chapel, *Our Lady of Peace,* is the oldest representation of the Madonna in the United States. Rescued from the old church during the 1680 Pueblo Rebellion, it was brought back by Don Diego de Vargas on his peaceful reconquest 12 years later, thus the name. Today *Our Lady of Peace* plays an important part in the annual Feast of Corpus Christi in June and July.

During a $600,000 renovation project in 1986, an early 18th-century wooden statue of St. Francis of Assisi was moved to the center of the altar screen. The cathedral's front doors feature 16 carved panels of historic note and a plaque memorializing the 38 Franciscan friars who were martyred during New Mexico's early years. There's also a large bronze statue of Bishop Lamy himself; his grave is under the main altar of the cathedral.

2 More Attractions

MUSEUMS

Catholic Museum and the Archbishop Lamy Commemorative Garden

223 Cathedral Place. ☎ **505/983-3811.** Donations appreciated. Mon–Fri 8:30am–4:30pm; Sat hours vary (call ahead).

Housed in a complex of buildings that date from 1832, the Catholic Museum is one of New Mexico's newest, where visitors have the opportunity to learn about the development and significance of Catholicism in New Mexico. Opened in 1994 by

Downtown Santa Fe Attractions

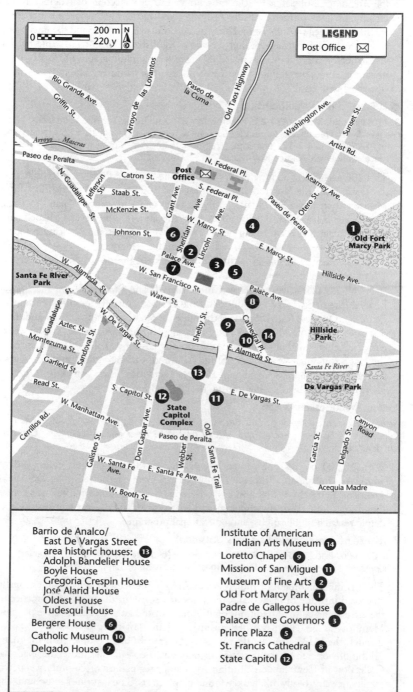

Barrio de Analco/
East De Vargas Street
area historic houses: **13**
Adolph Bandelier House
Boyle House
Gregoria Crespin House
José Alarid House
Oldest House
Tudesqui House
Bergere House **6**
Catholic Museum **10**
Delgado House **7**

Institute of American
Indian Arts Museum **14**
Loretto Chapel **9**
Mission of San Miguel **11**
Museum of Fine Arts **2**
Old Fort Marcy Park **1**
Padre de Gallegos House **4**
Palace of the Governors **3**
Prince Plaza **5**
St. Francis Cathedral **8**
State Capitol **12**

the Archdiocese of Santa Fe, the museum houses a collection of religious relics, including a book printed by Padre Antonio José Martinez of Taos, the Lamy chalice that was given to Archbishop Lamy by Pope Pius IX in 1854, and the document that formally reestablished royal possession of the Villa and Capital of Santa Fe and was signed by Diego de Vargas in 1692. There are also photographs on display, documenting events pertaining to the 11 archbishops of Santa Fe. The museum shop is stocked with books on New Mexico's history and religious items.

✪ El Rancho de las Golondrinas

334 Los Pinos Rd. ☎ **505/471-2261.** Admission $3.50 adults, $2.50 seniors and teens, $1.50 children 5–12. Free for children under 5. Festival weekends, $5 adults, $3.50 seniors and teens, $2.50 children 5–12. June–Sept, Wed–Sun 10am–4pm; Apr–May and Oct, open by advance arrangement. Closed Nov–Mar.

This 200-acre ranch, about 15 miles south of the Santa Fe Plaza via I-25 (take Exit 276), was once the last stopping place on the 1,000-mile El Camino Real from Mexico City to Santa Fe. Today it's a living 18th- and 19th-century Spanish village, comprising a hacienda, a village store, a schoolhouse, and several chapels and kitchens. There's also a working molasses mill, wheelwright and blacksmith shops, shearing and weaving rooms, a threshing ground, a winery and vineyard, and four water mills, as well as dozens of farm animals. A walk around the entire property is 1³/₄ miles in length.

Highlights of the year for Las Golondrinas ("The Swallows") are the Spring Festival (the first weekend of June) and the Harvest Festival (the first weekend of October). On these festival Sundays the museum opens with a procession and mass dedicated to San Ysidro, patron saint of farmers. Other festivals and theme weekends are held throughout the year. Authentically costumed volunteers demonstrate shearing, spinning, weaving, embroidery, wood carving, grain milling, blacksmithing, tinsmithing, soapmaking, and other activities. There's an exciting atmosphere of Spanish folk dancing, music, theater, and food.

Indian Art Research Center

School of American Research, 660 Garcia St. (off Canyon Rd.). ☎ **505/982-3584.** Free admission for Native Americans and SAR members; $15 per person for others. Open by appointment only.

With 10,000 objects, the center houses one of the world's best collections of Southwest Indian art. Admission, however, is highly restricted. The School of American Research, of which this is a division, was established in 1907 as a center for advanced studies in anthropology and related fields. It sponsors scholarship, academic research, publications, and educational programs.

Institute of American Indian Arts Museum

108 Cathedral Place. ☎ **505/988-6211.** Admission (two-day pass) $4 adults, $2 seniors and students, free for children 16 and under. Tues–Sat 10am–5pm; Sun noon–5pm.

The Institute of American Indian Arts (IAIA) is the nation's only congressionally chartered institute of higher education devoted solely to the study and practice of the artistic and cultural traditions of all American Indian and Alaska native peoples. Many of the best Native American artists of the last three decades have passed through the IAIA. Their works can often be seen in one or another of the many exhibitions offered at the museum throughout the year. The museum's National Collection of Contemporary Indian Art comprises painting, sculpture, ceramics, textiles, jewelry, beadwork, basketry, and graphic arts. The institute's museum is the official repository of the most comprehensive collection of contemporary Native

American art in the world and has loaned items from its collection to museums all over the world. The museum presents the artistic achievements of IAIA alumni, current students, and other nationally recognized Native American and Alaskan artists.

✪ Museum of Indian Arts and Culture

710 Camino Lejo. ☎ **505/827-6344.** Admission $5 adults, children under 17 free. Tues–Sun 10am–5pm.

Next door to the Museum of International Folk Art, this museum opened in 1987 as the showcase for the adjoining Laboratory of Anthropology. Interpretive displays detail tribal history and contemporary life-styles of New Mexico's Pueblo, Navajo, and Apache cultures. More than 50,000 pieces of basketry, pottery, clothing, carpets, and jewelry—much of it quite old—are on continual rotating display.

There are frequent demonstrations of traditional skills by tribal artisans and regular programs in a 70-seat multimedia theater. Native American educators run a year-round workshop that encourages visitors to try such activities as weaving and corn grinding. There are also regular performances of Native American music and dancing by tribal groups. Concession booths purvey Native American foods during the summer months.

The laboratory, founded in 1931 by John D. Rockefeller, Jr., is a point of interest in itself. Designed by the well-known Santa Fe architect John Gaw Meem, it is an exquisite example of Pueblo Revival architecture. Since the museum opened, the lab has expanded its research and library facilities into its former display wing.

✪ Museum of International Folk Art

706 Camino Lejo. ☎ **505/827-6350.** Admission $5 adults, free for children under 17. Tues–Sun 10am–5pm. The museum is located about two miles south of the Plaza, in the Sangre de Cristo foothills. Drive southeast on Old Santa Fe Trail, which becomes Old Pecos Trail, and look for signs pointing left onto Camino Lejo.

This branch of the Museum of New Mexico may not seem quite as typically southwestern as other Santa Fe museums, but it's the largest of its kind in the world. With a collection of around 130,000 objects from more than 100 countries, it is my personal favorite of the city museums.

It was founded in 1953 by the Chicago collector Florence Dibell Bartlett, who said: "If peoples of different countries could have the opportunity to study each others' cultures, it would be one avenue for a closer understanding between men." That's the basis on which the museum operates today.

The special collections include Spanish colonial silver, traditional and contemporary New Mexican religious art, Mexican tribal costumes, Mexican majolica ceramics, Brazilian folk art, European glass, African sculptures, East Indian textiles, and the marvelous Morris Miniature Circus. Particularly delightful are numerous dioramas—all done with colorful miniatures—of people around the world at work and play in typical town, village, and home settings. Recent acquisitions include American weathervanes and quilts, Palestinian costume jewelry and amulets, and Bhutanese and Indonesian textiles. Children love to look at the hundreds of toys on display. About half the pieces were given in 1982 by Alexander and Susan Girard. A new wing was built to hold the vast assemblage of dolls, animals, and dioramas of entire towns.

In 1989 the museum opened a new Hispanic Heritage Wing, which houses the country's finest collection of Spanish colonial and Hispanic folk art. Folk-art demonstrations, performances, and workshops are often presented here. The 80,000-square-foot museum also has a lecture room, a research library, and a gift shop where a variety of folk art is available for purchase.

Pueblo Pottery: A Glossary of Terms

Burnishing   Potters rub a smooth stone on the surface of a pot or bowl after slip (see below) has been applied in order to create a shiny surface on the finished product.

Coiling   Pieces of clay are rolled into long, snakelike pieces and then are "coiled" in order to build up the sides of a pot. After the desired size and shape have been achieved, the pot walls are thinned, scraped, and finally smoothed. Pueblo potters most frequently use this method.

Firing   Today most potters fire (bake in order to harden) their work in an electric or gas-fired kiln, but Pueblo potters fire their work in outdoor ovens using a variety of fuels, including animal dung.

Incising   The cutting of designs into the surface of a pot before the firing process.

Matte   As opposed to a burnished surface, a matte finish is dull. Many Pueblo Indians, including Acoma, Picuris, and Zia, use matte finishes.

Micaceous   The clay of micaceous pots contains small particles of mica, which sparkle when held up to the light. Taos and Picuris Pueblo clays contain quite a bit of mica.

Polychrome   If a potter uses three or more colors on a pot, it is referred to as polychrome.

Sgraffito   The scratching of a pot surface to create designs after it has been fired.

Slip   Put simply, slip is very watery clay. It is applied to a piece of pottery just before firing in order to fill in air holes and create a uniform color.

Wheelwright Museum of the American Indian

704 Camino Lejo. ☎ **505/982-4636.** Donations appreciated. Mon–Sat 10am–5pm; Sun 1–5pm. Closed Jan 1, Thanksgiving, and Dec 25.

Though not a member of the state museum system, the Wheelwright is often included when people plan a trip to the Folk Art and Indian Arts museums because of its proximity—it's next door. Once known as the Museum of Navajo Ceremonial Art, the Wheelwright was founded in 1937 by Boston scholar Mary Cabot Wheelwright in collaboration with a Navajo medicine man, Hastiin Klah, to preserve and document Navajo ritual beliefs and practices. Klah took the designs of sand paintings used in healing ceremonies and adapted them into the woven pictographs that are a major part of the museum's treasure.

In 1976 the museum's focus was changed to include the living arts of all Native American cultures. Built in the shape of a Navajo hogan, with its doorway facing east (toward the rising sun) and its ceiling formed in the interlocking "whirling log" style, it offers rotating shows of silverwork, jewelry, tapestry, pottery, basketry, and paintings. There's a permanent collection (although it is not always on display) plus an outdoor sculpture garden with works by Allan Houser and other noted artisans.

In the basement is the Case Trading Post, an arts-and-crafts shop built to resemble the typical turn-of-the-century trading post found on Navajo reservations. Storyteller Joe Hayes holds the attention of his listeners outside a tepee at dusk on certain days in July and August.

CHURCHES

Cristo Rey

Upper Canyon Rd. at Camino Cabra. ☎ **505/983-8528.** Free admission. Open most days, but call for hours.

This Catholic church, a huge adobe structure, was built in 1940 to commemorate the 400th anniversary of Coronado's exploration of the Southwest. Parishioners did most of the construction work, even making adobe bricks from the earth where the church stands. Architect John Gaw Meem designed the building, in missionary style, as a place to keep some magnificent stone reredos (altar screens) created by the Spanish during the colonial era and recovered and restored in the 20th century.

✪ Loretto Chapel Museum

207 Old Santa Fe Trail (between Alameda and Water Streets). ☎ **505/984-7971.** Admission $1 adults, free for children 6 and under. Daily 9am–5pm.

Though no longer consecrated for worship, the Loretto Chapel is an important site in Santa Fe. Patterned after the famous Sainte-Chapelle church in Paris, it was constructed in 1873—by the same French architects and Italian masons who were building Archbishop Lamy's cathedral—as a chapel for the Sisters of Loretto, who had established a school for young ladies in Santa Fe in 1852.

The chapel is especially notable for its remarkable spiral staircase: It makes two complete 360° turns with no central or other visible support! (A railing was added later.) Legend has It that the building was nearly finished in 1878 when workers realized the stairs to the choir loft wouldn't fit. Hoping for a solution more attractive than a ladder, the sisters made a novena to St. Joseph—and were rewarded when a mysterious carpenter appeared astride a donkey and offered to build a staircase. Armed with only a saw, a hammer, and a T-square, the master constructed this work of genius by soaking slats of wood in tubs of water to curve them and holding them together with wooden pegs. Then he disappeared without waiting to collect his fee.

Mission of San Miguel

401 Old Santa Fe Trail (at East De Vargas St.). ☎ **505/983-3974.** Donations appreciated. Mon–Sat 11:30am–4pm; Sun 1–4:30pm. Summer hours start earlier. Mass is said daily at 5pm.

This is one of the oldest churches in America, having been erected within a couple of years of the 1610 founding of Santa Fe. Tlaxcala tribe members, servants of early Spanish soldiers and missionaries, may have used fragments of a 12th-century pueblo that had been on this site in its construction. Severely damaged during the 1680 Pueblo Rebellion, the church was almost completely rebuilt in 1710 and has been altered numerous times since.

Because of its design, with high windows and thick walls, the structure was occasionally used as a temporary fortress during times of attack by raiding tribes. One painting in the sanctuary has holes that, according to legend, were made by arrows.

The mission and a nearby house—today a gift shop billed as "The Oldest House," though there's no way of knowing for sure—were bought by the Christian Brothers from Archbishop Lamy for $3,000 in 1881, and the order still operates both structures. Among the treasures in the mission are the San José Bell, reportedly cast in Spain in 1356 and brought to Santa Fe via Mexico several centuries later; and a series of buffalo hides and deerskins decorated with Bible stories for Native American converts.

Santuario de Nuestra Señora de Guadalupe

100 S. Guadalupe St. ☎ **505/988-2027.** Donations appreciated. Mon–Sat 9am–4pm. Closed weekends Nov–Apr.

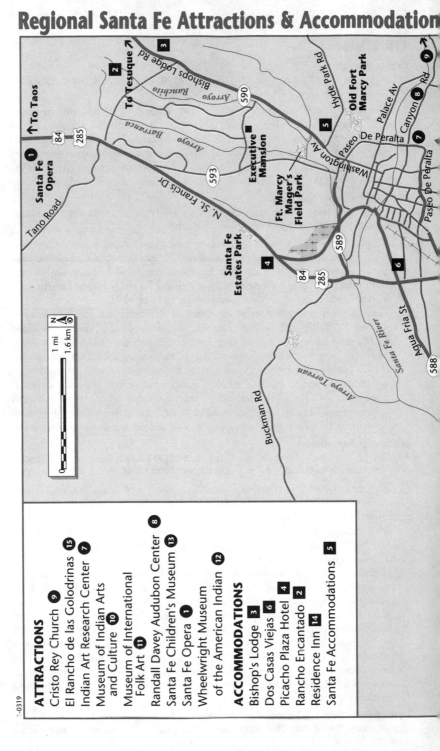

ATTRACTIONS
Cristo Rey Church ⑨
El Rancho de las Golodrinas ⑮
Indian Art Research Center ⑦
Museum of Indian Arts
and Culture ⑩
Museum of International
Folk Art ⑪
Randall Davey Audubon Center ⑧
Santa Fe Children's Museum ⑬
Santa Fe Opera ①
Wheelwright Museum
of the American Indian ⑫

ACCOMMODATIONS
Bishop's Lodge ③
Dos Casas Viejas ⑥
Picacho Plaza Hotel ④
Rancho Encantado ②
Residence Inn ⑭
Santa Fe Accommodations ⑤

7-0319

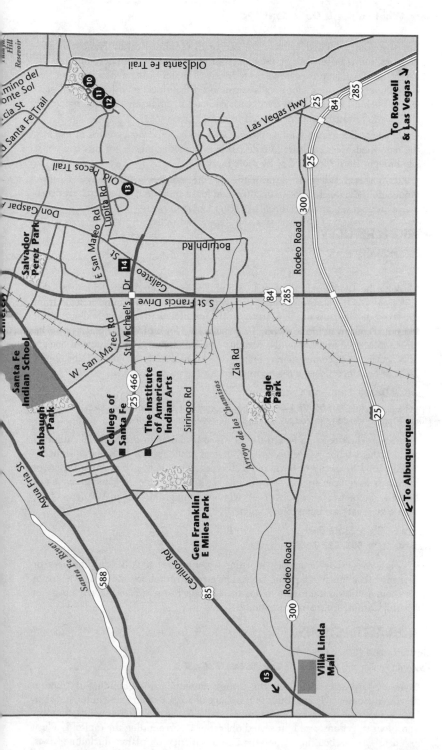

Built between 1795 and 1800 at the end of El Camino Real by Franciscan missionaries, this is believed to be the oldest shrine in the United States honoring the Virgin of Guadalupe, patroness of Mexico. Better known as Santuario de Guadalupe, the shrine's adobe walls are almost 3 feet thick, and the deep-red plaster wall behind the altar was dyed with oxblood in traditional fashion when the church was restored earlier in this century.

On one wall is a famous oil painting, *Our Lady of Guadalupe,* created in 1783 by the renowned Mexican artist José de Alzibar. Painted expressly for this church, it was brought from Mexico City by mule caravan.

Administered today as a museum by the nonprofit Guadalupe Historic Foundation, the sanctuary is frequently used for chamber music concerts, flamenco dance programs, dramas, lectures, and religious art shows.

PARKS & REFUGES

Old Fort Marcy Park

Artist Rd.

Marking the 1846 site of the first U.S. military reservation in the Southwest, this park overlooks the northeast corner of downtown. Only a few mounds remain from the fort, but the Cross of the Martyrs, at the top of a winding brick walkway from Paseo de Peralta near Otero Street, is a popular spot for bird's-eye photographs. The cross was erected in 1920 by the Knights of Columbus and the Historical Society of New Mexico to commemorate Franciscans killed during the Pueblo Rebellion of 1680. It has since played a role in numerous religious processions.

Randall Davey Audubon Center

Upper Canyon Rd. ☎ **505/983-4609.** $1 is charged for trail admission. Daily 9am–5pm. House tours conducted sporadically during the summer; call for hours.

Named for the late Santa Fe artist who willed his home to the National Audubon Society, this wildlife refuge occupies 135 acres at the mouth of Santa Fe Canyon. More than 100 species of birds and 120 types of plants live here, and a variety of mammals have been spotted—including black bears, mule deer, mountain lions, bobcats, raccoons, and coyotes. Trails winding through more than 100 acres of the nature sanctuary are open to day hikers.

Santa Fe River State Park

Alameda St. ☎ **505/827-7465.**

This is a lovely spot for an early morning jog, a midday walk beneath the trees, or perhaps a sack lunch at a picnic table. The green strip follows the midtown stream for about 4 miles as it meanders along the Alameda from St. Francis Drive upstream beyond Camino Cabra, near its source.

OTHER ATTRACTIONS

Roundhouse (State Capitol)

Paseo de Peralta and Old Santa Fe Trail. ☎ **505/986-4589.**

Some are surprised to learn that this is the only round capitol building in America. It's also the newest (1966). Built in the shape of a Zia Pueblo emblem (or sun sign, which is also the state symbol), it symbolizes the Circle of Life: four winds, four seasons, four directions, and four sacred obligations. Surrounding the capitol is a lush 6¹/₂-acre garden boasting more than 100 varieties of plants, including roses, plums, almonds, nectarines, Russian olive trees, and sequoias. Benches and sculptures (by local artists) have been placed around the grounds for the enjoyment of visitors. Inside you'll find standard functional offices. The walls are hung with New Mexican art. If you're interested in taking a tour, call the number above for information.

COOKING & ART CLASSES

If you have the time and you're looking for something to do that's a little off the beaten tourist path, take a cooking or art class.

You can master the flavors of Santa Fe with an entertaining three-hour demonstration cooking class at the ✪ **Santa Fe School of Cooking and Market,** on the upper level of the Plaza Mercado, 116 W. San Francisco St. (☎ **505/983-4511;** fax 505/983-7540). The class learns about the flavors and history of traditional New Mexican and contemporary southwestern cuisines. Cooking-light classes are offered for those who prefer to cook with less fat. Prices range from $35 to $55 and include a meal; call for a class schedule.

The adjoining market offers a variety of regional foods and cookbooks, with gift baskets available.

If southwestern art has you hooked, you can take a drawing and painting class led by Santa Fe artist Jane Shoenfeld. Students sketch such outdoor subjects as the Santa Fe landscape and adobe architecture. In case of inclement weather, classes are held in the studio. Each class lasts for three hours, and art materials are included in the $50 fee. All levels of experience are welcome. Children's classes can be arranged. Contact Jane at **Sketching Santa Fe,** P.O. Box 5912, Santa Fe, NM 87502 (☎ **505/986-1108**).

WINE TASTINGS

If you enjoy sampling regional wines, consider visiting the wineries within easy driving distance of Santa Fe: **Balagna Winery/San Ysidro Vineyards,** 223 Rio Bravo Dr., in Los Alamos (☎ **505/672-3678**), north on US 84/285 and then west on NM 502; **Santa Fe Vineyards,** (P.O. Box 216A) about 20 miles north of Santa Fe on US 84/285 (☎ **505/753-8100**); Madison Vineyards & Winery, in Ribera (☎ **505/421-8028**), about 45 miles east of Santa Fe on I-25 North; and the **Black Mesa Winery,** 1502 NM 68, in Velarde (☎ **800/852-MESA**), north on US 84/285 to NM 68.

Be sure to call in advance to find out when the wineries are open for tastings and to get specific directions.

3   Especially for Kids

Don't miss taking the kids to **the Museum of International Folk Art,** where they'll love the international dioramas and the toys, or to **El Rancho de las Golondrinas,** a living Spanish colonial village. (Both are discussed earlier in this chapter.)

Santa Fe Children's Museum

1050 Old Pecos Trail. ☎ **505/989-8359.** Admission $2.50 adults, $1.50 children under 12. Wed, Thurs, Sat 10am–5pm; Fri 9am–5pm; Sun noon–5pm. The first Friday every month the museum is open until 8pm.

Designed for whole families to experience, this museum offers interactive exhibits and hands-on activities in the arts, humanities, science, and technology. Special performances and hands-on sessions with artists and scientists are regularly scheduled.

4   Santa Fe Strolls

Santa Fe lends itself to walking. The city's historic downtown core extends only a few blocks in any direction from the Plaza, and the ancient Barrio de Analco and the Canyon Road artists' colony are a mere stone's throw away.

WALKING TOUR 1
The Plaza Area

Start: The Plaza.

Finish: Loretto Chapel.

Time: One to five hours, depending on how long you spend in the museums and churches.

Best Times: Any morning after breakfast (before the afternoon heat), but after the Native American traders have spread out their wares.

1. **The Plaza** has been the heart and soul of Santa Fe since it was established with the city in 1610. Originally designed as a meeting place, it has been the site of innumerable festivals and other historical, cultural, and social events. For many years it was a dusty hive of activity as the staging ground and terminus of the Santa Fe Trail. Today those who sit around its central fountain enjoy the best people-watching in New Mexico.

   Facing the Plaza on its north side is the:

2. **Palace of the Governors,** which has functioned continually as a public building since it was erected in 1610 as the capitol of Nuevo Mexico. Today it's the flagship of the New Mexico State Museum system (see "The Top Attractions," above). Every day Native American artisans spread out their crafts for sale beneath its portico.

   Immediately opposite the Palace, at Lincoln and Palace Avenues, is the:

3. **Museum of Fine Arts,** with its renowned St. Francis Auditorium (see "The Top Attractions" above, and "Major Performing-Arts Companies," in Chapter 9). The works of Georgia O'Keeffe and other famed 20th-century Taos and Santa Fe artists are one of the highlights of a visit here. The building is a fine example of Pueblo Revival–style architecture.

   Virtually across the street is the:

4. **Delgado House,** 124 W. Palace Ave., an 1890 Victorian mansion that now belongs to the Historic Santa Fe Foundation.

   If you continue west on Palace Avenue past numerous small shops and restaurants, you'll see a narrow lane—Burro Alley—cutting south toward San Francisco Street. Turn right on Grant Street to the:

5. **Tully House,** 136 Grant Ave., built in 1851 in Territorial style. This is the head-quarters of the Historic Santa Fe Foundation. (A publication of the foundation, *Old Santa Fe Today,* gives detailed descriptions, with a map and photos, of 50 sites within walking distance of the Plaza.)

   Across the street is the:

6. **Bergere House,** 135 Grant Ave., built around 1870. It hosted U.S. Pres. Ulysses S. Grant and his wife, Julia, during an 1880 visit to Santa Fe.

   Proceed north on Grant, turning right on Marcy. On the north side of this corner is the Sweeney Convention Center, host of major exhibitions and home of the Santa Fe Convention and Visitors Bureau.

   Three blocks farther east, through a residential, office, and restaurant district, turn left on Washington Avenue. A short distance along on your right, note the:

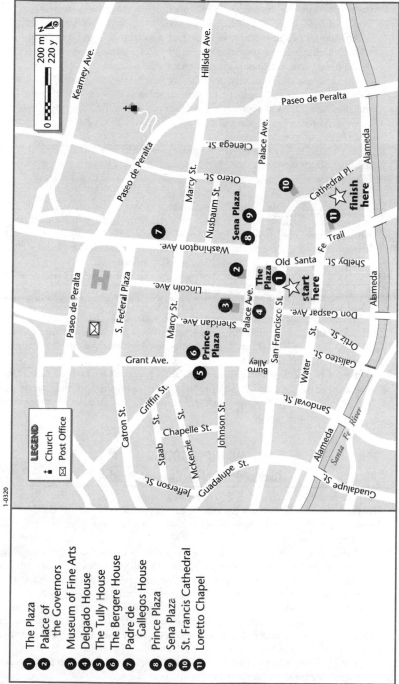

LEGEND
✝ Church
⊠ Post Office

1 The Plaza
2 Palace of
   the Governors
3 Museum of Fine Arts
4 Delgado House
5 The Tully House
6 The Bergere House
7 Padre de
   Gallegos House
8 Prince Plaza
9 Sena Plaza
10 St. Francis Cathedral
11 Loretto Chapel

1-0320

97

7. **Padre de Gallegos House,** 227–237 Washington Ave., built in 1857 in the Territorial style. Padre de Gallegos was a priest who, in the eyes of newly–arrived Archbishop Jean-Baptiste Lamy, kept too high a social profile and so was defrocked in 1852. Gallegos later represented the territory in Congress and eventually became the federal superintendent of Native American affairs.

   Reverse course and turn south again on Washington Avenue, passing en route the public library and some handsomely renovated accommodations—the Territorial Inn and the Plaza Real. On your right is the entrance to the Palace of the Governors' archives. As you approach the Plaza, turn left (east) on Palace Avenue. A short distance farther on your left is:

8. **Prince Plaza,** 113 E. Palace Ave., a former governor's home. This Territorial-style structure, which now houses the Shed restaurant, had huge wooden gates to keep out tribal attacks.

   Next door is:

9. **Sena Plaza,** 125 E. Palace Ave. This city landmark offers a quiet respite from the busy streets with its parklike patio. La Casa Sena restaurant is the primary occupant of what was once the 31-room Sena family adobe hacienda, built in 1831. The Territorial legislature met in the upper rooms of the hacienda in the 1890s.

   Turn right (south) on Cathedral Place to enter the doors of:

10. **St. Francis Cathedral,** built in Romanesque style between 1869 and 1886 by Archbishop Lamy. Santa Fe's grandest religious edifice, it has a famous 17th-century wooden Madonna known as *Our Lady of Peace* (see "The Top Attractions," above).

    After leaving the cathedral, walk around the back side of the illustrious La Fonda Hotel—south on Cathedral Place and west on Water Street—to the intersection of the Old Santa Fe Trail. Here, in the northwest corner of the Best Western Inn at Loretto, you'll find the:

11. **Loretto Chapel,** more formally known as the Chapel of Our Lady of Light. Lamy was also behind the construction of this chapel, built for the Sisters of Loretto. It is remarkable for its spiral staircase, which has no central or other visible support (see "More Attractions," above).

WALKING TOUR 2
Barrio de Analco/Canyon Road

Start: Don Gaspar Avenue and East De Vargas Street.
Finish: Any one of the quaint restaurants on Canyon Road.
Time: One to three hours, depending on how long you spend in the art galleries.
Best Times: Anytime.

The Barrio de Analco, now East De Vargas Street, is beyond question one of the oldest continuously inhabited avenues in the United States. Spanish colonists and their Mexican–Native American servants built homes here in the early 1600s, when Santa Fe was founded, and some of them survive to this day.

Most of the houses you'll see as you walk east on De Vargas are private residences, not open for inspection inside. But they are well worth looking at because of the feeling they give of Santa Fe life in bygone days. Most have interpretive historical plaques on their outer walls. The first you'll see is:

1. **Tudesqui House,** 129 E. De Vargas St., dating from the early 19th century, now recognizable for the wisteria growing over its adobe walls.

   Across the street is the:

Walking Tour—Barrio de Analco/Canyon Road

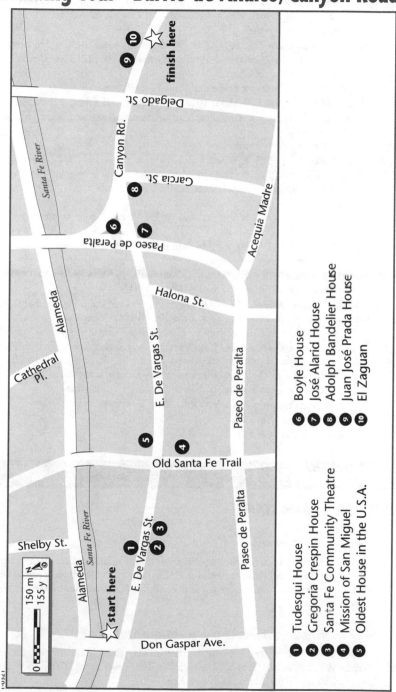

1. Tudesqui House
2. Gregoria Crespin House
3. Santa Fe Community Theatre
4. Mission of San Miguel
5. Oldest House in the U.S.A.
6. Boyle House
7. José Alarid House
8. Adolph Bandelier House
9. Juan José Prada House
10. El Zaguan

2. **Gregoria Crespin House,** 132 E. De Vargas St., whose records date back at least to 1747 (when it was sold for 50 pesos). Originally of pueblo design, it later had Territorial embellishments added in the trim of bricks along its roofline.

Just down the road is the:

3. **Santa Fe Community Theatre,** 142 E. De Vargas St., home of the oldest existing thespian group in New Mexico. Actors still perform in this original adobe theater (see "The Performing Arts," in Chapter 9).

In the next block, just east of the Old Santa Fe Trail, is the:

4. **Mission of San Miguel,** built about 1612 and certainly one of the oldest churches in America (see "More Attractions," above). Today it's maintained and operated by the Christian Brothers.

Across De Vargas Street is the so-called:

5. **Oldest House in the U.S.A.** Whether or not this is true is anybody's guess, but it's among the last of the poured-mud adobe houses and may have been built by Pueblo people. It's sad that modern graffiti has defiled some interior walls. The entrance is through a gift shop.

There are more homes at the east end of De Vargas, before its junction with Canyon Road. Among them is the:

6. **Boyle House,** 327 E. De Vargas St., built in the mid-18th century as a hacienda.

Nearby is the:

7. **José Alarid House,** 338 E. De Vargas St., built in the 1830s and now an art gallery.

A few houses farther down the road is the:

8. **Adolph Bandelier House,** 352 E. De Vargas St., home of the famous archaeologist who unearthed the prehistoric ruins at Bandelier National Monument.

De Vargas intersects narrow, winding Canyon Road after it crosses the Paseo de Peralta. Extending about 2 miles from the Paseo to Camino Cabra, Canyon Road today is lined with art galleries, shops, and restaurants. But it was once a Native American trail used by the Pueblo tribes when they came to launch their 1680 insurrection against the Spanish colonists. Historic buildings include the:

9. **Juan José Prada House,** 519 Canyon Rd., which dates from about 1760.

Farther up the road is:

10. **El Zaguan,** a hacienda at 545 Canyon Rd.

5 Organized Tours

BUS, CAR & TRAM TOURS

Gray Line Tours
1330 Hickox St. ☎ **505/983-9491.**

The trolleylike Roadrunner departs several times daily in summer (less often in winter) from the Plaza, beginning at 9am, for 2[1/2]-hour city tours. Buy tickets as you board. Daily tours to Taos, Chimayo, and Bandelier National Monument are also offered.

LorettoLine
At the Inn at Loretto, 211 Old Santa Fe Trail. ☎ **505/983-3701.**

For an open air tour of the city, contact LorettoLine. Tours last 1¹/₂ hours and are offered seven days a week from May to October. Tour times are at 10am, noon, and 2pm. Tickets are $9 for adults, $4 for children.

Rocky Mountain Tours
217 W. Manhattan St. ☎ **505/984-1684.**

With this service, you can arrange a custom tour with a private guide (in your car or a four-wheel-drive vehicle) to Chaco Canyon (usually requires an overnight stay), the "Four Corners" region (usually requires two nights on the road), and other areas. River-rafting trips, hot-air balloon flights, airplane sightseeing rides over Santa Fe, and horseback riding trips are also offered.

WALKING TOURS

Afoot in Santa Fe
At the Inn at Loretto, 211 Old Santa Fe Trail. ☎ **505/983-3701.**

Personalized 2¹/₂-hour tours are offered twice daily from the Inn at Loretto. Reservations are not required.

The Walking Tour of Santa Fe
107 Washington Ave. ☎ **800/338-6877** or 505/983-6565.

One of Santa Fe's best walking tours begins at the northwest corner of the Plaza (at 9:30am and 1:30pm) and lasts about 2¹/₂ hours. The tour costs $10 for adults. Children are free.

MISCELLANEOUS TOURS

Pathways Customized Tours
161-F Calle Ojo Feliz. ☎ **505/982-5382.**

Don Dietz offers several planned tours, including a downtown Santa Fe walking tour, a full city tour, a trip to the cliff dwellings and native pueblos, a "Taos adventure," and a trip to Georgia O'Keeffe country. He will try to accommodate any special requests you might have. These tours last anywhere from 1¹/₂ to 9 hours, depending on the one you choose. Don has extensive knowledge of the area's culture, history, geology, and flora and fauna and will help you make the most of your precious vacation time.

Rain Parrish
535 Cordova Rd., Suite 250. ☎ **505/984-8236.**

A Navajo anthropologist, artist, and freelance curator offers custom guide services focusing on cultural anthropology, Native American arts, and the history of the Native Americans of the Southwest. Ms. Parrish includes visits to local pueblo villages.

Recursos de Santa Fe
826 Camino de Monte Rey. ☎ **505/982-9301.**

This organization is a full-service destination management company, emphasizing custom-designed itineraries to meet the interests of any group. They specialize in the archaeology, art, literature, spirituality, architecture, environment, food, or history of the Southwest.

Rojo Tours & Services, Inc.
P.O. Box 15744. ☎ **505/474-8333**; fax 505/474-2992.

Customized private tours are arranged to pueblos, cliff dwellings, and ruins, as well as adventure travel such as river rafting and horseback riding.

Santa Fe Detours
107 Washington Ave. ☎ **800/DETOURS** or 505/983-6565.

Santa Fe's most extensive tour-booking agency accommodates almost all travelers' tastes, from bus and rail tours to river rafting, backpacking, and cross-country skiing.

Southwest Safaris
P.O. Box 945, Santa Fe, NM 87504. ☎ **800/842-4246** or 505/988-4246.

One-day combination air/land natural history tours are offered from Santa Fe to Monument Valley, Grand Canyon, Canyon de Chelly, Mesa Verde, and Arches/ Canyonlands.

6 Outdoor Activities

Note: In addition to all the activities and recreation centers listed below, there will be a new full-service family recreation center in Santa Fe by early to mid-1998. The complex will include a 25-meter pool, leisure and therapy pools, an ice-skating rink, three gyms, a workout room, racquetball courts, and an indoor running track. Contact the Santa Fe Convention and Visitors Bureau for more information.

BALLOONING New Mexico is known for its spectacular Balloon Fiesta, which takes place annually in Albuquerque. If you've always wanted to take a ride, this is the place to do it. **Rocky Mountain Tours,** at 217 W. Manhattan St. (☎ **800/ 231-7238** or 505/984-1684 outside New Mexico), offers year-round hot-air balloon flights daily on a reservations-only basis. Flights take place at dawn. The flight includes continental breakfast or snacks and champagne after the flight. Each passenger receives a certificate after the flight. Rates begin at around $135 a flight. If you've got your heart set on a balloon flight, I would suggest that you make your reservations early because flights are often canceled due to weather. This way, if you have to reschedule you'll have enough time to do so.

BIKING You can cycle along main roadways and paved country roads year round in Santa Fe, but be aware that traffic is particularly heavy around the Plaza and you need to be especially alert. Mountain biking is popular in the spring, summer, and fall. The Santa Fe Convention and Visitors Bureau can supply you with bike maps, and *The New Mexican Mountain Bike Guide* (Big Ring Press) by Brant Hayengand and Chris Shaw is an excellent guide to trails in Santa Fe, Taos, and Albuquerque. The book outlines tours for beginner, intermediate, and advanced riders. **Palace Bike Rentals,** 409 E. Palace Ave. (☎ **505/984-0455**), rents mountain bikes and caters to tourists. Half-day, full-day, and weekly rentals can be arranged. Accessories, maps, and trail information are also supplied.

In June cyclists participate in seven days of bicycle races known as the **Pedal the Peaks Bicycle Tour** (call 800/795-0898 for more information). Courses traverse areas around Santa Fe, Taos, and Albuquerque as well as Los Alamos and Las Vegas.

FISHING In the lakes and waterways around Santa Fe, anglers typically catch trout (there are five varieties in the area). Other local fish include bass, perch, and Kokanee salmon. The most popular fishing holes are Cochiti and Abiquiu Lakes as well as the Rio Chama and Pecos streams. Fly fishing is popular in the Rio Grande. Check with the **New Mexico Game and Fish Department** (☎ 505/827-7911 for information and licenses). **High Desert Angler,** 435 S. Guadalupe St. (☎ 505/ 988-7688), specializes in fly-fishing gear and guide service.

GOLF There are two public courses in the Santa Fe area: the 18-hole **Santa Fe Country Club,** on Airport Road (☎ 505/471-2626); and the often-praised, 18-hole **Cochiti Lake Golf Course,** 5200 Cochiti Hwy., Cochiti Lake, about 35 miles southwest of Santa Fe via I-25 and NM 16 and 22. The **Santa Fe Golf and Driving**

Range, 4680 Wagon Rd. (☎ **505/474-4680**) is also open to the public throughout the year. They have 42 practice tees, golf merchandise, and rental clubs, and will provide instruction.

HIKING   It's hard to decide which of the 1,000 miles of nearby national forest trails to challenge. Four wilderness areas are especially attractive: **Pecos Wilderness,** with 223,000 acres east of Santa Fe; **Chama River Canyon Wilderness,** 50,300 acres west of Ghost Ranch Museum; **Dome Wilderness,** 5,200 acres of rugged canyonland adjacent to Bandelier National Monument; and **San Pedro Parks Wilderness,** 41,000 acres west of Los Alamos. Also, visit the 58,000-acre Jemez Mountain National Recreation Area. Information on these and other wilderness areas is available from the **Santa Fe National Forest,** 1220 St. Francis Dr. (P.O. Box 1689), Santa Fe, NM 87504 (☎ **505/988-6940**). If you're looking for company on your trek, contact the Santa Fe branch of the **Sierra Club** (☎ **505/983-2703**) or **Tracks,** 417 San Pasqual, Santa Fe, NM 87501 (☎ **505/982-2586**). I enjoy taking a chairlift ride to the summit of the Santa Fe Ski Area (☎ **505/983-9155**) and hiking around up there in the spring and summer months. You might also consider purchasing *The Hiker's Guide to New Mexico* (Falcon Press Publishing Co., Inc.) by Laurence Parent; it outlines 70 hikes throughout the state.

HORSEBACK RIDING   Trips ranging in length from a few hours to overnight can be arranged by **Santa Fe Detours,** 107 Washington Ave. (☎ **800/338-6877** or 505/983-6565). You'll ride with "experienced wranglers," and can even arrange a trip that includes a cookout or brunch. Rides are also major activities at two local guest ranches: **The Bishop's Lodge** and **Rancho Encantado** (see "Santa Fe Accommodations," Chapter 5). In addition, **Rocky Mountain Tours,** 217 W. Manhattan St., Santa Fe, NM 87501 (☎ **505/984-1684**) arranges escorted rides for individuals of all ability levels as well as families. Trips can run from 90 minutes to a full day. Special packages such as "Raft and Ride," and "Design Your Own Ride," are also available.

HUNTING   Mule deer, and elk are taken by hunters in the Pecos Wilderness and Jemez Mountains, as well as occasional black bears and bighorn sheep. Wild turkeys and grouse are frequently bagged in the uplands, geese and ducks at lower elevations. Check with the **New Mexico Game and Fish Department** (☎ **505/ 827-7911**) for information and licenses.

JOGGING   Despite its elevation, Santa Fe is popular with runners and hosts numerous competitions, including the annual Old Santa Fe Trail Run on Labor Day. "Fun Runs," sponsored by **Santa Fe Striders** (☎ **505/983-2144**), begin at the Plaza on Wednesday at 6pm year round (5:30pm in winter).

RIVER RAFTING   Although Taos is the real rafting center of New Mexico, several companies serve Santa Fe during the April to October white-water season. They include the **Southwest Wilderness Adventures,** P.O. Box 9380, Santa Fe, NM 87501 (☎ **800/869-7238** or 505/983-7262); **New Wave Rafting,** 107 Washington Ave. (☎ **505/984-1444**); and the **Santa Fe Rafting Co.,** 80 E. San Francisco St. (☎ **505/988-4914**).

SOARING   Soaring is available for those who don't believe the sky is the limit. For information and rates, call **Santa Fe Soaring** (☎ **505/470-4571**).

SKIING   There's something available for every ability level at the **Ski Santa Fe,** about 16 miles northeast of Santa Fe via Hyde Park (Ski Basin) Road. Built on the upper reaches of 12,000-foot Tesuque Peak, the area has an average annual snowfall of 225 inches and a vertical drop of 1,650 feet. Seven lifts, including a 5,000-foot triple chair and a new quad chair, serve 39 runs and 590 acres of terrain, with a total capacity of 7,800 an hour. Base facilities, at 10,350 feet, center around La Casa Mall, with a cafeteria, lounge, ski shop, and boutique. Another restaurant, Totemoff's, has a midmountain patio.

The ski area is open daily from 9am to 4pm; the season often runs from Thanksgiving to early April, depending on snow conditions. Rates for all lifts are $37 for adults, $23 for children and seniors, free for kids less than 46 inches tall (in their ski boots), and free for seniors 73 and older. For more information, contact **Ski Santa Fe,** 1210 Luisa St., Suite 5, Santa Fe, NM 87505 (☎ **505/982-4429**). For 24-hour taped reports on snow conditions, call **505/983-9155.** The New Mexico Snow Phone (☎ **505/984-0606**) gives statewide reports. Ski packages are available through Santa Fe Central Reservations (☎ **800/776-7669** outside New Mexico or 505/983-8200 within New Mexico).

Cross-country skiers find seemingly endless miles of snow to track in the **Santa Fe National Forest** (☎ **505/988-6940**). A favorite place to start is at the Black Canyon campground, about nine miles from downtown en route to the Santa Fe Ski Area. In the same area are the Borrego Trail (high intermediate) and the Norski Trail, seven miles up from Black Canyon. Basic Nordic lessons and backcountry tours are offered by Bill Neuwirth's **Tracks,** 417 San Pasqual, Santa Fe, NM 87501 (☎ **505/982-2586**).

Other popular activities at the ski area in winter include snow-boarding, sledding, and inner-tubing. Snowboard rentals are available at the ski area.

SPAS A common stop for skiers coming down the mountain road from the Santa Fe Ski Area is **Ten Thousand Waves,** a Japanese-style health spa about three miles northeast of Santa Fe on Hyde Park Road (☎ **505/988-1047** or 505/982-9304). This serene retreat, nestled in a grove of piñon, offers hot tubs, saunas, and cold plunges, plus a variety of massage and other bodywork techniques.

Bathing suits are optional in the 10-foot communal hot tub, where you can stay as long as you want for $13. Nine private hot tubs cost $18 to $25 an hour, with discounts for seniors and children. You can also arrange therapeutic massage, hot-oil massage, in-water watsu massage, herbal wraps, salt glows, and facials. New in 1996 were four treatment rooms that feature dry brush aromatherapy treatments and Ayurvedic treatments; a women's communal tub; and lodging at the Houses of the Moon, a six-room Japanese-style inn. The spa is open on Sunday, Monday, Wednesday, and Thursday from 10am to 10pm; on Tuesday from 4:30 to 10pm; and on Friday and Saturday from 10am to 11:30pm. Reservations are recommended, especially on weekends.

SWIMMING The City of Santa Fe operates four indoor pools and one outdoor pool. The pool closest to downtown is the **Fort Marcy Complex** (☎ **505/ 984-6725**) on Camino Santiago, off Bishop's Lodge Road. Admission is $1.25 for adults, $1 for students, and 50¢ for children 8 to 13. Call the Santa Fe Convention and Visitors Bureau for information about the other area pools.

TENNIS Santa Fe has 44 public tennis courts and four major private facilities. The City Recreation Department (☎ **505/984-6862**) can locate all indoor, outdoor, and lighted public courts.

7 Spectator Sports

HORSE RACING   The ponies run from Memorial Day through September at **The Downs at Santa Fe** (☎ **505/471-3311**), about 11 miles south of Santa Fe off US 85, near La Cienega. Post time for 10-race cards is 3:30pm on Wednesday and Friday; for 12-race cards, 1:30pm on Saturday and Sunday, plus Memorial Day, the Fourth of July, and Labor Day. Admission starts at $1 and climbs depending on seating. A closed-circuit TV system shows instant replays of each race's final-stretch run and transmits out-of-state races for legal betting.

RODEO   The **Rodeo de Santa Fe,** 2801 Rodeo Rd. (☎ **505/471-4300**), is held annually the weekend following the Fourth of July. (See "Northern New Mexico Calendar of Events," in Chapter 2, for details.)

8 Santa Fe Shopping

For traditional Native American crafts as well as Hispanic folk art and abstract contemporary works, Santa Fe is the place to shop. Galleries speckle the downtown area, and Canyon Road is well known as an artists' thoroughfare. Of course, the greatest concentration of Native American crafts is displayed beneath the portal of the Palace of the Governors. And any serious arts aficionado will try to attend one or more of the city's great arts festivals—the Spring Festival of the Arts in May, the Spanish Market in July, the Indian Market in August, and the Fall Festival of the Arts in October.

1 The Shopping Scene

Few visitors to Santa Fe leave the city without buying at least one item from the Native American artisans at the Palace of the Governors. When you are thinking of making such a purchase, keep the following pointers in mind:

Silver jewelry should have a harmony of design, clean lines, and neatness in soldering. Navajo jewelry typically features large stones, with designs shaped around the stone. Zuni jewelry usually has patterns of small or inlaid stones. Hopi jewelry rarely uses stones; it usually has a motif incised into the top layer of silver and darkened.

Turquoise of a deeper color is usually higher quality, so long as it hasn't been color-treated. Heishi bead necklaces usually use stabilized turquoise.

Pottery is traditionally hand-coiled and of natural clay, not thrown on a potter's wheel using commercial clay. It is hand-polished with a stone, hand-painted, and fired in an outdoor oven rather than an electric kiln. Look for an even shape; clean, accurate painting; a high polish (if it is a polished piece); and an artist's signature.

Navajo rugs are appraised according to tightness and evenness of weave, symmetry of design, and whether natural (preferred) or commercial dyes have been used.

Kachina dolls are more highly valued according to the detail of their carving: fingers, toes, muscles, rib cages, feathers, etc. Elaborate costumes are also desirable. Oil staining is preferred to the use of bright acrylic paints.

How to Buy a Navajo Rug

After you arrive in New Mexico, you'll begin noticing beautiful hand-loomed Navajo rugs in shops, hotels, and museums. The colors and designs are so striking, chances are you'll quickly begin looking for one to take home.

There are several things to keep in mind when shopping for a Navajo rug. First of all, be sure the shop where you're browsing has a good reputation (ask for recommendations at your hotel). Although all Navajo rugs are authentic, they may not all be good quality (none is completely perfect, however). Of course, you want to buy a rug that pleases you aesthetically, but it is not wise to buy on impulse because you will be spending quite a lot of money. Take your time looking. Spread the rugs out completely to make sure there are no obvious flaws (holes or fraying wool). Then check to make sure the design and color are uniform throughout. The weave lines should be straight, without any visible loose ends. The rug should be of equal thickness throughout. If the rug you like meets all of the above criteria and the price is right, buy it—you'll regret it later if you don't.

Sand paintings should display clean narrow lines, even colors, balance, an intricacy of design, and smooth craftsmanship.

Local museums, particularly the Wheelwright Museum and the Institute of American Indian Art, can provide a good orientation to contemporary craftsmanship.

Contemporary artists are mainly painters, sculptors, ceramists, and fiber artists, including weavers. Peruse one of the outstanding **catalogs** that introduce local galleries—*The Collector's Guide to Santa Fe and Taos* by Wingspread Incorporated (P.O. Box 13566-M, Albuquerque, NM 87192), *Santa Fe and Taos Arts* by The Book of Santa Fe (535 Cordova Rd., Suite 241, Santa Fe, NM 87501), or *The Santa Fe Catalogue* by Modell Associates (P.O. Box 1007, Aspen, CO 81612). They're widely available at shops or can be ordered directly from the publishers.

An outstanding introduction to Santa Fe art and artists is the personalized studio tours offered by J **Studio Entrada,** P.O. Box 4934, Santa Fe, NM 87502 (☎ **505/983-8786**). For a cost of $100 for two people, director Linda Morton takes small groups into private studios to meet the artists and learn about their work. Each itinerary lasts about 2¹/₂ hours and includes two or three studio gallery visits.

Business hours vary quite a bit among establishments, but nearly everyone is open *at least* Monday through Friday from 10am to 5pm, with mall stores open until 9pm. Most shops are open similar hours on Saturday, and many are also open on Sunday afternoon during the summer. Winter hours tend to be more limited.

2 The Top Galleries

Alterman & Morris Galleries
225 Canyon Rd. ☎ **505/983-1590.**

Nineteenth and 20th-century American paintings and sculpture. Remington, Russell, Taos founders, Santa Fe artists, and members of the Cowboy Artists of America and National Academy of Western Art are represented here.

✪ Joshua Baer & Company
116 E. Palace Ave. ☎ **505/988-8944.**

Nineteenth-century Navajo blankets, pottery, jewelry, and tribal art.

Barclay Fine Art, Inc.
424 Canyon Rd. ☎ **505/986-1400.**

This private dealership specializes in 19th- and 20th-century master paintings, drawings, and sculptures. You'll find the works of Matisse, Braque, Cassatt, Caro, Degas, Lepine, Manet, Miro, Monet, Picasso, Wyeth, and many others. Call for an appointment.

Bellas Artes
653 Canyon Rd. ☎ **505/983-2745.**

Contemporary painting, sculpture, drawing, clay and fiber. African and pre-Columbian art as well as a sculpture garden.

Canyon Road Contemporary Art
403 Canyon Rd. ☎ **505/983-0433.**

This gallery represents some of the finest emerging U.S. contemporary artists as well as internationally known artists. Figurative, landscape, and abstract paintings, as well as raku pottery.

Deborah and Hudgins Fine Art Gallery
80 E. San Francisco St. ☎ **505/988-9298.**

Exclusive representation of R. C. Gorman lithographs, bronzes, and originals. Amado Peña is also represented.

Dreamtime Gallery
223¹/₂ Canyon Rd. ☎ **505/986-0344.**

If you're at all interested in Australian Aboriginal artwork, this is the place to visit. There are some very interesting Aboriginal paintings and sculptures, as well as original weavings, bark paintings, and digeridoos.

Gallery 821
821 Canyon Rd. ☎ **505/983-2000.**

Gallery 821 represents ten Santa Fe artists. Works are presented in a variety of different mediums and styles. Here you'll find pottery, paintings, sculpture, and etchings—among other things.

Glenn Green Galleries
50 E. San Francisco St. ☎ **505/988-4168.**

Exclusive representation for Allan Houser's bronze and stone sculptures. Paintings, prints, photographs, and jewelry by other important artists.

Hahn Ross Gallery
409 Canyon Rd. ☎ **505/984-8434.**

Owner Tom Ross, a children's book illustrator, specializes in representing artists who create colorful, fantasy-oriented works. Those represented here might include Rex Barron, Susan Contreras, Mary Ericksen, Peter Grieve, Kristina Hagman, Ted Larsen, Max Lehman, David Phelps, Kim Thomson, and Paul White.

Handsel Gallery
306 Camino del Monte Sol (at Canyon Rd.). ☎ **505/988-4030.**

Wonderful contemporary works that focus on images from myth, folklore, nature, and dreams.

Horwitch LewAllen Gallery
129 W. Palace Ave. ☎ **505/988-8997.**

Contemporary art gallery exhibiting works done on canvas and paper; sculpture in stone, bronze, and glass; and ceramics, all by midcareer artists from around the United States.

The Frank Howell Gallery
103 Washington Ave. ☎ **505/984-1074.**

Contemporary American and American Indian art. Original works by Frank Howell. Sculpture by award-winner Tim Nicola, as well as fine art, jewelry, and graphics.

Chuck Jones Showroom–Animation Gallery
135 W. Palace Ave., Suite 203. ☎ **800/290-5999** or 505/983-5999.

A comprehensive representation of animation artwork from Warner Bros. director Chuck Jones. Original production cels, lithographs, sculpture, drawings, and limited editions.

Adieb Khadoure Fine Art
610 Canyon Rd. ☎ **505/820-2666.**

This is a working artists' studio with contemporary artists Jeff Uffelman and Hal Larsen and Santa Fe artist Phyllis Kapp. Their works are shown in the gallery daily from 10am to 6pm, and Adieb Khadoure also features beautiful rugs, furniture, and pottery from around the world.

✪ Nedra Matteucci's Fenn Galleries
1075 Paseo de Peralta. ☎ **505/982-4631.**

Early Taos and Santa Fe painters; classic American impressionism, historical western modernism, as well as contemporary southwestern landscapes and sculpture, including monumental pieces displayed in the sculpture garden. Specialists in 19th- and 20th-century American art.

Mayans Galleries
601 Canyon Rd. ☎ **505/983-8068.**

Twentieth-century American and Latin American paintings, photography, prints, and sculpture.

✪ Owings-Dewey Fine Art
76 E. San Francisco St., upstairs. ☎ **505/982-6244.**

Nineteenth- and 20th-century American painting and sculpture. Georgia O'Keeffe, Robert Henri, Maynard Dixon, Fremont Ellis, and Andrew Dasburg are among those represented.

✪ Gerald Peters Gallery
439 Camino del Monte Sol (P.O. Box 908). ☎ **505/988-8961.**

Nineteenth- and 20th-century American painting and sculpture, featuring art from the New York, western, and southwestern schools. Contemporary art and photography.

Photogenesis: A Gallery of Photography
100 East San Francisco St. ☎ **505/989-9540.**

Photography by Eileen Benjamin, Howard Bond, Edouard Boubat, Ike Fordyce, Earnest Knee, Wright Morris, David Noble, Mark Nohl, Willy Roni, Nicholas Trofimuk, Flo Vogan, and John Youngblood.

✪ Photography: The Platinum Gallery

943 Canyon Rd. ☎ 505/982-2200.

The world's first (and only) gallery to specialize in platinum prints. Works by 19th- and 20th-century masters, including Evans, Curtis, Weston, Bravo, Horst, and Gilpin. This is a wonderful gallery!

Santos of New Mexico

2712 Paseo de Tularosa. ☎ 505/473-7941.

Work by award-winning Santero Charles M. Carillo. Traditional New Mexican santos crafted out of cottonwood root and decorated with homemade pigments. Also, hand-adzed panels. By appointment only.

✪ Shidoni Foundry and Gallery

Bishop's Lodge Rd. Tesuque. ☎ 505/988-8001.

Shidoni Foundry is one of the area's most exciting spots for sculptors and sculpture enthusiasts. At the foundry visitors may take a tour through the facilities to view casting processes. In addition, there is a 5,000-square-foot contemporary gallery, a bronze gallery, and a wonderful sculpture garden.

Wadle Galleries, Ltd.

128 W. Palace Ave. ☎ 505/983-9219.

Fine southwestern art, including paintings, bronzes, pottery, folk art, and traditional as well as contemporary jewelry.

3 More Shopping A to Z

ANTIQUES

Scarlett's Antique Shop & Gallery

225 Canyon Rd. ☎ 505/983-7092.

Early American antiques, fine crystal, vintage Hollywood jewelry, pre-1920 postcards, collected western books, jewelry "confections" by international artist Helga Wagner.

William R. Talbot Fine Art

129 W. San Francisco St. ☎ 505/982-1559.

Antique maps, natural-history paintings and prints.

Susan Tarman Antiques & Fine Art

923 Paseo de Peralta. ☎ 505/983-2336.

Seventeenth- to 19th-century American, Oriental, and European furniture, porcelain, silver, and paintings.

BELTS

Caballo

727 Canyon Rd. ☎ 505/984-0971.

The craftspeople at Caballo fashion "one of a kind, one at a time" custom-made belts. Everything is hand-tooled, handcarved, and hand-stamped. The buckles themselves are remarkable and worthy of special attention. This shop merits a stop.

BOOKS

Caxton Books & Maps
216 W. San Francisco St. ☎ **505/982-6911.**

A major downtown bookstore, Caxton's collection includes a wide choice of regional works, art books, music, and maps.

Dumont Maps & Books of the West
301 E. Palace Ave., #1. ☎ **505/988-1076.**

New and out-of-print works on western history, fiction, and antique maps.

Horizons—The Discovery Store
328 S. Guadalupe St. ☎ **505/983-1554.**

Adult and children's books, science-oriented games and toys, telescopes, binoculars, and a variety of unusual educational items.

Margolis & Moss
129 W. San Francisco St. ☎ **505/982-1028.**

Rare books, maps, photographs, and prints.

Nicholas Potter, Bookseller
203 E. Palace Ave. ☎ **505/983-5434.**

Rare and used hardcover books.

Palace Avenue Books
209 E. Palace Ave. ☎ **505/986-0536.**

Books on the Southwest as well as a nice collection of history and philosophy titles.

CRAFTS

Cristof's
106 W. San Francisco St. ☎ **505/988-9881.**

Fine contemporary Navajo weavings and jewelry.

Davis Mather Folk Art Gallery
141 Lincoln Ave. ☎ **505/983-1660.**

New Mexican animal wood carvings, as well as folk and Hispanic arts.

Gallery 10
225 Canyon Rd. ☎ **505/983-9707.**

Museum-quality Native American pottery, weavings, basketry, and contemporary paintings and photography.

Kania-Ferrin Gallery
662 Canyon Rd. ☎ **505/982-8767.**

Fine Native American baskets, kachinas, jewelry, textiles, beadwork, santos, retablos, and oceanic art and artifacts.

✪ Nambe Mills, Inc.
924 Paseo de Peralta (at Canyon Rd.). ☎ **505/988-5528.**

An exquisite alloy is sand-cast and handcrafted to create cooking, serving, and decorating pieces. Also available at Plaza Mercado, 112 W. San Francisco St. (☎ **505/988-3574**), and 216 Paseo del Pueblo Norte (Yucca Plaza), Taos (☎ **505/758-8221**).

Prairie Edge
In El Centro Mall, 102 E. Water St. ☎ **505/984-1336.**

Plains tribal art, artifacts, and jewelry.

Streets of Taos
200 Canyon Rd. ☎ **505/983-8268.**

Navajo rugs, Pueblo jewelry, pottery, and baskets.

FASHIONS
Dewey & Sons Trading Company
53 Old Santa Fe Trail. ☎ **505/983-5855.**

Native American trade blankets and men's and women's apparel.

Judy's Unique Apparel
714 Canyon Rd. ☎ **505/988-5746.**

Eclectic separates made either locally or imported from around the globe. You'll find a wide variety of items here.

Origins
135 W. San Francisco St. ☎ **505/988-2323.**

Wearable art, folk art, work of local designers, as well as imports and jewelry.

Rancho
554 Canyon Rd. ☎ **505/986-1688.**

Authentic, comfortable, functional Western wear. This store features clothing by Schaefer Outfitter for both men and women, as well as by The Great American Cowboy and Wild Mustangs.

Three Sisters
At the Inn at Loretto, 211 Old Santa Fe Trail. ☎ **505/988-5045.**

Casual southwestern clothing and fiesta ribbon shirts.

FOOD
The Chile Shop
109 E. Water St. ☎ **505/983-6080.**

If you want to take home some chile or other New Mexican specialties, the Chile Shop is a must. You'll find everything from salsas to cornmeal and tortilla chips. The shop also stocks cookbooks and pottery items.

Cookworks Gourmet
318 Guadalupe St. ☎ **505/988-7676.**

Gourmet food products and cooking items. Cookworks has two other shops, Cookworks Kitchen and Cookworks Tabletop, both next door.

Coyote Cafe General Store
132 Water St. ☎ **505/982-2454.**

This store is an adjunct to one of Santa Fe's most popular restaurants. The big thing here is the enormous selection of hot sauces; however, you can also get fresh fruits and vegetables, a wide variety of southwestern food items, T-shirts, and aprons.

Señor Murphy Candy Maker
100 E. San Francisco St. ☎ **505/982-0461.**

This candy store is unlike any you'll find in other parts of the country because everything is made with local ingredients. The chile piñon nut brittle is a taste sensation! Señor Murphy has another shop at 223 Canyon Road (☎ **505/983-9243**).

FURNITURE

Southwest Spanish Craftsmen
328 S. Guadalupe St. ☎ **505/982-1767.**

Spanish colonial and Spanish provincial furniture, doors, and home accessories.

Taos Furniture
232 Galisteo St. ☎ **505/988-1229.**

Classic southwestern furnishings handcrafted in solid Ponderosa pine—both contemporary and traditional pieces.

GIFTS & SOUVENIRS

El Nicho
227 Don Gaspar Ave. ☎ **505/984-2830.**

Handcrafted Navajo and Oaxacan folk art, metal sculpture, switchplates, kachinas, jewelry, and much, much more!

Wharton's Crafted Gifts
In the De Vargas Center Mall (N. Guadalupe St. and Paseo de Peralta). ☎ **505/983-3066.**

Native crafts including kachinas, sand paintings, jewelry, and art supplies.

JEWELRY

Mineral & Fossil Gallery of Santa Fe
127 W. San Francisco St. ☎ **505/984-1682.**

Natural mineral jewelry, fossils, and decorative items for the home, including lamps, wall clocks, furniture, art glass, and carvings.

James Reid Ltd.
114 E. Palace Ave. ☎ **505/988-1147.**

Gold and silver jewelry and buckle sets, contemporary furniture, paintings, and sculpture.

Tresa Vorenberg Goldsmiths
656 Canyon Rd. ☎ **505/988-7125.**

More than 30 artisans are represented in this fine jewelry store. All items are handcrafted and custom commissions are welcomed.

MALLS & SHOPPING CENTERS

De Vargas Center Mall
N. Guadalupe St. and Paseo de Peralta. ☎ **505/982-2655.**

There are more than 55 merchants and restaurants in this mall just northwest of downtown. Open Monday through Thursday from 10am to 7pm, Friday from 10am to 9pm, Saturday from 10am to 6pm, and Sunday from noon to 5pm.

Sanbusco Market Center
500 Montezuma St. ☎ **505/989-9390.**

Unique shops and restaurants occupy this remodeled warehouse near the old Santa Fe Railroad Yard. There's a farmers market in the south parking lot. Open from 7am to noon on Tuesday and Saturday in the summer.

Villa Linda Mall
4250 Cerrillos Rd. (at Rodeo Rd.). ☎ **505/473-4253.**

Santa Fe's largest mall (including department stores) is near the southwestern city limits, not far from the I-25 on-ramp. Open Monday through Friday from 10am to 9pm, Saturday from 10am to 6pm, and Sunday from noon to 5pm.

MARKETS

Farmers Market
In the parking lot of Sanbusco Market Center, 500 Montezuma St. No phone.

Every Saturday and Tuesday from 7 to 11:30am, you'll find a farmers market in the parking lot of Sanbusco Market Center. Everything is here from fruits, vegetables, and flowers to cheeses, cider, and salsas.

Trader Jack's Flea Market
US 84-285 (about 8 miles north of Santa Fe). No phone.

If you're a flea-market hound, you'll be happy to find Trader Jack's. More than 500 vendors here sell everything from used cowboy boots (you might find some real beauties) to clothing, jewelry, books, and furniture. The flea market is open from mid-April to late November on Friday, Saturday, and Sunday.

POTTERY AND TILES

Arius Santa Fe Art Tile
114 Don Gaspar Ave. ☎ **505/988-1196.**

Mexican tiles are popular in this part of the country, but here you'll find hand-painted art tiles of all sorts, shapes, and varieties. Tile murals are popular custom-made items. This is a great place for tile collectors and souvenir seekers.

Canyon Road Pottery
821 Canyon Rd. ☎ **505/983-9426.**

Handmade decorative and functional pottery. Items for sale include stoneware, raku, earthenware, and custom dinnerware.

Santa Fe Pottery
323 S. Guadalupe St. ☎ **505/989-3363.**

The work of more than 50 master potters from New Mexico and the Southwest is on display here. You'll find everything from mugs to lamps.

WINES

The Winery
500 Montezuma St. ☎ **505/982-WINE.**

Perhaps the best-stocked wine shop in New Mexico, The Winery also carries gourmet foods, beers, and gift baskets, and it publishes a monthly newsletter.

Santa Fe After Dark

Santa Fe is a city committed to the arts. Its night scene is dominated by high-brow cultural events, with the club and music scene running a distant second.

Complete information on all major cultural events can be obtained from the **Santa Fe Convention and Visitors Bureau** (☎ **800/777-CITY** or 505/984-6760) or from the **City of Santa Fe Arts Commission** (☎ **505/984-6707**). Current listings are published each Friday in the "Pasatiempo" section of *The New Mexican,* the city's daily newspaper, and in the *Santa Fe Reporter,* published every Wednesday.

The Galisteo News and Ticket Center, 201 Galisteo St. (☎ 505/984-1316), is the primary outlet for tickets to the opera and other major entertainment events. Nicholas Potter, Bookseller, 203 E. Palace Ave. (☎ 505/983-5434), also carries tickets to select events. You can order by phone from TicketMaster (☎ 505/842-5387 for information, 505/884-0999 to order). Discount tickets may be available on the night of a performance; the opera, for example, offers standing-room tickets at a greatly reduced price just one hour before curtain time.

A variety of free concerts, lectures, and other events are presented in the summer, cosponsored by the City of Santa Fe and the Chamber of Commerce under the name **Santa Fe Summerscene.** From mid-June through August, on Tuesday and Thursday at noon and 6pm, these events are held on the Plaza or in Fort Marcy Park. They run the gamut from light opera to blues, jazz, Cajun, and bluegrass to hot salsa and New Mexican folk music.

The **Santa Fe Summer Concert Series,** at the Paolo Soleri Outdoor Amphitheatre on the campus of the Santa Fe Indian School (Cerrillos Road), has brought such name performers as Frank Zappa, Kenny Loggins, and B. B. King to the city. More than two dozen concerts and special events are scheduled each summer.

Note: Many companies noted here perform at locations other than their listed addresses, so check the site of the performance you plan to attend.

1 The Performing Arts

No fewer than 24 performing-arts groups flourish in Santa Fe. Many of them perform year round, but others are seasonal. The internationally acclaimed Santa Fe Opera, for instance, has a two-month summer season: July and August.

MAJOR PERFORMING-ARTS COMPANIES

OPERA & CLASSICAL MUSIC

✪ Santa Fe Opera

P.O. Box 2408, Santa Fe, NM 87504-2408. ☎ **505/986-5959** for tickets. Tickets, $20–$104 Mon–Thurs; $26–$110 Fri–Sat. Wheelchair seating, $14 Mon–Thurs; $20 Fri–Sat. Standing room (sold on day of performance beginning at 10am), $6 Mon–Thurs; $8 Fri–Sat; $15 Opening Night Gala. Backstage tours: First Mon in July to last Fri in Aug, Mon–Sat at 1pm; $6 adults, free for children 15 and under.

Even if your visit isn't timed to coincide with the opera season, you shouldn't miss seeing the company's open-air amphitheater. Located on a wooded hilltop 7 miles north of the city off US 84/285, the sweeping curves of this serene structure seem perfectly attuned to the contour of the surrounding terrain. At night, the lights of Los Alamos can be seen in the distance under clear skies.

Many rank the Santa Fe Opera second only to the Metropolitan Opera of New York as the finest company in the United States today. Established in 1957 by John Crosby, still the opera's artistic director, it consistently attracts famed conductors, directors, and singers (the list has included Igor Stravinsky). At the height of the season the company is 500 strong, including the skilled craftspeople and designers who work on the sets.

The opera company is noted for its performances of the classics, little-known works by classical European composers, and American premières of 20th-century works.

The nine-week, 40-performance opera season runs from the first week in July through the last week in August. All performances begin at 9pm. At press time, the theater was undergoing a major renovation, but will be open for the 1997 season.

ORCHESTRAL & CHAMBER MUSIC

Oncydium Chamber Baroque

210 E. Marcy St., Suite 15, Santa Fe, NM 87501. ☎ **505/988-0703.**

This new chamber ensemble presents Renaissance, classical, and baroque concerts six times during the year at various gallery spaces in Santa Fe. On Sundays in August the Oncydium Chamber Baroque performs at brunch and afternoon teas. Call for information and schedules.

Santa Fe Pro Musica

320 Galisteo, Suite 502 (P.O. Box 2091), Santa Fe, NM 87504-2091. ☎ **505/988-4640.**

This chamber ensemble performs everything from Bach to George Crumb and William Wood (composer-in-residence at the University of New Mexico. During Holy Week the Santa Fe Pro Musica presents its annual Baroque Festival Concert. Christmas brings candlelight Christmas chamber ensemble concerts. Pro Musica's season runs from September through May.

✪ Santa Fe Symphony and Chorus

P.O. Box 9692, Santa Fe, NM 87504. ☎ **505/983-1414.** Tickets, $15–$35 (six seating categories).

This 60-piece professional symphony orchestra has grown rapidly in stature since its founding in 1984. Matinee and evening performances of classical and popular works are presented in a subscription series at Sweeney Center (Grant Ave. at Marcy St.) from August to May. There's a preconcert lecture before each performance. During the spring there are music festivals (call for details).

Serenata of Santa Fe

P.O. Box 5771, Santa Fe, NM 87502. ☎ **505/989-7988.** Tickets, $10 general admission, $15 reserved seats.

This professional chamber-music group specializes in bringing the lesser known works of the masters to the concert stage. Concerts are presented from September to May at the Santuario de Nuestra Señora de Guadalupe (100 S. Guadalupe St.). Call the number above for dates and details.

CHORAL GROUPS

Desert Chorale

219 Shelby St. (P.O. Box 2813), Santa Fe, NM 87501. ☎ **800/244-4011** or 505/988-7505. Tickets, $18–$34 adults; half price for students.

This 24- to 30-member vocal ensemble, New Mexico's only professional choral group, recruits members from all over the country. It's nationally recognized for its eclectic blend of both Renaissance melodies and modern avant-garde compositions. During the summer months the chorale performs classic concerts at both the historic Santuario de Nuestra Señora de Guadalupe and St. Francis Auditorium, as well as smaller cameo concerts at more intimate settings throughout Santa Fe and Albuquerque. The chorale also performs a popular series of Christmas concerts during December. Most concerts begin at 8pm (3 or 6pm on Sunday).

Sangre de Cristo Chorale

P.O. Box 4462, Santa Fe, NM 87502. ☎ **505/662-9717.** Tickets, Christmas $18–$35, for catered dinner and concerts; Spring $10 ($8 at the door).

This 34-member ensemble has a repertoire ranging from classical, baroque, and Renaissance works to more recent folk music and spirituals. Much of it is presented a cappella. The group gives concerts in Santa Fe, Los Alamos, and Albuquerque. The Christmas dinner concerts are extremely popular.

Santa Fe Women's Ensemble

424 Kathryn Place, Santa Fe, NM 87501. ☎ **505/983-2137.** Tickets, $12 general admission, $15 reserved seats.

This choral group of 12 semiprofessional singers, sponsored by the Santa Fe Concert Association (see below), offers classical works sung a cappella as well as with varied instrumental accompaniment during the spring and fall season. Both the "Christmas Offering" concerts (in mid-December) and the annual "Spring Offering" concerts are held in the Loretto Chapel (Old Santa Fe Trail at Water St.). Tickets are sold by Nicholas Potter, Bookseller (see "Books" in "More Shopping A to Z," in Chapter 8), through mail order, and at the door.

MUSIC FESTIVALS & CONCERT SERIES

Santa Fe Chamber Music Festival

640 Paseo de Peralta (P.O. Box 853), Santa Fe, NM 87504. ☎ **505/983-2075** or 505/982-1890 for the box office (after June 26). Tickets, $20–$32.

The festival brings an extraordinary group of international artists to Santa Fe every summer. Its six-week season of some 50 concerts runs from the second week of July through the third week of August and is held in the beautiful St. Francis Auditorium. Each festival season features chamber-music masterpieces, new music by a composer-in-residence, jazz, free youth concerts, preconcert lectures, and open rehearsals. Festival concerts are recorded for broadcast during a 13-week nationally syndicated radio series.

Performances are Monday through Friday at 8pm and on Saturday and Sunday at 6pm. Open rehearsals, youth concerts, and preconcert lectures are free to the public.

Santa Fe Concert Association

P.O. Box 4626, Santa Fe, NM 87502. ☎ **800/9905-3315** or 505/984-8759 for tickets. Tickets, $15–$65.

Founded in 1938, the oldest musical organization in northern New Mexico has a September to May season that includes approximately 20 annual events. Among them are a distinguished artists series featuring renowned instrumental and vocal soloists and chamber ensembles, a free youth concert series, a special Christmas Eve concert, and sponsored performances by local artists. All performances are held at the St. Francis Auditorium; tickets are sold by Nicholas Potter, Bookseller (see "Books" under "More Shopping A to Z" in Chapter 8).

THEATER COMPANIES

Greer Garson Theater Center

College of Santa Fe, St. Michael's Dr. ☎ **505/473-6511** or 505/473-6439. Tickets, $6–$12 adults; $5–$11 students and seniors ($15–$24 for summer season Santa Fe Stages performances).

The college's Performing Arts Department produces four plays annually, with five presentations of each, given between October and May. Usually there is a comedy, a drama, a musical, and a classic.

○ Santa Fe Community Theatre

142 E. De Vargas St., Santa Fe, NM 87504. ☎ **505/988-4262.** Tickets, $10 adults; $8 students and seniors; for previews people are asked to "pay what you like."

Founded in the 1920s, this is the oldest existing theater group in New Mexico. Still performing in a historic adobe theater in the Barrio de Analco, it attracts thousands for its dramas, avant-garde theater, and musical comedy. Its popular one-act melodramas call on the public to boo the sneering villain and swoon for the damsel in distress.

Shakespeare in Santa Fe

355 E. Palace Ave. (box office only), Santa Fe, NM 87501. ☎ **505/982-2910.** Tickets free. Reserved seating available for a donation.

Every Friday, Saturday, and Sunday during July and August, in the library courtyard of St. John's College (southeast of downtown—off Camino del Monte Sol), Shakespeare in Santa Fe presents Shakespeare in the Park.

DANCE COMPANIES

○ Maria Benitez Teatro Flamenco

Institute for Spanish Arts, P.O. Box 8418, Santa Fe, NM 87501. ☎ **800/905-3315** or 505/982-1237 for tickets. Tickets, $16–$27 (subject to change).

The Benitez Company's "Estampa Flamenca" summer series is performed from mid-June to mid-September. True flamenco is one of the most thrilling of all dance forms, displaying the inner spirit and verve of the gypsies of Spanish Andalusia.

MAJOR CONCERT HALLS & ALL-PURPOSE AUDITORIUMS

Center for Contemporary Arts

1050 Old Pecos Trail. ☎ **505/982-1338.** Tickets, films $6.

In case you want to see the world.

At American Express, we're here to make your journey a smooth one. So we have over 1,700 travel service locations in over 120 countries ready to help. What else would you expect from the world's largest travel agency?

do more

AMERICAN EXPRESS

Travel

http://www.americanexpress.com/travel

In case you want to be welcomed there.

We're here to see that you're always welcomed at establishments everywhere. That's why millions of people carry the American Express® Card – for peace of mind, confidence, and security, around the world or just around the corner.

do more

And just in case.

We're here with American Express® Travelers Cheques and Cheques *for Two*.® They're the safest way to carry money on your vacation and the surest way to get a refund, practically anywhere, anytime.

Another way we help you…

do more

AMERICAN
EXPRESS

Travelers Cheques

The Center for Contemporary Arts (CCA) presents the work of internationally, nationally, and regionally known contemporary artists in art exhibitions, dance, new music concerts, poetry readings, performance-art events, theater, and video screenings. The CCA Cinématique screens films from around the world nightly, with special series presented regularly. A permanent outdoor James Turrell Skyspace is located on the CCA grounds. The CCA Warehouse/Teen Project is a unique program designed to encourage creativity, individuality, and free expression by giving teens a safe, free place to create programs and events, including workshops, art exhibitions, a radio show and publication, theater ensemble, cafe (with open mike opportunities), and concerts featuring local teen bands. CCA's galleries are open Monday through Friday from noon to 8pm and on Saturday from 1pm to 8pm.

Paolo Soleri Amphitheatre
At the Santa Fe Indian School, 1501 Cerrillos Rd. ☎ **505/989-6318.**

This outdoor arena is the locale of many warm-weather events. A large number of concerts are presented here each summer. In recent years the facility has attracted such big-name acts as Joan Armatrading, the Grateful Dead, B. B. King, Kenny Loggins, Anne Murray, Suzanne Vega, Ziggy Marley, Lyle Lovett, Dave Matthews, Allan Parsons Project, and the Reggae Sunsplash. For information on scheduled performers while you're there, contact **Big River Corporation,** P.O. Box 8036, Albuquerque, NM 87198 (☎ **505/256-1777**).

✪ St. Francis Auditorium
In the Museum of Fine Arts, Lincoln and Palace Aves. ☎ **505/827-4455.** Tickets, $5–$25, depending on the event; see above for specific performing-arts companies.

This beautiful music hall, patterned after the interiors of traditional Hispanic mission churches, is noted for its acoustics. The hall hosts a wide variety of musical events, including the Santa Fe Chamber Music Festival in July and August. The Santa Fe Symphony Festival Series, the Santa Fe Concert Association, the Santa Fe Women's Ensemble, and various other programs are also held here.

Sweeney Convention Center
201 W. Marcy St. ☎ **800/777-2489** or 505/984-6760. Tickets, $10–$30, depending on seating and performances.

Santa Fe's largest indoor arena hosts a wide variety of trade expositions and other events during the year. It's also the home of the Santa Fe Symphony Orchestra and the New Mexico Symphony Orchestra's annual Santa Fe Series. *Note:* Tickets are never sold at Sweeney Convention Center; event sponsors handle ticket sales.

2 The Club & Music Scene

In addition to the clubs and bars listed below, there are a number of hotels whose bars and lounges feature some type of entertainment. (See the accommodations listings in Chapter 5.)

COUNTRY, JAZZ & FOLK

✪ El Farol
808 Canyon Rd. ☎ **505/983-9912.** Cover $2–$6.

The original neighborhood bar of the Canyon Road artists' quarter (its name means "The Lantern") is the place to head for local ambience. Its low ceilings and dark-brown walls are the home of Santa Fe's largest and most unusual selection of tapas (bar snacks and appetizers), from pulpo à la Gallega (octopus with Spanish paprika sauce) to grilled cactus with ramesco sauce. Jazz, folk, and ethnic musicians—some of national note—perform most nights.

Fiesta Lounge
In La Fonda Hotel, 110 E. San Francisco St. ☎ **505/982-5511.** No cover.

This lively lobby bar offers cocktails and live entertainment nightly.

Rodeo Nites
2911 Cerrillos Rd. ☎ **505/473-4138.** No cover Mon–Thurs, $3 Fri–Sat, $2 Sun.

There's live country dance music nightly at this popular club.

ROCK & DISCO

The Bull Ring
150 Washington Ave. ☎ **505/983-3328.** No cover Wed and Sun, $5 Thurs–Sat.

This steakhouse is also a lively bar with dance music Wednesday through Sunday after 9pm. Bands, normally booked for a week at a time, may play rock or tunes from the 1960s and 1970s.

Chelsea Street Pub & Grill
In the Villa Linda Mall, Rodeo and Cerrillos Rds. ☎ **505/473-5105.** No cover.

Burgers and beer are served here during the lunch and dinner hours, but when the shopping mall closes at 9pm the pub really starts hopping. Top bands from throughout the Southwest play dance music Monday through Saturday until 2am, Sunday until 7pm.

Edge
125 W. Palace Ave. ☎ **505/986-1700.**

Located on the third floor of the Palace Court, Edge is Santa Fe's hottest new night club. You'll hear everything from live blues to popular dance music. Edge has a state-of-the-art sound and light system, pool tables, a great video system, and an enormous bar. Food is served in the bar or on the balcony. Edge is open from 9pm to 2am daily.

3 The Bar Scene

Evangelo's
200 W. San Francisco St. ☎ **505/982-9014.** No cover.

Food is not offered at Evangelo's, but the tropical decor and mahogany bar are unique to Santa Fe. More than 250 varieties of imported beer are available, and pool tables are an added attraction. Evangelo's is extremely popular with the local crowd. Open daily from noon until 1 or 2am.

Vanessie of Santa Fe
434 W. San Francisco St. ☎ **505/982-9966.** No cover.

This is unquestionably Santa Fe's most popular piano bar. The talented Doug Montgomery and Charles Tichenor have a loyal local following. Their repertoire ranges from Bach to Billy Joel, Gershwin to Barry Manilow. They play Monday through Saturday from 8:30pm to 2am and Sunday from 8pm to midnight. Vanessie's offers a great bar menu.

Side Trips from Santa Fe 10

Native American pueblos and ruins, a national monument and national park, Los Alamos (the A-bomb capital of the United States), and the scenic and culturally fascinating High Road to Taos are all within an easy day trip of Santa Fe.

1 Exploring the Northern Pueblos

Of the Eight Northern Pueblos, Tesuque, Pojoaque, Nambe, San Ildefonso, San Juan, and Santa Clara are within about 30 miles of Santa Fe. Picuris (San Lorenzo) is on the High Road to Taos (see Section 3, below), and Taos Pueblo, of course, is just outside the town of Taos.

The six pueblos described in this section can easily be visited in a single day's round-trip from Santa Fe. Plan to focus most of your attention on San Juan and Santa Clara, including the former's arts cooperative and the latter's Puye Cliff Dwellings.

Certain **rules of etiquette** should be observed in visiting the pueblos. These are personal dwellings and/or important historic sites and need to be respected as such. Don't climb on the buildings or peek into doors or windows. Don't enter sacred grounds, such as cemeteries and kivas. If you attend a dance or ceremony, remain silent while it is taking place and refrain from applause when it's over. Many pueblos prohibit photography or sketches; others require you to pay a fee for a permit. Again, any rules that apply to visiting a pueblo must be followed. If you don't respect the privacy of the Native Americans who live at the pueblo, you'll be asked to leave (I've seen it happen more than once).

TESUQUE PUEBLO

Tesuque (Teh-*soo*-keh) Pueblo is located about 9 miles north of Santa Fe on US 84/285. You will know that you are approaching the pueblo when you see the unusual Camel Rock and a large roadside casino. Despite this concession to the late 20th century, the 400 pueblo dwellers are faithful to their traditional religion, ritual, and ceremony. Excavations confirm that a pueblo has been here at least since the year A.D. 1200; in fact, this pueblo is now on the National Register of Historic Places. A mission church and adobe houses surround the plaza, and visitors are asked to remain in that area.

Some Tesuque women are skilled potters; Ignacia Duran's black-and-white and red micaceous pottery and Teresa Tapia's miniatures and pots with animal figures are especially noteworthy. The **San**

Diego Feast Day, featuring buffalo, deer, flag, or Comanche dances, is November 12.

The address is Route 5, Box 360-T, Santa Fe, NM 87501 (☎ **505/983-2667**). Admission to the pueblo is free; however, there is a $10 charge for still cameras, $50 for movie cameras, and $100 for sketching. The pueblo is open daily from 9am to 5pm. Camel Rock Casino (☎ **505/984-8414**) is open 24 hours, and there is a snack bar on the premises. In addition, Tesuque Pueblo provides an RV and campground park (☎ **505/455-2661**), which is open year-round.

POJOAQUE PUEBLO

About 6 miles farther north on US 84/285, at the junction of NM 502, is Pojoaque (Po-*hwa*-keh). Though small (population 200) and without a definable village (more modern dwellings exist now), Pojoaque is important as a center for traveler services; in fact, Pojoaque, in its Tewa form, means "water drinking place." The historical accounts of the Pojoaque people are sketchy, but we do know that in 1890 smallpox took its toll on the Pojoaque population, forcing most of the Pueblo residents to abandon their village. Since the 1930s the population has gradually increased, and in 1990 a war chief and two war captains were appointed. Today visitors won't find much to look at, but the Poeh Center, operated by the Pueblo, features a museum and crafts store. Indigenous pottery, embroidery, silverwork, and beadwork are available for sale at the Pojoaque Pueblo Tourist Center.

A modern community center is located near the site of the old pueblo and church. **Our Lady of Guadalupe Day,** the annual feast day celebrated on December 12, features a bow-and-arrow or buffalo dance.

The pueblo's address is Route 11, Box 71, Santa Fe, NM 87501 (☎ **505/455-3460**). Admission is free. Contact the Governor's Office for information about sketching and camera fees. The pueblo is open every day during daylight hours.

NAMBE PUEBLO

Drive east about 3 miles from Pojoaque on NM 503, then turn right at the Bureau of Reclamation sign for Nambe Falls. Approximately 2 miles farther is Nambe (meaning "mound of earth in the corner"), a 700-year-old Tewa-speaking pueblo (population 450), with a solar-powered tribal headquarters, at the foot of the Sangre de Cristo range. Only a few of the original pueblo buildings still remain, including a large round kiva, used today in ceremonies. Pueblo artisans make woven belts, beadwork, and brown micaceous pottery.

Nambe Falls make a stunning three-tier drop through a cleft in a rock face about 4 miles beyond the pueblo, tumbling into Nambe Reservoir. A recreational site at the reservoir offers fishing, boating (nonmotor boats only), hiking, camping, and picnicking. The **Waterfall Dances** on July 4 and **the Saint Francis of Assisi Feast Day** on October 4, which has an elk dance ceremony, are observed at the sacred falls.

The address is Route 1, Box 117, Santa Fe, NM 87501 (☎ **505/455-2036** or 505/455-2304 for the Ranger Station). Admission to the pueblo is free, but there is a $5 charge for still cameras, $10 for movie cameras, and $10 for sketching. At the recreational site, the charge for fishing is $6 per day for adults, $4 per day for children; for camping it is $8 per night. The pueblo is open daily from 8am to 5pm. The recreational site is open March, September, and October from 7am to 7pm, April and May from 7am to 8pm, and June through August from 6am to 8pm.

SAN ILDEFONSO PUEBLO

If you turn left on NM 502 at Pojoaque, it's about 6 miles to the turnoff to this pueblo, nationally famous for the matte-finish black-on-black pottery developed by tribeswoman Maria Martinez in the 1920s. The pottery-making process is explained at the **San Ildefonso Pueblo Museum,** where exhibits of pueblo history, arts, and crafts are presented Monday through Friday. A couple of Westerns were filmed here in the 1940s. San Ildefonso is one of the most-visited pueblos in northern New Mexico, attracting more than 20,000 visitors a year.

San Ildefonso Feast Day (January 23) is a good time to observe the social and religious traditions of the pueblo, when buffalo, deer, and Comanche dances are presented. Dances may be scheduled for Easter, the Harvest Festival (early September), and Christmas.

The pueblo has a 4¹/₂-acre **fishing lake** which is open April through October. Picnicking is encouraged; camping is not.

The pueblo's address is Route 5, Box 315A, Santa Fe, NM 87501 (☎ **505/455-3549**). The admission charge is $3 for a noncommercial vehicle and $10 for a commercial vehicle, plus 50¢ per passenger. The charge for using a still cameras is $5; for a video camera or sketching, it is $15. If you plan to fish, the charge is $8 for adults, $4 for children 6 to 12 years of age, and free for children under 6. The pueblo is open in the summer, Monday through Friday from 8am to 4:30pm; call for weekend hours; in the winter, it is open Monday through Friday from 8am to 4.30pm. It is closed for major holidays and tribal events.

SAN JUAN PUEBLO

If you continue north on US 84/285, you will reach the pueblo via NM 74, a mile off NM 68, about 4 miles north of Española.

The largest (population 1,950) and northernmost of the Tewa-speaking pueblos and headquarters of the Eight Northern Indian Pueblos Council, San Juan is located on the east side of the Rio Grande—opposite the 1598 site of San Gabriel, the first Spanish settlement west of the Mississippi River and the first capital of New Spain. In 1598 when the Spanish first became acquainted with the people of San Juan, they were impressed with the openness and helpfulness of the Indians; thus they decided to establish a capital there (it was moved to Santa Fe 10 years later), making San Juan Pueblo the first to experience Spanish colonization. The Indians were generous with food, clothing, shelter, and fuel—they even helped sustain the settlement when its leader Conquistador Juan de Oñate became preoccupied with his search for gold and neglected the needs of his people. Unfortunately, the Indians became somewhat like slaves. They were forced to provide the Spanish with corn, venison, cloth, and labor. They were compelled to participate in Spanish religious ceremonies and to abandon their own religious practices. Under no circumstances were Indian ceremonials allowed, and those caught participating in them were punished. In 1676 several Indians were accused of "sorcery" and jailed in Santa Fe. Later they were led to the Plaza, where they were flogged or hanged. This incident became a turning point in Indian-Spanish relations, generating an overwhelming feeling of rage in the Indian community. One of the accused, a man named Popé, a San Juan Pueblo Indian, became a leader in the Great Pueblo Revolt, which led to freedom from Spanish rule for 12 years.

The past and present cohabit here. The San Juan tribe, though Roman Catholics, still practice traditional religious rituals; thus two rectangular kivas flank the church in the main plaza, and *caciques* (pueblo priests) share power with civil authorities.

The annual **San Juan Fiesta** is June 23 and 24, with buffalo and Comanche dances. Another annual ceremony is the **turtle dance** on December 26.

The address of the pueblo is P.O. Box 1099, San Juan Pueblo, NM 87566 (☎ 505/852-4400). Admission is free. Photography or sketching may be allowed with prior permission from the Governor's Office. The charge for fishing is $10 for adults, and $5 for children and seniors. Open every day during daylight hours.

The **Eight Northern Indian Pueblos Council** (☎ 505/852-4265) is a sort of chamber of commerce and social-service agency.

A crafts shop, **Oke Oweenge Arts and Crafts Cooperative** (☎ 505/852-2372), specializes in local wares. This is a fine place to seek out San Juan's distinctive red pottery, a lustrous ceramic incised with traditional geometric symbols. Also displayed for sale are seed, turquoise, and silver jewelry; wood and stone carvings; indigenous clothing and weavings; embroidery; and paintings. Artisans often work on the premises so that visitors can watch. The co-op is open Monday through Saturday from 9am to 4:30pm; closed San Juan Feast Day. **Sunrise Crafts,** another crafts shop, is located to the right of the co-op. There you'll find one-of-a-kind handcrafted pipes, beadwork, and burned and painted gourds.

Right on the main road that goes through the pueblo is the **Tewa Indian Restaurant,** serving traditional pueblo chile stews, breads, blue-corn dishes, posole, teas, and desserts. It's open Monday through Friday from 9am to 2:30pm; closed holidays and feast days.

Fishing and picnicking are encouraged at the **San Juan Tribal Lakes,** open year round.

As with most of the other pueblos, San Juan offers bingo. In summer, the doors open Wednesday through Sunday at 5:30pm; in winter, on Sunday at noon.

SANTA CLARA PUEBLO

Close to Española (on NM 5), Santa Clara, with a population of about 1,600, is one of the larger pueblos. If you contact the pueblo a week in advance, you can take one of the driving and walking tours that are offered Monday through Friday, including visits to the pueblo's historic church and artists' studios. Visitors can enter specified studios to watch artists making baskets and highly polished red-and-black pottery.

There are corn and harvest dances on **Santa Clara Feast Day** (August 12); other special days include buffalo and deer dances (early February) and children's dances (December 28).

The Puye Cliff Dwellings (see below) are on the Santa Clara reservation.

The pueblo's address is P.O. Box 580, Española, NM 87532 (☎ 505/753-7326). Admission is free. The charge for still cameras is $5; for movie cameras and sketching, the charge is $15. The pueblo is open every day during daylight hours; the visitor's center is open Monday through Friday from 9am to 4:30pm.

Puye Cliff Dwellings

The Santa Clara people migrated to their home on the Rio Grande in the 13th century from a former home high on the Pajarito Plateau to the west. Dwellings from their previous life have been preserved at this site, an 11-mile climb west of the pueblo. It is believed that this site at the mouth of the Santa Clara Canyon (now a National Historic Landmark) was occupied from about 1250 to 1577.

High on a nearly featureless plateau, the volcanic tuff rises in a soft tan façade 200 feet high. Here the Anasazi found niches to build their homes. Visitors can

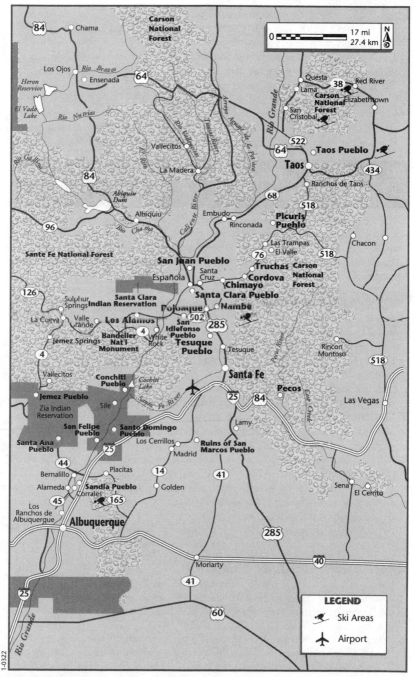

Excursions from Santa Fe

125

descend via staircases and ladders from the 7,000-foot mesa top into the 740-room pueblo ruin, which includes a ceremonial chamber and community house. Petroglyphs are evident in many of the rocky cliff walls.

About 6 miles farther west is the **Santa Clara Canyon Recreational Area,** a sylvan summer setting for camping that is open year-round for picnicking, hiking, and fishing in ponds and Santa Clara Creek.

If you would like to visit the cliff dwellings, call 505/753-7326. The admission is $5 for adults, $4 for children and seniors. There is an additional charge of $2 for guided tours (one week advance notice is required). The dwellings are open daily in the summer from 8am to 8pm; daily in the winter from 9am to 4:30pm.

2 Los Alamos & the Ancient Cliff Dwellings of Bandelier National Monument

Pueblo tribes lived in this rugged area for well over 1,000 years, and an exclusive boys' school operated atop the 7,300-foot plateau from 1928 to 1943. Then the Los Alamos National Laboratory was established here in secrecy—Project Y of the Manhattan Engineer District, the hush-hush wartime program that developed the world's first nuclear weapons.

Project director J. Robert Oppenheimer, later succeeded by Norris E. Bradbury, worked with a team of 30 to 100 scientists in research, development, and production of the weapons. Today 3,000 scientists and another 4,800 support staff work at the **Los Alamos National Laboratory,** making it the largest employer in northern New Mexico. Still operated by the University of California for the federal Department of Energy, its 32 technical areas occupy 43 square miles of mesa-top land.

The laboratory is known today as one of the world's foremost scientific institutions. It's still oriented primarily toward the defense industry—the Trident and Minuteman strategic warheads were created here, for example—but it has many other research programs, including studies in nuclear fusion and fission, energy conservation, nuclear safety, the environment, and nuclear waste. Its international resources include a genetic-sequence data bank, with wide implications for medicine and agriculture, and an Institute for Geophysics and Planetary Physics.

In 1995 workers at Los Alamos began preparations to build a plutonium core for a United States stockpile nuclear warhead—the first of its kind to be built in more than 40 years. It is reported that Los Alamos will build one or two cores a year for the U.S. Navy, beginning in 1997, to replace older warheads. It is possible that by then the government might want hundreds of new warheads.

ORIENTATION/USEFUL INFORMATION

Los Alamos is located about 35 miles west of Santa Fe and about 65 miles southwest of Taos. From Santa Fe, take US 84/285 north approximately 16 miles to the Pojoaque junction, then turn west on NM 502. Driving time is only about 50 minutes.

Los Alamos is a town of 18,000 spread over the colorful, fingerlike mesas of the Pajarito Plateau, between the Jemez Mountains and the Rio Grande valley. As NM 502 enters Los Alamos from Santa Fe, it follows Trinity Drive where accommodations, restaurants, and other services are located. Central Avenue parallels Trinity Drive and has restaurants, galleries, and shops, as well as the Los Alamos Historical Museum (free) and the Bradbury Science Museum (free).

The **Los Alamos Chamber of Commerce,** P.O. Box 460, Los Alamos, NM 87544 (☎ **505/662-8105,** fax 505/662-8399, e-mail lacoc@unix.nets.com), runs a visitor center that is open Monday through Friday from 8am to 5pm.

EVENTS

Los Alamos's events schedule includes a **Sports Skiesta** in late March or early April; **art-and-crafts fairs** in May, August, and November; **a county fair, rodeo,** and **arts festival** in August; and a **triathlon** in August/September.

WHAT TO SEE & DO

Aside from the sights described below, Los Alamos offers the **Pajarito Mountain ski area,** Camp May Road (P.O. Box 155), Los Alamos, NM 87544 (☎ **505/662-SNOW**), with five chair lifts—it's open only on Saturday, Sunday, Wednesday, and federal holidays; the **Los Alamos Golf Course,** 4250 Diamond Drive (☎ **505/662-8139**) at the edge of town; and the Larry R. Walkup Aquatic Center, 2760 Canyon Rd. (☎ 505/662-8170), the highest-altitude indoor Olympic-size swimming pool in the United States. There's even an outdoor **ice-skating rink.**

In Los Alamos

✪ Bradbury Science Museum

At the Los Alamos National Laboratory, 15th St. and Central Ave. ☎ **505/667-4444.** Free admission. Open Tues–Fri 9am–5pm, Sat Mon 1–5pm. Closed major holidays.

This outstanding museum is the lab's public showcase. Atomic research is emphasized in a wide variety of scientific and historical displays, including more than 35 hands-on exhibits. Visitors can peruse photographs and documents depicting the earliest days of Project Y, including a 1939 letter from Albert Einstein to Pres. Franklin D. Roosevelt suggesting research into uranium as a new and important source of energy. There are exhibits on weapons research, including an overview of the nation's nuclear arsenal; achievements in alternative-energy research, from solar and geothermal to laser and magnetic-fusion energy; biomedical research and development; computer technology; and basic research into the nature of nuclei, atoms, and molecules. Visitors can explore the museum, experiment with lasers, use computers, and view laboratory research in energy, defense, environment, and health. Self-guided exhibits have interesting hands-on features and video monitors. Educational and historical films are shown continuously.

Fuller Lodge Art Center

2132 Central Ave. ☎ **505/662-9331.** Free admission. Open Mon–Sat 10am–4pm, Sun 1–4pm.

Works of northern New Mexico artists and traveling exhibitions of regional and national importance are displayed here. Four annual arts-and-crafts fairs are also held here—in May, August, October, and November.

Los Alamos Historical Museum

2132 Central Ave. ☎ **505/662-4493.** Free admission. Open summer, Mon–Sat 9:30am–4:30pm, Sun 11am–5pm; winter, Mon–Sat 10am–4pm, Sun 1–4pm.

The massive log building that once housed the dining and recreation hall for the Los Alamos Ranch School for boys is now a National Historic Landmark known as the Fuller Lodge. Its current occupants include the museum office and research archives, the Fuller Lodge Art Center (see above), and the Los Alamos County Chamber of Commerce, which doubles as a visitor information center. The museum, located in the small log-and-stone building to the north of Fuller Lodge, depicts area history, from prehistoric cliff dwellers to the present. It also has exhibits ranging from Native American artifacts to school memorabilia and an excellent new permanent Manhattan Project exhibit. The museum sponsors guest speakers and operates a tax-free bookstore. Now you can even "visit" the museum on the World Wide Web at http://www.vla.com/lahistory or http://www.losalamos.com/lahistory.

NEARBY

✪ Bandelier National Monument

NM 4 (HCR 1, Box 1, Suite 15, Los Alamos, NM 87544). ☎ **505/672-3861.** Admission $5 per vehicle. Open every day during daylight hours. Closed Jan 1 and Dec 25.

Less than 15 miles south of Los Alamos along NM 4, this National Park Service area contains both extensive ruins of the ancient cliff-dwelling Anasazi pueblo culture and 46 square miles of canyon-and-mesa wilderness.

After an orientation stop at the visitor center and museum to learn about the culture that flourished here between A.D. 1100 and 1550, most visitors follow a trail along Frijoles Creek to the principal ruins. The pueblo site, including an underground kiva, has been stabilized. The biggest thrill for most folks, though, is climbing hardy Ponderosa pine ladders to visit an alcove 140 feet above the canyon floor that was once home to prehistoric people. Tours are self-guided or led by a National Park Service ranger.

On summer nights rangers offer campfire talks about the history, culture, and geology of the area. Some summer evenings, the guided night walks reveal a different, spooky aspect of the ruins and cave houses, outlined in the two-dimensional chiaroscuro of the thin cold light from the starry sky. During the day, nature programs are sometimes offered for adults and children. The small museum at the visitor center displays artifacts found in the area.

Elsewhere in the monument area, 70 miles of maintained trails lead to more tribal ruins, waterfalls, and wildlife habitats. The separate **Tsankawi** section, reached by an ancient 2-mile trail close to **White Rock,** has a large unexcavated ruin on a high mesa overlooking the Rio Grande valley. The town of White Rock, about 10 miles southeast of Los Alamos on NM4, offers spectacular panoramas of the river valley in the direction of Santa Fe; the White Rock Overlook is a great picnic spot.

Within Bandelier areas have been set aside for picnicking and camping. The national monument is named after the Swiss-American archaeologist Adolph Bandelier, who explored here in the 1880s.

Past Bandelier National Monument on NM4, beginning about 15 miles from Los Alamos, is Valle Grande, a vast meadow 16 miles in area—all that remains of a massive volcano that erupted nearly a million years ago. When the mountain spewed ashes and dust as far away as Kansas and Nebraska, its underground magma chambers collapsed, forming this great valley—the largest volcanic caldera in the world. However, lava domes that pushed up after the collapse obstruct a full view across the expanse. Valle Grande is now privately owned land.

3 Along the High Road to Taos

Unless you're in a hurry to get from Santa Fe to Taos, the "high road"—also called the Mountain Road or the King's Road—is by far the most fascinating route. It runs through tiny ridgetop villages where Hispanic life-styles and traditions continue much the same as a century ago.

CHIMAYO

About 28 miles north of Santa Fe on NM 84/285 is the historic weaving center of Chimayo. It's approximately 16 miles past the Pojoaque junction, at the junction of NM 520 and NM 76 via NM 503. In this small village, families such as the Ortegas maintain a tradition of crafting hand-woven textiles begun by their ancestors seven generations ago, in the early 1800s. Both **Ortega's Weaving Shop** and **Galeria Ortega** are fine places to take a close look at this ancient craft.

Today, however, many more people come to Chimayo to visit ✪ **El Santuario de Nuestro Señor de Esquipulas** (the Shrine of Our Lord of Esquipulas), better known simply as "El Santuario de Chimayo." Ascribed with miraculous powers of healing, this church has attracted countless thousands of pilgrims since it was constructed in 1814–16. Up to 30,000 people participate in the annual Good Friday pilgrimage, many of them walking from as far away as Albuquerque.

Although only the earth in the anteroom beside the altar has the presumed healing powers, the entire shrine offers a special serenity that's hard to ignore. It's quite moving to peruse the written testimonies of rapid recovery from illness or injury on the walls of the anteroom, and equally poignant to read the as-yet-unanswered entreaties made on behalf of loved ones.

A National Historic Landmark, the church has five beautiful reredos, or panels of sacred paintings, one behind the main altar and two on each side of the nave. Each year during the fourth weekend in July, the military exploits of the 9th-century Spanish saint Santiago are celebrated in a weekend fiesta, including the historic play *Los Moros y Cristianos* (Moors and Christians).

Lovely **Santa Cruz Lake** has a dual purpose: The artificial lake provides water for Chimayo valley farms and also offers a recreation site for trout fishing and camping at the edge of the Pecos Wilderness. To reach it, turn south 4 miles on NM 503, about 2 miles east of Chimayo.

WHERE TO DINE

✪ Restaurante Rancho de Chimayo

NM 76. ☎ **505/351-4444.** Reservations recommended. Lunch $6–$10; dinner $10–$15. MC, V. Tues–Sun noon–9pm. NEW MEXICAN.

Many travelers schedule their outings in order to have lunch at this well-known restaurant. The adobe home, built by Hermenegildo Jaramillo in the 1880s, has been in the food business for about three decades. Native New Mexican cuisine, prepared from generations-old Jaramillo family recipes, is served on terraced patios and in cozy dining rooms beneath hand-stripped vigas.

CORDOVA

Just as Chimayo is famous for its weaving, the village of Cordova, about 7 miles east on NM 76, is noted for its wood carvers. Small shops and studios along the highway display santos (carved saints) and various decorative items carved from aspen and cedar.

TRUCHAS

Anyone who saw Robert Redford's 1988 movie *The Milagro Beanfield War* has seen Truchas. A former Spanish colonial outpost built on top of an 8,000-foot mesa, 4 miles east of Cordova, it was chosen as the site for the film in part because traditional Hispanic culture is still very much in evidence. Subsistence (*acequia*) farming is prevalent here. The scenery is spectacular: 13,101-foot Truchas Peak dominates one side of the mesa and the broad Rio Grande valley dominates the other.

Georgia O'Keeffe: Development of a Great American Artist

In June 1917, during a short visit to the Southwest, painter Georgia O'Keeffe (born 1887) visited New Mexico for the first time. She was immediately enchanted by the scenery—her mind wandered frequently to the arid land and undulating mesas even after she returned to energy-filled New York City. Not until coaxed by arts patroness and "collector of people" Mabel Dodge Luhan 12 years later did O'Keeffe return to the multihued desert of her daydreams.

When she arrived in Santa Fe in April 1929, O'Keeffe was reportedly ill, both physically and emotionally. New Mexico seemed to soothe her spirit and heal her physical ailments almost immediately. Two days later, Mabel Dodge persuaded O'Keeffe to move into her home in Taos. There she would be free to paint and socialize as she liked.

In Taos, O'Keeffe began painting some of her best-known canvases—close-ups of desert flowers and objects such as cow and horse skulls. "The color up there is different . . .the blue-green of the sage and the mountains, the wild-flowers in bloom," O'Keeffe once said of Taos. "It's a different kind of color from any I've ever seen—there's nothing like that in north Texas or even in Colorado." Her personality, as well as her art, was transformed in Taos. She bought a car and learned to drive (in that order). Sometimes, on warm days, she ran stark naked through the sage fields. That August, a new, rejuvenated O'Keeffe rejoined her husband, photographer Alfred Stieglitz, in New York.

The artist returned to New Mexico year after year, spending time with Mabel Dodge as well as staying at isolated Ghost Ranch. She drove through the countryside in her snappy Ford, stopping to paint in her favorite spots along the way. Up until 1949, however, O'Keeffe always returned to New York in the fall. Three years after Stieglitz's death, though, she relocated permanently to New Mexico, spending each winter and spring in Abiquiu, and each summer and fall at Ghost Ranch. Georgia O'Keeffe died in Santa Fe in 1986.

About 6 miles east of Truchas on NM 76 is the small town of **Las Trampas,** noted for its **San José Church,** which some call the most beautiful of all churches built during the Spanish Colonial period.

PICURIS (SAN LORENZO) PUEBLO

Near the regional education center of **Peñasco,** about 24 miles from Chimayo near the intersection of NM 75 and NM 76, is the Picuris (San Lorenzo) Pueblo (☎ 505/587-2519). The 270 citizens of this 15,000-acre mountain pueblo, native Tiwa speakers, consider themselves a sovereign nation: Their forebears never made a treaty with any foreign country, including the United States. Thus they observe a traditional form of tribal council government. Their annual **feast day** at San Lorenzo Church is August 10.

Still, the people are modern enough to have fully computerized their public showcase operations, Picuris Tribal Enterprises. Besides running the Hotel Santa Fe in the state capital, they own the **Picuris Pueblo Museum,** where weaving, bead-work, and distinctive reddish-brown clay cooking pottery are exhibited Monday through Friday from 8am to 4:30pm. Guided tours through the old village ruins begin at the museum; camera fees start at $5. There's also an information center, crafts shop, grocery and other shops, and a cafe that serves Pueblo and American food at lunchtime. Permits ($5 for adults and children) are available to fish or camp at Pu-Na and Tu-Tah Lakes, regularly stocked with trout.

About a mile east of Peñasco on NM 75 is **Vadito,** the former center for a conservative Catholic brotherhood, the Penitentes, earlier in this century.

DIXON AND EMBUDO

Taos is about 24 miles north of Peñasco via NM 518. But day-trippers from Santa Fe can loop back to the capital by taking NM 75 west from Picuris Pueblo. **Dixon,** approximately 12 miles west of Picuris, and its twin village **Embudo,** a mile farther on NM 68 at the Rio Grande, are the homes of many artists and craftspeople who exhibit their works during the annual **autumn show** sponsored by the Dixon Arts Association. If you'd like to get something to drink, you can follow signs to **La Chiripada Winery** (☎ 505/579-4437), whose product is surprisingly good. Local pottery is also sold in the tasting room. The winery is open Monday through Saturday from 10am to 5pm.

Near Dixon is the **Harding Mine,** a University of New Mexico property where visitors can gather mineral specimens without going underground. If you haven't signed a liability release at the Albuquerque campus, ask at Labeo's Store in Dixon. They'll direct you to the home of a local resident who can get you started on your fossil hunt almost immediately.

Two more small villages lie in the Rio Grande valley at six-mile intervals south of Embudo on NM 68. **Velarde** is a fruit-growing center; in season, the road here is lined with stands selling fresh fruit or crimson chile ristras and wreaths of native plants. **Alcalde** is the site of Los Luceros, an early 17th-century home that is to be refurbished as an arts and history center. The unique Dance of the Matachines, a Moorish-style production brought from Spain by the conquistadors, is performed here on holidays and feast days.

ESPAÑOLA

The commercial center of Española (population 7,000) no longer has the railroad that led to its establishment in the 1880s, but it may have New Mexico's greatest concentration of "low riders." Their owners lavish attention on these late-model customized cars, so called because their suspension leaves them sitting quite close to the ground. You can't miss these cars since they cruise the main streets of town, especially on weekend evenings.

Significant sights in Española include the **Bond House Museum,** a Victorian-era adobe home that exhibits local history and art; and the **Santa Cruz Church,** built in 1733 and renovated in 1979, which houses many fine examples of Spanish Colonial religious art. Major events include the July **Fiesta de Oñate,** commemorating the valley's founding in 1596; the October **Tri-Cultural Art Festival** on the Northern New Mexico Community College campus; and the week-long **Summer Solstice** celebration staged in June by the nearby Ram Das Puri ashram of the Sikhs, located nearby (☎ 505/753-9438).

Complete information on Española and the vicinity can be obtained from the **Española Valley Chamber of Commerce,** 417 Big Rock Center, Española, NM 87532 (☎ 505/753-2831).

If you admire the work of Georgia O'Keeffe, try to plan a short trip to **Abiquiu,** a tiny town at a bend of the Rio Chama, 14 miles south of Ghost Ranch and 22 miles north of Española on US 84. Once you see the surrounding terrain, it will be clear that this was the inspiration for many of her startling landscapes. Since March 1995 O'Keeffe's adobe home (where she lived and painted) has been open for public tours. However, a reservation must be made in advance; the charge is $15 for a one-hour tour. As this book goes to press, seven tours are being given each week—on Tuesday, Thursday, and Friday—and a limited number of people are accepted per tour. Visitors are not permitted to take pictures. Fortunately, O'Keeffe's home remains as it was when she lived there (until 1986). For reservations, call **505/685-4539.**

4 Pecos National Monument

About 15 miles east of Santa Fe, I-25 meanders through **Glorieta Pass,** site of an important Civil War skirmish. In March 1862, volunteers from Colorado and New Mexico, along with Fort Union regulars, defeated a Confederate force marching on Santa Fe, thereby turning the tide of southern encroachment in the West.

Take NM 50 east to **Pecos,** a distance of about 7 miles. This quaint town, well off the beaten track since the interstate was constructed, is the site of a noted Benedictine monastery. About 26 miles north of here on NM 63 is the village of **Cowles,** gateway to the natural wonderland of the Pecos Wilderness. There are many camping, picnicking, and fishing locales en route.

Pecos National Historical Park (☎ **505/757-6414**), about 2 miles south of the town of Pecos off NM 63, contains the ruins of a 15th-century pueblo and 17th- and 18th-century missions. Coronado mentioned Pecos Pueblo in 1540: "It is feared through the land," he wrote. With a population of about 2,000, the Native Americans farmed in irrigated fields and hunted wild game. Their pueblo had 660 rooms and many kivas. By 1620 Franciscan monks had established a church and convent. Military and natural disasters took their toll on the pueblo, and in 1838 the 20 surviving Pecos went to live with relatives at the Jemez Pueblo.

The **E. E. Fogelson Visitor Center** tells the history of the Pecos people in a well-done, chronologically organized exhibit, complete with dioramas. A 1½-mile loop trail begins at the center and continues through Pecos Pueblo and the **Mission de Nuestra Señora de Los Angeles de Porciuncula** (as the church was formerly called). This excavated structure—170 feet long and 90 feet wide at the transept—was once the most magnificent church north of Mexico City.

Pecos National Historical Park is open Memorial Day to Labor Day, daily from 8am to 6pm; the rest of the year, daily from 8am to 5pm; closed Jan 1 and Dec 25. Admission is $2.

Getting to Know Taos

Situated where the western flank of the Sangre de Cristo range meets the semiarid high desert of the upper Rio Grande valley, Taos combines nature and culture, history and progress. There's much less commercialization here than in the state capital.

Located just 40 miles south of the Colorado border, about 70 miles north of Santa Fe, and approximately 135 miles from Albuquerque, Taos is best known for its thriving art colony, its historic Native American pueblo, and its nearby ski area, one of the most highly regarded in the Rockies. It also has several fine museums (including a brand-new one that opened in 1995) and a wide choice of accommodations and restaurants.

About 4,500 people consider themselves Taoseños (permanent residents of Taos) today. It is believed that this area may have been inhabited for 5,000 years; throughout the Taos valley there are ruins that date back more than 1,000 years.

The Spanish first visited this area in 1540 and then colonized it in 1598; in the last two decades of the 17th century, they put down three rebellions at the Taos Pueblo. During the 18th and 19th centuries Taos was an important trade center: New Mexico's annual caravan to Chihuahua, Mexico, couldn't leave until after the annual midsummer Taos Fair. French trappers began attending the fair in 1739. Even though the Plains tribes often attacked the pueblos at other times, they would attend the market festival under a temporary annual truce. By the early 1800s Taos had become a meeting place for American "mountain men," the most famous of whom, Kit Carson, made his home in Taos from 1826 to 1868.

Firmly Hispanic, Taos remained loyal to Mexico during the Mexican War of 1846. The town rebelled against its new U.S. landlord in 1847, killing newly appointed Gov. Charles Bent in his Taos home. Nevertheless, the town became part of the Territory of New Mexico in 1850. During the Civil War, Taos fell into Confederate hands for six weeks; afterward, Carson and two other men raised the Union flag over Taos Plaza and guarded it day and night. Since then Taos has had the honor of flying the flag 24 hours a day.

When the railroad bypassed Taos in favor of Santa Fe, the population declined. In 1898 two eastern artists—Ernest Blumenschein and Bert Phillips—discovered the dramatic effects of changing sunlight on the natural environment of the Taos valley and depicted them on canvas. By 1912, thanks to the growing influence of the Taos Society of Artists, the town had gained a worldwide reputation as a cultural center. Today it is estimated that more than 15% of the population are painters, sculptors, writers, musicians, or otherwise earn their income from an artistic pursuit.

The town of Taos is merely the focal point of the rugged 2,200-square-mile Taos County. Two features dominate this sparsely populated region: the high desert mesa, split in two by the 650-foot-deep chasm of the Rio Grande; and the Sangre de Cristo range, which tops out at 13,161-foot Wheeler Peak, New Mexico's highest mountain. From the forested uplands to the sage-carpeted mesa, the county is home to a large variety of wildlife. The human element includes Native Americans, who are still living in ancient pueblos, and Hispanic farmers who continue to irrigate their farmlands by centuries-old methods.

1 Orientation

ARRIVING

BY PLANE The **Taos Airport** (☎ 505/758-4995) is about eight miles northwest of town on US 64. Call for information on local charter services. It's easiest to fly into Albuquerque International Airport, rent a car, and drive up to Taos from there. The drive will take you approximately 2^1/2 hours. If you'd rather be picked up at Albuquerque International Airport, call **Pride of Taos** (☎ 505/758-8340). They offer charter bus service to Taos town and the Taos Ski Valley daily. **Faust's Transportation, Inc.** (☎ 800/535-1106 or 505/758-3410) offers a similar service.

BY BUS The **Taos Bus Center,** Paseo del Pueblo Sur at the Chevron station (☎ 505/758-1144), is not far from the Plaza. **Greyhound/Trailways** and **TNM&O Coaches** arrive and depart from this depot several times a day. For more information on these and two local bus services to and from Albuquerque and Santa Fe, see "Getting There," in Chapter 2.

BY CAR Most visitors arrive in Taos via either NM 68 or US 64. Northbound travelers should exit I-25 at Santa Fe, follow US 285 as far as San Juan Pueblo, and then continue on the divided highway when it becomes NM 68. Taos is about 79 miles from the I-25 junction. Southbound travelers from Denver on I-25 should exit about 6 miles south of Raton at US 64 and then follow it about 95 miles to Taos. Another major route is US 64 from the west (214 miles from Farmington).

VISITOR INFORMATION

The **Taos County Chamber of Commerce,** at the junction of US 64 and NM 68 (P.O. Drawer I), Taos, NM 87571 (☎ 800/732-TAOS or 505/758-3873), is open year round, daily from 9am to 5pm; closed major holidays. **Carson National Forest** also has an information center in the same building as the chamber. On the Internet you can access information about Taos at http://taoswebb.com/nmusa/TAOS. The e-mail address for the Taos County Chamber of Commerce is taos@taoswebb.com.

CITY LAYOUT

The Plaza is a short block west of Taos's major intersection—where US 64 (**Kit Carson Road**) from the east joins NM 68, **Paseo del Pueblo Sur** (also known as South Pueblo Road or South Santa Fe Road). US 64 proceeds north from the intersection as **Paseo del Pueblo Norte** (North Pueblo Road). **Camino de la Placita** (Placitas Road) circles the west side of downtown, passing within a block of the other side of the Plaza. Many of the streets that join these thoroughfares are winding lanes lined by traditional adobe homes, many of them over 100 years old.

Most of the art galleries are located on or near the Plaza, which was paved over with bricks several years ago, and along neighboring streets.

MAPS To find your way around town, pick up a free copy of the Taos map from the **Chamber of Commerce** at Taos Visitor Center, 1139 Paseo del Pueblo Sur (☎ 505/758-3873). Good, detailed city maps can be found at area bookstores as well (see "Shopping," in Chapter 8).

2 Getting Around

BY BUS AND TAXI

If you're in Taos without a car, you're in luck because there is now a local bus service, provided by **Taos Transit** (☎ 505/751-2000). It begins at around 6:30am and ends at about 11pm. The route runs from Kachina Lodge on Paseo del Pueblo Norte and ends at the Ranchos Post Office on the south side of town. Bus fares are 50¢ one way, $1 all day, and $5 for a seven-day pass.

In addition, Taos has two private companies. **Pride of Taos** (☎ 505/758-8340) operates a summer trolley that runs daily from 9am to 5pm from the Sagebrush Inn to Taos Pueblo on a 45-minute schedule, for $7 ($3 for children). In winter, Pride of Taos's shuttlebus service links town hotels and Taos Ski Valley four times a day for $7 round-trip. A night bus ($10) brings skiers staying at the ski valley into town for dinner and returns them to their lodgings.

Faust's Transportation (☎ 505/758-3410) offers town taxi service daily from 7am to 10pm, with fares of $8 anywhere within the city limits for up to two people ($2 per additional person), $35 to Albuquerque International Airport, and $25 to Taos Ski Valley from Taos town.

BY CAR

With offices at the Taos airport, **Dollar** (☎ 800/369-4226 or 505/758-9501) is reliable and efficient. Other car-rental agencies are available out of Albuquerque. See Chapter 15 for details.

PARKING Parking can be difficult during the summer rush, when the stream of tourists' cars moving north and south through town never ceases. If you can't find parking on the street or in the Plaza, check out some of the nearby roads (Kit Carson Road, for instance) because there are plenty of metered and unmetered lots in Taos town.

WARNING FOR DRIVERS Reliable paved roads lead to starting points for side trips up poorer forest roads to many recreation sites. Once you get off the main roads, you won't find gas stations or cafes. Four-wheel-drive vehicles are recommended on snow and much of the otherwise-unpaved terrain of the region. If you're doing some off-road adventuring, it's wise to go with a full gas tank, extra food and water, and warm clothing—just in case. At the higher-than-10,000-foot elevations of northern New Mexico, sudden summer snowstorms are not unheard of.

ROAD CONDITIONS Information on road conditions in the Taos area can be obtained free from the **State Police** (☎ 505/758-8878 or 505/983-0120 within New Mexico). Also, for highway conditions throughout the state, call the **State Highway Department** (☎ 800/432-4269).

BY BICYCLE/ON FOOT

Bicycle rentals are available from the **Gearing Up Bicycle Shop,** 129 Paseo del Pueblo Sur (☎ **505/751-0365**); **Hot Tracks Cyclery & Ski Touring Service,** 729 Paseo del Pueblo Sur (☎ **505/751-0949**); and **Native Sons Adventures,** 715 Paseo del Pueblo Sur (☎ **800/753-7559** or 505/758-9342).

Most of Taos's attractions can easily be reached by foot since they are within a few blocks of the Plaza.

FAST FACTS: Taos

Airport See "Orientation," above.

Area Code The telephone area code for all of New Mexico is **505.**

Business Hours Most **businesses** are open Monday through Friday from 10am to 5pm, though some may open an hour earlier and close an hour later. Many tourist-oriented **shops** are also open on Saturday mornings, and some **art galleries** are open all day Saturday and Sunday, especially during peak tourist seasons. **Banks** are generally open Monday through Thursday from 9am to 3pm and on Friday from 6am to 6pm. Call establishments for specific hours.

Car Rentals See "Getting Around," above.

Climate Taos's climate is similar to that of Santa Fe. Summer days are dry and sunny, except for frequent afternoon thunderstorms. Winter days are often bracing, with snowfalls common but rarely lasting too long. Average summer temperatures range from 50°F to 87°F. Winter temperatures vary between 9°F and 40°F. Annual rainfall is 12 inches; annual snowfall is 35 inches in town, 300 inches at Taos Ski Valley, elevation 9,207 feet. (A foot of snow is equal to an inch of rain.)

Currency Exchange Foreign currency can be exchanged at the Centinel Bank of Taos, 512 Paseo del Pueblo Sur (☎ **505/758-6700**).

Dentists If you need dental work, try Dr. Walter Jakiela, 536 Paseo del Pueblo Norte (☎ **505/758-8654**)**;** Dr. Michael Rivera (☎ **505/758-0531**); or Dr. Tom Simms, 623-B Paseo del Pueblo Sur (☎ **505/758-8303**).

Doctors Members of the Taos Medical Group, on Weimer Road (☎ **505/758-2224**), are highly respected. Also recommended are Family Practice Associates of Taos, on Don Fernando Street (☎ **505/758-3005**), a short distance west of the Plaza.

Driving Rules See "Getting Around," above.

Drugstores See "Pharmacies," below.

Embassies/Consulates See Chapter 3, "Fast Facts: For the Foreign Traveler."

Emergencies Dial **911** for police, fire, and ambulance.

Eyeglasses Taos Eyewear, in Cruz Alta Plaza (☎ **505/758-8758**), handles most needs Monday through Friday between 8:30am and 5pm. It also has emergency service.

Hospital Holy Cross Hospital, 1397 Weimer Road, off Paseo del Canyon (☎ **505/758-8883**), has 24-hour emergency service. Serious cases are transferred to Santa Fe or Albuquerque.

Hotlines The crisis hotline (☎ **505/758-9888**) is available for emergency counseling.

Information See "Visitor Information," above.

Library The Taos Public Library, on Ledoux Street (☎ 505/758-3063), has a general collection for Taos residents, a children's library, and special collections on the Southwest and Taos art.

Liquor Laws As in Santa Fe, bars must close by 2am Monday through Saturday and can open only between noon and midnight on Sunday. The legal drinking age is 21.

Lost Property Check with the police (☎ 505/758-2216).

Newspapers/Magazines The *Taos News* (☎ 505/758-2241) and the *Sangre de Cristo Chronicle* (☎ 505/377-2358) are published every Thursday. *Taos Magazine* is also a good source of local information. The *Albuquerque Journal*, *The New Mexican* from Santa Fe, and the *Denver Post* are easily obtained at the Fernandez de Taos Bookstore on the Plaza.

Pharmacies There are several full-service pharmacies in Taos. Furr's Pharmacy (☎ 505/758-1203), Smith's Pharmacy (☎ 505/758-4824, or 505/758-4823), and Wal-Mart Pharmacy (☎ 505/758-2743) are all located on Pueblo Sur and are easily seen from the road.

Photographic Needs Check Plaza Photo, Taos Main Plaza (☎ 505/758-3420). Minor camera repairs can be done the same day, but major repairs must be sent to Santa Fe and usually require several days. Plaza Photo offers a full line of photo accessories and 1-hour processing. April's 1-Hour Photos, at 613E N. Pueblo Rd. (☎ 505/758-0515) is another good choice.

Police In case of emergency, dial **911.** All other inquiries should be directed to Taos Police, Civic Plaza Drive (☎ 505/758-2216). The Taos County Sheriff, with jurisdiction outside the city limits, is located in the county courthouse on Paseo del Pueblo Sur (☎ 505/758-3361).

Post Offices The main Taos Post Office is at 318 Paseo del Pueblo Norte, Taos, NM 87571 (☎ 505/758-2081), a few blocks north of the Plaza traffic light. There are smaller offices in Ranchos de Taos (☎ 505/758-3944) and at El Prado (☎ 505/758-4810). The ZIP code for Taos is **87571.**

Radio Local stations are KRZA-FM (88.7); the National Public Radio Station—KKIT-AM (1340)—for news, sports, weather, and a daily event calendar at 6:30am (☎ 505/758-2231); and KTAO-FM (101.7), which broadcasts an entertainment calendar daily (☎ 505/758-1017).

Taxes Gross receipts tax for Taos town is 6.8125% and for Taos county it's 6.3125%. There is an additional local bed tax of 3.5% in Taos town and 3% on hotel rooms in Taos County.

Television Channel 2, the local access station, is available in most hostelries. For a few hours a day there is local programming. Cable networks carry Santa Fe and Albuquerque stations.

Time As is true throughout New Mexico, Taos is in the Mountain time zone. It's two hours earlier than New York, one hour earlier than Chicago, and one hour later than Los Angeles. Daylight saving time is in effect from early April to late October.

Useful Telephone Numbers For information on road conditions in the Taos area, call the state police at **505/758-8878** or dial **800/432-4269** (within New Mexico) for the state highway department. Taos County offices are at **505/758-8834.**

12 Taos Accommodations

Taos has some 1,450 rooms in 60 hotels, motels, condominiums, and bed-and-breakfasts. Most of the hotels and motels are located on Paseo del Pueblo Sur and Norte, with a few scattered just east of the town center along Kit Carson Road. The condos and bed-and-breakfasts are generally scattered throughout Taos's back streets.

During peak seasons, visitors without reservations may have difficulty trying to find a vacant room. **Taos Central Reservations,** P.O. Box 1713, Taos, NM 87571 (☎ **800/821-2437** or 505/758-9767), might be able to help.

There are another 400 or so rooms in 15 condo/lodges at or near the Taos Ski Valley. The **Taos Valley Resort Association,** P.O. Box 85, Taos Ski Valley, NM 87525 (☎ **800/776-1111** or 505/776-2233; fax 505/776-8842), can book these as well as more than 1,300 rooms in Taos, and unadvertised condominium vacancies. The World Wide Web address for Taos Valley Resort Association is http://taoswebb.com/nmusa/nmResv. If you'd rather e-mail for a reservation, the address is res@taoswebb.com.

Some three dozen bed-and-breakfasts are listed with the Taos Chamber of Commerce. The **Taos Bed and Breakfast Association** (☎ **800/876-7857** or 505/758-4747), with strict guidelines for membership, will provide information and make reservations for member homes.

And **Affordable Meetings & Accommodations,** P.O. Box 1258, Taos, NM 87571 (☎ **800/290-5384** or 505/751-1292), will help you find accommodations from bed-and-breakfasts to home rentals, hotels, and cabins throughout Taos and northern New Mexico. They'll also help you arrange rental cars and reservations for outdoor activities such as white-water rafting, horseback riding, fishing/hunting trips, and ski packages.

Unlike Santa Fe, there are two high seasons in Taos: winter (the Christmas-to-Easter ski season) and summer. Spring and fall are shoulder seasons, often with lower rates. The period between Easter and Memorial Day is notoriously slow in the tourist industry here, and many restaurants and other businesses take their annual vacations at this time. Book well ahead for ski holiday periods (especially Christmas) and for the annual arts festivals (late May to mid-June and late September to early October).

In these listings, the following categories have been used to describe peak-season prices for a double: **Expensive** applies to accommodations that charge over $100 per night; **Moderate** refers to $75 to $100; and **Inexpensive** indicates $75 and under. A tax of

11.38% in Taos town and 9.8125% in Taos County will be added to every hotel bill.

1   Best Bets

- **Best Historic Hotel: The Historic Taos Inn,** 125 Paseo del Pueblo Norte (☎ 505/758-2233), was once home to Taos's first doctor. It was also the first place in town to install indoor plumbing. Today, though the inn maintains much of its historic detail, it is equipped with all modern conveniences. It appears on both the State and National Registers of Historic Places.
- **Best for Families:** Without doubt, Taos's best full-service hotel for families is the **Best Western Kachina Lodge de Taos,** 413 Paseo del Pueblo Norte (☎ **505/758-2275**). The room prices are manageable, the location is excellent, there's an outdoor pool where kids can cool off during the summer, snack machines are helpful when Mom and Dad just don't feel like taking the car out again, and there are laundry facilities on the premises.
- **Best Moderately Priced Hotel:** For rooms in this category (that are not bed-and-breakfasts), you're best off with one of the chain hotels. The **Holiday Inn Don Fernando de Taos,** Paseo del Pueblo Sur (☎ **505/758-4444**) and **Rancho Ramada,** 615 Paseo del Pueblo Sur (☎ **505/758-2900**) are both good bets. You'll get large rooms, full-service restaurants, and swimming pools at both locations.
- **Best Bed-and-Breakfast:** In my opinion, the best bed-and-breakfast in Taos is the **Adobe and Pines Inn,** Box 837, Ranchos de Taos, NM 87557 (☎ **505/751-0947**). The rooms are beautiful and creatively decorated, hosts Chuck and Charil Fulkerson are more than gracious, and the atmosphere is warm and welcoming.
- **Best Modern Adobe Architecture:** While you'll find many bed-and-breakfasts in New Mexico in historic or old buildings that were constructed of true adobe bricks, you'd be hard pressed to find new, modern buildings using the same materials. **Little Tree Bed and Breakfast,** P.O. Box 960, El Prado, NM 87529 (☎ **505/776-8467**) is a beautiful, adobe inn. Even inside, you can see pieces of straw and mica in the walls.
- **Best Location for Skiers:** The **Inn at Snakedance,** P.O. Box 89, Taos Ski Valley, NM 87525 (☎ **505/776-2277**) is a modern hotel with ski-in/ski-out privileges.

2   The Taos Area

In addition to the hotels listed below, a brand-new luxury hotel, the **Fechin Inn** (227 Paseo del Pueblo Norte, Taos, NM 87571), was about to open at press time; it appears to be quite spectacular. Named for famed Russian artist, Nicolai Fechin, the hotel boasts beautiful handcarved ornamented doors, staircase, and reception desk. There will be a bar and lounge, an exercise room, an outdoor hot tub, and guest quarters that feature all the amenities you'd expect to find in a luxury hotel. For information and rates call **800/811-2939** or 505/751-1000.

EXPENSIVE

HOTELS/MOTELS

The Historic Taos Inn

125 Paseo del Pueblo Norte, Taos, NM 87571. ☎ **800/TAOS-INN** or 505/758-2233. Fax 505/758-5776. 37 rms. TEL. $85–$225 double, depending on the type of room and season. AE, DC, MC, V.

The last century of Taos history is alive and well within the walls of this atmospheric inn. It is made up of several separate adobe houses dating from the mid-1800s that surrounded a small plaza complete with communal town well. Dr. Thomas Paul Martin, the town's first (and for many years only) physician, purchased the complex in 1895. In 1936, a year after the doctor's death, his widow, Helen, enclosed the plaza—now the inn's magnificent two-story lobby—installed indoor plumbing (the first in Taos!) and opened the Hotel Martin. In 1981–82 the inn was restored; it's now listed on both the State and National Registers of Historic Places. Guests today find an inn of hospitality and charm, combining 20th-century elegance with 19th-century ambience. Interior balconies in the lobby overlook the old town well, now a tiered fountain. Above it rises a stained-glass cupola. Large ceiling vigas, hand-woven rugs, and outstanding artwork add to the atmosphere, and visitors can relax in Taos-style bancos facing a sunken Pueblo-style fireplace in one corner of the room.

No two guest rooms are alike. While all are furnished in regional style, they differ in size, shape, and craft items, giving each a distinct personality. Locally crafted Taos-style furniture, Spanish colonial antiques, and original Native American, Hispanic, and New Mexican artwork decorate the interiors. All rooms feature custom hand-loomed bedspreads and 30 have fireplaces.

Dining/Entertainment: Doc Martin's, with good southwestern cuisine, is one of Taos's leading dining establishments (see Chapter 13). The **Adobe Bar,** popular among Taos artists and other locals, offers live entertainment on certain weeknights as well as a full bar menu for light lunch or dinner, snacks, margaritas, and an espresso-dessert menu.

Services: Room service is available.

Facilities: Rooms for nonsmokers and travelers with disabilities; seasonal outdoor swimming pool, year-round Jacuzzi in greenhouse.

Quail Ridge Inn

Ski Valley Rd. (P.O. Box 707), Taos, NM 87571. ☎ **800/624-4448** or 505/776-2211. Fax 505/776-2949. 110 rms and suites. TV TEL. $75–$135 single or double; $170–$350 suite. Rates depend on season; 3% gratuity added to all rates. Extra person $10; children under 18 stay free in parents' room. DC, MC, V.

This sports-oriented Pueblo-style lodge bills itself as a family resort and conference center. Tennis and skiing are popular at this hotel, which spreads across several acres of open sagebrush about 4 miles north of Taos and 14 miles away from the ski valley.

Four types of rooms are available at the Quail Ridge Inn, which won an award from *Western Home* magazine for architect Antoine Predock when it opened in 1978. The smallest are "hotel rooms," which can each sleep four (two on a queen-size bed and two on a queen-size sleeper sofa). Next are studios, which are actually semisuites with full kitchens and patios or balconies. One-bedroom suites, the most popular accommodations, each consist of a studio with a connecting hotel room. Half a dozen separate casitas contain spacious two-bedroom suites. There are also two-bedroom suites that are made up of a studio and two connecting hotel rooms.

Every room, no matter what its size, has a fireplace, huge closets, and full shower/baths. Kitchenettes are fully stocked and each includes a stove, refrigerator, microwave oven, and dishwasher. The decor is breezy southwestern with light woods, dried-flower arrangements in handcrafted pottery, and various pieces of local art and artifacts.

Dining/Entertainment: The new **Renegade Cafe Bar and Grill** (☎ 505/776-1777) features Italian and southwestern specialties and is open daily for breakfast, lunch, and dinner (during the off season, the hours vary).

Facilities: Rooms for nonsmokers; year-round heated swimming pool, hot tubs and saunas, six outdoor and two indoor tennis courts, two racquetball and one squash court, summer volleyball pit, fitness center with weights and exercise room; coin-op laundry.

BED-AND-BREAKFASTS

✪ Adobe & Pines Inn

NM 68 (Box 837), Ranchos de Taos, NM 87557. ☎ **800/723-8267** or 505/751-0947. Fax 505/758-8423. 5 rms, 2 casitas. TV. $95–$150 double. Rates include breakfast. MC, V.

After traveling for some time in Europe, owners, Chuck and Charil Fulkerson, decided to open a bed-and-breakfast inn. The only problem was they didn't quite know where—until they happened to come to Taos and fell in love with what, after six months of renovation, is now the Adobe & Pines Inn. It's located directly off NM 68, just about 0.3 miles south of St. Francis Plaza. If you're driving from Santa Fe, look for the multicolored posts that mark the driveway on your right.

As you drive down to the house you'll be awed by the 80-foot long Grand Portal. The inn is a 150-year-old adobe home that is now one of the most beautiful and peaceful guesthouses I have ever stayed in. It rests amid pine and fruit trees on sacred land (the Native Americans once stopped here to pray for a good hunt on their way to the hunting grounds, and again on their way back to thank the gods for their successes). Each room has a private entrance, all have fireplaces (three even have a fireplace in the bathroom), and each is uniquely decorated. Puerta Azul is a wonderful, cozy room with an antique writing desk and royal-blue accents. Puerta Verde, done in deep greens, has a lovely old retablo (ask Chuck and Charil about it), a sitting area, and a queen-size canopy bed. Puerta Turquese, my favorite, is a separate guest cottage with a full kitchen. The "broken tile mosaic" floor, laid 100 years ago by a man who did only a select few in the whole town of Taos, runs throughout Puerta Turquese. The colors (turquoise, yellow, maroon, black, and peach) in the floor have been picked up in the rest of the decor. In Puerta Turquese you can relax in front of a fire either in bed or in a jet whirlpool bath. Two newer rooms, Puerta Violetta (the only second-story room, with a spectacular view of the Taos sky through a picture window at the foot of the bed and an outdoor patio) and Puerta Rosa (with a two-person soaking tub, cedar sauna, fireplaced bathroom, and a unique wrought-iron bed designed by Charil), are welcome competition for Puerta Turquese. Chuck and Charil have once again outdone themselves with the addition of two new casitas.

In the evening, Chuck, Charil, Rascal (their dog), and guests often gather in front of a roaring fire in the living room, which is decorated with local art (for sale). Morning brings a delicious full breakfast in front of the fire (in winter) in the glassed-in breakfast room. Chuck and Charil are most gracious hosts; they will help you plan activities to suit your interests and will even help you with dinner reservations. If I could give this place two stars I would!

✪ Casa de las Chimeneas

405 Cordoba Lane at Los Pandos Road (Box 5303), Taos, NM 87571. ☎ **505/758-4777**. Fax 505/758-3976. 4 rms, 1 suite. TV TEL. $125–$140 double; $150 suite (for two). Rates include breakfast. MC, V.

This qualifies as one of Taos's few luxury B&Bs. Its four rooms, each with a work of art and with a private entrance, look out on a beautifully landscaped private garden. The two-room suite includes an old library and two fireplaces; it's furnished with marble-topped antiques, a comfortable reading couch, a bentwood rocker, and a game table complete with chess and backgammon. Lace-trimmed bed linens cover a sheepskin mattress. The Blue Room and Willow Room have similar charm. The new Garden Room has a separate entrance off the herb, vegetable, and rose garden and features a fireplace as well as a skylit bathroom with an extra-deep soaking tub and shower. Original art and hand-quilted spreads hang throughout and are for sale. Room minirefrigerators are stocked with complimentary soft drinks, juices, and mineral water. Bathrobes are supplied in each room. A full gourmet breakfast as well as complimentary afternoon hors d'oeuvres are served daily. Massages are offered on the premises for an additional charge. There is a large hot tub in a courtyard. Smoking is not permitted.

MODERATE

Best Western Kachina Lodge de Taos

413 Paseo del Pueblo Norte (P.O. Box NN), Taos, NM 87571. ☎ **800/522-4462** or 505/ 758-2275. Fax 505/758-9207. 118 rms, 4 suites. A/C TV TEL. $85–$125 double. Extra person $8; children under 12 stay free in parents' room. AE, DC, DISC, MC, V.

A Pueblo-style motel with bright blue trim, this long-established lodge is an art lover's dream. The art gallery, which connects the lobby with the lodge's restaurants, displays paintings and other works from the Taos Gallery. The Navajo Living Room, a comfortable space for indoor games or fireside reading, is filled with valuable antique Navajo rugs. The varied guest rooms are each appointed with custom-made Taoseño furniture, including armoire, headboards, table, and chairs. Many are furnished with a couch or love seat; all feature huge bathrooms and a second sink at the vanity in an outer dressing area.

The **Hopi Dining Room** offers a family-style menu. The **Kiva Coffee House** serves filling breakfasts and Mexican-style lunches. The **Zuni Lounge** is open nightly, and the **Kachina Cabaret** (see Chapter 14) books big-name acts. A Taos Pueblo dance troupe performs nightly in summer. No pets are allowed.

There is a guest services desk (in summer) and the hotel van provides shuttle service. There are rooms for nonsmokers, an outdoor swimming pool, indoor hot tub, coin-op laundry, and a ski shop on the premises.

Holiday Inn Don Fernando de Taos

Paseo del Pueblo Sur (P.O. Drawer V), Taos, NM 87571. ☎ **800/759-2736** or 505/758-4444. Fax 505/758-0055. 124 rms, 26 suites. A/C TV TEL. $94–$110 double; $110–$149 suite. Rates depend on season; Christmas season rates higher. Extra person $10; children 19 and under stay free in parents' room. AE, CB, DC, DISC, JCB, MC, V.

Taos's newest major hotel (opened in 1989 is like a modern Pueblo village spread across landscaped grounds on the south side of town. Half a dozen adobe-style two-story building clusters, each named for a noted New Mexico artist, surround private courtyards. Standard rooms, appointed in a soft Southwest-motif decor with Pueblo paintings on the walls, each feature handcarved New Mexican wood furnishings, two double beds (or a king-size bed and sleeper sofa), and a special doorside niche for skis and boots. Each suite offers a sitting room, fireplace, and minirefrigerator.

Don Fernando's Restaurant serves a variety of regional breakfasts, lunches, and dinners. **Fernando's Hideaway** lounge, built around a large adobe fireplace, presents live entertainment and features a large hors d'oeuvres buffet.

The hotel offers room service, valet laundry, courtesy van, 24-hour desk, rooms for nonsmokers and the disabled, outdoor swimming pool, hot tub, and tennis court.

Central Taos Accommodations

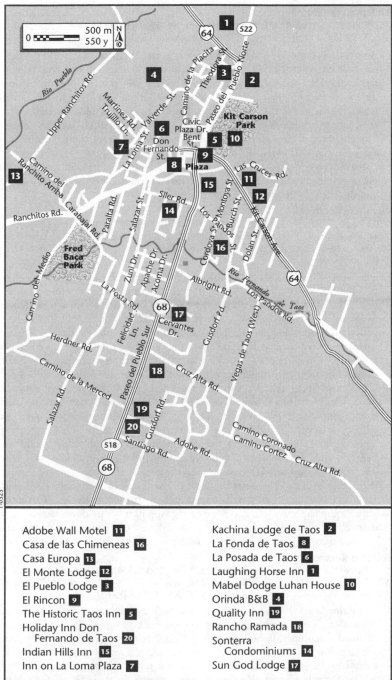

La Fonda de Taos

South Plaza (P.O. Box 1447), Taos, NM 87571. ☎ **800/833-2211** or 505/758-2211. Fax 505/758-8508. 24 rms, 3 suites. A/C TEL. $80 double; $120 suite. AE, MC, V.

An old-time, family owned hotel, La Fonda hosted many of Taos's most glamorous guests in the 1940s, 1950s, and 1960s. The only lodging on the Plaza, La Fonda has frankly seen better days. Today it's most often visited by drop-ins who want to see owner Saki Karavas's fine art collection (including Old West–style paintings), which is exhibited in the heavy-beamed lobby. Ten original nudes by author D. H. Lawrence are sealed away in a private room for viewing by special request; Lawrence brought them to Taos when they were banned in England, along with his novel *Lady Chatterley's Lover*, in 1929.

Rooms, gaily decorated with red carpets and blue trim, are equipped with double or twin beds. Furnishings include dressers and desks; local phone calls are free; and there is a TV room on the mezzanine.

Neon Cactus Hotel

1523 Paseo del Pueblo Sur (P.O. Box 5702), Taos, NM 87571. ☎ **800/299-1258** or 505/751-1258. 4 rms. A/C. Jan, Apr–June, and Sept–Dec 18, $65–$85 double; $105 quad. Rest of the year, $85–$125 double; $125–$145 quad. Rates include continental breakfast. AE, CB, DISC, MC, V.

The Neon Cactus is a delightful change of pace from some of the other hotels and bed-and-breakfasts in New Mexico. You won't find any hint of southwestern decor; each guest room here pays homage to a film star. For instance, there is the Marilyn Monroe Room; done mainly in black and white, it is decorated with authentic period furnishings and photographs that document the "many moods of Marilyn." There is a queen-size bed and a pull-out couch, making this room large enough for four. The bathroom here is something to behold: It features a Roman-style oversize sunken tub complete with bubble bath. Another room—the Rita Hayworth Room, is decorated in rich reds, has two queen-size beds, and features an inviting reading nook. The Hayworth Room adjoins the Casablanca Room (the Hayworth Room may be rented on its own, but the Casablanca Room must be rented in conjunction with the Hayworth), which is my favorite room. It is filled with Oriental rugs, tapestries, and pillows, but the best part is the built-in Turkish-style curtained twin bed. It is situated a couple of feet above the floor and is surrounded by bookshelves. The reading lamp invites guests to climb into bed, close the curtains, and read themselves to sleep. The other two rooms, the James Dean Room and the Billie Holiday Room, are equally well thought-out. Each room is stocked with biographies of the respective star, and there's a growing film library downstairs in the art deco sitting room. All rooms feature private decks; a Jacuzzi is available for guest use; and discount rates are offered at the adjacent Taos Spa.

Rancho Ramada

615 Paseo del Pueblo Sur, Taos, NM 87571. ☎ **800/RAMADA** or 505/758-2900. Fax 505/758-1662. 124 rms. A/C TV TEL. $84–$105 double. Rollaway $15 extra. Children under 18 stay free in parents' room. AE, CB, DC, DISC, MC, V. Free parking.

The Ramada is a large adobe-style building with a traditional bell tower. Each spacious room is equipped with a king-size bed (or two queen-size beds) and other standard furnishings, including a vanity table. Each suite consists of a living room with a pull-out couch, a gaslight kiva-style fireplace, a full bath, and a full-size bedroom (two beds) with a full bath. Each room can be entered separately.

The **Fireside Cantina Restaurant and Lounge,** located just off the lobby, is open daily for breakfast, lunch, and dinner. On Friday and Saturday evenings there's live entertainment in the fireside cantina.

The hotel offers limited room service, valet laundry (Monday through Friday), rooms for nonsmokers and travelers with disabilities, indoor swimming pool, Jacuzzi, sundeck, and gift shop.

At press time the hotel had just completed a renovation.

Sagebrush Inn

Paseo del Pueblo Sur (P.O. Box 557), Taos, NM 87571. ☎ **800/428-3626** or 505/758-2254. Fax 505/758-5077. 68 rms, 32 suites. A/C TV TEL. $70–$95 standard double; $90–$110 deluxe double; $95–$115 minisuite; $105–$140 executive suite. Extra person $10. Children under 12 stay free in parents' room. Rates include breakfast. AE, CB, DC, DISC, MC, V. Free parking.

Located about 3 miles south of Taos Plaza, this Pueblo Mission–style hotel (built in 1929) was originally called the Chamisa Inn. About 10 years after it opened, Georgia O'Keeffe came here to live and work for 10 months in a third-story room.

Most of the rooms face either an open grass courtyard or the outdoor swimming pool. Traditional viga ceilings are complemented by earth tones and standard furnishings. The suites in "Sagebrush Village" are outfitted with kiva fireplaces and beautiful handcarved furniture. Each has a king-size bed in the bedroom, a Murphy bed in the main living area, two full baths, and charcoal drawings of local Native Americans on the walls. In 1996 the hotel added 20 new deluxe units. If you decide to stay here, be aware that you're paying for the hotel's history—not its amenities.

Los Vaqueros Room is open for dinner daily. A complimentary full breakfast is served to guests daily in the **Sagebrush Dining Room.** The lobby bar is one of Taos's most active nightspots for live music and dancing (see Chapter 14).

The hotel provides a courtesy van, and it has a swimming pool, hot tub, and tennis courts.

✪ Sonterra Condominiums

206 Siler Rd. (P.O. Box 5244), Taos, NM 87571. ☎ **505/758-7989.** 9 suites. TV TEL. $49–$119 per day single or double, depending on the season. Extra person $10. AE, MC, V.

This pleasant and secluded complex is located four blocks from the Plaza. Surrounded by a high adobe wall and a cedar or latilla fence, these one-story, Pueblo-style condos face a central garden courtyard with a graceful Mexican fountain. Every unit has a well-stocked full kitchen, with a refrigerator, four-burner stove, microwave oven, and coffee-maker. Each has a private outdoor patio. Three have fireplaces, for which a complimentary firelog is provided. Regional art, from paintings to Taos-style drums employed as night tables, makes each room a bit different. Pets are not allowed. Facilities include a hot tub and solar-paneled guest laundry. Daily maid service is available for an extra charge.

BED-AND-BREAKFASTS

Casa Europa

840 Upper Ranchitos Rd. (HC 68, Box 3F), Taos, NM 87571. ☎ **505/758-9798.** 6 rms. $70–$135 double. Extra person $20. Rates include full breakfast and evening hors d'oeuvres or European pastries. AE, MC, V.

This cream-colored Territorial-style adobe (just 1¾ miles west of the Plaza) rests under giant cottonwoods, is surrounded by open pastures dotted with grazing horses, and offers lovely views of the mountains in the distance. Some rooms here date from the 1700s; however, a 1983 renovation made this a contemporary two-story luxury inn. Elegant rooms, each with a fireplace, sitting area, and full bath (two have two-person hot tubs and one has a whirlpool bath), vary in their furnishings.

Regional artwork in the rooms can be purchased. There's a common sitting room for reading and/or conversation, where coffee and pastries are offered each day between 3 and 4pm; during ski season hors d'oeuvres are served from 5 to 6pm. A full gourmet breakfast (specialties include cheese blintzes with a warm strawberry sauce and vegetarian eggs benedict) is served each morning in the formal dining room. In-room massages are available at an extra charge. Smoking is not permitted.

El Rincon Inn: An Historic Bed & Breakfast

114 Kit Carson Rd., Taos, NM 87571. ☎ **505/758-4874.** 16 rms. TV. $59–$125 double. Rates include continental breakfast. AE, DISC, MC, V.

Across the street from the Kit Carson Home and Museum of the West (see Chapter 14) is the former home of 19th-century cultural leader La Doña Luz Lucero de Martinez. The inn comprises two dwellings separated by a flower-filled courtyard where breakfast is served in warm weather. Fine art and handcarved furnishings representing the three cultures of Taos (Indian, Spanish, and Anglo) are scattered through both houses. Innkeepers Nina Meyers and Paul Castillo have created an incredibly pleasant and interesting environment in El Rincon. Paul spent a great deal of time working in a room known as the Rainbow Room, where he painted the ceiling latillas in an array of pastel shades, just as his grandfather once did for the famed Mabel Dodge Luhan. Nina, herself an artist, has a wonderful decorative sense which shows in all the rooms. Adjacent to the bed-and-breakfast is the Original Trading Post of Taos where visitors and guests can purchase all sorts of wondrous Native American craft items.

Hacienda del Sol

109 Mabel Dodge Lane (P.O. Box 177), Taos, NM 87571. ☎ **505/758-0287.** 9 rms. $90–$130 double. MC, V.

Not far from the Plaza on the north side of Taos, Hacienda del Sol is a lovely, quiet bed-and-breakfast in a surprising location—directly behind the Lottaburger. Housed within the main building is the original 190-year-old adobe structure, easily recognized by its low ceilings and Pueblo doorways. Like many of the homes in Taos, Hacienda del Sol has a wonderful history. The home was once owned by art patroness Mabel Dodge Luhan, and it was here that author Frank Waters wrote *The People of the Valley*. On the far side of the inn's well-manicured grounds is the adjoining Taos Pueblo. All of the guest rooms are constructed of adobe, and many of them feature kiva fireplaces built by Carmen Velarde, New Mexico's most sought-after kiva fireplace artist. Each room is furnished with handcrafted southwestern-style furnishings, antiques, and original art (for sale). Down comforters, clock radios with tape decks and a selection of cassettes, refrigerators, terry-cloth robes, and private baths (each supplied with a basket of items you might have forgotten to bring with you) are added luxuries here. The spacious Sala del Don, located in the main building, was once Tony Luhan's room; it features a beautiful screen hand-crafted by Lydia Garcia. The casita is a separate building, housing three guest rooms that can be rented separately or as a unit. These rooms have fireplaces and great mountain views through French doors. Los Amantes ("The Lovers") is indeed for lovers—the two-person black Jacuzzi, situated on a mahogany platform directly beneath a skylight, is the perfect place to spend a romantic evening of stargazing. One room even has a private steam room. A full breakfast might include buttery cinnamon apples and pumpkin pancakes with walnuts and warm maple syrup; or peach bread-pudding with blueberry sauce and a selection of fresh fruit. Refreshments are also served every evening from 5pm. An outdoor hot tub offering spectacular views of Taos Mountain is available for guest use in half-hour segments.

Hacienda del Sol is an excellent choice for those traveling with children—it's one of only a handful of bed-and-breakfasts that will accept children of any age.

Inn on La Loma Plaza

102 La Loma Plaza (P.O. Box 4159), Taos, NM 87571. ☎ **800/530-3040** or 505/758-1717. 7 rms. TV TEL. $95–$155 standard double; $170–$195 artist's studio; $150–$300 suite. Extra person $15. Discounts available. Rates include breakfast. AE, MC, V.

As you drive into the parking area, you'll see the Inn on La Loma Plaza perched atop a small hill. As you enter the reception area, your senses will be refreshed by the abundance of green plants and the slow, gurgling fountain. Local art (for sale) is displayed in the public areas of this comfortable and spacious adobe home (parts of which were built in the 1800s).

Each room is uniquely decorated, though all have the same amenities—such as bathrobes, fireplaces, fresh flowers, TVs, telephones, and queen- or king-size beds. Some rooms feature patios, and there are a couple of suites and artists' studios with kitchenettes. Cary's Studio—named for Cary Moore, a longtime resident of the home—has a full kitchenette and sleeps up to six. The Happy Trails Room, which is distinctly different from the other rooms, has wonderful pine paneling, a brass bed, and chaps and spurs hanging decoratively. A couple of the rooms offer incredible views of Taos Mountain. All of the furniture is handcrafted.

In the morning, a breakfast of fresh fruit, several kinds of juice, fresh breads, muffins, croissants, and a daily special hot item (perhaps a breakfast burrito with Jerry's special green chile) is served. In the early evening you'll find southwestern hors d'oeuvres or homemade cookies and coffee waiting for you to snack on while you're planning your evening.

La Posada de Taos

309 Juanita Lane (P.O. Box 1118), Taos, NM 87571. ☎ **800/645-4803** or 505/758-8164. 5 rms, 1 cottage. $80–$117 double. Extra person $15. Rates include breakfast. No credit cards.

There's room for 12 guests at La Posada de Taos, a secluded adobe inn, located just 2¹/₂ blocks from the Plaza. Now owned by Bill and Nancy Swan, who have recently completed an extensive renovation, La Posada was actually the first bed-and-breakfast in the town of Taos. There are five rooms and one self-contained honeymoon cottage, all of which have been charmingly decorated in a sort of Southwest/New England country style. International art and country pine antique furnishings predominate, and each room offers a private bath. La Casa de la Luna Miel, the cottage, has its own fireplace and a double bed in a loft with a skylight. The Beutler Room has a king-size bed, woodstove, and a Jacuzzi. Three other rooms also have a stove or fireplace. The sixth room has a queen-size bed, a small library, and a window that looks out to Taos Mountain. The Swans have recently added private patios for each of the rooms. A full breakfast is served in the dining room each morning, and during the day beverages and ice (from the much appreciated ice machine) are available.

✪ Little Tree Bed & Breakfast

P.O. Box 960, El Prado, NM 87529. ☎ **800/776334-8467** or 505/776-8467. 4 rms. $80–$105 double. Rates include breakfast. DISC, MC, V.

Little Tree is one of my favorite Taos bed-and-breakfasts, partly because it's located in a beautiful, secluded setting, and partly because it's constructed with real adobe—not stucco (used for most of the new buildings in the area). The Giddens, who call themselves "refugee Dallasites," came to New Mexico and fell in love with everything about this northern region, especially the architecture. When they decided to move to Taos, they began researching authentic adobe architecture and then developed a floor plan for their new home. They showed the plan to an architect and then, together with a couple of expert women adobe builders, began construction. (Interestingly, throughout history it has been women who built adobe homes because men felt that working with mud was too menial for them.)

The rooms are smallish, but charming and very cozy. They all have adobe floors, which are warm in the winter because radiant heat (which is healthier) has been installed there. All rooms feature queen-size beds, private baths, and access to the portal and courtyard garden, at the center of which is the "little tree" for which the inn is named. The Piñon and Juniper Rooms are equipped with fireplaces and private entrances. The Piñon and Aspen Rooms offer sunset views. The Spruce Room, which is western in feeling, is decorated with beautiful quilts.

In the main building, the living room has a traditional viga-and-latilla ceiling and tierra blanca adobe (adobe that's naturally white; if you look closely at it you can see little pieces of mica and straw). Two cats—Miss Kitty and Mister Mud—entertain, and the visiting hummingbirds enchant guests as they enjoy a healthy breakfast on the portal during warmer months. On arrival, guests are treated to refreshments.

Mabel Dodge Luhan House

240 Morada Lane (P.O. Box 3400), Taos, NM 87571. ☎ **800/84-MABEL** or 505/758-9456. 18 rms (13 with bath). $75–$150 double. Extra person $17.50. Rates include breakfast. MC, V.

This inn is also called "Las Palomas de Taos" because of the throngs of doves (palomas) that live in bird condominiums on the property. Like so many other free spirits, they were attracted by the flamboyant Mabel Dodge (1879–1962), who came to Taos in 1916. She and her fourth husband, a full-blooded Pueblo named Tony Luhan, enlarged this 200-year-old home to its present size of 22 rooms in the 1920s. The Spanish Colonial–style portal and flagstone placita are hidden behind an adobe wall and shaded by huge hardwood trees. All main rooms are decorated with viga ceilings, arched Pueblo-style doorways, handcarved Hispanic doors, kiva fireplaces, and dark hardwood floors. Guest rooms in the main building feature antique furnishings. Six have fireplaces; baths are either private or shared. Eight more guest rooms were recently added with the completion of a second building. All new accommodations are equipped with fireplaces. Many educational workshops are held here throughout the year, and so the rooms are often reserved for the participants. The Mabel Dodge Luhan House is now a National Historic Landmark.

Orinda B&B

461 Valverde St. (P.O. Box 4451), Taos, NM 87571. ☎ **800/847-1837** or 505/758-8561. 3 rms, 1 suite. $75–$85 double; $115 suite. Extra person $15. Rates include full breakfast. AE, MC, V.

This bed-and-breakfast has the delightful advantage of being both in town and in the country. Though only a 10-minute walk from the Plaza, it's tucked beneath huge trees with a view across pasture land to Taos Mountain. Thick adobe walls keep it warm in winter and cool in summer. Innkeepers Cary and George Pratt share their living room (including a TV, sound system, and wood-burning stove) with guests. Works by local artists adorn the walls of the dining room, where a hearty continental breakfast is served daily. The Vigil Suite is made up of a sitting room, with a fireplace and refrigerator, and two bedrooms (each of which has a private bath). The Truchas Room, with traditional southwestern decor, has a private entrance, fireplace, and bath. The inn is home to a cat, dog, and some llamas. Smoking is not permitted, and guests may not bring pets.

Salsa del Salto

P.O. Box 1468, El Prado, NM 87529. ☎ **800/530-3097** or 505/776-2422. Fax 505/776-2422. 10 rms (all with bath). $85–$160 double. Extra person $20. MC, V.

Situated between Taos town and the Taos Ski Valley, Salsa del Salto is a good choice for those seeking a secluded retreat not far from Taos's major tourist attractions. The rooms here are tastefully decorated with pastel shades in a southwestern motif, and the beds are covered with cozy down comforters. Each room offers views of the mountains or mesas of Taos, and the private bathrooms are modern and spacious. The Master's Room features a beautiful fireplace with copper detailing as well as a private door to a covered portal, and the Lobo Room faces Lobo Peak, one of the largest aspen stands in the Taos area. La Familia, made up of two connecting rooms, is, as its name suggests, ideal for families.

The focus here is on relaxation and outdoor activities. Innkeeper Mary Hockett, a native New Mexican and avid sportswoman, is extremely knowledgeable about the surrounding area. She's eager to share information about her favorite activities with her guests. Mary's husband, Dadou Mayer, who was born and raised in Nice, France, is an accomplished chef. Dadou has also been a member of the French National Ski Team and was recently named "The Fastest Chef in the United States" when he won the Grand Marnier Ski Race. Mayer has authored a cookbook, *Cuisine à Taos*, and has been a supervisor at the Ski School of Taos for more than 20 years. Salsa del Salto is the only bed-and-breakfast in Taos with a pool and hot tub as well as private tennis courts; it's certainly the only place in Taos where you'll be treated to a full gourmet breakfast whipped up by a true French chef. Mary bakes the muffins and breads, while Dadou creates such specialties as green chile and Brie omelets—all of which you can savor each morning in front of the massive fireplace. If you're at Salsa del Salto during the winter, you'll get the added bonus of an early morning briefing about ski conditions. In short, you'll want for nothing here.

INEXPENSIVE

Abominable Snowmansion Skiers' Hostel

Taos Ski Valley Rd., Arroyo Seco (P.O. Box 3271), Taos, NM 87571. ☎ **505/776-8298.** Fax 505/776-2107. 60 beds. $15.50–$55 per bed, depending on size of accommodation and season. Rates include full breakfast in winter. MC, V.

Located in the small community of Arroyo Seco, about 8 miles north of Taos and 10 miles from the Taos Ski Valley, this lodging attracts many young people. It's clean and comfortable for those who like the advantages of dormitory-style accommodations. Toilets, shower rooms, and dressing rooms are segregated by sex. A two-story lodge room features a circular fireplace as well as a piano and games area. Lodging is also offered in traditional teepees and smaller bunkhouses in the campfire area. Tent camping is permitted outside. Guests can either cook their own meals or indulge in home-cooked fare.

Adobe Wall Motel

227 E. Kit Carson Rd. (P.O. Box 1081), Taos, NM 87571. ☎ **505/758-3972.** 20 rms. TV. $56 double. Extra person $6; children under 12 stay free in parents' room. AE, MC, V.

Once a stagecoach stop, this motel offers cozy units featuring king- or queen-size beds, handmade Mexican furniture, and leather-upholstered chairs. All rooms are equipped with showers; some also have tubs. There are no private phones, but guests can use a pay phone in the lobby, where complimentary coffee, tea, soft drinks, and snacks are available. There are rooms for nonsmokers.

El Monte Lodge

317 Kit Carson Rd. (P.O. Box 22), Taos, NM 87571. ☎ **505/758-3171.** Fax 505/758-1536. 13 rms. TV TEL. $75–$125 double. Kitchenette units $10 extra. AE, DISC, MC, V.

Century-old cottonwood trees stand in a parklike picnic area, complete with barbecue grills and children's playground, outside this friendly 1930s motel. Four blocks east of the Plaza, El Monte is old-fashioned but homey, built in traditional adobe style with protruding vigas and framed by flower gardens. The rooms, many with fireplaces, occupy eight small buildings. The eclectic decor features a large amount of Pueblo art. Four rooms come with fully stocked kitchenettes; there's a free guest laundry. Pets are permitted for an extra $5.

El Pueblo Lodge

412 Paseo del Pueblo Norte (P.O. Box 92), Taos, NM 87571. ☎ **800/433-9612** or 505/758-8700. Fax 505/758-7321. 60 rms, 4 suites. TV TEL. $55–65 double; $58–$215 suite. Extra person $5–$10. Rates include continental breakfast. AE, DISC, MC, V.

The setting here is special: nicely landscaped $3^{1}/_{2}$-acre grounds, complete with cottonwood and towering fir trees, gardens, barbecue pits, and lawn furniture. Throw in a year-round outdoor swimming pool and hot tub, and it's no surprise that this lodge is popular with families. All the brightly colored rooms feature southwestern decor and refrigerators. There are also rooms with kitchenettes and fireplaces. Twelve new rooms were added to the property in 1996. Guests have free use of laundry facilities.

Indian Hills Inn

233 Paseo del Pueblo Sur (P.O. Box 1229), Taos, NM 87571. ☎ **800/444-2346** or 505/758-4293. 55 rms. A/C TV TEL. $59–$79 double. Rates include continental breakfast. AE, DISC, MC, V.

Just a short walk south of the Plaza, this stuccoed adobe-style building (home of "Taos's most unusual totem poles")—the Indian Hills Inn—has undergone a major facelift. Its well-lit units (which surround almost an acre of landscaped grounds) feature king- or queen-size beds, southwestern design furnishings, and cable TV. Local phone calls are free. Some rooms are equipped with kitchens; 30 have gas-log fireplaces. Behind the hotel are a swimming pool and picnic area with barbecues. There are three gift shops on premises.

⑤ Laughing Horse Inn

729 Paseo del Pueblo Norte (P.O. Box 4889), Taos, NM 87571. ☎ **800/776-0161** or 505/758-8350. 14 rms (3 with bath). TV. $49–$95 double; $98–$125 suite. AE, MC, V.

In 1924 a man named Spud Johnson bought the building now occupied by the Laughing Horse Inn (an unmistakable stucco structure with lilac-purple trim located just a mile north of the Plaza), whereupon he established a print shop known as "The Laughing Horse Press." Johnson was a central figure in the cultural development of Taos, and he often provided rooms to writers (for example, D. H. Lawrence) who needed a place to hang their hats. Today guests can choose between sunny dorm rooms, cozy private rooms, a deluxe solar-heated penthouse, or guesthouses. The private rooms feature sleeping lofts, cassette decks, TVs, VCRs, and some have fireplaces. Bathrooms are shared. The penthouse has a private solar bedroom and enclosed sleeping loft, a private bath, a woodstove, a big-screen TV, and video and audio decks. The guest houses include living rooms, fireplaces, private baths, and queen lofts; one has a full kitchen. The two guesthouses adjoin for large parties. The inn offers a common room around a big fireplace, a games room, a cafe

ⓘ Family-Friendly Hotels

Best Western Kachina Lodge de Taos *(see p. 143)* An outdoor swimming pool and snack machines in the summer here make a great late-afternoon diversion for hot, tired, and cranky kids.

El Pueblo Lodge *(see p. 150)* A slide, year-round swimming pool, and hot tub set on 3¹/₂ acres of land will please the kids; a barbecue, some minikitchens with microwave ovens, laundry facilities, and the rates will please their parents.

Quail Ridge Inn *(see p.140)* The year-round swimming pool and tennis courts will keep active kids busy during the day when it's time for a parent's siesta.

where continental breakfasts (not included in the rates) are served, and a refrigerator (which is stocked for use on the honor system). There's an outdoor hot tub, a masseuse (by appointment), and mountain bikes for guests' free use.

Quality Inn

1043 Camino del Pueblo Sur, Taos, NM 87571. ☎ **800/845-0648** or 505/758-2200. Fax 505/758-9009. 99 rms. 2 suites. A/C TV TEL. $55–$109 single or double; $115–$179 suite. Extra person $7. Children under 18 stay free in parents' room. Rates include continental breakfast. AE, CB, DC, DISC, EU, JCB, MC, V.

This Quality Inn is closer to Carson National Forest (a short trek east) than to Taos Plaza (about 2 miles north). The rooms have nice decorative touches such as mirrors framed with copperwork and R. C. Gorman prints. There are 11 units with king-size beds; two suites offer kitchenettes, and some rooms have microwaves and minirefrigerators. There's a restaurant, lounge, and a heated outdoor swimming pool and hot tub.

Sun God Lodge

919 Paseo del Pueblo Sur (5513 NDCBU), Taos, NM 87571. ☎ **800/821-2437** or 505/758-3162. Fax 505/758-1716. 40 rms, 8 suites. TV TEL. $45–$95 single or double; $100–$140 casita. AE, MC, DISC, V.

An adobelike structure, this motel is set on 1¹/₂ acres of landscaped grounds. The rooms were recently redecorated in a southwestern style, all with ceiling fans, double, queen-, or king-size beds (and Navajo-patterned spreads), prints and lithographs by Taos artists on the walls, and complimentary bedside coffee service. There are some new accommodations with kitchenette areas (fully supplied with dishes and utensils, coffee-makers, and minirefrigerators) and living rooms with kiva fireplaces (wood and a fire-starter are supplied), remote-controlled TVs, and niches with howling coyotes or kachinas. Outdoor grills and a hot-tub room are available. Pets are allowed.

Taos Motel

1798 Paseo del Pueblo Sur (P.O. Box 729F), Ranchos de Taos, NM 87557. ☎ **800/323-6009** or 505/758-2524. Fax 505/758-1989. 28 rms. TV TEL. $34–$52 double. Children under 12 stay free in parents' room. DISC, MC, V.

Taos's southernmost motel is a Spanish Colonial–style building with spiral pillars and corbels and a red tile roof (it is about 3¹/₂ miles from the Plaza). The rooms are furnished with double beds and built-in desk/dressers; local phone calls are free. Complimentary coffee is served in the lobby every day from 7am to 11pm. The Taos RV Park, open all year, is located next door. Pets are welcome.

3 Taos Ski Valley

For information on the skiing and the facilities offered at Taos Ski Valley, see "Skiing" in Chapter 14.

EXPENSIVE

HOTELS

Hotel Edelweiss
P.O. Box 83, Taos Ski Valley, NM 87525. ☎ **800/I-LUV-SKI** or 505/776-2301. Fax 505/776-2533. 21 rms, 3 condos. A/C TV TEL. May–Oct, hotel room $69 double; condo $125 for up to six people. Ski season hotel room $170 double; condo $245 for up to six people. AE, MC, V.

This quiet, elegant hotel offers family-style accommodations right on the ski slopes. The large hotel rooms, which were recently redecorated, all offer either a queen- or king-size bed covered with a down comforter. Each of the two-bedroom/two-bathroom condominiums provides a fully equipped kitchen, living room with a fireplace, and a Jacuzzi tub in the master bathroom. There's French cuisine for breakfast and lunch, with après-ski coffees and pastries. An outdoor hot tub gazebo, indoor sauna, sundeck, and television (in the lounge) are available for guest use. There is also a masseuse on the premises.

Inn at Snakedance
P.O. Box 89, Taos Ski Valley, NM 87525. ☎ **800/322-9815** or 505/776-2277. Fax 505/776-1410. 60 rms. TV TEL. June 15–Sept 29, $75 double; Nov 27–Dec 20, $125 double; Dec 21–Dec 25, Jan 1–Jan 3, and Feb 8–Mar 29, $195 standard double; $215 fireplace double; Dec 26–Dec 31, $250 standard double, $270 fireplace double; Jan 4–Feb 7, $175 standard double, $195 fireplace double; Mar 30–Apr 5, $145 double. MC, V. Free parking at Taos Ski Valley parking lot.

Located in the heart of Taos Ski Valley, the Inn at Snakedance is the only modern hotel in the area that offers ski-in/ski-out privileges. The most attractive feature of this hotel is that it's literally only 10 yards from the ski lift, which means that you won't have to drag your skis, boots, and children onto a shuttle bus to reach the lift and you can ski right back to the hotel if you get cold or tired. The original structure that stood on this site (part of which has been restored for use today) was known as the Hondo Lodge. Before there was a Taos Ski Valley, Hondo Lodge served as a refuge for fishermen, hunters, and artists. Constructed from enormous pine timbers that had been cut for a copper mining operation in the 1890s, it was literally nothing more than a place for the men to bed down for the night. The Inn at Snakedance today offers comfortable guest rooms, many of which feature wood-burning fireplaces. All of the furnishings are modern, the decor is jade and maroon with floral-print draperies, and the windows (many of which offer mountain views) open to let in the fresh mountain air. All rooms provide cable TV, minirefrigerators and wet bars (not stocked), and bathrooms with standard shower/tubs and a separate vanity area. Some rooms adjoin, connecting a standard hotel room with a fireplace room—perfect for families. Smoking is prohibited in the guest rooms and most public areas. Children under 6 are not welcome.

Dining/Entertainment: The **Hondo Restaurant and Bar** offers dining and entertainment daily during the ski season (schedules vary off-season), and also sponsors wine tastings and wine dinners. Grilled items, salads, and snacks are available on an outdoor deck. The slopeside bar provides great views.

Services: Shuttle service to nearby hotels, shops, and restaurants.

Facilities: Minispa (with hot tub, sauna, exercise equipment, and massage facilities), massage therapist on site, in-house ski storage and boot dryers, convenience store (with food, sundries, video rental, and alcoholic beverages).

CONDOMINIUMS

Hacienda de Valdez
Ski Valley Rd. (Box 357), Arroyo Seco, NM 87514. ☎ **800/837-2218** or 505/776-2218. Fax 505/776-2218. 13 units. A/C TV TEL. Ski season $150–$300. May–Oct, $85–$145. Rates are based on four to six people per unit. AE, DISC, MC, V.

Located about 8 miles from the Ski Valley, these Pueblo-style luxury condo units come with fully equipped kitchens (including microwave ovens), fireplaces (firewood is provided), queen-size beds, and color TVs. There are outdoor hot tubs and daily maid service.

Kandahar Condominiums
P.O. Box 72, Taos Ski Valley, NM 87525. ☎ **800/7556-2226** or 505/776-2226. Fax 505/776-2481. 27 units. A/C TV TEL. May–Oct, $75–$120; ski season (four to six people per unit), $150–$350. AE, MC, V.

These condos have the highest location on the slopes—and with it, ski-in/ski-out access. Facilities include an exercise room, Jacuzzi, steam room, professional masseur, laundry, and conference/party facility. American Educational Institute seminars are held here each week during the season.

Sierra del Sol Condominiums
P.O. Box 84, Taos Ski Valley, NM 87525. ☎ **800/523-3954** or 505/776-2981. Fax 505/776-2347. 32 units. TV TEL. $125–$185. AE, DISC, MC, V.

Located just a two-minute walk from the lifts, these condo units offer fully equipped kitchens, fireplaces, and balconies. There are two hot tubs and saunas on the premises. Two-bedroom units sleep up to six; one-bedrooms and studios are also available.

Twining Condominiums
P.O. Box 696, Taos Ski Valley, NM 87525. ☎ **800/828-2472** or 505/776-8873. Fax 505/776-8873. 19 units. TV TEL. $95–$355 depending on the season and number of people. AE, DISC, MC, V.

Studios and two-bedroom units with lofts come with fireplaces, color TVs, and fully equipped kitchens (including dishwashers). There are also a hot tub and sauna. The main lift area is just a three-minute walk away.

MODERATE

LODGES & CONDOMINIUMS

Amizette Inn
Taos Ski Valley Rd. (P.O. Box 756), Taos Ski Valley, NM 87525. ☎ **800/446-8267** or 505/776-2451. 12 rms. A/C TV TEL. May–Oct, $55–$110 single or double; ski season, $95–$150 single or double. AE, CB, DC, DISC, MC, V.

Open year round, this lodge offers a hot tub and redwood sauna, tanning deck, and full-service restaurant. The spacious rooms with separate sitting areas that offer panoramic river and mountain views are perfect for a romantic getaway.

Austing Haus
Taos Ski Valley Rd. (P.O. Box 8), Taos Ski Valley, NM 87525. ☎ **800/748-2932** or 505/776-2649. Fax 505/776-8751. 53 rms. TV TEL. $49–$170 double. Rates include continental breakfast. CB, DC, DISC, MC, V.

About 1¹/₂ miles from the ski resort, the Austing Haus features a restaurant and hot tub. Guests have a choice of rooms, ranging from a standard hotel unit to luxury fireplace rooms with four-poster beds. Incidentally, this is the largest and tallest timber frame building in the United States.

Taos Mountain Lodge

Taos Ski Valley Rd. (P.O. Box 698), Taos Ski Valley, NM 87525. ☎ **800/530-8098** or 505/776-2229. Fax 505/776-2229. 10 suites. A/C TV TEL. May–Oct, $69–$79 suite; ski season (based on four to six people per unit), $138–$205 suite. AE, MC, V.

About 1 mile west of the valley these loft suites (which can accommodate up to four) provide queen-size beds, fully equipped kitchenettes (with microwave ovens), living rooms, and private spa rooms.

Thunderbird Lodge

P.O. Box 87, Taos Ski Valley, NM 87525. ☎ **800/776-2279** or 505/776-2280. Fax 505/776-2238. 32 rms. $99–$142 double. Seven-day Ski Week Package $1,080–$1,350 per adult, depending on season and type of accommodation. Seven-day Lodge Packages are also available. Rates include three meals. AE, MC, V.

Located 150 yards from the slopes on the north ("sunny") side of the valley, the Thunderbird's extras include a superb restaurant with a large wine cellar, an excellent Saturday-evening buffet, and nightly entertainment in the bar. International jazz stars are booked annually during early January. Seven-day Ski Week Packages include seven nights, 20 meals, six days of unlimited use of all ski lifts, six daily morning ski lessons, use of all lodge facilities, a weekly wine-tasting session, and two-step lessons. The lodge is equipped with saunas, Jacuzzi, and conference facilities. Twenty-four rooms in the main lodge each have a double and a single bed or a set of bunk beds. Eight rooms in the chalets are larger (including some family rooms) with king-size beds.

4 RV Parks & Campgrounds

Carson National Forest

P.O. Box 558, Taos, NM 87571. ☎ **505/758-6200.**

There are nine national forest campsites within 20 miles of Taos, all open from April or May until September or October, depending on snow conditions. For information on other public sites, contact the **Bureau of Land Management,** 224 Cruz Alta Rd., Taos, NM 87571 (☎ **505/758-8851**).

Enchanted Moon Campground

#7 Valle Escondido Rd. (on US 64 E.), Valle Escondido, NM 87571. ☎ **505/758-3338.** 69 sites. Full RV hookup, $17 per day. Closed Nov–mid-Apr.

Questa Lodge

Two blocks from NM 522 (P.O. Box 155), Questa, NM 87556. ☎ **505/586-0300.** 24 sites. Full RV hookup, $17 per day, $175 per month. Closed Nov–Apr.

Taos RV Park

Paseo del Pueblo Sur (P.O. Box 729), Ranchos de Taos, NM 87557. ☎ **800/323-6009** or 505/758-1667. Fax 505/758-1989. 29 spaces. $12 without RV hookup, $18 with RV hookup. Senior discounts are available.

Taos Valley RV Park and Campground

120 Estes Rd. off NM 68; 7204 NDCBU, Taos, NM 87571. ☎ 800/999-7571 or 505/758-4469. Fax 505/758-4469. 92 spaces. $14.50–$15.50 without RV hookup, $18.50–$22.50 with RV hookup. MC, V. Closed Nov 1–Mar 15.

13 Taos Dining

Restaurants in Taos are quite informal. Nowhere is a jacket and tie mandatory. In the winter you'll see diners in ski sweaters and blue jeans even at the finest restaurants. This informality doesn't extend to reservations, however; especially during the peak season, it is important to make reservations well in advance and keep them or else cancel.

In the listings below, **Expensive** refers to restaurants where most main courses are $15 or higher; **Moderate** includes those where main courses generally range from $10 to $15; and **Inexpensive** indicates that most main courses are $10 or less.

1 Expensive

Casa Cordova
Arroyo Seco, 8 miles north of town on NM 150. ☎ **505/776-2500.** Reservations recommended. Main courses $10.95–$21.95. Mon–Sat 6–10pm. CONTINENTAL.

The cozily elegant Casa Cordova comprises two softly lit dining rooms—both with working fireplaces—under log-beamed, rough-hewn ponderosa-pine ceilings. Romantically candlelit white-linen-covered tables are surrounded by whitewashed adobe walls hung with Navajo rugs and paintings by acclaimed Navajo artist R. C. Gorman. A big plus here is a lamp-lit piano bar, comfortably furnished with velvet upholstered sofas and armchairs, where a wonderfully talented pianist entertains Friday and Saturday nights. If you're here on a weekend, retreat to this simpatico lounge for dessert or after-dinner drinks.

Most of the seafood served here is farm-raised, and only free-range chickens, chemical-free beef, organic greens, and naturally fed veal are used. Moreover, this being Taos, chef Alan Kinner personally "blesses" each item as it leaves the kitchen. You might begin with an order of plump farm-raised oysters. A bowl of five pastas (which vary nightly), tossed with roasted garlic, chicken, and red chile butter is scrumptious. Main courses, such as pan-fried trout crusted with herbs and garlic, are served with soup, a baked potato or curried rice, a medley of five or six sautéed seasonal vegetables, and a basket of fresh-baked herb breads. Owners and genial hosts Johnny and Elaine Montano are always on hand to welcome guests; try Elaine's fresh-baked chocolate raspberry torte for dessert.

Doc Martin's
In the Historic Taos Inn, 125 Paseo del Pueblo Norte. ☎ **505/758-1977.** Reservations recommended. Main courses at breakfast $3.95–$7.50; at lunch

$4.50–$8.50; at dinner $15.50–$28, early diner's menu $12.95 per person. AE, DC, MC, V. Daily 8am–2:30pm and 5:30–9:30pm. CONTEMPORARY SOUTHWESTERN.

Doc Martin's restaurant comprises Dr. Thomas Paul Martin's former home, office, and delivery room. In 1912, painters Bert Philips (Doc's brother-in-law) and Ernest Blumenschein hatched the concept of the Taos Society of Artists in the Martin dining room. Art still predominates here, from paintings to cuisine. The food is widely acclaimed, and the wine list has received numerous "Awards of Excellence" from *Wine Spectator* magazine.

Breakfast might include the local favorites: huevos rancheros (fried eggs on a blue-corn tortilla smothered with chile and Jack cheese) or "The Kit Carson" (eggs benedict with a southwestern flair). Lunch might include a Pacific ahi tuna sandwich, Caesar salad, or for the heartier appetite, the northern New Mexican casserole (layers of blue-corn tortillas, pumpkin-seed mole, calabacitas, and Cheddar). For dinner appetizer, I'd recommend the salmon gravlax (with blue corn tortilla points, red chile aioli, red chile oil, capers, cilantro, and chives) or the chile relleno. This might be followed by sesame-crusted tuna mignon (served on a noodle cake with spicy eggplant sauce, tomato jam, house pickled ginger, and bok choy) or the Southwest lacquered duck (poached, roasted, and grilled duck breast served over julienne duck-leg meat and red-chile broth with posole and mango relish). If you still have room, there's always a nice selection of desserts—try Leroy's citrus cheesecake, a lemon, lime, and orange scented cheesecake perfected by baker Leroy Torres and served with an orange-tarragon sauce.

✪ Lambert's of Taos

309 Paseo del Pueblo Sur. ☎ **505/758-1009.** Reservations recommended. Main courses at lunch $5.50–$11.50, at dinner $8–$18.50. AE, DC, MC, V. Mon–Fri 11:30am–2pm; daily 6–9pm. CONTEMPORARY AMERICAN.

Zeke Lambert, a former San Francisco restaurateur who was head chef at Doc Martin's for four years, opened this fine dining establishment in late 1989 in the historic Randall Home near Los Pandos Road. Now, in simple but elegant surroundings, he presents a new and different menu every night.

At lunch start with the chile-dusted rock shrimp; they're a house specialty and they're great. I enjoyed the mandarin steak salad (mixed greens with a ginger vinaigrette, grilled steak with orange sauce served on fried wontons). It was served with just the right amount of vinaigrette, and the combined flavors of the steak, orange sauce, and ginger was perfect. For dinner I recommend the fresh dungeness crab cakes with Thai dipping sauce and pickled vegetables to start, followed by the pepper-crusted lamb (served with garlic pasta and a red wine demiglace). If you'd rather have something a bit lighter, try the grilled tuna served on braised Oriental greens with mashed yams. To accommodate different appetites, most main courses are offered in two sizes. For dessert the white chocolate ice cream and Zeke's chocolate mousse with raspberry sauce are outstanding. Espresso coffees, beers, dinner and dessert wines are available.

✪ Stakeout Grill & Bar

Stakeout Dr., just off NM 68. ☎ **505/758-2042.** Reservations recommended. Main courses $11.95–$25.95. AE, CB, DC, DISC, MC, V. Daily 5–10pm. CONTINENTAL.

I love this restaurant. Maybe it's because you have to drive about a mile up a dirt road toward the base of the Sangre de Cristo mountains, but once you get there (you'll think I'm insane for sending you up Stakeout Drive at night, and you'll think you're never going to get there) you'll have one of the greatest views of Taos (and the sunset). Or maybe it's because after you're inside, you're enveloped in the

Central Taos Dining

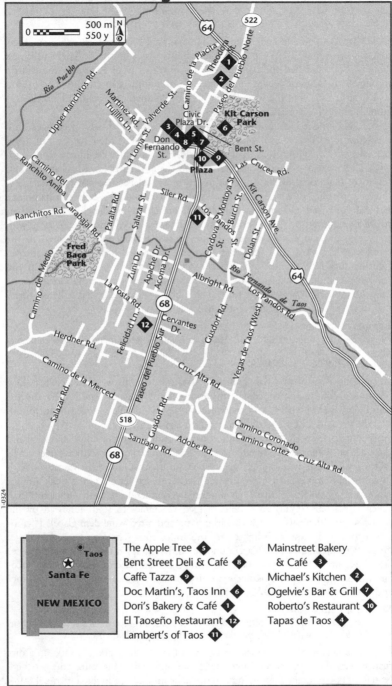

The Apple Tree ◆5
Bent Street Deli & Café ◆8
Caffè Tazza ◆9
Doc Martin's, Taos Inn ◆6
Dori's Bakery & Café ◆1
El Taoseño Restaurant ◆12
Lambert's of Taos ◆11

Mainstreet Bakery & Café ◆3
Michael's Kitchen ◆2
Ogelvie's Bar & Grill ◆7
Roberto's Restaurant ◆10
Tapas de Taos ◆4

158

warmth of its rustic decor (which is a great contrast to the almost-white exterior). There are paneled walls, creaking hardwood floors, and a crackling fireplace in the winter. The food, which focuses on steak and seafood, is marvelous. You can start with baked Brie with sliced almonds and apples or escargots baked with walnuts, herbs, white wine, and garlic. Move on to a wonderful filet mignon, served with béarnaise sauce and cooked to your liking or my favorite, duck Cumberland (half a duck roasted with apples and prunes and served with an orange-currant sauce); this dish is never fatty and always leaves you feeling satisfied. Among the seafood offerings are salmon, Alaskan king crab legs (steamed and served with drawn butter), scallops, and shrimp. Finish your meal with a fresh pastry and a cappuccino. You'll really be missing something if you don't get to Stakeout while you're in Taos. Try to time your reservation so you can see the spectacular sunset.

✪ Villa Fontana

NM 522, 5 miles north of Taos. ☎ **505/758-5800.** Reservations recommended. Main courses $19–$25. AE, CB, DC, DISC, JCB, MC, V. Lunch (June–Oct only) Mon–Sat 11:30am–2pm; dinner Mon–Sat 6–11pm. ITALIAN.

Carlo and Siobhan Gislimberti like to talk about "peccato di gola" (lust of the palate). The couple brought it with them to Taos when they left their home in the Italian Dolomites, near the Austrian border. They have their own herb garden, and Carlo, a master chef, is a member of the New Mexico Mycological Society—wild mushrooms play an important role in many of his kitchen preparations. Also something of an artist, Carlos displays his own works throughout the restaurant.

Meals are truly gourmet. Diners can start with scampi alla Veneziana (shrimp in a brandy Aurora sauce) or pâté ricco de fegatini alla moda (homemade chicken-liver pâté). Main courses include whole Dover sole with fresh herbs, pheasant breast with dried blueberries and demiglace, and grilled beef tenderloin with brandy, balsamic vinegar, and green peppercorns. Dinners are served with salad, fresh vegetables, and potatoes or rice. Outdoor dining in the summer offers pleasant mountain and valley views.

2 Moderate

The Apple Tree

123 Bent St. ☎ **505/758-1900.** Reservations recommended. Main courses at lunch $5.25–$9.95, at dinner $10.95–$18.95. CB, DC, DISC, MC, V. Mon–Fri 11:30am–3pm; light meals and snacks daily 3–5:30pm; daily 5:30–9pm. Brunch Sat 11:30am–3pm; Sun 10am–3pm. INTERNATIONAL.

Eclectic music pervades the four elegant adobe rooms of this fine restaurant, a block north of the Plaza. Original paintings by Taos masters overlook the candlelit service indoors. Outside, diners sit at wooden tables on a graveled courtyard beneath a spreading apple tree.

Daily specials supplement the regular international-accented menu. A very popular and excellent dish is mango chicken enchiladas (chicken simmered with onions and spices, layered between blue-corn tortillas with mango chutney, sour cream, and salsa fresca and smothered with green chile). There's also a Thai red curry (either vegetarian or with shrimp), chicken moutard (boneless, skinless breast of chicken sautéed with spinach in apple cider and served with a Dijon brandy cream sauce). The Apple Tree has an award-winning wine list, and the desserts are prepared fresh daily.

✪ Casa de Valdez

1401 South Santa Fe Rd. ☎ **505/758-8777.** Reservations recommended. Main courses $8.95–$18.95. AE, DC, DISC, MC, V. Mon–Tues and Thurs–Sat 11:30am–9:30pm; Sun 3:30–9:30pm. NEW MEXICAN.

Located 2¹/₂ miles south of the Plaza, Casa de Valdez has recently been renovated. The interior is warm and welcoming and the extremely friendly staff know many of their customers by name. The menu is predictable as far as New Mexican cuisine goes, with blue-corn enchiladas, bean burritos, and tamales. The chile rellenos are exceptionally good. You can also order spareribs, barbecued chicken, steak, and shrimp. Personally, I think the sopaipillas served at the Casa de Valdez are the best around—they practically melt in your mouth.

Jacquelina's Restaurant

1541 Paseo del Pueblo Sur. ☎ **505/751-0399.** Reservations recommended. Main courses $8.25–$14.95. AE, MC, V. Tues–Fri and Sun 11am–2pm; Tues–Sun 5–9pm. CREATIVE SOUTH-WESTERN.

The decor here isn't much to talk about, but the food is quite good. To start, I have enjoyed the grilled crabcakes with spicy black bean sauce, and I particularly liked the portobello mushrooms with polenta French fries (you should be aware that I'm a great fan of the combination of flavors and textures in the pairing of mushrooms and polenta). I also tried the southwestern-style spring rolls with a red bell pepper dipping sauce and was pleased. For a main course I would recommend the fresh salmon with sesame crust served with a Chinese special sauce or Jacquelina's signature dish—chipotle chile and honey-marinated pork tenderloin with roasted corn red chile. Southwestern specialties include a variety of burritos and fajitas as well as chile rellenos. In short, if you're not a fanatic about ambience, Jaquelina's will more than satisfy.

La Luna Ristorante

223 Paseo del Pueblo Sur. ☎ **505/751-0023.** Reservations recommended. Main courses $8.50–$12. MC, V. Daily 5–10pm (last order is taken at 10pm; restaurant closes at midnight). ITALIAN.

During the six years that I have been covering New Mexico as a travel writer, there have been at least four restaurants (including this one) at this location; I'm hoping that this restaurant will survive. The atmosphere is bright and colorful. Black-and-white squares have been painted in trompe l'oeil fashion on the floor to resemble tiles, and the walls, hung with interesting original works, are done in rich, warm tones. Outside, in front, there are several tables shaded by deep blue market umbrellas. The food is good. Start with the focaccia de patate (pizza bread drizzled with olive oil, topped with thin slices of potato, and spiced with rosemary leaves) or—if it's listed as a special—the Brie served with toast points and peach salsa. The restaurant offers several pizzas as well as a wide variety of pasta choices. The vegetarian lasagne was good, and I've also enjoyed the spaghetti alla carbonara (spaghetti with Italian bacon, peas, cream, and Parmesan cheese, finished with egg yolk). There are also a couple of meat dishes on the menu. The desserts change regularly, but tira misu is usually available.

Ogelvie's Bar & Grill

1031 East Plaza. ☎ **505/758-8866.** No reservations. Main courses $5.95–$9.50 at lunch, $8.50–$18.50 at dinner. AE, MC, V. Daily 11am–closing. INTERNATIONAL.

This is a casual restaurant with rich wood decor. Homemade soups, burgers and other sandwiches, and huevos (eggs) de casa Ogelvie's are hits on the lunch menu.

℗ Family-Friendly Restaurants

El Taoseño Restaurant *(see p. 162)*   The jukebox and games room will keep
the kids happy while you wait for tacos and enchiladas at low prices.
Casa de Valdez *(see p. 160)*   Parents will feel comfortable dining with children here, and the menu is simple enough to please even the pickiest of palates.

Dinner might include shrimp Hawaiian (jumbo shrimp and fresh vegetables simmered in teriyaki sauce and pineapple juice), fresh trout piñon (broiled in lemon
butter and pine nuts), steaks, and regional specialties (such as fajitas, burritos, and
enchiladas), as well as a few pasta dishes. A lively bar with an outdoor deck overlooks the Plaza.

✪ Trading Post Café
4179 Paseo del Pueblo Sur. Ranchos de Taos ☎ **505/758-5089.** No reservations. Menu items
$4–$17. AE, MC, V. Mon–Sat 11am–9:30pm. ITALIAN/INTERNATIONAL.

Without doubt, this is Taos's hottest new restaurant. In fact, it's so popular that it
has undergone several expansions in the last two years. As you enter this bright, airy
restaurant, to your right you'll see high metal stools surrounding a bar (where meals
can be taken). The bar itself encloses an open, exhibition kitchen. If you're dining
alone or just don't feel like waiting for a table, the bar is a fun place to sit. I like the
Trading Post's menu since it lists a nice variety of items without distinguishing
between appetizers and main courses. This small detail speaks volumes about the
restaurant. Although the focus is on the food, diners can feel comfortable here. You
can order whatever you want; if you feel like trying three appetizers and skipping
the main course, that's fine. The Caesar salad is traditional with an interesting
twist—garlic chips. I guarantee you've never had a Caesar salad this good. If you like
pasta you'll find a nice variety on the menu. The angel hair pasta with chicken, wild
mushrooms, and Gorgonzola cream is surprisingly light and flavorful. There's also
a fresh fish of the day. For dessert there are delicious tarts.

3 Inexpensive

⑤ Bent Street Deli & Cafe
120 Bent St. ☎ **505/758-5787.** Reservations recommended. Breakfast $1.25–$6; lunch
$2.50–$8; dinner $10–$16. MC, V. Mon–Sat 8am–9pm. DELI/INTERNATIONAL.

This popular cafe is a short block north of the Plaza. Outside, a flower box sur-
rounds sidewalk cafe–style seating beneath large blue-and-white umbrellas. Inside,
baskets and bottles of homemade jam provide a homey, country feel. The menu
features breakfast burritos and homemade granola in the morning; 18 deli sandwiches, plus a "create-your-own" column, for lunch. At dinner, the menu becomes
a bit more sophisticated with dishes such as beef tenderloin medallions served over
fettuccine with a chipotle, Fontina cream or roja shrimp (black tiger shrimp, red
chile, and jicama, cilantro, and corn relish). All dinner entrées are served with a
salad and freshly baked bread. There's heated patio dining in the winter. If you'd like
to grab a picnic to go, Bent Street Deli and Cafe offers carry-out service.

Caffè Tazza
122 Kit Carson Rd. ☎ **505/758-8706.** No reservations. All menu items under $10. No
credit cards. Daily 8am–6pm (to 10pm on performance nights). CAFE.

This cozy three-room cafe is a gathering spot for local community groups, artists, performers, and poets—in fact, it's home to SOMOS, the Society of the Muse of the Southwest. Plays, films, comedies, and musical performances are given here on weekends (and some weeknights in summer) in the cafe's main room. The walls are always hung with the works of local emerging artists who have not yet made it to the Taos gallery scene. Locals and tourists alike enjoy sitting in the cafe, taking in the scene or reading one of the assorted periodicals available while sipping a cappuccino or espresso. Of course, the food is also quite good. Soups, sandwiches, tamales, croissants, and pastries are all popular.

Dori's Cafe
402 Paseo del Pueblo Norte. ☎ **505/758-9222.** Breakfast and lunch $3.50–$7. MC, V. Mon–Sat 7am–2:30pm; brunch Sun 8am–1pm. AMERICAN/NORTHERN NEW MEXICAN.

This delightful find, next door to the Taos Post Office, is a gathering place for the Taos literary and artistic crowd. In fact, if you read John Nicholl's *Nirvana Blues,* you'll recognize the Prince Whales Cafe as Dori's. Twenty-four years ago, when Dori's opened, bagels were a mainstay on the menu, but they turned out to be a hard sell since no one in Taos had ever heard of a bagel before. Now it's a different story. Dori's regulars come here so often that they keep their own personal coffee mugs hanging above the kitchen doorway. The cafe also hosts changing art exhibits and musical performances by local artists. Breakfast burritos and "hash brown heaven" are popular in the morning, as are bagels, eggs, pancakes, and granola. In the afternoon the menu offers sandwiches, soups, salads, and pizzas. Pastries are homemade daily, and gourmet coffees are served all day. Beer and wine are also available.

El Taoseño Restaurant
819 South Santa Fe Rd. ☎ **505/758-4142.** Main courses $1.25–$11.95. MC, V. Mon–Sat 6am–10pm, Sun 6:30am–3pm. NEW MEXICAN/AMERICAN.

A long-established local diner, El Taoseño features a jukebox in the corner and local art (for sale) on the walls. There are daily specials such as barbecued chicken and Mexican plates; standard fare includes everything from huevos rancheros to enchiladas and tacos. Locals flock here for the breakfast burrito. A low-fat menu is also available.

Mainstreet Bakery & Cafe
Guadalupe Plaza, Camino de la Placita. ☎ **505/758-9610.** $4.95–$12.95. No credit cards. Daily 7:30am–9pm. NATURAL FOODS.

Located about 1 1/2 blocks west of the Plaza, this is one of Taos's biggest counterculture hangouts. The image is fostered by the health-conscious cuisine and the wide selection of newspapers, magazines, and other reading material presenting alternative life-styles. Coffee and pastries are served all day. At breakfast omelets, pancakes, French toast, and huevos rancheros are popular. The lunch menu focuses on sandwiches and pasta, but there are also several chicken dishes (like poulet Joelle, braised chicken breast with a mushroom-hazelnut cream sauce) and fish selections. In keeping with the spirit of good health promoted here, alcoholic beverages are not served, and smoking is not permitted.

✪ Michael's Kitchen
304 C Paseo del Pueblo Norte. ☎ **505/758-4178.** No reservations. Breakfast $1.55–$7.95; lunch $3.25–$9.50; dinner $2.45–$16.95. AE, DISC, MC, V. Daily 7am–8:30pm. NEW MEXICAN/AMERICAN.

A couple of blocks north of the Plaza is this eatery, a throwback to earlier days. Between its hardwood floor and viga ceiling are various knickknacks on posts, walls, and windows: a deer head here, a Tiffany lamp there, and several scattered antique woodstoves. Seating is at booths and tables. Meals, too, are old-fashioned, as far as quality and quantity for price. Breakfast dishes, including a large selection of pancakes and egg preparations (with names like the "Moofy," "Omelette Extraordinaire," and "Pancake Sandwich"), are served all day (because they're so good), as are luncheon sandwiches (including Philly cheesesteak, tuna melt, chile burger, and a veggie sandwich). One of my favorite lunch dishes is "Health Food," a double order of fries with red or green chile and cheese. Dinners range from veal Cordon Bleu to knockwurst and sauerkraut, plantation-fried chicken to enchiladas rancheros, fish and chips to New York steak. Michael's has its own excellent full-service bakery.

Roberto's Restaurant

122 Kit Carson Rd. ☎ **505/758-2434.** Reservations recommended. Main courses $9.45–$10.65. MC, V. Summer, Wed–Mon noon–2:30pm and 6–9pm. Winter, most weekends. NEW MEXICAN.

Hidden within a warren of art galleries opposite the Kit Carson Museum (see Chapter 14) is this local gem, which, for more than 25 years, has focused on authentic native dishes. Within this 160-year-old adobe building are three small high-ceilinged dining rooms, each with hardwood floors and a maximum of five tables; one room has a corner fireplace. Everyday dishes include tacos, enchiladas, tamales, and chile rellenos. All meals start with sopaipillas and come with homemade refried beans and chicos (dried kernels of corn). Beer and wine are the only alcoholic beverages served. Since Roberto is an avid skier, the restaurant's winter hours are unpredictable at best.

Tapas de Taos Cafe

136 Bent St. ☎ **505/758-9670.** No reservations. Tapas $3.95–$7.95; main courses $3.95–$12.95. MC, V. Lunch Mon–Fri 11:30am–3pm; dinner Mon–Sat 3–9:30pm; Sun 3–9pm. NEW MEXICAN/TAPAS.

If you're familiar with Mexican culture, you'll recognize the theme decor at Tapas de Taos Cafe; it represents the Mexican Day of the Dead (Dia de los Muertos). The rows of black skulls lining the walls of the dining room in this 300-year-old adobe may not be to everyone's liking, but they certainly are unique. The tapas menu is short but excellent; it includes such items as spicy Vietnamese fried calamari, pork-and-ginger potstickers, and a shrimp-and-vermicelli fritter. Other menu offerings include chile rellenos, fajitas, enchiladas, tacos, and chimichangas. A wide variety of coffees are available, including cafe macchiata, cappuccino, caffè latte, and espresso. Outdoor patio dining is available during the warmer months. There's also a kids' menu.

Wild & Natural Cafe

812 Paseo del Pueblo Norte. ☎ **505/751-0480.** Reservations accepted for parties of six or more. All menu items under $10. MC, V. Mon–Sat 7am–9pm. ORGANIC/VEGETARIAN.

When vegetarians are traveling, it's often difficult to find a place to eat (many restaurants provide a couple of vegan entrées on their menus), but in Taos the choice is easy. In fact, the Wild & Natural Cafe was voted "Natural Food Restaurant of the Year" by *New Mexico Naturally* in 1994. Lunch features soups, salads, sandwiches, veggie burgers, steamed vegetables, southwestern dishes, and low-fat daily specials. At dinner you might try the Thai peanut pasta, the East Indian plate, lemon-ginger squash, black bean enchiladas, or a steamed vegetable plate. There's an espresso bar, as well as organic wine, fresh vegetable juices, local beer, fruit smoothies, and dairy-free desserts. Take-out orders are available.

14 What to See & Do in Taos

With a history shaped by pre-Columbian civilization, Spanish colonialism, and the Wild West; outdoor activities that range from ballooning to world-class skiing; and a clustering of artists, writers, and musicians, Taos has something to offer almost everybody. Its pueblo is the most accessible in New Mexico, and its museums, including the new Van Vechten Lineberry Taos Art Museum, offer a world-class display of regional history and culture. (*Note:* If you would like to visit all seven museums that comprise the museum association of Taos—the Blumenschein Home, the Fechin Institute, Hacienda Martinez, Harwood Museum, Kit Carson Home and Museum, Millicent Rogers Museum, and the Van Vechten Lineberry Taos Art Museum—it might be worthwhile to purchase a combination ticket for $20.) Spectacular scenery embraces even those who prefer the comfort of a car.

SUGGESTED ITINERARIES

If You Have Only 1 Day

Spend at least two hours at the Taos Pueblo. You'll also have time to see the Millicent Rogers Museum and to browse in some of the town's fine art galleries. Try to make it to Ranchos de Taos to see the San Francisco de Asis Church.

If You Have 2 Days

Spend the first day as outlined above. On the second day, explore the Kit Carson Historic Museums—the Martinez Hacienda, the Kit Carson Home, and the Ernest L. Blumenschein Home. Then head out of town to enjoy the view from the Rio Grande Gorge Bridge.

If You Have 3 Days or More

Spend the first two days as outlined above. On your third day, drive the "Enchanted Circle" through Red River, Eagle Nest, and Angel Fire or head to the Van Vechten Lineberry Taos Art Museum. You may want to allow a full day for shopping or perhaps drive up to the Taos Ski Valley for a chairlift ride or a short hike. Of course, if you're here in the winter with skis, that's your first priority.

1 The Top Attractions

TAOS PUEBLO

No other site in Taos is as important or as famous. The community of 1,500—about 2¹/₂ miles north of the Plaza—comprises a world of its own. The northernmost of New Mexico's 19 pueblos, it has been the home of the Tiwa tribes for more than 900 years.

Two massive, multistoried adobe apartment buildings look much the same today as they did when a regiment from Coronado's expedition first saw them in 1540. Houses are built one upon another to form porches, balconies, and roofs reached by ancient ladders. The distinctive flowing lines of shaped mud, with a straw-and-mud exterior plaster, are typical of Pueblo architecture throughout the Southwest. The buildings blend in with the surrounding land since they are made of the earth itself. Bright-blue doors are the same shade as the sky that frames the brown buildings. Between the complexes trickles a fast-flowing creek, the Rio Pueblo de Taos. A footbridge joins the two shores. To the northeast looms Taos Mountain, its long fir-covered slopes forming a timeless backdrop to the old pueblo.

Though the Tiwa were essentially a peaceful agrarian people, they are perhaps best remembered because they spearheaded the only successful revolt by Native Americans in U.S. history. Launched by Pope (Po-*pay*) in 1680, the uprising drove the Spanish from Santa Fe until 1692 and from Taos until 1698.

Native American culture and religion have prevailed here over the centuries. Taos is one of the most conservative of all North American tribal communities, still eschewing such modern conveniences as electricity and plumbing. Arts and crafts and other tourism-related businesses support the economy, along with government services, ranching, and farming.

As you explore the pueblo and gain insights into its people's life-style, you can visit their studios, munch on homemade bread, look into the new **San Geronimo Chapel,** and wander past the fascinating ruins of the old church and cemetery. You're expected to ask permission from individuals before taking their photos; some will ask for a small payment, but that's for you to negotiate. Kivas and other ceremonial underground areas are taboo.

San Geronimo is the patron saint of the Taos Pueblo and his feast day (September 30) combines Catholic and pre-Hispanic traditions. **The Old Taos Trade Fair** on that day is a joyous occasion, with footraces, pole climbs, and crafts booths. Dances are performed the evening of September 29. Other annual events include a turtle dance on **New Year's Day,** deer or buffalo dances on **Three Kings Day** (January 6), and corn dances on **Santa Cruz Day** (May 3), **San Antonio Day** (June 13), **San Juan Day** (June 24), **Santiago Day** (July 23), and **Santa Ana Day** (July 24). The **Taos Pueblo Powwow,** a dance competition and parade that brings together tribes from throughout North America, is held the weekend after July 4 on reservation land off NM 522. **Christmas Eve** bonfires mark the start of the children's corn dance, the **Christmas Day** deer dance, or the three-day-long Matachines dance.

During your visit to the pueblo you will have the opportunity to purchase traditional fried and oven-baked bread as well as a variety of arts and crafts. If you would like to try some traditional feast day-style meals, Tiwa Kitchen, near the entrance to the pueblo, is a good place to stop. Close to Tiwa Kitchen is the Oo-oonah Children's Art Center, where you can see the creative works of pueblo children.

The address is P.O. Box 1846, Taos Pueblo, NM 87571 (☎ 505/758-8626). The admission charge is $5 per car or $10 per van. If you would like to use a still camera, the charge is $5; for a video camera $10; if you would like to sketch, the charge is $15, to paint $35. Photography is not permitted on feast days. The pueblo is open daily from 8am to 5:30 pm, with a few exceptions. Taos Pueblo closes for one month every year in late winter or early spring (call to find out if it will be open at the time you expect to be in Taos).

As with many of the other pueblos in New Mexico, Taos Pueblo has opened a casino featuring slot machines, blackjack, and poker. Free local transportation is available. Call **505/751-0991** for details.

✪ Millicent Rogers Museum

Off NM 522, 4 miles north of Taos. ☎ **505/758-2462.** Admission $4 adults, $3 seniors and students, $2 children 6–16. Daily 10am–5pm. Closed Mon Nov–Mar, Easter, San Geronimo Day (Sept 30), Thanksgiving, Christmas, and Jan 1.

Taos's most interesting collection is in this museum, founded in 1953 by family members after the death of Millicent Rogers. Rogers was a wealthy Taos émigré who in 1947 began acquiring a magnificent collection of aesthetically beautiful Native American arts and crafts. Included are Navajo and Pueblo jewelry, Navajo textiles, Pueblo pottery, Hopi and Zuni kachina dolls, paintings from the Rio Grande Pueblo people, and basketry from a wide variety of southwestern tribes. The collection continues to grow through gifts and museum acquisitions. The museum also presents changing exhibitions of southwestern art, crafts, and design.

Since the 1970s the scope of the museum's permanent collection has been expanded to include Anglo arts and crafts and Hispanic religious and secular arts and crafts, from Spanish and Mexican colonial to contemporary times. Included are santos (religious images), furniture, weavings, colcha embroideries, and decorative tinwork. Agricultural implements, domestic utensils, and craftspeople's tools dating from the 17th and 18th centuries are also displayed. A special exhibition, "Animal Friends," which focuses on the artistic and cultural significance of animals in the Southwest, is scheduled for January 18 to May 4, 1997.

The museum gift shop has a fine collection of superior regional art. Classes and workshops, lectures, and field trips are held throughout the year.

✪ Kit Carson Historic Museums

P.O. Drawer CCC, Taos, NM 87571. ☎ **505/758-0505.** Three museums, $8 adults, $6 seniors, $5 children 6–16; family rate, $15. Two museums, $6 adults, $5 seniors, $4 children; family rate, $13. One museum, $4 adults, $3 seniors, $2.50 children; family rate, $6. All museums free for children under 5. Summer: Kit Carson Home, daily 8am–6pm; Martinez Hacienda, daily 9am–5pm; Blumenschein Home, daily 9am–5pm. Winter: all museums, daily 9am–5pm.

Three historical homes are operated as museums, affording visitors a glimpse of early Taos life-styles. The Martinez Hacienda, Kit Carson Home, and Ernest Blumenschein home each has a unique appeal.

The **Martinez Hacienda,** Lower Ranchitos Road, Hwy. 240 (☎ **505/758-1000**), is the only Spanish Colonial hacienda in the United States that's open to the public year round. This was the home of the merchant and trader Don Antonio Severino Martinez, who bought it in 1804 and lived here until his death in 1827. Located on the west bank of the Rio Pueblo de Taos about two miles southwest of the Plaza, the hacienda was built like a fortress, with thick adobe walls and no exterior windows, to protect against raids by Plains tribes.

Twenty-one rooms were built around two *placitas,* or interior courtyards. Most of the rooms that are open to visitors contain period furnishings: They include the bedrooms, servants' quarters, stables, a kitchen, and even a large fiesta room. Exhibits in one newly renovated room tell the story of the Martinez family and life in Spanish Taos between 1598 and 1821, when Mexico gained control.

Don Antonio Martinez, who for a time was *alcalde* (mayor) of Taos, owned several caravans that he used in trade on the Chihuahua Trail to Mexico. This business

Central Taos Attractions

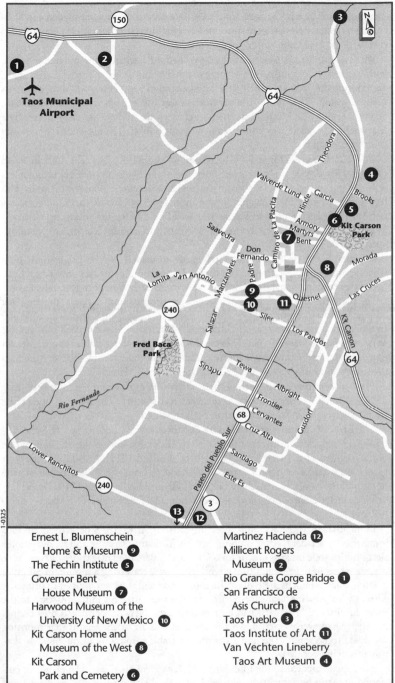

Taos Municipal Airport

Kit Carson Park

Fred Baca Park

was carried on by his youngest son, Don Juan Pascual, who later owned the hacienda. His eldest son was Padre Antonio José Martinez, northern New Mexico's controversial spiritual leader from 1826 to 1867.

Kit Carson Historic Museums has developed the hacienda into a living museum with weavers, blacksmiths, and wood carvers. Demonstrations are scheduled daily, even during the Taos Trade Fair (the last weekend in September) when they run virtually nonstop. The Trade Fair commemorates the era when Native Americans, Spanish settlers, and mountain men met here to trade with each other. The Martinez Hacienda is now home to a new santos exhibit. The hacienda is open daily from 9am to 5pm.

The **Kit Carson Home and Museum of the West,** East Kit Carson Road (☎ 505/758-4741), located a short block east of the Plaza intersection, is the town's only general museum of Taos history. The 12-room adobe home, with walls $2^1/2$ feet thick, was built in 1825 and purchased in 1843 by Carson, the famous mountain man, Indian agent, and scout, as a wedding gift for his young bride, Josefa Jaramillo. It remained their home for 25 years, until both died (exactly a month apart) in 1868.

A living room, bedroom, and kitchen are furnished as they might have been when occupied by the Carsons. The Indian Room contains artifacts crafted and utilized by the original inhabitants of Taos Valley; the Early American Room has a variety of pioneer items, including many antique firearms and trappers' implements; and the Carson Interpretive Room presents memorabilia from Carson's unusual life. In the kitchen is a Spanish plaque that reads: *Nadie sabe lo que tiene la olla mas que la cuchara que la menea* (Nobody better knows what the pot holds than the spoon that stirs it). New permanent exhibits in the Carson home include Native American prehistory and history as well as "Kit Carson: Life and Times."

The museum bookshop, with perhaps the town's most comprehensive inventory of New Mexico historical books, is adjacent to the entry. The home is open daily from 8am to 6pm in summer, 9am to 5pm in winter.

The **Ernest L. Blumenschein Home & Museum,** 222 Ledoux St. (☎ 505/758-0505), $1^1/2$ blocks southwest of the Plaza, recalls and re-creates the life-style of one of the founders of the Taos Society of Artists (founded 1915). An adobe home with garden walls and a courtyard, parts of which date from the 1790s, it became the home and studio of Blumenschein (1874–1960) and his family in 1919. Period furnishings include European antiques and handmade Taos furniture in Spanish colonial style.

Blumenschein was born and raised in Pittsburgh. In 1898 he arrived in Taos somewhat by accident. After training in New York and Paris, he and fellow painter Bert Phillips were on assignment for *Harper's* and *McClure's* magazines of New York when a wheel of their wagon broke while they were traversing a mountain 30 miles north of Taos. Blumenschein drew the short straw and thus was obliged to bring the wheel by horseback to Taos for repair. He later recounted his initial reaction to the valley he entered: "No artist had ever recorded the New Mexico I was now seeing. No writer had ever written down the smell of this air or the feel of that morning sky. I was receiving . . . the first great unforgettable inspiration of my life. My destiny was being decided."

That spark later led to the foundation of Taos as an art colony. An extensive collection of works by early 20th-century Taos artists is on display in several rooms of the home, including some by Blumenschein's daughter, Helen. The home and museum are open daily from 9am to 5pm.

2   More Attractions

D. H. Lawrence Ranch
San Cristobal. ☎ **505/776-2245.**

The shrine of the controversial early 20th-century author is a pilgrimage site for literary devotees. A short uphill walk from the ranch home, it's littered with various mementos—photos, coins, messages from fortune cookies—placed by visitors. The guestbook is worth a long read.

Lawrence lived in Taos on and off between 1922 and 1925. The ranch was a gift to his wife, Frieda, from art patron Mabel Dodge Luhan. Lawrence repaid Luhan the favor by giving her the manuscript of *Sons and Lovers.* Lawrence died in southern France in 1930 of tuberculosis; his ashes were returned here for burial. The grave of Frieda, who died in 1956, is outside the shrine.

The shrine is the only public building at the ranch, which is operated today by the University of New Mexico as an educational and recreational retreat. To reach the site, head north from Taos about 15 miles on NM 522, then another 6 miles east into the forested Sangre de Cristo range via a well-marked dirt road.

✪ The Fechin Institute
227 Paseo del Pueblo Norte (P.O. Box 832), Taos, NM 87571. ☎ **505/758-1710.** Admission $3. May–Oct, Wed–Sun 1–5pm; Nov–Apr, by appointment.

The home of Russian artist Nicolai Fechin (Feh *shin*) from 1927 until 1933, this historic building commemorates the career of a 20th-century Renaissance man. Born in Russia in 1881, Fechin came to the United States in 1923, already acclaimed as a master of painting, drawing, sculpture, architecture, and woodwork. In Taos, he built a huge adobe home and embellished it with handcarved doors, windows, gates, posts, fireplaces, and other features of a Russian country home. The house and adjacent studio are now used for Fechin Institute educational activities, as well as concerts, lectures, and other programs. Fechin died in 1955.

Governor Bent House Museum
117 Bent St. ☎ **505/758-2376.** Admission $1 adults, 50¢ children. Summer, daily 9am–5pm; winter, daily 10am–4pm.

Located a short block north of the Plaza, this was the residence of Charles Bent, New Mexico Territory's first American governor. Bent, a former trader who established Fort Bent, Colorado, was murdered during the 1847 Native American and Hispanic rebellion, while his wife and children escaped by digging through an adobe wall into the house next door. The hole is still visible. Period art and artifacts are on display.

Harwood Museum of the University of New Mexico
238 Ledoux St. ☎ **505/758-9826.** Admission $4. Mon–Fri 10am–5pm, Sat 10am–4pm.

Some of the finest works of art ever produced in or about Taos hang in this Pueblo-style library-and-museum complex, a cultural and community center since 1923.

The museum displays paintings, drawings, prints, sculpture, and photographs by Taos-area artists from 1800 to the present. Featured are paintings from the early days of the art colony by members of the Taos Society of Artists, including Oscar Berninghaus, Ernest Blumenschein, Herbert Dunton, Victor Higgins, Bert Phillips, and Walter Ufer. Also included are works by Emil Bisttram, Andrew Dasburg, Leon Gaspard, Louis Ribak, Bea Mandelman, Agnes Martin, Larry Bell, and Thomas Benrimo.

On display are 19th-century retablos, religious paintings of saints that have traditionally been used for decoration and inspiration in the homes and churches of New Mexico. The permanent collection includes sculptures by Patrociño Barela, one of the leading Hispanic artists of 20th-century New Mexico, as well as artists Marsden Hartley and John Marin.

The museum also schedules five or six changing exhibitions a year, many of which feature works by the best artists currently living in Taos.

Note: The Harwood, which is planning a renovation beginning at the end of 1996 and continuing through the spring of 1997, will be closed during that period. Call the number given above for up-to-date information.

Kit Carson Park and Cemetery

Paseo del Pueblo Norte.

Major community events are held in the park in summer. The cemetery, established in 1847, contains the graves of Carson and his wife, Gov. Charles Bent, the Don Antonio Martinez family, Mabel Dodge Luhan, and many other noted historical figures and artists. Their lives are described briefly on plaques.

✪ Rio Grande Gorge Bridge

US 64, 10 miles west of Taos.

This impressive bridge, west of the Taos airport, spans the Southwest's greatest river. At 650 feet above the canyon floor, it's one of America's highest bridges. If you can withstand the vertigo, it's interesting to come more than once, at different times of day, to observe how the changing light plays tricks with the colors of the cliff walls. An interesting aside is that the wedding scene in the hit movie, *Natural Born Killers*, was filmed here.

✪ San Francisco de Asis Church

Ranchos de Taos. ☎ **505/758-2754.** Donations appreciated, $2 minimum. Open Mon–Sat 9am–4pm; closed Sun and daily from noon to 1pm. Visitors may attend mass Sat at 5:30pm and Sun at 7am (Spanish), 9am, and 11:30am.

From NM 68, about four miles south of Taos, this famous church appears as a modernesque adobe sculpture with no doors or windows. It has often been photographed (by Ansel Adams, among others) and painted (for example, by Georgia O'Keeffe) from this angle. Visitors must walk through the garden on the west side of this remarkable two-story church to enter and get a full perspective on its massive walls, authentic adobe plaster, and beauty.

Displayed on the wall is an unusual painting, *The Shadow of the Cross* by Henri Ault (1896). Under ordinary light it portrays a barefoot Christ at the Sea of Galilee; in darkness, however, the portrait becomes luminescent, and the perfect shadow of a cross forms over the left shoulder of Jesus's silhouette. The artist reportedly was as shocked as everyone else to see this. The reason for the illusion remains a mystery.

The church office and gift shop are just across the driveway north of the church. A video presentation is given here every hour on the half hour. Several crafts shops surround the square.

Van Vechten Lineberry Taos Art Museum

501 Paseo del Pueblo Norte (P.O. Box 1848). ☎ **505/758-2690.** Admission $5 adults, $3 students and seniors. Tues–Fri 11am–4pm, Sat–Sun 1:30–4pm.

Taos's newest museum is the Van Vechten Lineberry Taos Art Museum. It was the brainchild of Ed Lineberry, who lives in the spectacular home adjacent to the museum; he conceived of it as a memorial to his late wife, Duane Van Vechten. An artist herself, Duane spent much time working in her studio, which now serves as the entryway to the 20,000-square-foot main gallery of the museum. The entryway features, among other things, John Dunn's roulette wheel. Lineberry traveled throughout Europe studying techniques for preservation and storage, as well as the display space, climate control, and lighting of fine museums. As a result, the Van Vechten Lineberry Taos Art Museum is state-of-the-art. The museum displays the extraordinary works of Van Vechten (by far the best works in the museum), as well as those of the original Taos artists. Each artist is represented by at least one piece. Mr. Lineberry hopes to acquire more works in the next few years. Besides the main gallery space, there are smaller areas available for traveling exhibitions and a wonderful library that will be open by appointment to researchers.

ART & COOKING CLASSES

Perhaps you're visiting Taos because of its renown as an art community, but galleries and studio visits may not satisfy your own urge to create. Well, if you'd like to pursue an artistic adventure of your own here, check out the week-long classes in such media as sculpture, painting, jewelry making, photography, clay working, and textiles that are available at the **Taos Institute of Arts,** Box 5280 NDCBU, Taos, NM 87571 (☎ **505/758-2793;** e-mail tia@taosnet.com; URL: http://www.taosnet.com/tia/). Class sizes are limited, so if you're thinking about giving these workshops a try, call for information well in advance. The fees vary from class to class but are generally quite reasonable; however, they usually don't include the cost of materials.

If you've fallen in love with New Mexican and southwestern cooking during your stay (or even before you arrived), you might like to sign up for cooking classes with Jane Butel, a leading Southwest cooking authority and author of 14 cookbooks. At **Jane Butel's Cooking School,** 800 Rio Grande NW, Suite 14 (☎ **800/473-8229;** fax 505/243-8297), you'll learn the history and techniques of southwestern cuisine and have ample opportunity for hands-on preparation. If you choose the week-long session, you'll start by learning about chiles. The second and third days you'll try your hand at native breads and dishes, the fourth focuses on more innovative dishes, and the fifth and last day covers appetizers, beverages, and desserts. Weekend sessions are also available. Call or fax for current schedules and fees.

3 Organized Tours

Damaso and Helen Martinez's **Pride of Taos Tours,** P.O. Box 1192, Taos, NM 87571 (☎ **505/758-8340**), offers several packages, including a Taos historical tour that lasts an hour and takes tourists to the Plaza, Martinez Hacienda, and Ranchos de Taos Church ($6 adults, $3 children 12 and under).

An excellent opportunity to explore the historic downtown area is offered by **Taos Historic Walking Tours** (☎ **505/758-4020**). Call for schedule and prices.

4 Skiing

DOWNHILL

Five alpine resorts are located within an hour's drive of Taos. All offer complete facilities, including equipment rentals. Although exact opening and closing dates vary according to snow conditions, skiing usually begins around Thanksgiving and continues into early April.

Ski clothing can be purchased, and ski equipment rented or bought, from several Taos outlets. Among them are **Cottam's Ski & Outdoor Shops,** with four locations, call **800/322-8267** or 505/758-2822 for the one nearest you; **Taos Ski Valley Sportswear, Ski & Boot Co.,** in Taos Ski Valley (☎ **505/776-2291**); and **Looney Tunes Ski Shop,** also in the ski valley (☎ **505/776-8839**).

✪ **Taos Ski Valley,** (Box 90) Taos Ski Valley, NM 87525 (☎ **505/776-2291**), World Wide Web http://taoswebb.com/nmusa/skitaos/), is the preeminent ski resort in the southern Rocky Mountains. It was founded in 1955 by a Swiss-German immigrant, Ernie Blake. According to local legend, Blake searched for two years in a small plane for the perfect location for a ski resort comparable to what he was accustomed to in the Alps. He found it at the abandoned mining site of Twining, high above Taos. Today, under the management of two younger generations of Blakes, the resort has become internationally renowned for its light, dry powder (320 inches annually), its superb ski school (one of the best in the country), and its personal, friendly manner.

Taos Ski Valley, however, can best be appreciated by the more experienced skier. It offers steep, high-alpine, high-adventure skiing. The mountain is more intricate than it might seem at first glance, and it holds many surprises and challenges—even for the superexpert. The esteemed London *Times* called the valley "without any argument the best ski resort in the world. Small, intimate, and endlessly challenging, Taos simply has no equal." And, if you're sick of dealing with those yahoos on snowboards, you will be pleased to know that they're not permitted on the slopes of Taos Ski Valley (the only ski area in New Mexico that forbids them). The quality of the snow here (light and dry) is believed to be due to the dry southwestern air and abundant sunshine.

Between the 11,819-foot summit and the 9,207-foot base, there are 72 trails and bowls, and more than half of them are designated for superexpert and advanced skiers. Most of the remaining trails are suitable for advanced-intermediates; there is little flat terrain for novices to gain experience and mileage. The area has an uphill capacity of 15,000 skiers per hour on its five double chairs, one triple, four quads, and one surface tow. Tickets for all lifts, depending on the season, cost $26–$41 for adults for a full day, $25 half day; $16–$24 for children 12 or younger for a full day, $17 half day; $18 seniors 65–69 for a full day; free for seniors over 70. Novice lift tickets cost $22 for adults, $16 for children. Full rental packages are $14 for adults and $7 for children. Taos Ski Valley is open daily from 9am to 4pm from Thanksgiving to the first week of April. It should be noted that Taos Ski Valley has one of the best ski schools in the country. This school specializes in teaching people how to negotiate steep and challenging runs.

With its children's ski school, Taos Ski Valley has always been an excellent location for skiing families, but with the 1994 addition of an 18,000-square-foot children's center (Kinderkäfig Center), skiing with your children in Taos is even better. Kinderkäfig offers every service imaginable, from equipment rental for children to baby-sitting services. Call ahead for more information.

Taos Ski Valley has 13 lodges and condominiums with nearly 700 beds. (See "Taos Ski Valley," in Chapter 12, for details on accommodations.) All offer ski-week packages; four of them have restaurants. There are two more restaurants on the mountain in addition to the many facilities of Village Center at the base. For reservations, call the **Taos Valley Resort Association** (☎ **800/776-1111** or 505/776 2233).

Not far from Taos Ski Valley is **Red River Ski Area** (P.O. Box 900, Red River, NM 87558; ☎ **800/348-6444** or 505/754-2223 for reservations). One of the bonuses of this ski area is the fact that lodgers at Red River can walk out their doors and be on the slopes. Two other factors make this 37-year-old, family-oriented area special: First, most of its 57 trails are geared to the intermediate skier, though beginners and experts also have some trails; and second, good snow is guaranteed early and late in the year by snowmaking equipment that can work on 75% of the runs, more than any other in New Mexico. There's a 1,600-foot vertical drop here to a base elevation of 8,750 feet. Lifts include four double chairs, two triple chairs, and a surface tow, with a skier capacity of 7,920 skiers per hour. The cost of a lift ticket for all lifts is $36 for adults for a full day, $26 for a half day; $22 for children 12 and under and seniors (60 and over) for a full day, $15 for a half day. Full rental packages start at $13 for adults, $9 for children. Red River Ski Area is open daily from 9am to 4pm from Thanksgiving to March 30.

Also quite close to Taos is **Angel Fire Resort** (P.O. Drawer B, Angel Fire, NM 87710; ☎ **800/633-7463** or 505/377-6401). The 32 miles of ski runs here are heavily oriented to beginning and intermediate skiers. Still, with a vertical drop of 2,180 feet to a base elevation of 8,500 feet, advanced skiers are certain to find something they like. The area's lifts—one Poma surface tow, four doubles, and one high-speed quad—have an hourly capacity of 8,600 skiers. All-day lift tickets cost $32 for adults and $20 for children. Open from approximately Thanksgiving to April (depending on the weather) daily from 8:30am to 4:30pm.

The oldest ski area in the Taos region, founded in 1952, **Sipapu Ski Area** (P.O. Box 29, Vadito, NM 87579; ☎ **505/587-2240**) is 25 miles southeast, on NM 518 in Tres Ritos canyon. It prides itself on being a small local area, especially popular with schoolchildren. There are just one triple chair and two surface lifts, with a vertical drop of 865 feet to the 8,200-foot base elevation. There are 18 trails, half classified as intermediate. Many types of overnight lodging are available, from duplexes to a bunkhouse to camping. All-day lift tickets are $28 for adults and $21 for children under 12. Open from Thanksgiving to April daily from 8am to 4pm.

Just south of the Colorado border is **Ski Rio** (P.O. Box 159, Costilla, NM 87524; ☎ **800/2-ASK-RIO** or 505/758-7707), a rapidly expanding ski area. Half of its 83 named trails are for the intermediate skier, 30% for beginners, and 20% for advanced skiers. Also within Ski Rio are Snowboard and Snow Skate Parks, as well as 13 miles of cross-country trails. Annual snowfall here is about 260 inches, and there are three chair lifts (two triple, one double) and three tows. At the ski base you can rent skis, snowboards, snowshoes, and snow skates, as well as find lodgings, restaurants, and a sports shop. Sleigh rides, dogsled tours, and snowmobile tours are also available. The ski school offers private and group clinics (for adults and children) in cross-country and downhill skiing, snow skating, and snowboarding. Lift tickets are $33 for adults ($22–$27 during the value season), $23 for juniors 7–12, free for children 6 and under with a paying adult. Ski Rio is open daily from 9am to 4pm from November 27 to April 6.

For information via the World Wide Web, try: http://laplaza.com/tp/skirio/.

CROSS COUNTRY

There are numerous popular Nordic trails in Carson National Forest. If you call or write ahead, they'll send you a booklet titled, "Where to Go in the Snow," which gives cross-country skiers details about the maintained trails in Carson National Forest. One of the more popular trails is **Amole Canyon,** off NM 518 near the Sipapu Ski Area, where the Taos Nordic Ski Club maintains set tracks and signs along a 3-mile loop. It's closed to snowmobiles, a comfort to lovers of serenity. Several trails are open only to cross-country skiers.

Just east of Red River, with 31 miles of groomed trails in 600 acres of forestland atop Bobcat Pass, is the **Enchanted Forest Cross Country Ski Area** (☎ 505/ 754-2374). Full-day trail passes, good from 9am to 4:30pm, are $9 for adults, much less for children. Equipment rentals and lessons can be arranged at **Miller's Crossing** ski shop on Main Street in Red River (☎ 505/754-2374). Nordic skiers can get instruction in "skating," mountaineering, and telemarking.

Taos Mountain Outfitters, 114 South Plaza (☎ 505/758-9292), offers tele- mark and cross-country sales, rentals, and guide service, as do **Los Rios Whitewater Ski Shop** (☎ 505/776-8854) and **Southwest Nordic Center** (☎ 505/758-4761).

5 More Outdoor Activities

Taos County's 2,200 square miles embrace a great diversity of scenic beauty, from New Mexico's highest mountain, 13,161-foot **Wheeler Peak,** to the 650-foot-deep chasm of the **Rio Grande Gorge. Carson National Forest,** which extends to the eastern city limits of Taos and cloaks a large part of the county, contains several major ski facilities as well as hundreds of miles of hiking trails through the Sangre de Cristo range.

Recreation areas are mainly in the national forest, where pines and aspen provide refuge for abundant wildlife. Forty-eight areas are accessible by road, including 38 with campsites. There are also areas on the high desert mesa, carpeted by sagebrush, cactus, and frequently wildflowers. Both terrains are favored by hunters, fishermen, and horseback riders. Two beautiful areas within a short drive of Taos are the **Valle Vidal Recreation Area,** north of Red River, and **the Wild Rivers Recreation Area,** near Questa. For complete information, contact **Carson National Forest,** P.O. Box 558, Taos, NM 87571 (☎ 505/758-6200 or 505/758-6390), or the **Bureau of Land Management,** 224 Cruz Alta Rd. (P.O. Box 6168), Taos, NM 87571 (☎ 505/758-8851).

BALLOONING As in many other towns throughout New Mexico, hot-air bal- looning is a top attraction. Recreational trips are offered by **Paradise Hot Air Balloon Adventure** (☎ 505/751-6098).

The **Taos Mountain Balloon Rally,** P.O. Box 3096, Taos, NM 87571 (☎ 505/758-8321), is held each year the last full weekend of October. (See "Northern New Mexico Calendar of Events," in Chapter 2, for details.)

BIKING Even if you're not an avid cyclist, it won't take long for you to realize that getting around Taos by bike is preferable to driving. You won't have the usual parking problems, and you won't have to sit in the line of traffic as it snakes through the center of town. If you feel like exploring the surrounding area, Carson National Forest rangers recommend several biking trails in the greater Taos area, including those in Garcia Park and Rio Chiquito for beginner to intermediate mountain bik- ers, and a number of Gallegos and Picuris peaks for experts. Inquire at the U.S. Forest Service office next to the Chamber of Commerce for excellent materials that map out trails; tell you how to get to the trailhead; specify length, difficulty, and ele- vation; and inform you about safety tips. You can also purchase the Taos Trails map (created jointly by the Carson National Forest, Native Sons Adventures, and Trail Illustrated). It's readily available at area bookstores and is designed to withstand water damage. Once you're out riding in Carson National Forest, you'll find trails marked in green (easy), blue (moderate), or gray (expert). **Gearing Up Bicycle Shop** (129 Paseo del Pueblo Sur; ☎ 505/751-0365) and **Native Sons Adventures** (715 Paseo del Pueblo Sur; ☎ 505/758-9342), offer mountain bike and equipment rentals. Rates range from $15 to $20 for a full day and $10 to $15 for a half day.

Annual touring events include Red River's **Enchanted Circle Century Bike Tour** (☎ 505/754-2366) in mid-September.

FISHING The fishing season in the high lakes and streams opens April 1 and continues through December, though spring and fall tend to be the best times. Naturally, the Rio Grande is a favorite fishing spot, but there is also excellent fishing in the streams around Taos. Taoseños favor the Rio Hondo, Rio Pueblo (near Tres Ritos), Rio Fernando (in Taos Canyon), Pot Creek, and Rio Chiquito. Rainbow, cutthroat, and German brown trout and kokanee (a freshwater salmon) are commonly stocked and caught. Pike and catfish have been caught in the Rio Grande as well. Jiggs, spinners, or woolly worms are recommended as lure, or worms, corn, or salmon eggs as bait, but many experienced anglers prefer fly fishing.

Licenses are required, of course; they are sold, along with tackle, at several Taos sporting-goods shops. For backcountry guides, try **Deep Creek Wilderness Outfitters and Guides,** P.O. Box 721, El Prado, NM 87529 (☎ 505/776-8423) or **Taylor Streit Flyfishing Service** (P.O. Box 2759; ☎ 505/751-1312) in Taos.

FITNESS FACILITIES The **Taos Spa and Court Club,** 111 Dona Ana Dr. (☎ 505/758-1980), is a fully equipped fitness center that rivals any you'd find in a big city. There are treadmills, step machines, climbing machines, rowing machines, exercise bikes, NordicTrack, weight-training machines, saunas, indoor and outdoor hot tubs, a steam room, and indoor and outdoor pools. Thirty-five step aerobic classes a week, as well as stretch aerobics, aqua aerobics, and classes specifically designed for senior citizens are also offered. In addition, there are five tennis and two racquetball courts. Therapeutic massage is available daily by appointment. Children's programs include tennis and swimming camp, and baby-sitting programs are available in the morning and evening. The spa is open Monday through Friday from 5:30am to 9pm; Saturday and Sunday from 7am to 8pm. Monthly, weekly, and daily memberships are available for individuals and families. For visitors there's a daily rate of $10.

The **Northside Health and Fitness Center,** at 1307 Paseo del Pueblo Norte, in Taos (☎ 505/751-1242), is also a full-service facility, featuring top-of-the-line Cybex equipment, free weights, and cardiovascular equipment. Aerobics and Jazzercise classes are scheduled daily, and there are indoor/outdoor pools and four tennis courts, as well as children's and senior citizens' programs.

GOLF Since the summer of 1993 the 18-hole golf course at the **Taos Country Club,** Ranchos de Taos (☎ 800/758-7375 or 505/758-7300), has been open to the public. Located on NM 570, just 4 miles south of the Plaza, it's a first-rate championship golf course designed for all levels of play—in fact, it is ranked as the third best course in New Mexico. It's a links-style course with open fairways and no hidden greens. In addition, there's a driving range, practice putting and chipping green, and a 9-hole course and instruction by PGA professionals. Greens fees in 1996 were $27 during the week, $35 on weekends and holidays for 18 holes. Cart and club rentals are also available. It's always advisable to call ahead for tee times, but it's not unusual for people to show up unannounced and still manage to find a time to tee off.

The par-72, 18-hole course at the **Angel Fire Country Club and Golf Course** (☎ 505/377-3055) has been endorsed by the Professional Golfers Association. Surrounded by stands of ponderosa pine, spruce, and aspen, at 8,500 feet, it's one of the highest regulation golf courses in the world. It also has a driving range and putting green. Carts and clubs can be rented at the course, and the club pro provides instruction.

For 9-hole play, stop at the golf course at Valle Escondido residential village just off US 64. It's a par-36 course with mountain and valley views. Greens fees are $12 for the day (children under 12 are free), clubs and pull-carts are available for rental, and the clubhouse serves refreshments.

Another golf course is under construction in Red River. Call the chamber of commerce to check on its status when you're in town.

HIKING   There are hundreds of miles of hiking trails in Taos County's mountain and high-mesa country. They're especially well traveled in the summer and fall, although nights turn chilly and mountain weather may be fickle by September.

Maps (for a nominal fee) and free materials and advice on all **Carson National Forest** trails and recreation areas can be obtained from the **Forest Service Building,** 208 Cruz Alta Rd. (☎ 505/758-6200), and from the office adjacent to the Chamber of Commerce on Paseo del Pueblo Sur. Both are open Monday through Saturday from 8am to 4:30pm. Detailed USGS topographical maps of backcountry areas can be purchased from **Taos Mountain Outfitters** on the Plaza (☎ 505/758-9292). This is also the place to rent camping gear, if you came without your own. Tent rentals and sleeping bags are $10 each per day. Backpacks can be rented for $8 a day.

Two wilderness areas close to Taos offer outstanding hiking possibilities. The 19,663-acre **Wheeler Peak Wilderness** is a wonderland of alpine tundra encompassing New Mexico's highest peak (13,161 feet). The 20,000-acre **Latir Peak Wilderness,** north of Red River, is noted for its high lake country. Both are under the jurisdiction of the **Questa Ranger District,** P.O. Box 110, Questa, NM 87556 (☎ 505/586-0520).

HORSEBACK RIDING   The **Taos Indian Horse Ranch,** on Pueblo land off Ski Valley Road, just before Arroyo Seco (☎ 800/659-3210 or 505/758-3212), offers a variety of guided rides. Open from 10am to 4pm daily and by appointment, the ranch provides horses for all types of riders (English, western, bareback) and ability levels. Call ahead to reserve. Rates start at $65 to $125 for a two-hour trail ride. Horse-drawn trolley rides are also offered in summer. From late November to March, the ranch provides evening sleigh rides to a bonfire and marshmallow roast at $45 per person; for an extra $17.50, dinner will be included.

Horseback riding is also offered by the **Shadow Mountain Guest Ranch,** 6 miles east of Taos on US 64 (☎ 505/758-7732), **Rio Grande Stables** (P.O. Box 2122, El Prado ☎ 505/776-5913), and **Llano Bonito Ranch** (P.O. Box 99, Penasco, about 40 minutes from Taos ☎ 505/587-2636; fax 505/587-2636). Rates at Llano Bonito Ranch are $15 for a one-hour trail ride, $50 per person for a half-day ride ($60 if breakfast is included), and $85 per person for a full-day ride. In addition to trail rides, Llano Bonito Ranch offers three-day pack trips for $600 per person. On the three-day trip you'll spend two nights in the high country wilderness, and during the day you'll ride to an altitude of 12,500 feet. Meals are included on the pack trip.

Most riding outfitters offer lunch trips and overnight trips. Call for further details.

HUNTING   Hunters in Carson National Forest bag deer, turkey, grouse, band-tailed pigeons, and elk by special permit. On private land, where hunters must be accompanied by qualified guides, there are also black bear and mountain lions. Hunting seasons vary year to year, so it's important to inquire ahead with the **New Mexico Game and Fish Department** in Santa Fe (☎ 505/827-7882).

Several Taos sporting-goods shops sell hunting licenses. Backcountry guides include **Agua Fria Guide Service** (☎ 505/377-3512) in Angel Fire, **AAA Outfitters** (☎ 505/751-5474 or 505/751-1198) in Taos, and **Rio Costilla Park** (☎ 505/586-0542) in Costilla.

ICE-SKATING   For ice-skating, **Kit Carson Park Ice Rink** (☎ 505/758-8234), located in Kit Carson Park, is open from Thanksgiving through February. Skate rentals are available for adults and children.

JOGGING   You can jog anywhere (except on private property) in and around Taos. I would especially recommend stopping by the Carson National Forest office in the Chamber of Commerce building to find out what trails they might recommend.

LLAMA TREKKING   **El Paseo Llama Expeditions** (☎ 800/455-2627 or 505/758-3111) utilizes U.S. Forest Service–maintained trails that wind through canyons and over mountain ridges. The llamas will carry your gear and food, allowing you to walk and explore, free of any heavy burdens. They're friendly, gentle animals that have a keen sense of sight and smell. Often, other animals, like elk, deer, and mountain sheep, are attracted to the scent of the llamas and will venture closer to hikers if the llamas are present. Llama expeditions are scheduled from June to early October. Day hikes cost $80 per person. Three- to five-day hikes cost $130 per person per day. **Taos Llama Adventures** (☎ 800/758-LAMA or 505/776-1044) also offers half- or full-day, as well as overnight llama treks.

RIVER RAFTING   Half- or full-day white-water rafting trips down the Rio Grande and Rio Chama originate in Taos and can be booked through outfitters in Red River. The wild **Taos Box,** a steep-sided canyon south of the Wild Rivers Recreation Area, is especially popular. May and June, when the water is rising, is a good time to go. Experience is not required, but you will be required to wear a life jacket (provided), and you should be willing to get wet.

One convenient rafting service is **Rio Grande Rapid Transit,** P.O. Box A, Pilar, NM 87571 (☎ 800/222-RAFT or 505/758-9700). In addition to Taos Box ($65 per person), Rapid Transit also runs the Pilar Racecourse ($30 per person) on a daily basis. Its headquarters are at the entrance to the BLM-administered **Orilla Verde Recreation Area,** 16 miles south of Taos, where most excursions through the Taos Box end. Several other serene but thrilling floats through the Pilar Racecourse start at this point.

Other rafting outfitters in the Taos area **include Native Sons Adventures,** 715 Paseo del Pueblo Sur (☎ 800/753-7559 or 505/758-9342) and **Far Flung Adventures** (☎ 800/359-2627 or 505/758-2628).

Safety Warning: Taos is not the place to experiment if you are not an experienced rafter. Do yourself a favor and check with the Bureau of Land Management (☎ 505/758-8851) to make sure that you're fully equipped to go white-water rafting without a guide. Have them check your gear to make sure that it's sturdy enough—this is serious rafting!

SPAS   **Ojo Caliente Mineral Springs,** Ojo Caliente, NM 87549 (☎ 800/222-9162 or 505/583-2233), is on US 285, 50 miles (a one-hour drive) southwest of

Taos. This National Historic Site was considered sacred by prehistoric tribes. When Spanish explorer Cabeza de Vaca discovered and named the springs in the 16th century, he called them "the greatest treasure that I found these strange people to possess." No other hot spring in the world has Ojo Caliente's combination of iron, soda, lithium, sodium, and arsenic. The resort offers herbal wraps and massages, lodging, and meals. It's open in summer daily from 8am to 9pm; in winter (November through March) the springs are open from 9am to 5pm.

SWIMMING   The **Don Fernando Pool,** on Civic Plaza Drive at Camino de la Placita, opposite the new Convention Center, admits swimmers over age 6 without adult supervision.

TENNIS   **Quail Ridge Inn** (see Chapter 12) has six outdoor and two indoor tennis courts. **Taos Spa and Tennis Club** (see Fitness Facilities above) has five courts, and the **Northside Health and Fitness Center** (see above) in El Prado has three tennis courts. In addition there are four free public courts in Taos, two at **Kit Carson Memorial State Park**, on Paseo del Pueblo Norte, and two at **Fred Baca Memorial Park,** on Camino del Medio south of Ranchitos Road.

6   Shopping

Many visitors come to Taos to buy fine art. Some 50-odd galleries are located within easy walking distance of the Plaza, and a couple of dozen more are a short drive from downtown. Most artists exhibit in one or more of the galleries, which are generally open seven days a week, especially in high season. Some artists show their work by appointment only.

The best-known artist in modern Taos is R. C. Gorman, a Navajo from Arizona who has made his home in Taos for more than two decades. Now in his fifties, Gorman is internationally acclaimed for his bright, somewhat surrealistic depictions of Navajo women. His **Navajo Gallery**, at 210 Ledoux St. (☎ **505/758-3250**), is a showcase for his widely varied work: acrylics, lithographs, silk screens, bronzes, tapestries, hand-cast ceramic vases, etched glass, and more.

A good place to begin exploring galleries is the **Stables Fine Art Gallery,** operated by the Taos Art Association at 133 Paseo del Pueblo Norte (☎ **505/ 758-2036**). A changing group of fine arts exhibits feature many of Taos's emerging and established artists. All types of work are exhibited, including painting (from expressionism to nonrepresentationalism), sculpture, printmaking, photography, and ceramics. Admission is free; it's open year-round Monday through Saturday from 10am to 5pm and Sunday from 1 to 5pm.

Other places to shop, listed according to their specialties, include the following:

ART

Act I Gallery
226D Paseo del Pueblo Norte. ☎ **800/666-2933** or 505/758-7831.

Watercolors, retablos, furniture, paintings, Hispanic folk art, pottery, jewelry, and sculpture.

✪ Philip Bareiss Contemporary Exhibitions
15 Ski Valley Rd. ☎ **505/776-2284.**

The works of some 30 leading Taos artists, including sculptor Gray Mercer and watercolorist Patricia Sanford, are exhibited here. In 1995 Philip Bareiss opened "Circles and Passageways," a sculptural installation by Gray Mercer, on the 2,500-

acre Romero Range located just west of Taos. A four-wheel-drive vehicle is recommended in order to get there.

Brooks Indian Shop

108G Cabot Plaza Mall. ☎ **505/758-9073.**

Gold and silver Native American jewelry and fine pottery.

Desurmont-Ellis Gallery

121 North Plaza (P.O. Box 1011). ☎ **505/758-3299.**

Abstract and impressionist oils and watercolors, sculpture, ceramics, and jewelry.

✪ El Taller de Taos Gallery and Native American Arts

119A Kit Carson Rd. ☎ **505/758-4887.**

Exclusive representation of Amado Peña, as well as fine art by an excellent group of southwestern artists and Native American art and artifacts.

The Fenix Gallery

228B N. Pueblo Rd. ☎ **505/758-9120.**

The Fenix Gallery focuses on Taos artists with national and/or international collections and reputations who live and work in Taos. The work is primarily non-objective in nature and very contemporary. Some "historic" artists are represented as well.

Franzetti Metalworks

127B Bent St. ☎ **505/758-7872** or 505/758-8741.

Functional metal sculpture and metal art.

Gallery A

105–107 Kit Carson Rd. ☎ **505/758-2343.**

The oldest gallery in town, Gallery A has contemporary and traditional paintings, sculpture, and graphics, including Gene Kloss oils, watercolors, and etchings.

Hirsch Fine Art

146 Kit Carson Rd. ☎ **505/758-5460.**

Watercolors, etchings and lithographs, and drawings by early Southwest artists, including the original Taos Founders.

Lizard of Oz

156 Vista del Valle ☎ **505/758-0708.**

This gallery has a great collection of fine Australian art, textiles, pottery, jewelry, and other items.

✪ Lumina of New Mexico

239 Morada Rd. (P.O. Box LL). ☎ **505/758-7282.**

Located in the historic Victor Higgins home, next to the Mabel Dodge estate, Lumina is one of the loveliest galleries in New Mexico. You'll find a large variety of fine art, including paintings, sculpture, and photography. This place is as much a tourist attraction as any of the museums and historic homes in town.

✪ New Directions Gallery

107B North Plaza. ☎ **505/758-2771.**

Features Larry Bell's unique mixed-media "Mirage paintings" and work by acclaimed sculptor Ted Egri.

Quast Galleries—Taos

229 and 133 E. Kit Carson Rd. ☎ **505/758-7160** or 505/758-7779.

Representational landscapes and figurative paintings and distinguished sculpture. Rotating national and international exhibits are shown here.

Second Phase Gallery
110 Dona Luz. ☎ **505/751-0159.**

Fine antique Native American art, including Navajo rugs and blankets, Pueblo pottery, and Plains beadwork.

Shriver Gallery
401 Paseo del Pueblo Norte. ☎ **505/758-4994.**

Traditional paintings, drawings, etchings, and bronze sculpture.

Spirit Runner Gallery
303 Paseo del Pueblo Norte. ☎ **505/758-1132.**

Southwestern weavings, furniture, and sculpture as well as contemporary watercolors. Spirit Runner is also located at North Plaza.

The Taos Gallery
403 North Pueblo Rd. ☎ **505/758-2475.**

Southwestern impressionism, traditional Western art, contemporary fine art, and bronze sculpture.

BOOKS

The Brodsky Bookshop
218 Paseo del Pueblo Norte. ☎ **505/758-9468.**

Exceptional inventory of fiction, nonfiction, southwestern and Native American studies, children's books, topographical and travel maps, cards, tapes, and CDs.

Fernandez de Taos Bookstore
109 North Plaza. ☎ **505/758-4391.**

A substantial offering of books on southwestern subjects, along with local and regional newspapers and a large selection of magazines.

Kit Carson Home
E. Kit Carson Rd. ☎ **505/758-4741.**

Fine collection of books about regional history.

❂ Moby Dickens Bookshop
124A Bent St. ☎ **505/758-3050.**

Children's and adults' collections of Southwest, Native American, and out-of-print books. This is one of Taos's best bookstores. A renovation to add 600 square feet more of store space is currently in progress.

Taos Book Shop
122D Kit Carson Rd. ☎ **505/758-3733.**

Founded in 1947, this is the oldest general bookstore in New Mexico. Taos Book Shop specializes in out-of-print and southwestern titles.

CRAFTS

Clay & Fiber Gallery
126 W. Plaza Dr. ☎ **505/758-8093.**

Clay & Fiber represents over 150 artists from around the country; merchandise changes frequently, but you should expect to see a variety of ceramics, fiber arts, jewelry, and wearables.

Open Space Gallery
103B East Plaza, Taos Plaza. ☎ **505/758-1217.**

An artist-owned cooperative gallery of contemporary arts and crafts.

Southwestern Arts
In the Dunn House, Bent St. ☎ **505/758-8418.**

Historic and contemporary Navajo weavings, Pueblo pottery, and jewelry. Also photography by Dick Spas.

Southwest Moccasin & Drum
803 Paseo del Pueblo Norte. ☎ **800/447-3630** or 505/758-9332.

Home of the All One Tribe Drum, this favorite local shop carries a large variety of drums in all sizes and styles, handmade by master Native American drum makers from Taos Pueblo. Southwest Moccasin & Drum also has the country's second-largest selection of moccasins, as well as an incredible inventory of indigenous world instruments and tapes, sculpture, weavings, rattles, fans, fetishes, bags, decor, and many handmade one-of-a-kind items. A percentage of the store's profits goes to support Native American causes.

✪ Taos Artisans Cooperative Gallery
107A Bent St. ☎ **505/758-1558.**

Local handmade jewelry, wearables, claywork, glass, drums, baskets, leather work, garden sculpture, and woven Spirit Women. This is an eight-member cooperative gallery, owned and operated by local artists. You'll always find an artist in the shop.

Taos Blue
101A Bent St. ☎ **505/758-3561.**

Fine Native American and contemporary handcrafts gallery; it specializes in clay and fiber work.

Weaving Southwest
216 Paseo del Pueblo Norte. ☎ **505/758-0433.**

Contemporary tapestries by New Mexico artists, as well as one-of-a-kind rugs, blankets, and pillows. In May and September of 1997 Weaving Southwest will hold tapestry exhibits.

FASHIONS

Blue Fish
140 E. Kit Carson Rd. ☎ **505/758-3520.**

If you love unique articles of clothing, you'll love Blue Fish, where you'll find hand-blocked pieces of art clothing. Blue Fish also carries jewelry and gifts.

Twining Weavers and Contemporary Crafts
135 Paseo del Pueblo Norte. ☎ **505/758-9000.**

Handwoven wool rugs and pillows by owner Sally Bachman, as well as creations by other gallery artists in fiber, basketry, and clay.

FOOD

Casa Fresen Bakery
Ski Valley Rd., Hwy 150. ☎ **505/776-2969.**

Located on the road to the Taos Ski Valley in Arroyo Seco, this is a wonderful place to buy fresh pastries, cakes, cheeses, pâtés, specialty meats, pastas, sauces, preserves, and oils. You can enjoy a sandwich right there or select a box lunch to take along on a picnic. It's open daily from 7:30am to 6pm.

FURNITURE

Country Furnishings of Taos
534 Pueblo Norte. ☎ **505/758-4633.**

Here you'll find unique hand-painted folk-art furniture that has become popular all over the country. The pieces are as individual as the styles of the local folk artists who make them. There are also home accessories, unusual gifts, clothing, and jewelry.

Lo Fino
201 Paseo del Pueblo Sur. ☎ **505/758-0298.**

Handcrafted traditional and contemporary Southwest furniture and home accessories by northern New Mexico artisans. Lo Fino specializes in custom building furniture.

The Taos Company
124K John Dunn Plaza, Bent St. ☎ **800/548-1141** or 505/758-1141.

Interior design showroom, specializing in unique southwestern antique furniture and decorative accessories.

GIFTS & SOUVENIRS

Broken Arrow Ltd.
222 North Plaza. ☎ **505/758-4304.**

Ceramics, weaving, jewelry, baskets, paintings, and sculpture.

Charley's Corner
NW corner of Taos Plaza. ☎ **505/758-9470.**

Charley's is jam-packed full of T-shirts, pottery, jewelry, and a variety of southwestern souvenirs.

JEWELRY

Artwares
Taos Plaza (P.O. Box 2825). ☎ **800/527-8850** or 505/758-8850.

Artwares gallery owners call their contemporary jewelry "a departure from the traditional." Indeed, each piece here is a new twist on traditional Southwest and Native American design.

Taos Gems & Minerals
637 Paseo del Pueblo Sur. ☎ **505/758-3910.**

Now in its 30th year of business, Taos Gems & Minerals is a fine lapidary showroom. Here you can get jewelry, specimens, carvings, and antique pieces at reasonable prices.

MUSICAL INSTRUMENTS

Taos Drum Company
Five miles south of Taos Plaza, off NM 68. ☎ **505/758-3796.**

Drum making is an age-old tradition that local artisans are continuing in Taos. The drums are made of hollowed-out logs stretched with rawhide, and they come in all different shapes, sizes, and styles. Taos Drums has the largest selection of Native

American log and hand drums in the world. In addition to drums, the showroom displays southwestern and wrought-iron furniture, cowboy art, and lamps, as well as a constantly changing selection of primitive folk art, ethnic crafts, Native American music tapes, books, and other information on drumming. To find Taos Drum Company, look for the teepees and drums off NM 68.

POTTERY & TILES

Stephen Kilborn Pottery

136D Paseo del Pueblo Norte. ☎ **505/758-5760.**

Head up to Stephen Kilborn Pottery and you'll find some wonderful handmade pieces—both functional and decorative.

Vargas Tile Co.

NM 68. ☎ **505/758-5986.**

Vargas Tile has a great little collection of hand-painted Mexican tiles at good prices. My favorite pieces are the cabinet doorknobs and the beautiful sinks.

7 Taos After Dark

For a small town, Taos has its share of top entertainment; performers are attracted to Taos because of the resort atmosphere and the arts community. Taos enjoys annual programs in music and literary arts, and state troupes—the New Mexico Repertory Theater and New Mexico Symphony Orchestra make regular visits.

Many events are scheduled by the **Taos Art Association,** 145 Paseo del Pueblo Norte (P.O. Box 198), Taos, NM 87571 (☎ **505/758-2052**), at the **Taos Community Auditorium** (☎ **505/758-4677**). The TAA imports local, regional, and national performers in theater, dance, and concerts (Dave Brubeck, the late Dizzy Gillespie, the American String Quartet, and the American Festival Ballet have performed here) and offers two weekly film series, including one for children.

You can obtain information on current events in the *Taos News,* published every Thursday. The **Taos County Chamber of Commerce** (☎ **800/732-TAOS** or 505/758-3873) publishes semiannual listings of "Taos County Events," as well as an annual Taos Country Vacation Guide which also lists events and happenings around town.

THE PERFORMING ARTS

MAJOR ANNUAL PROGRAMS

Fort Burgwin Research Center

On NM 518 south of Taos. ☎ **505/758-8322.**

This historic site (of the 1,000-year-old Pot Creek Pueblo), located about ten miles south of Taos, is a summer campus of Southern Methodist University. From mid-May through mid-August, the SMU-IN-TAOS curriculum (such as studio arts, humanities, and sciences) includes courses in music and theater. There are regularly scheduled orchestral concerts, guitar and harpsichord recitals, and theater performances available to the community, without charge, throughout the summer.

Music from Angel Fire

P.O. Box 502, Angel Fire, NM 87710. ☎ **505/377-3233.**

This acclaimed program of chamber music begins in mid-August with weekend concerts and continues up to Labor Day. Based in the small resort community of

The Major Concert and Performance Halls

Taos Civic Plaza and Convention Center, 121 Civic Plaza Dr., ☎ **505/758-4160.**
Taos Community Auditorium, Kit Carson Memorial State Park, ☎ **505/758-4677.**

Angel Fire (located about 21 miles east of US 64), it also presents numerous concerts in Taos and Raton.

Taos Poetry Circus
☎ **505/758-1800.**

Aficionados of the literary arts appreciate this annual event, held during eight days in mid-June. Billed as "a literary gathering and poetry showdown among nationally known writers," it includes readings, seminars, performances, public workshops, and a poetry video festival. The main event is the World Heavyweight Championship Poetry Bout, 10 rounds of hard-hitting readings—with the last round extemporaneous.

Taos School of Music
360 State Rd., Arroyo Seco, Taos, NM 87514. ☎ **505/776-2388.**

Sponsored by the Taos Art Association, the Taos School of Music was founded in 1963. It is located at the Hotel St. Bernard in Taos Ski Valley. From mid-June to mid-August there is an intensive eight-week study and performance program for advanced students of violin, viola, cello, and piano. Students receive daily coaching by the American String Quartet and pianist Robert McDonald.

The eight-week Chamber Music Festival, an important adjunct of the school, offers 16 concerts and seminars for the public; performances are given by the American String Quartet, pianist Robert McDonald, guest violist Michael Tree (of the Guarneri Quartet), and the international young student artists. Performances are held at the Taos Community Auditorium and the Hotel St. Bernard.

THE CLUB & MUSIC SCENE

Adobe Bar
In the Historic Taos Inn, 125 Paseo del Pueblo Norte. ☎ **505/758-2233.** No cover. Because the hours vary, be sure to call ahead.

A favorite gathering place for locals as well as visitors, the Adobe Bar is known for its live music series (Tuesday through Thursday and Sunday) devoted to the eclectic talents of Taos musicians. The schedule offers a little of everything—classical, jazz, folk, Hispanic, and acoustic. The Adobe Bar features a wide selection of international beers, wines by the glass, light New Mexican dining, desserts, and an espresso menu.

Fireside Cantina
At Rancho Ramada, 615 Paseo del Pueblo Sur. ☎ **505/758-2900.** No cover.

Live entertainment on Friday and Saturday nights. Call for information and schedule.

Hideaway Lounge
At the Holiday Inn, 1005 Paseo del Pueblo Sur. ☎ **505/758-4444.** No cover.

This hotel lounge, built around a large adobe fireplace, offers live entertainment and an extensive hors d'oeuvres buffet. Call for schedule.

Kachina Cabaret

At the Kachina Lodge, 413 Paseo del Pueblo Norte. ☎ **505/758-2275.** Cover varies according to performer, but usually $5 Fri–Sat.

Top-name country and Hispanic acts—including the Desert Rose Band, the Nitty Gritty Dirt Band, and Eddie Rabbit—have performed here. Saturday night is the big event night, starting at 9pm. The adjacent Zuni Lounge features rock bands nightly.

Sagebrush Inn

Paseo del Pueblo Sur. ☎ **505/758-2254.** No cover.

Taos's highest energy dancing spot offers country or rock performers nightly, year-round, from 9pm.

Thunderbird Lodge

Taos Ski Valley. ☎ **505/776-2280.** Cover for Jazz Festival $10 and up.

Throughout January, the Thunderbird Jazz Festival brings leading contemporary jazz musicians to perform week-long gigs at the foot of the ski slopes. The rest of the year there's live entertainment and two-step dance lessons.

8 Exploring Beyond Taos: A Driving Tour of the Enchanted Circle

The one "don't-miss" trip from Taos is an excursion around the Enchanted Circle. This 90-mile loop, a National Forest Scenic Byway, runs through the towns of Questa, Red River, Eagle Nest, and Angel Fire, incorporating portions of NM 522, NM 38, and US 64. Although one can drive the entire loop in two hours from Taos, most folks prefer to take a full day, and many take several days, to accomplish it.

QUESTA Traveling north from Taos via NM 522, it's a 24-mile drive to Questa, most of whose residents are employed at a molybdenum mine about 5 miles east of town. En route north, the highway passes near **San Cristobal,** where a side road turns off to the D. H. Lawrence Shrine, and **Lama,** site of an isolated spiritual retreat.

If you turn west off NM 522 onto NM 378 about 3 miles north of Questa, you'll descend 11 miles on a gravel road into the gorge of the Rio Grande at the Bureau of Land Management–administered **Wild Rivers Recreation Area** (☎ **505/758-8851**). Here, where the Red River enters the gorge, is the most accessible starting point for river-rafting trips through the infamous Taos Box. Some 48 miles of the Rio Grande, south from the Colorado border, are protected under the national Wild and Scenic River Act of 1968. Information on geology and wildlife, as well as hikers' trail maps, can be obtained at the visitors center here. Ask for directions to the impressive petroglyphs in the gorge. River-rafting trips can be booked in Taos, Santa Fe, Red River, and other communities. (See the "Outdoor Activities" sections in Chapter 7 and above for booking agents in Santa Fe and Taos, respectively.)

The village of **Costilla,** near the Colorado border, is 20 miles north of Questa. This is the turnoff point for four-wheel-drive jaunts into **Valle Vidal,** a huge U.S. Forest Service–administered reserve with 42 miles of roads.

RED RIVER Turn east at Questa onto NM 38 for a 12-mile climb to Red River, a rough-and-ready 1890s gold-mining town that has parlayed its Wild West ambience into a pleasant resort village that's especially popular with families from Texas and Oklahoma.

This community at 8,750 feet is a center for skiing and snowmobiling, fishing and hiking, off-road driving and horseback riding, mountain biking, river rafting, and other outdoor pursuits. Frontier-style celebrations, honky-tonk entertainment, and even staged shootouts on Main Street are held throughout the year.

The **Red River Chamber of Commerce,** P.O. Box 870, Red River, NM 87558 (☎ 800/348-6444 or 505/754-2366), lists more than 40 accommodations, including lodges and condominiums. Some are open winters or summers only.

EAGLE NEST   About 16 miles east of Red River, on the other side of 9,850-foot Bobcat Pass, is the village of Eagle Nest, resting on the shore of Eagle Nest Lake in the Moreno Valley. Gold was mined in this area as early as 1866, starting in what is now the ghost town of Elizabethtown about 5 miles north; but Eagle Nest itself (population 200) wasn't incorporated until 1976. The 4-square-mile lake is considered one of the top trout producers in the United States and attracts ice fishermen in winter as well as summer anglers. Sailboats and windsurfers also use the lake, although swimming, waterskiing, and camping are not permitted.

If you're heading to Cimarron or Denver, proceed east on US 64 from Eagle Nest. But if you're circling back to Taos, continue southwest on US 38 and US 64 to Agua Fria and Angel Fire.

Shortly before the Agua Fria junction, you'll see the **DAV Vietnam Veterans Memorial.** It's a stunning structure with curved white walls soaring high against the backdrop of the Sangre de Cristo range. Consisting of a chapel and underground visitor center, it was built by Dr. Victor Westphall in memory of his son, David, a marine lieutenant killed in Vietnam in 1968. The chapel has a changing gallery of photographs of Vietnam veterans who gave their lives in the Southeast Asian war, but no photo is as poignant as this inscription written by young Davis Westphall, a promising poet:

> *Greed plowed cities desolate.*
> *Lusts ran snorting through the streets.*
> *Pride reared up to desecrate*
> *Shrines, and there were no retreats.*
> *So man learned to shed the tears*
> *With which he measures out his years.*

ANGEL FIRE   The year-round, full-service resort community of **Angel Fire**, approximately 150 miles north of Albuquerque, 21 miles east of Taos, and 2 miles south of the Agua Fria junction on NM 38, dates only from the late 1960s but already has a wide variety of lodging choices—from condos and lodges to hotels and cabins. Winter nordic and alpine skiing and summer golf are the most popular activities, but there's also ample opportunity for sailing and fishing on Eagle Nest Lake, tennis, hiking, snowmobiling, mountain biking, river rafting, and horseback riding. A variety of special events attracts visitors to the area throughout the year, including a hot-air balloon festival, Winterfest, and concerts of both classical and popular music. The **Angel Fire Chamber of Commerce** can be reached at **800/446-8117** for more information.

The unofficial community center is **The Legends Hotel and Conference Center,** North Angel Fire Road (P.O. Drawer B), Angel Fire, NM 87710

Taos Area (Including Enchanted Circle)

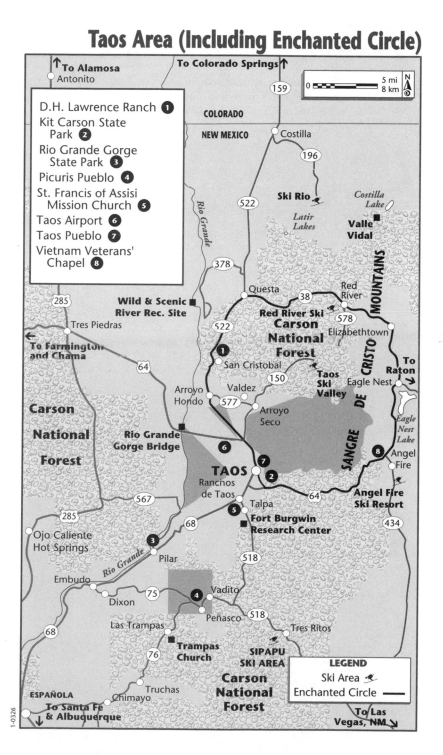

D.H. Lawrence Ranch ❶
Kit Carson State Park ❷
Rio Grande Gorge State Park ❸
Picuris Pueblo ❹
St. Francis of Assisi Mission Church ❺
Taos Airport ❻
Taos Pueblo ❼
Vietnam Veterans' Chapel ❽

To Alamosa
Antonito
To Colorado Springs
159
COLORADO
NEW MEXICO
Costilla
196
Ski Rio
Costilla Lake
Latir Lakes
522
Valle Vidal
378
Questa
Red River
38
285
Wild & Scenic River Rec. Site
522
Red River Ski
578
Carson National Forest
Elizabethtown
Tres Piedras
To Farmington and Chama
64
❶
San Cristobal
150
Taos Ski Valley
To Raton
Eagle Nest
Arroyo Hondo
577
Valdez
Arroyo Seco
Eagle Nest Lake
Carson
National
Forest
Rio Grande Gorge Bridge
❻
❼
❷
❽
Angel Fire
TAOS
Ranchos de Taos
567
285
Talpa
64
Angel Fire Ski Resort
❺
Fort Burgwin Research Center
434
Ojo Caliente Hot Springs
68
❸
Pilar
518
SANGRE DE CRISTO MOUNTAINS
Embudo
Rio Grande
75
❹
Vadito
Dixon
Peñasco
518
Las Trampas
Tres Ritos
68
76
Trampas Church
SIPAPU SKI AREA
LEGEND
Ski Area
Enchanted Circle
ESPAÑOLA
Truchas
Carson National Forest
Chimayo
To Santa Fe & Albuquerque
To Las Vegas, NM

0   5 mi
0   8 km
N

1-0326

187

(☎ **505/633-7463**), a 139-room hotel with rates starting at $75 in the summer, $105 in the winter.

For more information on, and full accommodations listings in, the Moreno Valley, contact the **Angel Fire Chamber of Commerce,** P.O. Box 547, Angel Fire, NM 87710 (☎ **800/446-8117** or 505/377-6353; fax 505/377-3034).

Albuquerque 15

Albuquerque is the gateway to fascinating northern New Mexico, the portal through which most domestic and international visitors pass before traveling on to Santa Fe and Taos.

From the rocky crest of Sandia Peak at sunset, one can see the lights of this city of almost half a million people spread out like shiny sequins on an enormous quilt. As the sun drops beyond the western horizon, it reflects off the Rio Grande, flowing through Albuquerque more than a mile below.

The 10,378-foot Sandia Peak can be reached by aerial tramway; from the northeastern outskirts of the city, it passes high above cathedral-like crags and sparse ponderosa and aspen forest. From the summit, you can—with keen eyes and a little imagination—see the site where Spanish colonists established a villa on the Old Chihuahua Trail in 1706 and named it after regional governor Don Francisco Cuervo y Valdez, the 13th Duke of Alburquerque (the first "r" was later deleted from the city's name).

Reminders of the colonial past of the "Duke City" still abound. Today Albuquerque is a major metropolis that sprawls 16 miles from the lava-crested mesas on the west side of the Rio Grande to the steep alluvial slopes of the Sandia Mountains on the east and another 14 miles north-south through the Rio Grande valley. It boomed as a transportation center with the arrival of the railroad in 1880, but that economic explosion was nothing compared with what has happened since World War II, when Albuquerque was designated a major national center for military research and production. Its population has increased more than tenfold in the past five decades.

1 Orientation

ARRIVING

Since Albuquerque is the transportation hub for New Mexico, getting in and out of town is easy. For more detailed information about doing that, see "Getting There" in Chapter 2.

BY PLANE The **Albuquerque International Airport** is in the south-central part of the city, between I-25 on the west and Kirtland Air Force Base on the east, just south of Gibson Boulevard. Sleek and efficient, the airport is served by eight national airlines and two local ones.

Most hotels have courtesy vans to meet their guests and take them to their respective destinations. In addition, **Shuttlejack**

(☎ **505/243-3244**) and **Checker Airport Express** (☎ **505/765-1234**) run services to and from city hotels. **Sun Tran** (☎ **505/843-9200**), Albuquerque's public bus system, also makes airport stops. There is efficient taxi service to and from the airport, plus numerous car-rental agencies.

BY TRAIN   Amtrak's "Southwest Chief" arrives and departs daily from and to Los Angeles and Chicago. The station is at 214 First St. SW, two blocks south of Central Avenue (☎ **800/USA-RAIL** or 505/842-9650). *Note:* A new train station is currently in the planning stage, so call ahead to make sure the address listed here is still current.

BY BUS   **Greyhound/Trailways** (☎ **800/231-2222** for schedules, fares, and information) and **TNM&O Coaches** (☎ **505/243-4435**) arrive and depart from the Albuquerque Bus Transportation Center, 300 Second St. SW (near the train station).

BY CAR   If you're driving, you'll probably arrive via either the east-west Interstate 40 or the north-south Interstate 25. Exits are well marked. For information and advice on driving in New Mexico, see "Getting There," in Chapter 2.

VISITOR INFORMATION

The main office of the **Albuquerque Convention and Visitors Bureau** is at 20 First Plaza NW. (☎ **800/284-2282** or 505/243-3696). It's open Monday through Friday from 8am to 5pm. There are information centers at the airport, on the lower level at the bottom of the escalator, open daily from 9:30am to 8pm; and in Old Town at 303 Romero St. NW (Suite 107), open daily from 9am to 5pm. Tape-recorded information about current local events is available from the bureau after 5pm weekdays and all day Saturday and Sunday. Call **800/284-2282.** If you have access to the World Wide Web, the address for the Albuquerque Convention and Visitors Bureau is http://www.abqcvb.org

CITY LAYOUT

The city's sprawl takes a while to get used to. A visitor's first impression is of a grid of arteries lined with shopping malls and fast-food eateries, with residences tucked behind on side streets.

If you look at a map of Albuquerque, the first thing you'll notice is that it lies at the crossroads of **Interstate 25** north-south and **Interstate 40** east-west. Refocus your attention on the southwest quadrant of the **+**: Here you'll find both **downtown** Albuquerque and **Old Town**, site of many tourist attractions. **Lomas Boulevard** and **Central Avenue,** the old "Route 66" (US 66), flank downtown on the north and south. They come together 2 miles west of downtown near the **Old Town Plaza,** the historical and spiritual heart of the city. Lomas and Central continue east across I-25, staying about half a mile apart as they pass by the University of New Mexico and the New Mexico State Fairgrounds. The airport is directly south of the UNM campus, about 3 miles via Yale Boulevard. Kirtland Air Force Base—site of Sandia National Laboratories and the National Atomic Museum—is an equal distance south of the fairgrounds on Louisiana Boulevard.

Roughly paralleling I-40 to the north is Menaul Boulevard, focus of **midtown** and **uptown** shopping as well as the hotel districts. As Albuquerque expands northward, the **Journal Center** business park area, about 4¹/₂ miles north of the freeway interchange, is getting more attention. East of Eubank Boulevard are the **Sandia Foothills,** where the alluvial plain slants a bit more steeply toward the mountain.

Great Albuquerque

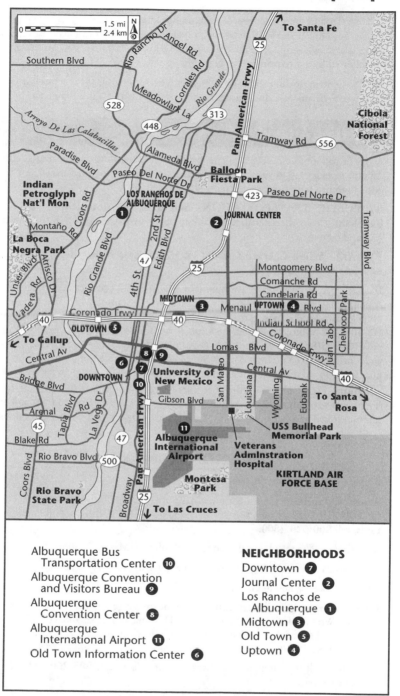

Albuquerque Bus
  Transportation Center ❿
Albuquerque Convention
  and Visitors Bureau ❾
Albuquerque
  Convention Center ❽
Albuquerque
  International Airport ⓫
Old Town Information Center ❻

NEIGHBORHOODS

Downtown ❼
Journal Center ❷
Los Ranchos de
  Albuquerque ❶
Midtown ❸
Old Town ❺
Uptown ❹

When looking for an address, it is helpful to know that Central Avenue divides the city into north and south, and the railroad tracks—which run just east of First Street downtown—comprise the dividing line between east and west. Street names are followed by a directional: NE, NW, SE, or SW.

MAPS   The most comprehensive Albuquerque street map is the one published by First Security Bank and distributed by the Convention and Visitors Bureau.

2   Getting Around

A city of half a million people might seem intimidating to maneuver, but actually Albuquerque is easy to get around, thanks to its wide thoroughfares and grid layout, combined with its efficient transportation systems.

BY PUBLIC TRANSPORTATION   Sun Tran of Albuquerque (☎ **505/ 843-9200**) cloaks the arterials with its city bus network. Call for information on routes and fares.

BY TAXI   Yellow-Checker Cab (☎ **505/765-1234**) serves the city and surrounding area 24 hours a day.

BY CAR   The *Yellow Pages* list more than 30 car-rental agencies in Albuquerque. Among them are these well-known national firms: **Alamo,** 2601 Yale Blvd., SE (☎ **505/842-4057**); **Avis,** at the airport (☎ **505/842-4080**); **Budget,** at the airport (☎ **505/768-5900**); **Dollar,** at the airport (☎ **505/842-4304**); **Hertz,** at the airport (☎ **505/842-4235**); **Rent-A-Wreck,** 501 Yale Blvd. SE (☎ **505/242-9556**); and **Thrifty,** 2039 Yale Blvd. SE (☎ **505/842-8733**). Those not located at the airport itself are close by and can provide rapid airport pickup and delivery service.

Parking is generally not difficult in Albuquerque—nor, for that matter, is rush hour a serious problem (yet). Meters operate weekdays from 8am to 6pm and are not monitored at other times. Only the large downtown hotels charge for parking.

FAST FACTS: Albuquerque

Airport   See "Orientation," above.

American Express   The American Express office is at 6600 Indian School Road (☎ **800/219-1023** or 505/883-3677; fax 505/884-0008). To report lost credit cards, call **800/528-4800.**

Area Code   The telephone area code for all of New Mexico is **505.**

Car Rentals   See "Getting There," in Chapter 2 or "Getting Around," above.

Climate   See "When to Go," in Chapter 2.

Currency Exchange   Foreign currency can be exchanged at any of the branches of Sun West Bank (its main branch is at 303 Roma St. NE ☎ **505/765-2211**); or at any of the branches of First Security Bank (its main office is at Twenty-First Plaza ☎ **505/765-4000**).

Dentists   Call the Albuquerque District Dental Society at **505/260-7333** for emergency service.

Doctors   Call The University of New Mexico Medical Center Physician Referral Service at **505/843-0124** for a recommendation.

Embassies/Consulates   See "Fast Facts: For the Foreign Traveler," in Chapter 3.

Emergencies   For police, fire, or ambulance, dial **911.**

Hospitals   The major facilities are **Presbyterian Hospital,** 1100 Central Ave. SE (☎ **505/841-1234,** 505/841-1111 for emergency services); and **University of New Mexico Hospital,** 2211 Lomas Blvd. NE (☎ **505/843-2411** for emergency services).

Liquor Laws   See "Fast Facts: Santa Fe," in Chapter 4.

Newspapers and magazines   The two daily newspapers are the *Albuquerque Tribune,* published mornings, and the *Albuquerque Journal,* published evenings. *Albuquerque Monthly* magazine, which covers many aspects of city life, is widely available.

Police   For emergencies, call **911.** For other business, contact the Albuquerque City Police (☎ **505/768-1986**) or the New Mexico State Police (☎ **505/841-9256**).

Post Offices   The Main Post Office, 1135 Broadway NE (☎ **505/245-9561**) is open daily from 7:30am to 6pm. There are 18 branch offices, with another 13 in surrounding communities.

Radio/TV   Albuquerque has some 30 local radio stations catering to all musical tastes. Albuquerque television stations include KOB, Channel 4 (NBC affiliate); KOAT, Channel 7 (ABC affiliate); KGGM, Channel 13 (CBS affiliate); KNME, Channel 5 (PBS affiliate); and KGSW, Channel 14 (Fox and independent). There are, of course, numerous local cable channels as well.

Taxes   In Albuquerque, the hotel tax is 10.81%; it will be added to your bill.

Taxis   See "Getting Around," above.

Time Zone   Albuquerque is on Mountain Time, one hour ahead of the West Coast and two hours behind the East Coast.

Transit Info   **Sun Tran of Albuquerque** is the public bus system. Call **505/843-9200** for schedules and information.

Useful Telephone Numbers   For **time and temperature** call **505/247-1611; road information 800/432-4269; emergency road service (AAA) 505/291-6600.**

3 Accommodations

Albuquerque's hotel glut is good news to travelers looking for quality rooms at reasonable cost. Except during peak periods—specifically, the New Mexico Arts and Crafts Fair (late June), the New Mexico State Fair (September), and the Kodak Albuquerque International Balloon Fiesta (early October)—most of the city's hotels have vacant rooms, so guests can frequently request and get a lower room rate than the one posted.

In the following listing, hotels are categorized by price range: **Expensive** means that a double room costs $110 or more per night; **Moderate** includes doubles for $75 to $110; and **Inexpensive** refers to doubles for $75 and under.

A tax of 10.81% is added to every hotel bill.

EXPENSIVE

Casas de Sueños

310 Rio Grande Blvd. SW, Albuquerque, NM 87104. ☎ **800/CHAT-W/US** or 505/247-4560. 19 rms. TV TEL. $85–$250 single or double. Rates include breakfast and afternoon snacks. AE, CB, DC, DISC, MC, V.

You'll recognize Casas de Sueños by the bright sign and the snail-shaped front of the main building (you'll understand exactly what I mean when you see it—you can't miss it), which was designed by famed architect Bart Prince. The buildings that comprise Casas de Sueños were once private homes—a compound that was all part of a gathering place for artists and their admirers. Most of them face a garden court-yard that was cooperatively maintained for many years by the residents. In the spring and summer the gardens, filled with roses, are maintained by a resident gar-dener, making this place an urban oasis.

Each of the rooms has an individual theme; for instance, one room is designed to follow the color schemes of Monet's paintings, while another is reminiscent of an English drawing room. Some of the rooms are equipped with kitchens, and La Miradora has two bedrooms (with king- and queen-size beds), a living room with a fireplace, a full bath (with a two-person Jacuzzi), and a back porch with a swing overlooking a golf course. Four rooms and several private hot tubs have recently been added, and the owners are currently designing a full spa facility that will be constructed next door to the inn (it is projected to be completed by the fall of 1996). Every accommodation has its own entrance.

A delicious full breakfast is served in the main building every morning. Works by local artists are displayed in Studio 310, an art gallery and sculpture garden. Massage therapists are available. No smoking is permitted indoors. Children 12 and older are welcome, but pets are not accepted.

Doubletree Hotel Albuquerque, "A Merv Griffin Hotel"

201 Marquette St. NW, Albuquerque, NM 87102. ☎ **800/222-TREE** or 505/247-3344. Fax 505/247-7025. 294 rms, 13 suites. A/C TV TEL. $84–$134 double. AE, CB, DC, DISC, MC, V. Self-parking $5 a day.

A two-story waterfall cascades down a marble backdrop adjacent to the registration area, setting the mood in this totally renovated hotel (purchased a couple of years ago by entertainer Merv Griffin). Marble is the trademark of the pillared lobby; ele-gance also extends to the guest rooms, which feature custom-made contemporary southwestern furnishings and other regional touches. Each room is outfitted with a hair dryer and a coffee-maker. The hotel is the only one directly connected to the Albuquerque Convention Center. On the hotel's lower level is a photo gallery of Merv Griffin and celebrities from the popular *Merv Griffin Show.*

Dining/Entertainment: La Cascada Restaurant, at the foot of the waterfall, is an airy, sidewalk cafe–style coffee shop serving three meals daily. Adjacent is the **Bistro Bar.** Upstairs, the **Lobby Lounge** features live music daily during happy hour.

Services: Limited room service, courtesy van to airport and Old Town, valet laundry, newspaper delivery to rooms on the Executive Level, twice-daily maid ser-vice, baby-sitting service, secretarial service, in-room massage.

Facilities: Rooms for nonsmokers and travelers with disabilities; outdoor swim-ming pool, weight and exercise room; gift shop; American Airlines desk; under-ground passage to the Convention Center and Galeria shopping center; access to nearby health club (for a nominal fee) which features a lap pool, exercise equip-ment, aerobics classes, handball, racquetball, saunas, and a Jacuzzi.

✪ Hyatt Regency Albuquerque

330 Tijeras Ave. NW, Albuquerque, NM 87102. ☎ **800/233-1234** or 505/842-1234. Fax 505/842-1184. 395 rms, 14 suites. A/C TV TEL. $139–$164 double weekdays, $89 weekends; $310–$725 suite. AE, CB, DC, DISC, MC, V. Self parking $8, valet $11.

This $60-million hotel opened in 1990 with a great deal of hoopla. Already a city landmark, the 20-story structure—which incorporates the offices of Albuquerque Plaza—makes a bold architectural statement uncharacteristic of New Mexico. The lobby features a palm-shaded fountain beneath a pyramidal skylight, and throughout the hotel's public areas there is an extensive art collection, including original Frederic Remington sculptures. The spacious guest rooms enhance the feeling of richness with mahogany furnishings, full-length mirrors, even data-port phone jacks for busy businesspeople.

Dining/Entertainment: McGrath's serves three meals daily in a luxurious setting of forest-green upholstery and black-cherry furniture. **Bolo Saloon** is noted for its whimsical oils of "where the deer and the antelope play" (at the bar).

Services: Room service, valet laundry.

Facilities: Rooms for nonsmokers and travelers with disabilities; outdoor swimming pool, health club (with weight/exercise equipment and masseur); shopping block (including art galleries, hair salon, florist, optician, and travel agency).

MODERATE

In Albuquerque

Albuquerque Hilton Hotel

1901 University Blvd. NE, Albuquerque, NM 87102. ☎ **800/27-HOTEL** or 505/884-2500. Fax 505/889-9118. 264 rms, 7 suites. A/C TV TEL. $95–$135 double; $375–$475 suite. Weekend discounts are available. AE, CB, DC, DISC, MC, V. Free parking.

White stuccoed corridors with petroglyph-style paintings are a trademark of this hotel. Many of the rooms are in a high-rise tower that offers panoramic views of the Sandia Mountains or of the downtown area and western mesa. Two floors of rooms comprise a VIP level for business travelers. Cabaña rooms with 15-foot-high cathedral ceilings surround the outdoor pool. Pets are not permitted.

Dining/Entertainment: The **Ranchers Club,** built like a British hunting lodge transported to the high plains, is one of Albuquerque's finest restaurants. **Casa Chaco** is open daily for three meals. **The Cantina,** with its fajitas grill and piano bar, serves as the hotel lounge.

Services: Room service (during restaurant hours), valet laundry, shoeshine stand, Avis car-rental desk.

Facilities: Rooms for nonsmokers and travelers with disabilities; indoor and outdoor swimming pools, whirlpool, saunas, tennis courts, fitness center, gift shop, and business center.

Best Western Fred Harvey

2910 Yale Blvd. SE, Albuquerque, NM 87106. ☎ **800/227-1117** or 505/843-7000. Fax 505/843-6307. 266 rms. A/C TV TEL. $93–$103 double. AE, CB, DC, DISC, MC, V. Free parking.

No accommodation is closer to the airport than the Best Western Fred Harvey, which is literally a stone's throw north of the main terminal. It caters to air travelers with a 24-hour desk, shuttle service, and overnight valet laundry. The rooms have been decorated in pastel colors with a southwestern flair and are furnished with king-size or double beds, four-drawer dressers, leather easy chairs with ottomans,

Central Albuquerque Accommodations

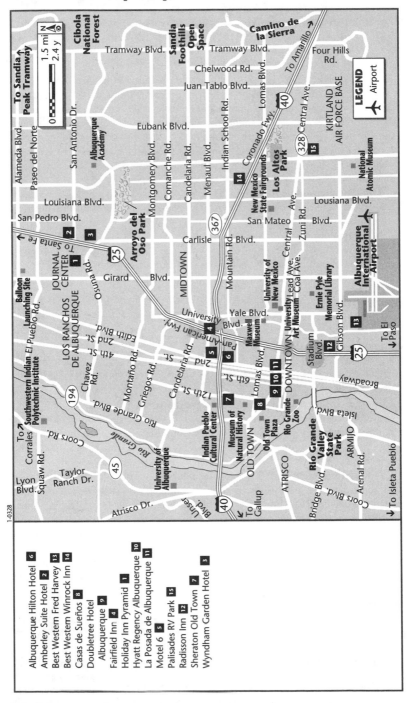

Albuquerque Hilton Hotel **6**
Amberley Suite Hotel **2**
Best Western Fred Harvey **13**
Best Western Winrock Inn **14**
Casas de Sueños **8**
Doubletree Hotel
Albuquerque **9**
Fairfield Inn **4**
Holiday Inn Pyramid **1**
Hyatt Regency Albuquerque **10**
La Posada de Albuquerque **11**
Motel 6 **5**
Palisades RV Park **15**
Radisson Inn **12**
Sheraton Old Town **7**
Wyndham Garden Hotel **3**

cable TV/radios, and phones. There are two restaurants on the premises that serve meals at reasonable prices. Room service, courtesy van, valet laundry, complimentary shoeshine, and rooms for nonsmokers and travelers with disabilities are available. Pets are not permitted. Facilities include an outdoor swimming pool, self-service laundry, coed sauna, two all-weather tennis courts, and a gift shop.

✪ Casa del Granjero

414 C de Baca Lane NW, Albuquerque, NM 87114. ☎ **800/701-4144** or 505/897-4144. Fax 505/897-4144. 7 rms. $79–$149 double. Extra person $20. Rates include breakfast. MC, V.

From the pygmy goats to the old restored wagon out front, Casa del Granjero ("The Farmer's House") is true to its name. It might come as more of a surprise, however, that the innkeepers actually are the Farmers—Butch and Victoria Farmer—and they have transformed their home into an exquisite bed-and-breakfast. The Great Room has an enormous sculptured adobe fireplace, comfortable bancos for lounging, a library, and scores of Old West and Native American artifacts. As a guest here you can curl up in front of the fire and read a book or listen to Butch's stories about an Indian fighter relative who was a scout for George Washington. If you'd rather spend a couple of hours watching a movie but are too tired to head to downtown Albuquerque, the 52-inch television in the den fits the bill. The guest rooms are beautifully furnished and decorated. Most have fireplaces. Cuarto del Rey, with queen-size and day beds, features Mexican furnishings and handmade quilts and comforters. Cuarto de Flores has French doors that open onto a portal, and Cuarto Allegrehas, a king-size canopy bed done up in lace and satin. All the bathrooms are unique and quite beautiful. The one in Cuarto Allegre has wooden beams, corbels, and handmade Mexican tiles. In the morning, breakfast is served at the spectacular dining room table or on the portal. It includes fresh fruit, homemade pastries and breads, and a hot dish. Catered lunches and dinners are also available by arrangement. There's an outdoor hot tub available for guest use. Smoking is permitted outdoors only, and pets are not permitted.

Hacienda Antigua

6708 Tierra Dr., NW, Albuquerque, NM 87107. ☎ **800/201-2986** or 505/345-5399. 5 rms (all with bath). A/C. $85–$125 double. Extra person $25. Rates include breakfast. AE, CB, DISC, MC, V.

Located on the north side of Albuquerque, just off Osuna Road, is Hacienda Antigua, a 200-year-old adobe home that was once the first stagecoach stop out of Old Town in Albuquerque. Owned for two centuries by the Yrissaris family, the hacienda retained its old world charm. When Ann Dunlap and Melinda Moffit bought it, they were careful to preserve the building's historic aspects while transforming it into a beautiful bed-and-breakfast. The inn's exterior walls are remarkable in their simplicity—only the heavy carved gates hint of the treasures that lie within. The beautifully landscaped courtyard, with its large cottonwood tree and abundance of greenery (including a large raspberry patch), offers a welcome respite for today's tired travelers just as it did during the days when the hacienda served as a mercantile and cantina.

The five guest rooms are furnished with antiques. The Don Pablo Suite features a king-size bed (covered with a stunning blue quilt), a sitting room with a kiva fireplace, and a bathroom with a wonderful old pedestal bathtub/shower. A traditional "ducking door" allows guests access to the courtyard. La Capilla, the home's former chapel, is furnished with a queen-size bed, a fireplace, and a beautiful carving of San Ysidro (the patron saint of farmers). Doña Manuelita features antique iron beds (full-size and twin) and traditional bancos by the window. The bathroom is separated from the rest of the room by a curving adobe wall, which offers bathers who sink into the clawfoot tub a view of the fireplace. The Emilia Room features a private courtyard entrance, a massive adobe fireplace, and an oversize clawfoot bathtub that dates from 1897. The Antonia Teresa Room also has a private entrance and features antique oak furnishings and a 19th-century slipper tub. All rooms are equipped with unstocked minirefrigerators. A gourmet breakfast is served in the garden during warm weather and by the fire in winter. Guests also have use of the pool and hot tub. Just a 20-minute drive from the airport, Hacienda Antigua is a welcome change from the anonymity of the downtown Albuquerque high-rise hotels, and Ann and Melinda are terrific hosts.

✪ Holiday Inn Pyramid

5151 San Francisco Rd., NE, Albuquerque, NM 87109. ☎ **800/544-0623** or 505/821-3333. Fax 505/828-0230. 311 rms, 54 suites. A/C TV TEL. $120–$150 double; $115–$325 suite. Ask about special weekend and package rates. AE, CB, DC, MC, V. Free parking.

As you drive north from Albuquerque toward Santa Fe, a spectacular stepped Aztec pyramid seems to rise from nowhere on the west side of I-25. This major hotel and convention complex, reached via the Paseo del Norte exit (Exit 232) from I-25, is a monument to what modern hotel architecture can be like. The 10 guest floors are grouped around a "hollow" skylit core. Vines drape from planter boxes on the balconies, and water falls five stories to a pool between the two glass elevators. There is a restaurant and two lounges on the premises. The hotel offers shuttle service to and from the airport, guest laundry, rooms and facilities for travelers with disabilities, a health club, indoor and outdoor pools, hot tub, and sauna.

An associated hostelry is the 363-room **Holiday Inn Midtown Albuquerque,** 2020 Menaul Blvd. NE, Albuquerque, NM 87102 (☎ **505/884-2511**), where rates run slightly less than those at the Pyramid.

⑤ La Posada de Albuquerque

125 Second St. NW (at Copper Ave.), Albuquerque, NM 87102. ☎ **800/777-5732** or 505/242-9090. Fax 505/242-8664. 114 rms, 3 suites. A/C TV TEL. $92–$102 double; $175–$225 suite. AE, CB, DC, DISC, MC, V. Free valet parking.

Built in 1939 by Conrad Hilton as the famed hotelier's first inn in his home state of New Mexico, this twice-sold hostelry on the National Register of Historic Places feels more like Old Mexico. An elaborate Moorish brass-and-mosaic fountain stands in the center of the tiled lobby floor; old-fashioned tin chandeliers hang from the two-story ceiling. The lobby is surrounded on all sides by high archways, creating the feel of a 19th-century hacienda courtyard.

As in the lobby, all guest-room furniture is handcrafted, but here it's covered with cushions of southwestern design. There are limited-edition lithographs by R. C. Gorman and Amado Peña on the white walls, adobe-tone ceramic lamps on the tables flanking the couch, and an ample desk opposite the wood-shuttered windows.

Conrad's Downtown, La Posada's elegantly redesigned restaurant, features Spanish/Yucatán cuisine (see below for full description). **The Lobby Bar** is a favorite gathering place for evening cocktails. The hotel offers room service, courtesy car, valet laundry, and rooms for nonsmokers and travelers with disabilities.

⑤ Radisson Inn

1901 University Blvd. SE, Albuquerque, NM 87106. ☎ **800/333-3333** or 505/247-0512. Fax 505/843-7148. 148 rms. A/C TV TEL. $75–$85 double. AE, CB, DC, DISC, MC, V. Free parking.

The Spanish Colonial–style Radisson (which is scheduled for renovation in 1997) is a mile from the airport. It's nice to be away from the hubbub, especially when you can lounge on the spacious deck of the swimming pool on the landscaped grounds. Decorated in emerald green and navy blue, the rooms are furnished with king- or queen-size beds, two-drawer credenzas, tables and chairs, and Spectravision movie channels. In addition, each room is equipped with a hair dryer and every guest room features voice-mail phone systems with data ports. Small pets are accepted.

Diamondback's Restaurant specializes in southwestern and American cuisine. Coyote's Cantina is a popular watering hole. The hotel offers limited room service, valet laundry, 24-hour courtesy van, rooms for nonsmokers, year-round outdoor swimming pool and whirlpool, and guest use of a nearby health club.

Sarabande

5637 Rio Grande Blvd., NW, Albuquerque, NM 87107. ☎ **800/506-4923** or 505/345-4923. Fax 505/345-9130. 3 rms (all with bath or shower). A/C TV. $85–$125 double. Rates include breakfast. MC, V. Free parking.

"Absolutely charming" is the best way I can describe this bed-and-breakfast and its owners, Betty Vickers and Margaret Magnussen. Once you pass through the front gate and into the beautifully tended, fountained courtyard gardens, you'll forget that you're staying on the fringes of this big city. When you enter the building, you'll immediately notice the gorgeous kitchen with a wood-burning cookstove. Further exploration of the viga-and-latilla ceilinged living room will reveal a Peter Rockwell work known as *Crack the Whip* and a lovely wooden piece titled *Eagle* by Native American artist Durango. The rooms are modern and bright. The Rose Room has a wonderful Japanese soaking tub and kiva fireplace. The Iris Room, with its stained-glass window depicting irises, has a king-size bed. Both rooms open out onto a wisteria-shaded patio where breakfast can be taken in the morning. Out back are a 50-foot heated lap pool and a hot tub (which can be used through the winter). On the other side of the lap pool is the Garden Room, which is my favorite. The light is spectacular, and one of the focal points of the room is an enormous old-time refrigerator (now used for storage). The Garden Room has a shower only. There is a library stocked with magazines, books by local authors, and books about New Mexico (including local sports and recreation). Betty and Margaret are avid hikers and will be happy to recommend hiking options for you. All-terrain bikes are available for guest use free of charge. Breakfast (fresh fruit, fresh squeezed juice, coffee, and homemade breads) may be served in the courtyard or the dining room.

Sheraton Old Town

800 Rio Grande Blvd. NW, Albuquerque, NM 87104. ☎ **800/325-3535** or 505/843-6300. Fax 505/842-9863. 190 rms, 20 suites. A/C TV TEL. $110–$120 double; $140 suite. Children stay free in parents' room. AE, CB, DC, DISC, MC, V. Free parking.

No Albuquerque hotel is closer to top tourist attractions than the Sheraton. Five minutes' walk from the Old Town Plaza and overlooking two important museums, it's an ideal spot for visitors without their own car who don't want to be at the mercy of taxis or rental cars. Mezzanine-level windows light the adobe-tone lobby, which is separated from the Fireside Lounge by a double-sided fireplace. Each of the guest rooms is characterized by a pueblo craft on the wall over the beds. The southside rooms, facing Old Town, are equipped with private balconies. All rooms now offer coffee-makers, hair dryers, and irons and ironing boards.

The Customs House Restaurant, specializing in seafood and regional cuisine, serves weekday lunches and nightly dinners. The Café del Sol is the Sheraton's coffee shop. Taverna Don Alberto, serving drinks off the main lobby, features dance bands on weekend nights. The hotel provides room service, concierge, valet laundry, secretarial and baby-sitting services, rooms for nonsmokers and travelers with disabiities, and an outdoor swimming pool. Old Town Place, an attached shopping center, has arts-and-crafts dealers, a bookstore, beauty salon, and manicurist.

NEARBY

Hacienda Vargas

El Camino Real (P.O. Box 307), Algodones, NM 87001. ☎ **800/261-0006 or** 505/867-9115. Fax 505/867-1902. 7 rms. $79–$149 double. Extra person $15. Rates include breakfast. MC, V.

Unassuming in its elegance, Hacienda Vargas is located right on old Route 66. Owned and operated by the DeVargas family, the inn is situated in the small town of Algodones (about 20 miles from Albuquerque) and is a good place to stay if you're planning to visit both Santa Fe and Albuquerque but don't want to stay in one of the downtown hotels in either city. The walls of the entry hallway are hung with the works of local artists (for sale), and each guest room has a private entrance. All rooms are furnished with New Mexico antiques, are individually decorated, and have handmade kiva fireplaces. The Santa Fe Room looks out onto the courtyard and features a Jacuzzi tub and fireplace, as does the Kiva Room. The Piñon Room offers direct access to the outdoor hot tub and has a beautiful antique clawfoot bathtub. The main attractions in the Peña Room are the unique bed and headboard and the authentic adobe walls. Hosts Jule and Paul DeVargas are extremely gracious and helpful—they'll make you feel right at home. Two suites, each with a private Jacuzzi tub, fireplace, and private patio, were recent additions to Hacienda Vargas. A full breakfast is served every morning in the dining room. The only drawback here is that there are train tracks near the back of the house, and during my stay the last train went by around midnight. At all other times the inn is quiet and restful.

La Hacienda Grande

21 Baros Lane, Bernalillo, NM 87004. ☎ **505/867-1887.** Fax 505/867-4621. 6 rms (all with bath). A/C. $89–$115 double. Extra person $10. Rates include breakfast. AE, DISC, MC, V. Free parking.

Opened in 1993, La Hacienda Grande, run by a brother-and-sister team Daniel Buop and Shoshana Zimmerman, has a wonderful history. The completely restored adobe home, with 2-foot-thick walls, is more than 250 years old. It was one of two original stagecoach stops and is reported to have had the very first adobe stables and an adobe corral, built to prevent horse theft. It sits on 4 acres of land that was once part of the original 100-square-mile Spanish land grant; the kitchen was once used as a chapel for this area before churches were built. The courtyard, surrounded by high adobe walls, has a vortex, which had special significance to the local native tribespeople who often came here to pray and hold ceremonies. Not long after the present owners purchased the property, they learned that during the Civil War gold and silver were often stored here because the walled courtyard was a perfect fortress (its roofline was easily patrolled).

The guest rooms, all featuring custom-crafted furniture, are comfortable and inviting. Much of the furniture is made of bent willow, which lends a rustic air to the hacienda. One room has a queen-size wrought-iron canopy bed, all rooms have small sitting areas and southwestern-style armoires, and five have wood-burning kiva fireplaces (one is a lovely freestanding clay fireplace). Brick or tile floors are covered with throw rugs. There are phone jacks in each room, and phones are available at the front desk. In addition, televisions and VCRs are available upon request.

Early each morning thermoses of coffee are left outside each guest room; later on breakfast is served in the dining room. Favorite breakfast entrées include amaretto French toast, cheese strata, and cranberry cinnamon pancakes. At breakfast there are also homemade breads, specialty honeys, fresh-ground coffees, egg dishes, fruit, and granola. The emphasis is on healthy eating. Guests may make use of the living room, including the TV and VCR; tea and snacks are served in the afternoon. Smoking is prohibited except on the patio.

The Sandhill Crane Bed & Breakfast

389 Camino Hermosa, Corrales, NM 87048 ☎ **800/375-2445** or 505/898-2445. Fax 505/898-2445. 3 rms. A/C TV TEL. $75–$145 double. Rates include breakfast. AE, MC, V. Free parking.

This lovely bed-and-breakfast, run by Carol Hogan and Phil Thorpe, is located about 20 minutes from Albuquerque in the sleepy little town of Corrales. It's a great place to stay if you want to explore the city but don't want to stay right downtown. Wisteria-draped walls surround the renovated adobe hacienda, and each room is uniquely decorated in a Southwest-type style. For families or friends traveling together, the Outlaw Wing (two rooms with connecting bath, small kitchen, and private entrance) is a great choice. All rooms have cable TV and phone jacks for those who want a TV or telephone. Carol, a former university professor and private-practice psychologist from Bucks County, Pennsylvania, has decorated the cozy guest rooms with her charming collection of bird decoys and birdhouses. Phil, a hypnotherapist and financial planner, is responsible for breakfasts that include fruit drinks, bagels, muffins, or homemade bread, as well as a special hot entrée on weekends. Breakfast is served on the patio in warmer weather.

INEXPENSIVE

Ⓢ Amberley Suite Hotel

7620 Pan American Fwy. NE, Albuquerque, NM 87109. ☎ **800/333-9806** or 505/823-1300. Fax 505/823-2896. 170 suites. A/C TV TEL. $106–$121 suite for one or two; $20 higher during balloon fiesta. Discounts for longer stays, weekend arrivals, or corporate or government travelers. Extra person $10; children under 16 stay free in parents' room. AE, CB, DC, DISC, MC, V. Free parking.

Every accommodation in the recently renovated Amberley Suite Hotel is a one- or two-room suite, most with a living room/kitchenette and separate bedroom; the deluxe king is an efficiency studio with a kitchen area. Kitchen facilities include a refrigerator (with complimentary beverages), microwave oven, coffee-maker, and pots, pans, and utensils. Each living room has a swivel rocker with ottoman and a cable TV. Every bathroom (each of which has recently been renovated) comes with a built-in hair dryer.

Watson's Café and Deli serves an all-you-can-eat breakfast buffet and a summer patio barbecue. The hotel manager hosts a happy-hour reception with cocktails and hors d'oeuvres daily.

There is a 24-hour courtesy car (within a two-mile radius), free airport shuttle, guest laundry, rooms for nonsmokers and travelers with disabilities, and outdoor swimming pool.

Best Western Airport Inn

2400 Yale Blvd. SE, Albuquerque, NM 87106. ☎ **800/528-1234** or 505/242-7022. Fax 505/243-0620. 120 rms, 3 suites. A/C TV TEL. $63–$69 double. Rates include continental breakfast. AE, CB, DC, DISC, MC, V.

A landscaped garden courtyard behind the hotel is a lovely place to relax on cloudless days. The rooms, not the most attractive in town, contain standard furnishings plus cable TV and free local phone calls. Deluxe units are equipped with refrigerators. Continental breakfast is served in the rooms, or guests can request a coupon good for $3 off their morning meal at the adjacent Village Inn. A courtesy van is available from 6am to midnight, and the hotel also offers valet laundry service. There are rooms for nonsmokers and travelers with disabilities, and guests can enjoy an outdoor swimming pool and Jacuzzi.

Best Western Winrock Inn

18 Winrock Center NE, Albuquerque, NM 87110. ☎ **800/528-1234** or 505/883-5252. Fax 505/889-3206. 173 rms. A/C TV TEL. $59–$135 double. Rates include breakfast. AE, CB, DC, DISC, MC, V. Free parking.

Located just off I-40 at the Louisiana Boulevard interchange, the Winrock is attached to Albuquerque's second-largest shopping center: Winrock Center. A hotel that appeals primarily to international visitors, its two separate buildings are wrapped around a garden and private lagoon with Mandarin ducks, giant *koi* (carp), and an impressive waterfall. The comfortable rooms, many of which provide private patios overlooking the lagoon, feature a pastel southwestern-motif decor. A breakfast buffet is served in the Club Room every morning. Valet laundry service is available, as are rooms for nonsmokers and the disabled. On the premises you will find a heated outdoor pool and guest laundry.

Fairfield Inn

1760 Menaul Rd. NE, Albuquerque, NM 87102. ☎ **800/228-2800** or 505/889-4000. 188 rms. A/C TV TEL. $62.95 double. Extra person $6; children 18 and under stay free in parents' room. AE, CB, DC, DISC, MC, V.

The Fairfield Inn, owned by Marriott, has exceptionally clean rooms, with cable TV with pay movies, a king-size or two double beds, and free local phone calls. Complimentary coffee and tea are served in the morning (in the lobby). Valet service is available and vending machines are located on every floor. There's an indoor swimming pool with saunas and a Jacuzzi. You probably couldn't get more for your money (in a chain hotel) anywhere else. There are rooms for both nonsmokers and travelers with disabilities.

ⓢ Wyndham Garden Hotel

6000 Pan American Fwy. NE (I-25 at San Mateo Blvd.), Albuquerque, NM 87109. ☎ **800/996-3426** or 505/821-9451. Fax 505/858-0239. 151 rms. A/C TV TEL. $94 double. AE, CB, DC, DISC, MC, V.

The Wyndham doesn't try to be as grand as the Pyramid (see above), but it does feature a five-story lobby atrium with fountains of its own. All rooms offer private balconies (patios on the ground floor), as well as standard, comfortable furnishings, coffee-makers, in-room safes, and computer dataports. *USA Today* is delivered to guest rooms Monday through Friday.

The **Garden Cafe** is open daily for the breakfast buffet, lunch, and dinner. The **Atrium Lounge** is a quiet, comfortable place to enjoy cocktails or after-dinner drinks. There are limited room service, complimentary airport shuttle (from 7am to 11pm), guest laundry, fax and copy service, rooms for nonsmokers and travelers with disabilities, and indoor/outdoor heated swimming pool.

RV Parks

Albuquerque Central Koa

12400 Skyline Rd. NE, Albuquerque, NM 87123. ☎ **505/296-2729.**

Bathhouse, guest laundry, outdoor swimming pool (open summers only), convenience store. Cabins available.

Albuquerque North Koa
555 Hill Rd., Bernalillo, NM 87004. ☎ **505/867-5227.**

Laundry, outdoor swimming pool (open May to October), playground, convenience store, cafe, free outdoor movies. Free pancake breakfast daily. Reservations recommended.

Palisades RV Park
9201 Central Ave. NW, Albuquerque, NM 87121. ☎ **505/831-5000.** 110 sites.

Bathhouse, guest laundry, reception room, small convenience store, propane available, near Old Town.

4 Dining

In these listings, the following categories define price ranges: **Expensive,** most dinner main courses are priced over $15; **Moderate,** most dinner main courses $10 to $15; **Inexpensive,** $10 and under.

EXPENSIVE

Antiquity
112 Romero NW (in Old Town). ☎ **505/247-3545.** Reservations recommended. Main courses $16.95–$24.95. AE, DC, DISC, MC, V. Daily 5–9pm. FRENCH/CONTINENTAL.

Antiquity is something of a surprise in this Old Town neighborhood, which is filled with snack shops and Mexican restaurants that have been around for decades, but it's a nice surprise. Antiquity has been around long enough now (about 10 years) to have earned a fine reputation. Small dining rooms, punctuated by an enormous open grill, are subtly decorated in Southwest style with Mexican touches, making this an intimate spot for a romantic dinner. Classical music adds a finishing touch. Appetizers include standard, well-prepared dishes, such as escargots and French onion soup. The house special, known as Henry the Fourth (fillet of beef served with an artichoke heart and béarnaise), is excellent. The salmon en papillote, my favorite, is perfectly done, tender and flaky. Desserts such as chocolate mousse and crêpes are normally quite rich but well worth the workout you might want to do the next morning.

Conrad's Downtown
125 Second St. NW (at Copper Ave.) (in La Posada de Albuquerque). ☎ **505/242-9090.** Reservations recommended. Main courses at lunch $5.95–$7.25, at dinner $12.50–$18.75. AE, CB, DC, DISC, MC, V. Daily 6:30–2pm and 5:30–10pm. Tapas bar daily 11am–10pm. SPANISH/MEXICAN.

Conrad's, one of Albuquerque's best restaurants, is located on the first floor of the historic La Posada hotel, just off the lobby. A large, classic bar is the focal point around which diners enjoy Spanish and Mexican specialties such as tapas and a delicious huachinango con tequila toronja vinagre (sautéed red snapper topped with tequila vinaigrette and grapefruit) at lunch. Dinner entrées include a delicious cordoorniz negrado con chipotle y mantequilla con tequila (blackened quail with a mixture of lime and tequila, chipotle, and cilantro in a creamy butter sauce) and an interestingly textured trucha con maiz azul y tequila mantequilla (red trout breaded in a spicy blue-corn meal with a lime and tequila butter). A few beef and pork dishes are offered as well. All entrées are served with polenta, black beans, and

Spanish rice or pesto poblano. The paellas (for one or two) are quite good here as well, though you'll have to wait 20 to 30 minutes for them. The atmosphere is casual. Conrad's offer's complimentary valet parking.

High Finance Restaurant & Tavern

40 Tramway Rd. NE (atop Sandia Peak). ☎ **505/243-9742.** Reservations recommended. Main courses at lunch $6.50–$8.95, at dinner $13.95–$23.95. Tramway, $10 with dinner reservations, $13.50 without. AE, CB, DC, DISC, MC, V. Daily 11am–4pm and 5–9:30pm. CONTINENTAL/ITALIAN.

Perched atop Sandia Peak, 2 miles above Albuquerque and the Rio Grande valley, High Finance offers diners a breathtaking panorama of New Mexico's largest city. The atmosphere inside is elegant yet casual.

The lunch menu features sandwiches, pastas, and New Mexico specialties. A recommendation from that menu is linguine Sandia (linguine tossed with bacon, green chile, corn, sage, and fresh Parmesan). Dinner brings such entrées as chicken fettuccine with sun-dried tomatoes, fresh basil, and cream; chile-dusted seared beef tips; and marinated pork chops served with apple green-chile chutney, garlic potato purée, and grilled squash. I always enjoy High Finance's slow roasted prime rib with ancho chile jus, roasted potatoes, and horseradish crema. There are nightly specials and a fish of the day. Many tram riders just drop in for the view and a drink at the casual full-service bar. Smoking is permitted only in the bar.

✪ Le Marmiton

5415 Academy Blvd. NE. ☎ **505/821-6279.** Reservations recommended. Dinner $13.95–$18.95. AE, DC, MC, V. Mon–Thurs 5–9pm, Fri–Sat 5:30–9:30pm, Sun 5:30–9pm. FRENCH.

The name means "The Apprentice," but there's nothing novice about the food or presentation. The 15 tables seat 45 people in a romantic French provincial atmosphere, accented with lace curtains and a lovely collection of antique plates.

Recommended main courses include fantaisie aux fruits de mer, a mixture of shrimp, scallops, and crab sautéed with shallots, basil, white wine, and mushrooms and finished with a cream sauce, served on a puff pastry shell; and cailles, two whole quail, lightly seasoned, sautéed, and finished with a shallot-sherry cream sauce. For vegetarians, the menu now includes a vegetarian appetizer and entrée. If you arrive early for dinner (between 5 and 6pm) Monday through Thursday, you can take advantage of the fixed-price light dinners, which include soup or salad, a choice of main course, and coffee or tea for $7.50. There's a long wine list, and the crème aux framboises makes a great dessert.

✪ Prairie Star

1000 Jemez Canyon Dam Rd., Bernalillo. ☎ **505/867-3327.** Reservations recommended. Main courses $15–$24. AE, DISC, MC, V. Daily 5–10pm (lounge opens at 4pm); brunch Sun 11am–2:30pm. CONTEMPORARY REGIONAL.

A sprawling adobe home, with a marvelous view across the high plains and a golf course adjacent to Sandia Peak, is host to this intimate dining experience. The 6,000-square-foot house, on a rural site leased from Santa Ana Pueblo, was built in the 1940s in Mission architectural style. Exposed vigas and full latilla ceilings, as well as handcarved fireplaces and bancos, complement the thick adobe walls in the dining room. The art displayed on the walls is for sale. There is a lounge at the top of the circular stairway.

Diners can start with smoked quail or baked cheese in puff pastry (a blend of mascarpone and Gruyère cheese scented with toasted hazelnuts and fresh tarragon). Main courses include shrimp margarita (shrimp sautéed and flambéed with tequila,

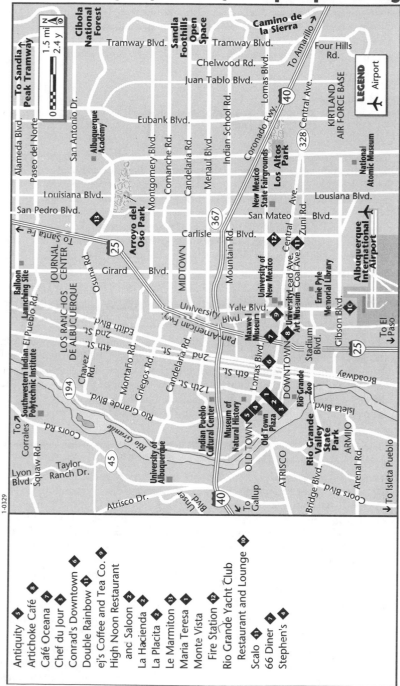

Antiquity ⑤
Artichoke Café ⑧
Café Oceana ⑦
Chef du Jour ③
Conrad's Downtown ⑥
Double Rainbow ⑪
ej's Coffee and Tea Co. ⑨
High Noon Restaurant
  anc Saloon ②
La Hacienda ②
La Placita ②
Le Marmiton ⑬
Maria Teresa ①
Monte Vista
Fire Station ⑫
Rio Grande Yacht Club
  Restaurant and Lounge ⑩
Scalo ⑪
66 Diner ⑦
Stephen's ④

fresh tomatoes, and roasted poblano chiles, and finished with lime juice and butter), veal sweetbreads (served in puff pastry with a tarragon and wild-mushroom cream sauce), lamb loin (stuffed with roast garlic, pine nuts, basil, and goat cheese), and pan-fried Truchas trout with piñon nuts. There are daily specials.

MODERATE

✪ Artichoke Cafe

424 Central Ave. SE. ☎ **505/243-0200.** Reservations recommended. Main courses $8.95–$19.95. AE, CB, DC, DISC, MC, V. Mon–Fri 11am–2:30pm; Mon–Sat 5:30–10pm. CONTINENTAL.

The no-frills decor here is clean and tasteful, with modern art prints on azure walls, white linens on tables shaded by standing plants, and classical music playing in the background. Start your meal with an artichoke appetizer, then go on to a main dish such as baked chicken stuffed with goat cheese, spinach, and roasted red peppers (wonderful!), or baby clams in a sauce of white wine, garlic, leeks, and cream. Crêpes, pastas, salads, sandwiches, and the like are popular at lunch. The cafe has an excellent list of Californian and French wines. Over the years, the Artichoke Cafe has, in my opinion, consistently been one of the area's best restaurants.

Cafe Oceana

1414 Central Ave. SE. ☎ **505/247-2233.** Reservations recommended. Main courses $11.95–$13.95. AE, DC, DISC, MC, V. Mon–Thurs 11am–11pm, Fri 11am–11:30pm, Sat dinner only 5–11:30pm. Oyster hour Mon–Thurs 3–6:30pm and 10–11pm, Fri 3–6:30pm and 10:30–11:30pm, Sat 5–7pm and 10:30–11:30pm. SEAFOOD.

The Cafe Oceana is and has long been Albuquerque's favorite oyster bar and fresh seafood cafe. In a New Orleans–style dining room with high ceilings and hardwood floors, you can enjoy fresh oysters, fresh fish daily, scallops, crab rellenos (for the New Mexican touch), and the house special—beer-batter-fried shrimp Oceana. The daily oyster hour features two-for-one oysters and boiled shrimp. If you're really in the mood for New Orleans cuisine, you can also order red beans and rice here.

Cafe Spoleto

2813 San Mateo Blvd. NE. ☎ **505/880-0897.** Reservations recommended, especially on weekends. Main courses $10–$16.25. DISC, MC, V. Tues–Sun 6–9:30pm. MEDITERRANEAN.

If you've grown a bit weary of New Mexican cuisine (if that's possible) and are looking for a nice, unpretentious Mediterranean restaurant with a casual atmosphere, try Cafe Spoleto. Salads include a grilled raddichio wrapped in pancetta with melon, which is quite nice. My pasta choice was the farfalle with sugar snap peas, mushrooms, applewood smoked bacon, and shaved Spanish manchego cheese. The natural chicken under a brick with grilled portobello mushrooms and sherry is also very tasty, and the grilled homemade sausages are definitely worth trying. There's also always a fish selection (like sautéed halibut with a spicy sweet pepper sauce with Pernod). You won't be disappointed here.

The County Line

9600 Tramway Blvd. NE. ☎ **505/856-7477.** No Reservations. Main courses $8.95–$14.95. AE, CB, DC, DISC, MC, V. Mon–Thurs 5–9pm, Fri–Sat 5–10pm, Sun 4–9pm. BARBECUE.

Although this extremely popular spot doesn't take reservations, if you call before you leave your hotel, they'll put your name on the waiting list, and by the time you get there you'll probably be next in line. If not, you can always wait at the ever-crowded bar. The restaurant is loud and always busy, but it has a spectacular view of the city lights and great food.

When you finally get a table, you'll be given a Big Chief Writing Tablet menu offering great southwestern barbecue at very reasonable prices. You might opt for barbecued chicken or a steak grilled to perfection, along with a baked potato (with your choice of toppings), beans, and coleslaw. If you're not very hungry you should probably consider going somewhere else.

High Noon Restaurant and Saloon

425 San Felipe St. NW. ☎ 505/765-1455. Reservations recommended. Main courses $8.75–$19.25. AE, CB, DC, DISC, MC, V. Mon–Sat 11am–3pm and 5–10pm, Sun noon–9pm. STEAKS/SEAFOOD/NEW MEXICAN.

One of Albuquerque's oldest buildings, this restaurant (now in business for over 20 years) boasts a 19th-century saloon atmosphere with stuccoed walls, high and low ceiling beams, and historical photos on the walls. One photo depicts the original 1785 structure, which now comprises the building's foyer and santo room. The dinner menu offers a choice of beef dishes, such as the house-specialty pepper steak sautéed with brandy; fish dishes, including red trout amandine; game dishes, including buffalo, venison, and caribou; and regional favorites, such as burritos, enchiladas, and fajitas.

La Hacienda Restaurant

302 San Felipe St. NW (at North Plaza). ☎ 505/242-3131. Reservations recommended for large parties. Main courses at lunch $4.50–$8.95, at dinner $7.25–$14.95. AE, CB, DC, MC, V. Daily 11am–9:30pm. NEW MEXICAN/AMERICAN.

A mural girding La Hacienda's outer wall depicts the establishment of Albuquerque and the construction of this Villa de Albuquerque at the turn of the 18th century. Diners enter this cozy restaurant through a large gift shop. The interior, with an intimate, laid-back atmosphere, is adorned with hanging plants and chile ristras. The menu is predominantly regional, with such house specialties as beef or chicken fajitas, carne adovada (sautéed dried pork smothered in red chile), tostadas compuestas (a corn tortilla cup topped with beef, beans, melted cheese, and red or green chile), and tortilla-chile soup. Steaks, shrimp, and other American meals are also offered. Desserts include the traditional flan and fried ice cream.

✪ Maria Teresa

618 Rio Grande Blvd. NW. ☎ 505/242-3900. Reservations recommended. Main courses $13–$26. AE, MC, V. Daily 11am–2:30pm, 5–9pm. NEW MEXICAN/CONTINENTAL.

The city's most beautiful and classically elegant restaurant, Maria Teresa is located in the 1840s Salvador Armijo House, a National Historic property furnished with Victorian antiques and paintings. Built with 32-inch-thick adobe walls, the house exemplifies 19th-century New Mexican architecture, when building materials were few and defense a prime consideration. The house had 12 rooms, seven of which (along with a large patio) are now reserved for diners. Another room is home to the 1840 bar and lounge.

The menu features salads, pastas, sandwiches, seafood, and New Mexican specialties for lunch; and a wide choice of traditionally continental gourmet dinners, from seared filet mignon with béarnaise sauce or seared New York cut venison with sun dried tomatoes and olives to poached salmon with Dijon basil hollandaise.

Monte Vista Fire Station

3201 Central Ave. NE (Nob Hill). ☎ 505/255-2424. Reservations recommended. Main courses at lunch $5.95–$8.95, at dinner $12.95–$17.95. AE, MC, V. Mon–Fri 11am–2:30pm, Sun–Thurs 5–10:30pm, Fri–Sat 5–11pm. Bar, Mon–Fri 11am–2am, Sat noon–2am, Sun noon–midnight. CONTEMPORARY AMERICAN.

The Fire Station has been a city landmark since it was built in pure Pueblo Revival style in 1936. Its occupants no longer make fire calls, however; the focus now is on creative New American cuisine in an art deco setting. A great way to start is with the ancho chile–dusted calamari served with a vegetable cake, tomatillo-pineapple salsa, and hot avocado. Follow this with the sautéed Pacific red snapper served with a sun-dried tomato mint sauce, or the grilled loin of lamb surrounded by polenta diamonds served with a juniper rosemary fumet sauce. The presentation is as well planned as the dishes themselves. Try the tira misu for dessert. There's a popular singles bar on the second-floor landing.

✪ Rio Grande Yacht Club Restaurant & Lounge

2500 Yale Blvd. SE. ☎ **505/243-6111.** Reservations recommended at dinner. Main courses $4.25–$7.95 at lunch, $9.95–$32.95 at dinner. AE, DC, DISC, MC, V. Mon–Fri 11am–2pm, daily 5:30–10:30pm. SEAFOOD.

Red, white, and blue sails are draped beneath the skylight of a large room dominated by a tropical garden. The walls, hung with yachting prints and photos, are of wood strips like those of a ship's deck. The lunch menu features burgers, sandwiches, salads, and a few New Mexican specialties. At dinner, however, fresh fish is the main attraction. Catfish, whitefish, bluefish, sole, salmon, grouper, mahimahi, and other denizens of the deep are prepared broiled, poached, blackened, teriyaki, Vera Cruz, au gratin, mornay, amandine, and more. If you'd rather have something else, the chef here also prepares certified Angus beef, shrimp, Alaskan king crab, several chicken dishes, and even barbecued baby back pork ribs. If you find it difficult to choose one of these, you might want to try a steak and seafood combination.

✪ Scalo

3500 Central Ave. SE (Nob Hill). ☎ **505/255-8782.** Reservations recommended. Main courses $5.75–$9 at lunch, $7.95–$16.95 at dinner. AE, CB, DC, DISC, MC, V. Mon–Sat 11:30am–2:30pm and 5:30–11:30pm, Sun 5–9pm. Bar, Mon–Sat 11am–1am. NORTHERN ITALIAN.

Scalo has a simple bistro-style elegance, with white linen-clothed tables indoors, plus outdoor tables in a covered, temperature-controlled patio. The kitchen, which makes its own pasta and breads, specializes in contemporary adaptations of classical northern Italian cuisine.

Seasonal menus focus on New Mexico–grown produce. Featured appetizers include calamaretti fritti (fried baby squid served with a spicy marinara and lemon aioli) and caprini con pumante (local goat cheese with fresh foccacia, capers, tapenade, and a roasted garlic spread). There's a selection of pastas for lunch and dinner, as well as meat, chicken, and fish dishes. The filetto con salsa balsamica (grilled fillet of beef with rosemary, green peppercorns, garlic, and a balsamic demiglace sauce) is one of my favorites, and the Battuta di Vitello Mandorlata (veal scallopine prepared with toasted almonds, sun-dried cranberries, and Pinot Grigio) is also quite good. Dessert selections change daily.

✪ Stephens

1311 Tijeras Ave. NW (at 14th St. and Central Ave.). ☎ **505/842-1773.** Reservations recommended. Main courses $7.25–$24.95. AE, DC, MC, V. Mon–Fri 11am–2pm, Sun–Thurs 5:30–9:30pm, Fri–Sat 5:30–10:30pm. CONTEMPORARY AMERICAN.

This modern, open, and airy restaurant was inspired by Mexico City's Hacienda Angel and features interior decor by the noted designer Richard Worthen. French windows provide a view of the European-style garden and elegant fountain. Start with a fine baked Brie with almonds, apples, and honey in puff pastry or the black bean pasta ravioli stuffed with Montrachet and Fontina cheeses served with a roasted red pepper sauce. If you're dining on a Friday or Saturday night, I would recommend the chicken Anasazi (chicken breast stuffed with spinach, sun-dried tomatoes, and pistachio pesto served on spinach fettuccine); otherwise, the shrimp and scallop pastry box (with fresh mushrooms in a light champagne sauce) is a good choice. Other dishes on the menu include filet mignon, loin lamb chops, New York strip steak, and several pasta creations. There is a spa menu, and the award-winning wine list features more than 300 choices. There are daily dessert specials.

INEXPENSIVE

Chef du Jour
119 San Pasquale Ave. SW. ☎ **505/247-8998.** Reservations not required. Menu items $2.50–$6.75. No credit cards. Mon–Fri 11am–2pm. ECLECTIC.

The decor certainly isn't much to talk about at Chef du Jour, but that's not why people are flocking to this popular lunch spot located just a block from Old Town. Once you get a taste of what's on the menu (which changes every week), you'll be coming back for more. Recent menu offerings included spicy garlic soup, a great garden burger, green-corn tamales (served with Southwest mango salsa), and marinated grilled chicken breast (on whole-wheat fruit and nut bread with Jamaican banana ketchup). There are also sandwiches and a salad du jour. Chef du Jour has both indoor and some outdoor tables; if you call in advance, the restaurant will fax you a copy of their current menu.

Double Rainbow
3416 Central Ave. SE. ☎ **505/255-6633.** No reservations. All menu items under $8. AE, DISC, MC, V. Daily 6:30–midnight. CAFE/BAKERY.

If you're a people-watcher worth your salt, you shouldn't miss the Double Rainbow, located in Albuquerque's historic Nob Hill district. Of course, people-watching is only one reason to stop by—Double Rainbow has great sandwiches, ice cream, breads, pastries, cakes, and coffee. All baking is done on the premises daily. And one of the best things about this place is its enormous selection of magazines. In fact, there are more than 700 titles, ranging from comic books to film and fashion magazines to a travel magazine for gays and lesbians. Among the unusual titles are *Tricycle* (a Buddhist review) and *Blues Review Quarterly*. The selection of newspapers spans the globe. No one will feel out of place here! Double Rainbow has another branch at 4501 Juan Tabo NE (☎ **505/275-8311**), which features a large outdoor patio, a slightly more extensive menu, and live music on Thursday nights as well as Saturday and Sunday mornings.

✪ ej's Coffee and Tea Co.
2201 Silver Ave. SE. ☎ **505/268-CAFE.** No reservations. Breakfast $2.50–$5.95; lunch $3.95–$7.50; dinner $5.25–$8.75. MC, V. Mon–Thurs 7am–11pm, Fri 7am–midnight, Sat 8am–midnight, Sun 8am–9pm. NATURAL FOODS.

A popular coffeehouse just a couple of blocks from the UNM campus, ej's roasts its own specialty coffees and caters to natural-foods lovers. Breakfast includes granola and croissants from ej's own bakery. Lunch features homemade vegetarian soups, tempeh burgers, organic turkey sandwiches, and cheese enchiladas. The gourmet dinner menu lists shrimp linguine, spinach fettuccine Alfredo, Monterey chicken, and a vegetarian stir-fry.

✪ La Placita
208 San Felipe St. NW (Old Town Plaza). ☎ **505/247-2204.** Reservations recommended for large parties. Lunch $4.25–$7.25; dinner $6.25–$14.50. AE, DISC, MC, V. Daily 11am–9pm. NEW MEXICAN/AMERICAN.

Native American artisans spread their wares on the sidewalk outside the old Casa de Armijo, built by a wealthy Hispanic family in the early 18th century. The 283-year-old adobe hacienda, which faces the Old Town Plaza, features handcarved wooden doorways, deep-sunk windows, and an ancient patio. Fine regional art and furnishings decorate the five dining rooms and an upstairs gallery. The house favorite is a full Mexican dinner, which includes an enchilada colorado de queso, chile rellenos, taco de carne, frijoles con queso, arroz español, ensalada, and two sopaipillas. There is also a variety of beef, chicken, and fish selections.

Rudy's Country Store and Bar-B-Q

2321 Carlisle Blvd. NE (at I-40). ☎ **505/884-4000.** Main courses $3.75–$10.95. AE, DISC, MC, V. Daily 10am–1pm. BARBECUE.

Don't be put off by the picnic tables in this otherwise nondescript barbecue spot. There are three counters where you can order your meal. Start at the first counter by ordering your side dishes (for example, traditional pinto beans, potato salad, and creamed corn) by the pint. The second counter is where you order what you came for, delectable (and I'm not kidding) barbecue brisket, spare ribs, short ribs, chicken, and turkey—among other things. Finally, head to the third counter for beer, soda, and iced tea. The sauce, which is quite thin and spicy with lots of vinegar, is up to you (bottles are on each table). The dessert selections aren't worth mentioning, but chances are you won't have any room left anyway.

66 Diner

1405 Central Ave. NE. ☎ **505/247-1421.** Menu items $3–$6.25. AE, DISC, MC, V. Mon-Thurs 11am–11pm, Fri 11am–midnight, Sat 8am–midnight, Sun 8am–10pm. AMERICAN.

Like a trip back in time to the days when Martin Milner and George Maharis got "their kicks on Route 66," this thoroughly 1950s-style diner comes complete with Seeburg jukebox and full-service soda fountain. The white caps make great green-chile cheeseburgers, along with meat loaf sandwiches, grilled liver and onions, and chicken-fried steaks. Ham-and-egg and pancake breakfasts are served every morning. Beer and wine are available. After a devastating fire, 66 Diner has now been completely rebuilt (with the help of extraordinary community support). The owners hope to have the restaurant reopened by the time this book is published.

5 What to See & Do

Albuquerque's original town site, known today as Old Town, is the central point of interest for visitors. Here, grouped around the Plaza, are the venerable Church of San Felipe de Neri and numerous restaurants, art galleries, and crafts shops. Several important museums are situated close by.

But don't get stuck in Old Town. Elsewhere you will find the Sandia Peak Tramway, Kirtland Air Force Base and the National Atomic Museum, the University of New Mexico with its museums, and a number of natural attractions. Within day-trip range are several pueblos and a trio of significant monuments (see "Exploring Nearby Pueblos & Monuments," below.)

Note: As this book goes to press, the Albuquerque Aquarium and the Rio Grande Botanic Garden (near Central Ave. and Tingley Dr. NW) are under construction. It is hoped that the project, which will include a 25,000-square-foot aquarium and a 50-acre botanical garden, will be completed by October 1996. If you would like to visit them, call the Albuquerque Convention and Visitors Bureau to see if they are open.

THE TOP ATTRACTIONS

✪ Old Town

Northeast of Central Ave. and Rio Grande Blvd. NW.

A maze of cobbled courtyard walkways leads to hidden patios and gardens where many of Old Town's 150 galleries and shops are located. Adobe buildings, many refurbished in the Pueblo Revival style in the 1950s, are grouped around the tree-shaded **Plaza**, created in 1780. Pueblo and Navajo artisans often display their pottery, blankets, and silver jewelry on the sidewalks lining the Plaza.

The buildings of Old Town once served as mercantile shops, grocery stores, and government offices, but the importance of Old Town as Albuquerque's commercial center declined after 1880, when the railroad came through 1¼ miles east of the Plaza and businesses relocated to be closer to the trains. Old Town clung to its historical and sentimental roots, but the quarter fell into disrepair until the 1930s and 1940s, when it was rediscovered by artisans and other shop owners, and tourism burgeoned as an industry.

When Albuquerque was established in 1706, the first building erected by the settlers was the **Church of San Felipe de Neri,** which faces the Plaza on its north side. This house of worship has been in almost continuous use for about 290 years.

Guided **walking tours** of Old Town's historic buildings are offered by **Old Town Walking Tours** (Plaza Don Luis, 303 Romero NW #S 202 ☎ 505/246-9424). From March to November there are two tours daily (9:30am and 1:30pm) that last approximately 2½ hours. Reservations are not necessary. Call for current prices.

✪ Sandia Peak Tramway

10 Tramway Loop NE. ☎ **505/856-7325.** $13.50 adults, $10 seniors and children 5–12, free for children under 5. Memorial Day–Labor Day, daily 9am–10pm; spring and fall, Thurs–Tues 9am–8pm, Wed 5–8pm; ski season, Mon–Tues and Thurs–Fri 9am–8pm, Wed noon–8pm, Sat–Sun 8:30am–8pm. To reach the base of the tram, take I-25 north to the Tramway Road (exit 234), then proceed east about 5 miles on Tramway Road (NM 556); or take Tramway Boulevard, exit 167, (NM 556) north of I-40 approximately 8½ miles. Turn east the last half mile on Tramway Road.

The Sandia Peak tram is a "jigback"; in other words, as one car approaches the top, the other nears the bottom. The two pass half-way through the trip, in the midst of a 1½-mile "clear span" of unsupported cable between the second tower and the upper terminal.

Several hiking trails are available on Sandia Peak; one of them—La Luz Trail—is flat and quite easy. The views in all directions are extraordinary. *Note:* The trails on Sandia may not be suitable for children.

There is a popular and expensive restaurant at Sandia's summit, **High Finance** (see "Dining," earlier in this chapter). Special tram rates apply with dinner reservations.

✪ Indian Pueblo Cultural Center

2401 12th St. NW. ☎ **800/766-4405** or 505/843-7270. $3 adults, $2 seniors, $1 students, free for children 4 and under. Daily 9am–5:30pm; restaurant daily 7:30am–4pm. Closed Jan 1, Thanksgiving, and Dec 25. From Lomas Boulevard, turn north on 12th Street. The Cultural Center is on the left, just beyond the I-40 underpass. From midtown, head west on Menaul Boulevard and turn left onto 12th Street; the center will be on the right.

Owned and operated as a nonprofit organization by the 19 pueblos of New Mexico, this is a fine place to begin exploring local Native American culture. Situated about a mile northeast of Old Town, this museum—modeled after Pueblo Bonito, a spectacular 9th-century ruin in Chaco Culture National Historic Park—consists of several parts.

Traditional Native American Bread Baking

While visiting the pueblos in New Mexico, you'll probably notice outdoor ovens (they look a bit like giant anthills), known as *hornos*, which Native Americans have used for baking bread for hundreds of years. As is true for many cultural groups, Native Americans consider bread the staple of daily life. For Native Americans, making their typical bread is more than simply preparing food; it is a tradition that links them directly to their ancestors. The long process of mixing and baking also brings mothers and daughters together for what we today might call "quality time."

Usually in the evening the bread dough (ingredients: white flour, lard, salt, yeast, and water) is made and kneaded, and the loaves are shaped. They are allowed to rise overnight. Then, in the morning, the oven is filled with wood and a fire lighted. After the fire burns down to ashes and embers, the oven is cleared and the ashes are shoveled away. Unlike modern ovens, *hornos* don't come equipped with thermometers, so the baker must rely on her senses to determine when the oven is the proper temperature. At that point the loaves are placed into the oven with a long-handled wooden paddle. They bake for about an hour.

If you would like to try a traditional loaf, you can buy one at the Indian Pueblo Cultural Center in Albuquerque (and elsewhere throughout the state).

In the basement, a permanent exhibit depicts the evolution (from prehistory to the present) of the various pueblos, including displays of the distinctive handcrafts of each community. Note, especially, how pottery differs in concept and design from pueblo to pueblo. The displays include a series of remarkable photographs of Pueblo tribe members taken between 1880 and 1910, a gift of the Smithsonian Institution. The Pueblo House Children's Museum, also on the premises, is a hands-on museum that gives children the opportunity to learn about and understand the evolution of Pueblo culture.

Upstairs is an enormous gift shop—a fine place to check the price of the Pueblo peoples' colorful ceramics, weavings, and paintings before you barter with private artisans. The Indian Arts and Crafts Association's code of ethics guarantees that the work here is stylistically authentic and that everything was made by Native Americans only. A gallery displays a variety of ancient and modern works from different pueblos, and the exhibits change monthly.

Local Native American dancers perform and artisans demonstrate their craft expertise in an outdoor arena surrounded by original murals. **Craft fairs** are held on July 4th weekend, the first weekend in October, and Thanksgiving weekend.

A **restaurant,** open for breakfast and lunch daily from 7:30am to 4pm, emphasizes the cornmeal-based foods of the Pueblo people. An ample meal might consist of posole, treated dried corn with beef, chile, and oven-fried bread.

✪ Albuquerque Museum

2000 Mountain Rd. NW. ☎ **505/243-7255.** Free admission, but donations are appreciated. Tues–Sun 9am–5pm. Closed major holidays.

The largest U.S. collection of Spanish colonial artifacts is housed here. Included are arms and armor used during the Hispanic conquest, medieval religious artifacts and weavings, maps from the 16th to 18th centuries, and coins and domestic goods traded during that era. A multimedia audiovisual presentation, *Four Centuries: A History of Albuquerque*, depicts the history of the mid–Rio Grande region from the Spanish conquest to the present. "History Hopscotch" is a hands-on history exhi-

Central Albuquerque Attractions

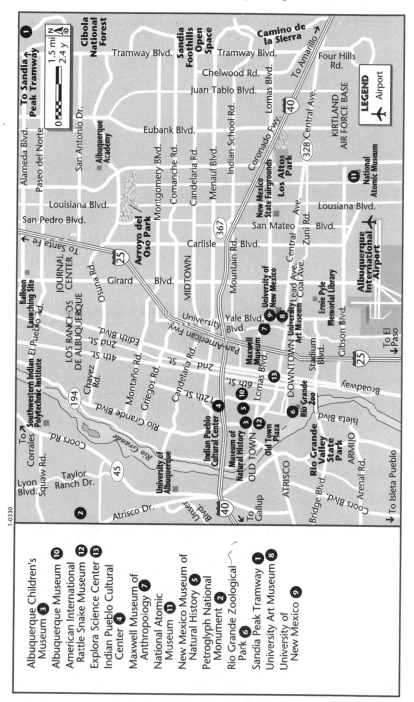

213

bit designed specifically for children. There's also a gallery of early and modern New Mexico art, with permanent and changing exhibits; a major photo archive; and a sculpture garden. Some of the exhibits scheduled for 1997 are: *Rodin: Sculpture from the B. Gerald Cantor Collection, Larry Bell Retrospective, Inventing the Southwest: Fred Harvey Company & Southwest Native Art,* and *The Art of Tibet.* From time to time children's exhibits and classes are offered. A gift shop sells a variety of souvenirs and other wares.

MORE ATTRACTIONS

✪ National Atomic Museum

Wyoming Blvd. and K St. (P.O. Box 5800), Kirtland Air Force Base. ☎ **505/284-3243.** Free admission. Visitors must obtain passes (and a map) at the Wyoming or Gibson Gate of the base. Children under 12 not admitted without parent or adult guardian. Daily 9am–5pm. Closed Jan 1, Easter, Thanksgiving, and Dec 25.

This museum is the next-best introduction to the nuclear age after the Bradbury Science Museum in Los Alamos. It traces the history of nuclear weapons development beginning with the top-secret Manhattan Project of the 1940s, including a copy of the letter Albert Einstein wrote to Pres. Franklin D. Roosevelt suggesting the possible development of an atomic bomb. A 51-minute film, *Ten Seconds That Shook the World,* is shown every hour.

There are full-scale models of the "Fat Man" and "Little Boy" bombs, and displays and films on the peaceful application of nuclear technology and other alternative energy sources. Fusion is explained in a manner that a layperson could understand; other exhibits deal with the problem of nuclear waste. Outdoor exhibits include a B-52 "Stratofortress," an F-1015D "Thunderchief," and a 280mm atomic cannon. An hour-long tour takes visitors through the development of the first nuclear weapons to today's technology. You'll also see a solar-powered TV and be able to test your budgeting skills as you use the Energy-Environment Simulator to manipulate energy allocations to make the planet's supplies last longer. The museum is directly across the street from the International Nuclear Weapons School, adjacent to Sandia National Laboratory.

Petroglyph National Monument

4735 Unser Blvd. NW (west of Coors Rd.). ☎ **505/839-4429** or 505/899-0205. $1 per vehicle weekdays, $2 weekends. Summer, daily 9am–6pm; winter, daily 8am–5pm. Closed state holidays.

Albuquerque's western city limits are marked by five extinct volcanoes. Adjacent lava flows became a hunting and gathering area for prehistoric Native Americans, who lived here and left a chronicle of their beliefs etched and chipped in the dark basalt boulders. Some 15,000 of these petroglyphs have been found in several concentrated groups at this archaeological preserve. Plaques interpret the rock drawings—animal, human, and ceremonial forms—to visitors, who have a choice of four hiking trails, ranging from easy to moderately difficult, winding through the lava. The 45-minute Mesa Point trail is the most strenuous but also the most rewarding.

Camping is not permitted in the park; it's strictly for day use, with picnic areas, drinking water, and restrooms provided.

Rio Grande Nature Center State Park

2901 Candelaria Rd. NW. ☎ **505/344-7240.** Admission $1 adults, 50¢ children 6 and older, free for children under 6. Daily 10am–5pm. Closed Jan 1, Thanksgiving, and Dec 25.

Located on the Rio Grande Flyway, an important migratory route for many birds, this wildlife refuge extends for nearly a mile along the east bank of the Rio Grande. Numerous nature trails wind through the cottonwood bosque, where a large variety of native and migratory species can be seen at any time of year. The center publishes a checklist to help visitors identify them, as well as several self-guiding trail brochures.

Housed in a unique building constructed half above ground and half below, the visitor center houses classrooms, laboratory space, a library, a gift shop, and exhibits describing the history, geology, and ecology of the Rio Grande valley. Informative hikes are scheduled every weekend.

University of New Mexico

Yale Blvd. NE (north of Central Ave.). ☎ **505/277-0111.**

The state's largest institution of higher learning stretches across an attractive 70-acre campus about 2 miles east of downtown Albuquerque, north of Central Avenue and east of University Boulevard. The five campus museums, none of which charges admission, are constructed (like other UNM buildings) in a modified Pueblo style. Popejoy Hall, in the south-central part of the campus, hosts many performing-arts presentations, including those of the New Mexico Symphony Orchestra; other public events are held in nearby Keller Hall and Woodward Hall.

The **Maxwell Museum of Anthropology,** situated on the west side of the campus on Redondo Drive at Ash Street NE (☎ **505/277-4404**), is an internationally acclaimed repository of southwestern anthropological finds. It's open Monday through Friday from 9am to 4pm, Saturday from 10am to 4pm, and Sunday from noon to 4pm; closed holidays.

The **University of New Mexico Art Museum** (☎ **505/277-4001**) is located in the UNM College of Fine Arts Center, just north of Central Avenue and Cornell Street. The museum features changing exhibitions of 19th- and 20th-century art. Its permanent collection includes Old Masters paintings and sculpture, significant New Mexico artists, Spanish colonial art work, the Tamarind Lithography Archives, and one of the largest university-owned photography collections in the country. It's open Tuesday through Friday from 9am to 4pm; Tuesday evenings from 5 to 8pm; and Sunday from 1 to 4pm; closed holidays. A gift shop offers a variety of gifts and posters. Admission is free.

A branch of the University of New Mexico's Art Museum, **5·1·6 university art museum downtown** (☎ **505/242-8244**) is located at 516 Central Ave. SW. Its two floors of exhibition space feature changing exhibits of 19th- and 20th-century art and a variety of featured artists. It's open Tuesday through Saturday from 11am to 4pm (closed holidays). There is a gift shop offering cards, posters, jewelry, and art gift items. Admission is free.

The intimate **Jonson Gallery** at 1909 Las Lomas Blvd. NE (☎ **505/277-4967**), on the north side of the central campus, displays more than 2,000 works by the late Raymond Jonson, a leading modernist painter in early 20th-century New Mexico, as well as works by contemporary artists. The gallery is open Tuesday from 9am to 4pm and 5 to 8pm, and Wednesday through Friday from 9am to 4pm.

In Northrop Hall (☎ **505/277-4204**), about halfway between the Maxwell Museum and Popejoy Hall in the southern part of the campus, the adjacent **Geology Museum** and **Meteorite Museum** (☎ **505/277-1644**) cover the gamut of recorded time from dinosaur bones to moon rocks. The 550 meteorite specimens here comprise the sixth-largest collection in the United States. The Geology

Museum is open Monday through Friday from 8am to 5pm; the Meteorite Museum, Monday through Friday from 9am to noon and 1 to 4pm.

Finally, the **Museum of Southwestern Biology,** in the basement of the Biology Department at Castetter Hall (☎ **505/277-5340**), has few displays but rather extensive research holdings of global flora and fauna, especially representative of southwestern North America, Central America, South America, and parts of Asia. Call for times and other information.

6 Especially for Kids

Albuquerque Children's Museum

800 Rio Grande Blvd. NW., Suite 10. ☎ **505/842-1537.** Admission $3 children 2–12, $1 ages 13 and up, free for kids under 2. Tues–Sat 10am–5pm, Sun noon–5pm.

At the Albuquerque Children's Museum there's something for everyone: bubbles, whisper disks, a puppet theater, a giant loom, a dress-up area, zoetropes, a capture-your-shadow wall, art activities, science demonstrations, and a giant pin-hole camera. The museum also sponsors wonderful educational workshops. "The Me I Don't Always See" was a health exhibit designed to teach children about the mysteries of the human body, and a Great Artists Series featured live performances about artists' lives and work followed by a related art activity.

American International Rattlesnake Museum

202 San Felipe St. NW ☎ **505/242-6569.** Admission $2 adults, $1 children. Daily 10am–6:30pm.

This unique museum, located just off Old Town Plaza, has living specimens of common, uncommon, and very rare rattlesnakes of North, Central, and South America in naturally landscaped habitats. Oddities such as albinos and patternless rattlesnakes are included, with a popular display for youngsters—baby rattlesnakes. More than 30 species can be seen, followed by a seven-minute film on this contributor to the ecological balance of our hemisphere. Throughout the museum are rattlesnake artifacts of early American history, Native American culture, medicine, the arts, and advertising.

You'll also find a gift shop that specializes in Native American jewelry, T-shirts, and other memorabilia related to the natural world and the Southwest, all with an emphasis on rattlesnakes.

Explora Science Center

40 1st Plaza/Galleria #68 (at Second St. and Tijeras Ave. NW). ☎ **505/842-6188.** Admission $2 adults, $1 children 5–17 and seniors 62 and older, free for children 4 and under. Wed–Sat 10am–5pm, Sun noon–5pm.

Children and adults alike will enjoy a trip to the Explora Science Center, a hands-on science and technology museum. Kids will learn about air pressure by firing an air cannon, flying a model plane, and floating a ball on a stream of air. The light and electricity exhibits allow museum-goers to create their own laser shows and freeze their shadows. Furthermore, there are motion, health and body, fluid, and sound exhibits—all hands on.

✪ New Mexico Museum of Natural History & Science

1801 Mountain Rd. NW. ☎ **505/841-2800.** Admission $5.25 adults, $4.20 seniors, $2.10 children 3–11. Museum and Dynamax, $8.40 adults, $6.30 seniors, $3.15 children 3–11.

Children under 12 must be accompanied by an adult. Daily 9am–5pm. Closed Mon in Jan and Sept, and Christmas Day.

Two life-size bronze dinosaurs stand outside the entrance to this modern museum, opposite the Albuquerque Museum. Inside, innovative video displays, polarizing lenses, and black lighting enable visitors to stroll through geologic time. You can walk a rocky path through the Hall of Giants, as dinosaurs fight and winged reptiles swoop overhead; step into a seemingly live volcano, complete with simulated magma flow; or share an Ice Age cave, festooned with stalagmites, with saber-toothed tigers and woolly mammoths. Hands-on exhibits in the Naturalist Center permit use of a video microscope, viewing of an active beehive, and participation in a variety of other activities. For an additional charge, the giant-screen Dynamax Theater puts you into the on-screen action.

There's a gift shop on the ground floor, and a Subway Sandwich shop on the mezzanine. At press time, a new space for changing exhibits was being completed.

Rio Grande Zoological Park

903 10th St. SW. ☎ **505/764-6200.** Admission $4.25 adults, $2.25 children and seniors. Children under 12 must be accompanied by an adult. Mon–Thurs 9am–4:30, Sat–Sun 9am–5:30pm. Closed Jan 1, Thanksgiving, and Dec. 25.

Open-moat exhibits with animals in naturalized habitats are a treat for zoo-goers. Major exhibits include the giraffes, sea lions (with underwater viewing), the cat walk, the bird show, and ape country with its gorilla and orangutans. More than 1,200 animals of 300 species live on 60 acres of riverside bosque among ancient cottonwoods. The zoo has an especially fine collection of elephants, mountain lions, koalas, reptiles, and native southwestern species. A children's petting zoo is open during the summer, and in the fall of 1996 an aquarium and botanical garden were scheduled to open. There are numerous snack bars on the zoo grounds, and La Ventana Gift Shop carries film and souvenirs.

7 Outdoor Activities

BALLOONING Visitors not content to watch the colorful craft rise into the clear-blue skies have a choice of several hot-air balloon operators; rates start at about $100 per person:

Braden's Balloons Aloft, 3212 Stanford Dr. NE (☎ 505/281-2714).

Rainbow Ryders, 10305 Nita Pl. NE (☎ **505/293-0000**).

World Balloon Corporation, 4800 Eubank Blvd. NE (☎ **505/293-6800**).

The annual **Kodak Albuquerque International Balloon Fiesta®** is held the first through second weekends of October (see "Northern New Mexico Calendar of Events," in Chapter 2, for details).

BIKING Albuquerque is a major bicycling hub in the summer, both for road racers and mountain bikers. Bikes can be rented from **Big River Bike** (1613 Virginia St. NE ☎ 505/294-6800), **R.E.I.** (1905 Mountain Rd. NW ☎ **505/247-1191**), and **Rio Mountain Sport** (1210 Rio Grande NW ☎ **505/766-9970**). Big River Bike and R.E.I. supply bikers with helmets, maps, and locks. A great place to bike is Sandia Peak in Cíbola National Forest. You can't take your bike on the tram, but Chairlift no. 1 is available for up- or downhill transportation with a bike. If you'd rather not rent a bike from one of the above-mentioned sports stores, bike rentals are available at the top and bottom of the chairlift. The lift ride one way with a bike is $6, all day with a bike will cost you $10. Helmets are mandatory. Bike maps are available; the clearly marked trails range from easy to very difficult. Mountain Bike

Challenge Events are held on Sandia Peak in May, July, and August. For information about other mountain bike areas, contact the Albuquerque Convention and Visitors Bureau or ask for bike maps at the bike-rental outlets listed above.

FISHING   There are no real fishing opportunities in Albuquerque as such, but there is a nearby fishing area known as Shady Lakes. Nestled among cottonwood trees, it's located near I-25 on Albuquerque's north side. The most common catches are rainbow trout, black bass, bluegill, and channel catfish. To reach Shady Lakes, take I-25 north to the Tramway Exit. Follow Tramway Road west for a mile and then go right on NM 313 for a half mile. Call **505/898-2568** for information. **Sandia Lakes Recreational Area** (☎ **505/897-3971**), also located on NM 313, is another popular fishing spot. There is a bait and tackle shop there.

GOLF   There are quite a few public courses in the Albuquerque area. The Championship Golf Course at the University of New Mexico (3601 University Blvd, SE; ☎ **505/277-4546**) is one of the best in the Southwest and was rated one of the country's top 25 public links by *Golf Digest*. Paradise Hills Golf Course (10035 Country Club Ln., NW; ☎ **505/898-7001** for tee times and information) is a popular 18-hole golf course that has recently been completely renovated.

Other Albuquerque courses to check with for tee times are **Ladera,** located at 3401 Ladera Dr., NW (☎ **505/836-4449**); **Los Altos** at 9717 Copper Ave. NE (☎ **505/298-1897**); **Puerto del Sol,** 1800 Girard Blvd. SE (☎ **505/265-5636**); and **Arroyo del Oso,** 7001 Osuna Rd. NE (☎ **505/888-8115**).

If you're willing to drive a short distance just outside Albuquerque, you can play at the **Santa Ana Golf Club at Santa Ana Pueblo** (288 Prairie Star Rd. [P.O. Box 1736], Bernalillo, NM 87004; ☎ **505/867-9464**), which was rated by *The New York Times* as one of the best public golf courses in the country. Rentals are available (call for information), and greens fees range from $20 to $50 depending on where you want to play.

In addition, **Isleta Pueblo** is currently in the process of building an 18-hole golf course. It is expected to open for play in the summer of 1996.

HIKING   The 1.6-million-acre **Cíbola National Forest** offers ample opportunities. In the Sandia Ranger District alone there are 16 recreation sites, though only two allow overnight camping. For details, contact Sandia Ranger Station, NM 337 south toward Tijeras (☎ **505/381-3304**).

Elena Gallegos/Albert G. Simms Park, near the base of the Sandia Peak Tramway at 1700 Tramway Blvd. NE (☎ **505/291-6224** or 505/768-3550), is a 640-acre mountain picnic area with hiking-trail access to the Sandia Mountain Wilderness.

For a guided tour, contact **South Mountain Wilderness Tours, Inc.,** P.O. Box 638, Edgewood, NM 87015; ☎ **505/281-9638.** You'll do the hiking and mules will carry the load. Women-only hiking trips are available.

HORSEBACK RIDING   There are a couple of places in Albuquerque that offer guided or unguided horseback rides. At **Sandia Trails Horse Rentals** (10601 N. 4th St. ☎ **505/898-6970**), you'll have the opportunity to ride on Sandia Indian Reservation land along the Rio Grande. The horses are friendly and are accustomed to children. In addition, **Turkey Track Stables, Inc.** (1306 US 66 East Tijeras ☎ **505/281-1772**), located about 15 miles east of Albuquerque, offers rides on trails in the Manzano foothills. Riding lessons are available.

RIVER RAFTING   This sport generally takes place farther north, in the area surrounding Santa Fe and Taos.

In mid-May each year, the **Great Race** takes place on a 14-mile stretch of the Rio Grande through Albuquerque. Eleven categories of craft, including rafts, kayaks, and canoes, race down the river. Call ☎ **505/768-3490** for details.

SKIING   The **Sandia Peak Ski Area** has twin base-to-summit chairlifts to its upper slopes at 10,360 feet, and a 1,700-foot vertical drop. There are 25 runs (35% beginner, 55% intermediate, 10% advanced) above the day lodge and ski-rental shop. Four chairs and two pomas accommodate 3,400 skiers an hour. All-day lift tickets are $30 for adults, $21 for children; rental packages are $14 for adults, $11 for kids. The season runs from mid-December to mid-March. Contact 10 Tramway Loop NE (☎ **505/242-9133**) for more information, or call the hotline for ski conditions (☎ **505/242-9052**).

Cross-country skiers can enjoy the trails of the Sandia Wilderness from the ski area, or they can go an hour north to the remote Jemez Wilderness and its hot springs.

TENNIS   There are 29 public parks in Albuquerque with tennis courts. Because of the city's size, your best bet is to call the Albuquerque Convention and Visitors Bureau to find out which park is closest to your hotel.

8   Spectator Sports

BASEBALL   The Albuquerque Dukes, 1994 champions of the Class AAA Pacific Coast League, are a farm team of the Los Angeles Dodgers. They play 72 home games from mid-April to early September in the city-owned 10,500-seat Albuquerque Sports Stadium, 1601 Stadium Blvd. SE (at University Boulevard) (☎ **505/243-1791**).

BASKETBALL   The University of New Mexico team, nicknamed "The Lobos," plays an average of 16 home games from late November to early March. Capacity crowds cheer the team at the 17,121-seat University Arena (fondly called "The Pit") at University and Stadium Boulevards. The arena was the site of the National Collegiate Athletic Association championship tournament in 1983.

FOOTBALL   The UNM Lobos football team plays a September to November season, usually with five home games, at the 30,000-seat University of New Mexico Stadium, opposite both Albuquerque Sports Stadium and University Arena at University and Stadium Boulevards.

HORSE RACING   **The Downs at Albuquerque,** New Mexico State Fairgrounds (☎ **505/266-5555** for post times), is near Lomas and Louisiana Boulevards NE. Racing and betting—on thoroughbreds and quarter horses—take place on Wednesday, Friday, and Saturday from late January to June and during the state fair in September. The Downs has a glass-enclosed grandstand, exclusive club seating, valet parking, and complimentary racing programs and tip sheets. General admission is free; reserved second floor seating is $2.

9   Shopping

Visitors interested in regional specialties will find many artists and galleries, although they are not so concentrated as they are in Santa Fe and Taos. The galleries and regional fashion designers around the Plaza in Old Town comprise sort of a shopping center for tourists, with more than 40 merchants represented. The Sandia

Pueblo people run their own crafts market at their reservation off I-25 at Tramway Road, just beyond Albuquerque's northern city limits.

Albuquerque has the two largest shopping malls in New Mexico within two blocks of one another, both on Louisiana Boulevard just north of I-40—Coronado Center and Winrock Center.

Business hours vary, but shops are generally open Monday through Saturday from 10am to 6pm; many have extended hours; some have reduced hours; and a few, especially in shopping malls or during the high tourist season, are open on Sunday.

The Albuquerque sales tax is 5.8125%.

BEST BUYS

The best buys in Albuquerque are southwestern regional items, including **arts and crafts** of all kinds, from traditional Native American and Hispanic to contemporary works. In local Native American art, look for silver and turquoise jewelry, pottery, weavings, baskets, sand paintings, and Hopi kachina dolls. Hispanic folk art, including handcrafted furniture, tinwork and retablos, and religious paintings, is worth seeking out. The best contemporary art is in paintings, sculpture, jewelry, ceramics, and fiber art, including weaving.

By far the greatest concentration of **galleries** is in Old Town; others are spread around the city, with smaller groupings in the university district and the northeast heights. Consult the brochure published by the Albuquerque Gallery Association, "A Select Guide to Albuquerque Galleries," or Wingspread Communications' annual *The Collector's Guide to Albuquerque,* widely distributed at shops. Once a month, usually from 5 to 9pm on the third Friday, the **Albuquerque Art Business Association** (☎ **800/284-2282** or 505/842-9918 for information) sponsors an ArtsCrawl to dozens of galleries and studios. If you're in town, it's a great way to meet the artists.

Other items of potential interest are **fashions** in southwestern print designs; **gourmet foods/ingredients,** including blue-corn flour and chile ristras; and unique regional **souvenirs,** especially local Native American and Hispanic creations.

10 Albuquerque After Dark

Albuquerque has an active performing-arts and nightlife scene, as befits a city of half a million people. The performing arts are multicultural, with Hispanic and (to a lesser extent) Native American productions sharing time with Anglo works, including theater, opera, symphony, and dance. Albuquerque also attracts many national touring companies. Country music predominates in nightclubs, though aficionados of rock, jazz, and other forms of music can find them here as well.

Complete information on all major cultural events can be obtained from the **Albuquerque Convention and Visitors Bureau** (☎ **800/284-2282** for recorded information after 5pm). Current listings appear in the two daily newspapers; detailed weekend arts calendars can be found in the Thursday evening *Tribune* and the Friday morning *Journal.* The monthly *On the Scene* also carries entertainment listings.

Tickets for nearly all major entertainment and sporting events can be obtained from **TicketMaster,** 4004 Carlisle Blvd. NE (☎ **505/884-0999** for information, or

505/842-5387 to place credit or charge-card orders on American Express, MasterCard, or Visa). Discount tickets are often available for midweek and matinee performances. Check with specific theaters or concert halls.

THE PERFORMING ARTS

CLASSICAL MUSIC

Chamber Orchestra of Albuquerque

2730 San Pedro Dr. NE, Suite H-23. ☎ **505/881-0844.** Tickets, $12–$25, depending on seating and performance.

This 31-member professional orchestra, conducted by music director David Oberg, performs from September to June, primarily at St. John's United Methodist Church, 2626 Arizona St. NE. There is a subscription series of six classical concerts (in October, November, January, March, May, and June), an all-baroque concert in February, concerts for children in February and April, and a joint concert with the University of New Mexico Chorus. The orchestra regularly features guest artists of national and international renown.

New Mexico Symphony Orchestra

3301 Menaul Blvd. NE, Suite 4. ☎ **800/251-6676** or 505/881-9590 for tickets and information. Ticket prices vary with concert; call for details.

NMSO musicians may be the busiest performing artists in New Mexico. During its 1996–97 season, the orchestra will perform about 30 classical, pops, baroque, and family concerts from September to May, plus ensemble programs in all Albuquerque elementary schools and tours to a dozen communities throughout the state. Concert venues range from Popejoy Hall on the University of New Mexico campus to the 2,500-seat Hoffmantown Baptist Church to the outdoor bandshell at the Rio Grande Zoo.

DANCE

New Mexico Ballet Company

3620 Wyoming Blvd. NE (P.O. Box 21518). ☎ **505/292-4245.** Tickets, $10–$16 adults, $5–$8 students.

Founded in 1972, the state's oldest ballet company performs an October-to-April season at Popejoy Hall. Typically there is a fall production such as *The Legend of Sleepy Hollow*, a December performance of *The Nutcracker* or *A Christmas Carol*, and a contemporary spring production.

THEATER

Albuquerque Civic Light Opera Association

4201 Ellison Rd. NE. ☎ **505/345-6577.** Ticket prices vary. $10–$18.50 adults, $8–$16.50 students and seniors.

Five major Broadway musicals are presented each year at Popejoy Hall during a March-to-December season. Each production is staged for three consecutive weekends, including two Sunday matinees. In 1996, its 29th season, ACLOA presented *Oliver*.

The Major Concert and Performance Halls

Keller Hall, University of New Mexico, Cornell St. at Redondo Drive South, ☎ 505/277-4402.

KiMo Theatre, 423 Central Ave., ☎ 505/764-1700.

Popejoy Hall, University of New Mexico, Cornell St. at Redondo Drive South, ☎ 505/277-3121.

South Broadway Cultural Center, 1025 Broadway Blvd., ☎ 505/848-1320.

Albuquerque Little Theatre

224 San Pasquale Ave. SW. ☎ **505/242-4750.**

The Albuquerque Little Theatre has been offering a variety of productions ranging from comedies to dramas to musicals since 1930. Six plays are presented here annually during a September-to-May season. Located across from Old Town, Albuquerque Little Theatre offers plenty of free parking. The 1996–97 schedule includes *The Cemetery Club, Sleuth, The Secret Garden, A Comedy of Errors, A Few Good Men,* and *The Good Doctor.*

La Companía de Teatro de Albuquerque

518 First St. NW. ☎ **505/242-7929.** Tickets, $9 adults Thurs and Sun, $10 Fri–Sat; $8 students, seniors, and children Thurs and Sun, $9 Fri–Sat.

One of the few major professional Hispanic companies in the United States and Puerto Rico, La Companía stages a series of productions every year between October and June. Comedies, dramas, and musicals are offered, along with one Spanish-language play a year.

Vortex Theatre

Buena Vista (just South of Central Ave.). ☎ **505/247-8600.** Tickets, $8 adults, $7 students and seniors, $6 children 13 and under; $6 for everyone Sun.

An 18-year-old community theater known for its innovative productions, the Vortex is Albuquerque's "Off-Broadway" theater, presenting a range of plays from classic to original. The company mounts 10 shows a year, including (in 1996) *Six Degrees of Separation.* Performances take place on Friday and Saturday at 8pm and on Sunday at 6pm. The black-box theater seats 90.

THE CLUB & MUSIC SCENE

COMEDY CLUBS/DINNER THEATER

Laffs Comedy Caffè

3100-D Juan Tabo Blvd. (at Candelaria Rd. NE). ☎ **505/296-JOKE.**

Top acts from each coast, including comedians who have appeared on the *Late Show with David Letterman* and HBO, are booked at Albuquerque's top comedy club. Show times are Tuesday through Sunday at 8pm, with second shows on Friday and Saturday at 10:30pm. Tuesday is "Best of Albuquerque Night." Wednesday is smoke-free night; Thursday and Sunday are Laff's T-shirt nights. The Laffs Comedy Caffè serves dinner nightly from 6pm.

Mystery Cafe

In La Posada de Albuquerque, 125 Second St. NW. ☎ **505/237-1385.**

If you're in the mood for a little interactive dinner theater, the Mystery Cafe might be just the ticket. You'll help the characters in this ever popular, delightfully funny show solve the mystery as they serve you a four-course meal. Reservations are a must. Call for show times and prices.

COUNTRY MUSIC

Midnight Rodeo

4901 McLeod Rd. NE (near San Mateo Blvd.). ☎ **505/888-0100.** No cover Sun–Thurs, $3 Fri–Sat.

The Southwest's largest nightclub of any kind, Midnight Rodeo has bars in all corners of its enormous domicile and even has its own shopping arcade, including a boutique and gift shop. A DJ spins records daily until closing; the hardwood dance floor is so big (5,000 square feet) that it resembles an indoor horse track. Free dance lessons are offered on Sunday from 5:30 to 7pm. A busy kitchen serves simple but hearty meals to dancers who work up appetites.

ROCK/JAZZ

Brewsters Pub

312 Central Ave. SW. ☎ **505/247-2533.**

Wednesday through Saturday nights, Brewsters Pub offers live entertainment in a "sports bar"–type setting. There are 24 beers on tap, as well as a wide variety of bottled beer. Sports fans can enjoy the game on a big-screen TV. Barbecue is served at lunch and dinner.

The Cooperage

7220 Lomas Blvd. NE. ☎ **505/255-1657.** Cover $3–$5.

Jazz, rhythm-and-blues, rock, and salsa keep dancers hopping on Friday and Saturday nights inside this gigantic wooden barrel.

Dingo Bar

313 Gold Ave. SW. ☎ **505/243-0663.** Cover charge varies with performance, but can run up to $20 per person.

The Dingo Bar is one of Albuquerque's premier rock clubs. Nightly live entertainment runs from punk rock to classic rock 'n' roll and jazz.

MORE ENTERTAINMENT

Albuquerque's best nighttime attraction is the **Sandia Peak Tramway** (see "What to See & Do," above) and the restaurant High Finance at the summit (see "Dining," above). Here you can enjoy a view nonpareil of the Rio Grande valley and the city lights.

The best place to catch foreign films, art films, and limited-release productions is the **Guild Cinema,** 3405 Central Ave. NE (☎ **505/255-1848**). For film classics, check out the **Southwest Film Center,** on the UNM campus (☎ **505/277-5608**), with double features Wednesday through Sunday, changing nightly.

Major Albuquerque **first-run theaters** include the **Coronado Six Theater,** 6401 Uptown Blvd. NE (☎ **505/881-5266**); **Del Norte Cinema Four,** 7120 Wyoming Blvd. NE (☎ **505/823-6666**); **United Artists Four Hills 10 Theater,** 13160 Central Ave. SE, at Tramway Boulevard (☎ **505/275-2114**); **Ladera Six Cinema,** 3301 Coors Blvd. NW (☎ **505/836-5606**); **United Artists Montgomery Plaza-5,** 165 Montgomery Plaza NE (at San Mateo Blvd.) (☎ **505/881-1080**); **General Cinemas San Mateo Cinema 8,** 631 San Mateo Blvd. NE (☎ **505/889-3051**);

United Artists 8 at High Ridge, Tramway Boulevard (at Indian School Road) (☎ **505/275-0038**); and **Winrock 6 UA Cinema,** 201 Winrock Center NE (☎ **505/883-6022**).

The **Isleta Gaming Palace,** 11000 Broadway SE (☎ **800/460-5686** or 505/ 869-2614), is a luxurious, air-conditioned casino (blackjack, poker, slots, bingo, and keno) with a full-service restaurant, no-smoking section, and free bus transportation on request. It's open 24 hours a day. At press time, the casino had plans to open a hotel.

11 Exploring Nearby Pueblos & Monuments

Ten Native American **pueblos** are located within an hour's drive from central Albuquerque. One national and two state monuments preserve another five ancient pueblo ruins.

The active pueblos nearby include Acoma, Cochiti, Isleta, Jemez, Laguna, Sandia, San Felipe, Santa Ana, Santo Domingo, and Zia. Of these, Acoma is the most prominent.

When you visit pueblos, it is important to observe certain **rules of etiquette:** Remember to respect the pueblos as people's homes; don't peek into doors and windows or climb on top the buildings. Stay out of cemeteries and ceremonial rooms (such as kivas), since these are sacred grounds; don't speak during dances or ceremonies or applaud after their conclusion; silence is mandatory. Most pueblos require a permit to carry a camera or to sketch or paint on location. Several pueblos prohibit picture taking at any time.

✪ Acoma Pueblo

To reach Acoma from Albuquerque, drive west on I-40 approximately 52 miles to the Acoma-Sky City exit (Exit 108), then about 12 miles southwest.

The spectacular "Sky City," a walled adobe village perched high atop a sheer rock mesa 365 feet above the 6,600-foot valley floor, is believed to have been inhabited at least since the 11th century—the longest continuously occupied community in the United States. Native legend claims that it has been inhabited since before the time of Christ. Both the pueblo and **San Estevan del Rey Mission** are National Historic Landmarks.

The Keresan-speaking Acoma (*Ack*-oo-mah) Pueblo boasts about 6,005 inhabitants, but only about 50 people reside year round on the 70-acre mesa top. They make their living from tourists who come to see the large church containing examples of Spanish colonial art and to purchase the pueblo's thin-walled white **pottery** with polychrome designs.

The pueblo's address is P.O. Box 309, Acoma, NM 87034. ☎ **505/470-4966.** The admission charge is $6 for adults, $5 for seniors, $4 children 6 through 17, free for children under 6. The charge to take still photographs is $5, *video cameras are allowed by special permission only.* The pueblo is open daily in the summer from 8am to 7pm; daily in the spring, fall, and winter from 8am to 4:30pm. One-hour tours begin every 30 minutes; the last tour is scheduled one hour before closing. The pueblo is closed the first or second weekend in October and also July 10 to 13.

Start your tour at the **visitor center** at the base of the mesa. There is a **museum** and **cafe** here. A 16-seat **tour bus** climbs through a rock garden of 50-foot sandstone monoliths and past precipitously dangling outhouses to the mesa's summit.

There's no running water or electricity in this medieval-looking village; a small reservoir collects rainwater for most purposes, but drinking water is transported up from below. Wood-hole ladders and mica windows are prevalent among the 300-odd adobe structures.

Salinas Pueblo Missions National Monument

P.O. Box 496, Mountainair, NM 87036. ☎ **505/847-2585.** Free admission. Sites, daily 9am–6pm in summer, 9am–5pm the rest of the year. Visitor center in Mountainair, daily 8am–5pm. Closed Jan 1 and Dec 25. Abo is 9 miles west of Mountainair on US 60. Quarai is 8 miles north of Mountainair on NM 55. Gran Quivira is 25 miles south of Mountainair on NM 55. All roads are paved.

The Spanish conquistadors' Salinas Jurisdiction, on the east side of the Manzano Mountains (southeast of Albuquerque), was an important 17th-century trade center because of the salt extracted by the Native Americans from the salt lakes. Franciscan priests, utilizing native labor, constructed missions of Abo red sandstone and blue-gray limestone for the native converts. The ruins of some of the most durable missions—along with evidence of preexisting Anasazi and Mogollon cultures—are highlights of a visit to Salinas Pueblo Missions National Monument. The monument consists of three separate units: the ruins of Abo, Quarai, and Gran Quivira. They are situated around the quiet town of Mountainair, 75 miles southeast of Albuquerque at the junction of US 60 and NM 55.

Abo (☎ **505/847-2400**) boasts the 40-foot-high ruins of the Mission of San Gregorio de Abo, a rare example of medieval architecture in the United States. **Quarai** (☎ **505/847-2290**) preserves the largely intact remains of the Mission of La Purísima Concepción de Cuarac (1630). Its vast size, 100 feet long and 40 feet high, contrasts with the modest size of the pueblo mounds. A small museum in the visitor center has a scale model of the original church, along with a selection of artifacts found at the site. **Gran Quivira** (☎ **505/847-2770**) once had a population of 1,500. Las Humanes has 300 rooms and seven kivas. Rooms dating back to 1300 can be seen. There are indications that an older village, dating back to 800, may have previously stood here. Ruins of two churches (one almost 140 feet long) and a *convento* have been preserved. A museum with many artifacts from the site, a 40-minute movie showing the excavation of some 200 rooms, plus a short history video of Las Humanes can be seen at the visitor center.

All three pueblos and the churches that were constructed above them are believed to have been abandoned in the 1670s. Self-guided tour pamphlets can be obtained at the units' respective visitor centers and at the Salinas Pueblo Missions National Monument Visitor Center in Mountainair, on US 60 one block west of the intersection of US 60 and NM 55. The visitor center offers an audiovisual presentation on the region's history, a bookstore, and an art exhibit.

Coronado State Monument

NM 44 (P.O. Box 95), Bernalillo, NM 87004. ☎ **505/867-5351.** Admission $3 adults, free for children 16 and under. Summer, daily 9am–6pm; winter, daily 8am–5pm. Closed major holidays. To get to the site (20 miles north of Albuquerque), take I-25 to Bernalillo and NM 44 West.

When the Spanish explorer Coronado traveled through this region in 1540–41 while searching for the Seven Cities of Cíbola, he wintered at a village on the west bank of the Rio Grande—probably one located on the ruins of the ancient Anasazi pueblo known as Kuaua. Those excavated ruins have been preserved in this state monument.

Hundreds of rooms can be seen, and a kiva has been restored so that visitors can descend a ladder into the enclosed space, once the site of sacred rites. Unique multicolored murals, depicting human and animal forms, were found on successive layers of wall plaster in this and other kivas here; some examples are displayed in the monument's small archaeological museum.

Jemez State Monument

NM 4 (P.O. Box 143) Jemez Springs. ☎ **505/829-3530.** $2.50 adults, free for children 16 and under. May–Sept 15, daily 9:30am–5:30pm; Sept 16–Apr, daily 8:30am–4:30pm. Closed Jan 1, Thanksgiving, and Dec 25. From Albuquerque, take NM 44 to NM 4, and then continue on NM 4 for about 18 miles.

All that's left of the Mission of San José de los Jemez, founded by Franciscan missionaries in 1621, is preserved at this site. Visitors will find massive walls standing alone; sparse, small door and window openings underscore the need for security and permanence in those times. The mission was excavated between 1921 and 1937, along with portions of a prehistoric Jemez pueblo. The pueblo, near the Jemez Hot Springs, was called Giusewa—"place of the boiling waters."

A small **museum** at the site displays artifacts found during the excavation, describes traditional crafts and foods, and weaves the thread of history of the Jemez peoples to the 20st century in a series of exhibits. An instructional trail winds through the ruins.

THE TURQUOISE TRAIL

New Mexico 14 begins about 16 miles east of downtown Albuquerque, at I-40's Cedar Crest exit, and winds some 46 miles to Santa Fe along the east side of the Sandia Mountains. Best known as "The Turquoise Trail," this state-designated scenic and historic route traverses the revived "ghost towns" of Golden, Madrid, and Cerrillos, where gold, silver, coal, and turquoise were once mined in great quantities. Modern-day settlers, mostly artists and craftspeople, have brought a renewed frontier spirit to the old mining towns.

GOLDEN   Golden is approximately 10 miles north of the Sandia Park junction on NM 14. Its sagging houses, with their missing boards and the wind whistling through the broken eaves, make it a purist's ghost town. There's a general store widely known for its large selection of well-priced jewelry, as well as a bottle seller's "glass garden." Nearby are the ruins of a pueblo called **Paako,** abandoned around 1670. Such communities of mud huts were all that the Spaniards ever found during their avid quest for the gold of Cíbola.

MADRID   Madrid (pronounced with the accent on the first syllable) is about 12 miles north of Golden. Madrid and neighboring Cerrillos were in a fabled turquoise-mining area dating back into prehistory. Gold and silver mines followed, and when they faltered, there was coal. The Turquoise Trail towns supplied fuel for the locomotives of the Santa Fe Railroad until the 1950s, when the railroad converted to diesel fuel. Madrid used to produce 100,000 tons of coal a year, but the mine closed in 1956. Today this is a village of artists and craftspeople seemingly stuck in the 1960s: Its funky, ramshackle houses have many counterculture residents—the "hippies" of yore—who operate several crafts stores and import shops.

The **Old Coal Mine Museum** (☎ 505/473-0743) invites visitors to go down into a real mine, saved when the town was abandoned. You can see the old mine's offices, steam engines, machines, and tools. It's called a "living" museum because blacksmiths, metalworkers, and leatherworkers ply their trades here in restoring

Excursions from Albuquerque

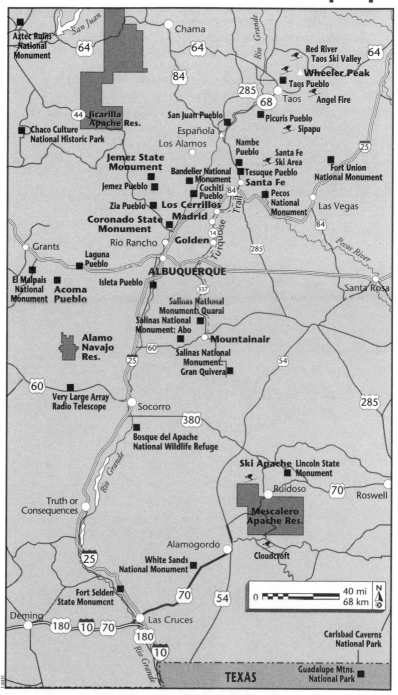

parts and tools found in the mine. It's open daily; admission is $3.50 for adults, $2.50 for seniors, and $1.50 for children under 12.

Next door, the **Mine Shaft Tavern** continues its colorful career by offering buffalo steaks on the menu and presenting live music daily; it attracts folks from Santa Fe and Albuquerque. Next door is the **Madrid Opera House,** possibly the only such establishment on earth with a built-in steam locomotive on its stage. (The structure had been an engine repair shed; the balcony is made of railroad track.)

CERRILLOS   Cerrillos, about 3 miles north of Madrid, is a village of dirt roads that sprawls along Galisteo Creek. It appears to have changed very little since it was founded during a lead strike in 1879; the old hotel, the saloon, and even the sheriff's office look very much like an Old West movie set. It's another 15 miles to Santa Fe and I-25.

Appendix

Useful Toll-Free Numbers and Web Sites

LODGINGS

Best Western International, Inc.
800/528-1234 in Continental U.S. and Canada
800/528-2222 TDD

Days Inn
800/325-2525 in Continental U.S. and Canada
800/325-3297 TDD
http://www.daysinn.com/daysinn.html

Hilton Hotels Corporation
800/HILTONS in Continental U.S. and Canada
800/368-1133 TDD
http://www.hilton.com

Holiday Inn
800/HOLIDAY in Continental U.S. and Canada
800/238-5544 TDD
http://www.holiday-inn.com

Hyatt Hotels and Resorts
800/233-1234 in Continental U.S. and Canada
800/228-9548 TDD
http://www.hyatt.com

ITT Sheraton
800/325-3535 in Continental U.S. and Canada
800/325-1717 TDD

La Quinta Motor Inns, Inc.
800/531-5900 in Continental U.S. and Canada
800/426-3101 TDD

Quality Inns
800/228-5151 in Continental U.S. and Canada
800/228-3323 TDD
http://www.hotelchoice.com/cgi-bin/res/webres?quality.html

Radisson Hotels International
800/333-3333 in Continental U.S. and Canada

Residence Inn by Marriott
800/331-3131 in Continental U.S. and Canada
800/228-7014 TDD
http://www.marriott.com/lodging/resinn.htm
Super 8 Motels
800/800-8000 in Continental U.S. and Canada
800/533-6634 TDD
http://www.super8motels.com/super8.html

CAR-RENTAL AGENCIES

Alamo Rent A Car
800/327-9633 in Continental U.S. and Canada
http://www.goalamo.com
Avis Rent A Car
800/331-1212 in Continental U.S.
800/TRY-AVIS Canada
800/331-2323 TDD
http://www.avis/com
Budget Rent A Car
800/527-0700 in Continental U.S. and Canada
800/826-5510 TDD
Dollar Rent A Car
800/800-4000 in Continental U.S. and Canada
Enterprise Rent-A-Car
800/325-8007 in Continental U.S. and Canada
Hertz Rent A Car
800/654-3131 in Continental U.S. and Canada
800/654-2280 TDD
Rent-A-Wreck
800/535-1391 in Continental U.S.
Thrifty Rent-A-Car
800/367-2277 in Continental U.S. and Canada
800/358-5856 TDD

AIRLINES

America West Airlines
800/235-9292 in Continental U.S.
American Airlines
800/433-7300 in Continental U.S. and Western Canada
800/543-1586 TDD
http://www.americanair.com/aa_home/aa_home.htm
Continental Airlines
800/525-0280 in Continental U.S.
800/343-9195 TDD
http://www.flycontinental.com:80/index.html
Delta Air Lines
800/221-1212 in Continental U.S.
800/831-4488 TDD
http://www.delta-air.com/index.html
Southwest Airlines
800/435-9792 in Continental U.S.

Trans World Airlines
800/221-2000 in Continental U.S.
http://www2.twa.com/TWA/Airlines/home/home.htm
United Airlines
800/241-6522 in Continental U.S. and Canada
http://www.ual.com
USAir
800/428-4322 in Continental U.S. and Canada
http://www.usair.com

Index

ACCOMMODATIONS

ALBUQUERQUE

ANGEL FIRE

SANTA FE

TAOS

FROMMER'S COMPLETE TRAVEL GUIDES

(Comprehensive guides to destinations around the world, with selections in all price ranges—from deluxe to budget)

Acapulco/Ixtapa/Zihuatenjo
Alaska
Amsterdam
Arizona
Atlanta
Australia
Austria
Bahamas
Bangkok
Barcelona, Madrid & Seville
Belgium, Holland & Luxembourg
Berlin
Bermuda
Boston
Budapest & the Best of Hungary
California
Canada
Cancún, Cozumel & the Yucatán
Caribbean
Caribbean Cruises & Ports of Call
Caribbean Ports of Call
Carolinas & Georgia
Chicago
Colorado
Costa Rica
Denver, Boulder & Colorado Springs
Dublin
England

Florida
France
Germany
Greece
Hawaii
Hong Kong
Honolulu/Waikiki/Oahu
Ireland
Italy
Jamaica & Barbados
Japan
Las Vegas
London
Los Angeles
Maryland & Delaware
Maui
Mexico
Mexico City
Miami & the Keys
Montana & Wyoming
Montréal & Québec City
Munich & the Bavarian Alps
Nashville & Memphis
Nepal
New England
New Mexico
New Orleans
New York City
Northern New England
Nova Scotia, New Brunswick & Prince Edward Island

Paris
Philadelphia & the Amish Country
Portugal
Prague & the Best of the Czech Republic
Puerto Rico
Puerto Vallarta, Manzanillo & Guadalajara
Rome
San Antonio & Austin
San Diego
San Francisco
Santa Fe, Taos & Albuquerque
Scandinavia
Scotland
Seattle & Portland
South Pacific
Spain
Switzerland
Thailand
Tokyo
Toronto
U.S.A.
Utah
Vancouver & Victoria
Vienna
Virgin Islands
Virginia
Walt Disney World & Orlando
Washington, D.C.
Washington & Oregon

FROMMER'S FRUGAL TRAVELER'S GUIDES

(The grown-up guides to budget travel, offering dream vacations at down-to-earth prices)

Australia from $45 a Day
Berlin from $50 a Day
California from $60 a Day
Caribbean from $60 a Day
Costa Rica & Belize from $35 a Day
Eastern Europe from $30 a Day

England from $50 a Day
Europe from $50 a Day
Florida from $50 a Day
Greece from $45 a Day
Hawaii from $60 a Day
India from $40 a Day
Ireland from $45 a Day
Italy from $50 a Day

Israel from $45 a Day
London from $60 a Day
Mexico from $35 a Day
New York from $70 a Day
New Zealand from $45 a Day
Paris from $60 a Day
Washington, D.C. from $50 a Day

FROMMER'S PORTABLE GUIDES

(Pocket-size guides for travelers who want everything in a nutshell)

Charleston & Savannah · · · Las Vegas · · · Washington, D.C. · · · New Orleans · · · San Francisco

FROMMER'S FAMILY GUIDES

(The complete guides for successful family vacations)

California with Kids	New England with Kids	San Francisco with Kids
Los Angeles with Kids	New York City with Kids	Washington, D.C. with Kids

FROMMER'S AMERICA ON WHEELS

(Everything you need for a successful road trip, including full-color road maps and ratings for every hotel)

California & Nevada	Midwest & the Great	Northwest & the	Southwest
Florida	Lake States	Great Plains States	Texas & the South-
Mid-Atlantic	New York & the New	Southeast	Central States
	England States		

FROMMER'S WALKING TOURS

(Memorable neighborhood strolls through the world's great cities)

Berlin	Montréal & Québec City	Spain's Favorite Cities
Chicago	New York	Tokyo
England's Favorite Cities	Paris	Venice
London	San Francisco	Washington, D.C.

SPECIAL-INTEREST TITLES

Arthur Frommer's Branson!
Arthur Frommer's New World of Travel
The Civil War Trust's Official Guide to the
 Civil War Discovery Trail
Frommer's America's 100 Best-Loved State
 Parks
Frommer's Caribbean Hideaways
Frommer's Complete Hostel Vacation Guide to
 England, Scotland & Wales
Frommer's Food Lover's Companion to France
Frommer's Food Lover's Companion to Italy
Frommer's Great European Driving Tours

Frommer's National Park Guide
Outside Magazine's Adventure Guide to New
 England
Outside Magazine's Adventure Guide to
 Northern California
Places Rated Almanac
Retirement Places Rated
USA Sports Traveler's and TV Viewer's
 Golf Tournament Guide
USA Sports Minor League Baseball Book
USA Today Golf Atlas
Wonderful Weekends from NYC

FROMMER'S IRREVERENT GUIDES

(Wickedly honest guides for sophisticated travelers)

Amsterdam	Manhattan	Paris	U.S. Virgin Islands
Chicago	Miami	San Francisco	Walt Disney World
London	New Orleans	Santa Fe	Washington, D.C.

UNOFFICIAL GUIDES

(Get the unbiased truth from these candid, value-conscious guides)

Atlanta	Euro Disneyland	Mini-Mickey
Branson, Missouri	The Great Smoky & Blue	Skiing in the West
Chicago	Ridge Mountains	Walt Disney World
Cruises	Las Vegas	Walt Disney World Companion
Disneyland	Miami & the Keys	Washington, D.C.

WHEREVER YOU TRAVEL, *H*ELP IS NEVER FAR AWAY.

From planning your trip to providing travel assistance along the way, American Express® Travel Service Offices are always there to help.

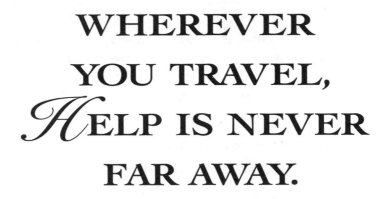

Santa Fe

Pajarito Travel (R)
2801 Rodeo Road
Suite B
Santa Fe
505/474-7177

Travel

http://www.americanexpress.com/travel

**American Express Travel Service Offices
are located throughout New Mexico.
For the office nearest you, call 1-800-AXP-3429.**